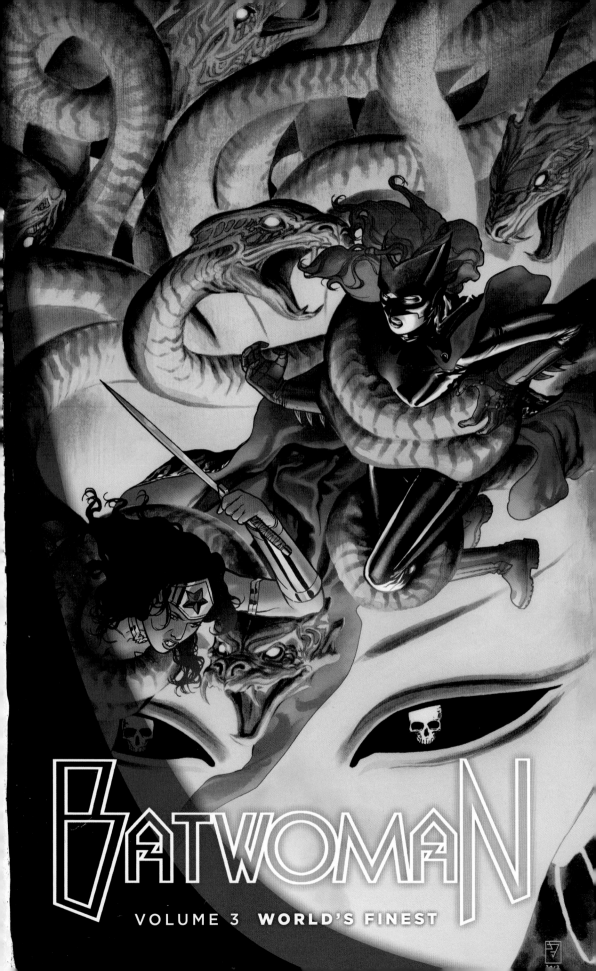

BATWOMAN

VOLUME 3 WORLD'S FINEST

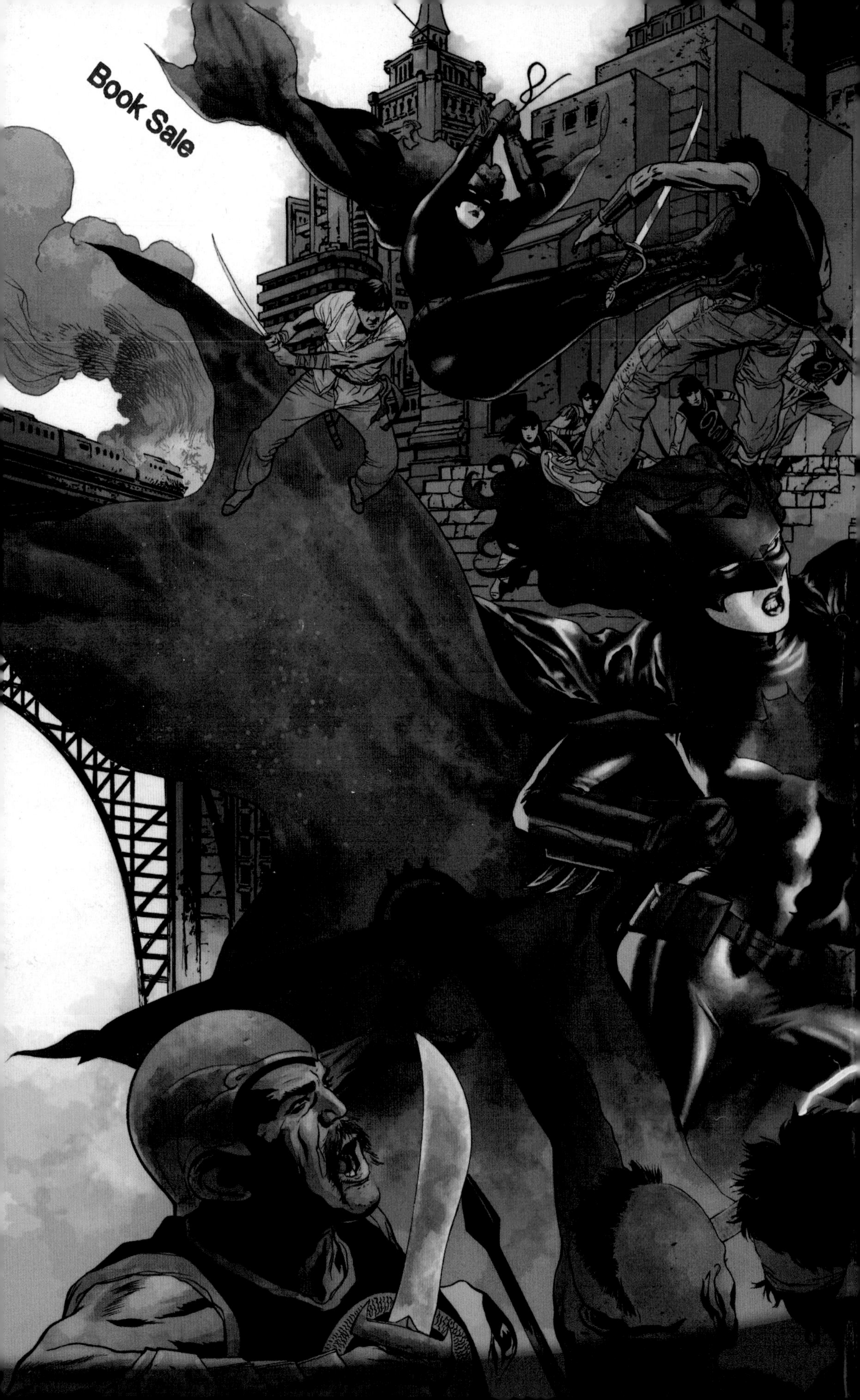

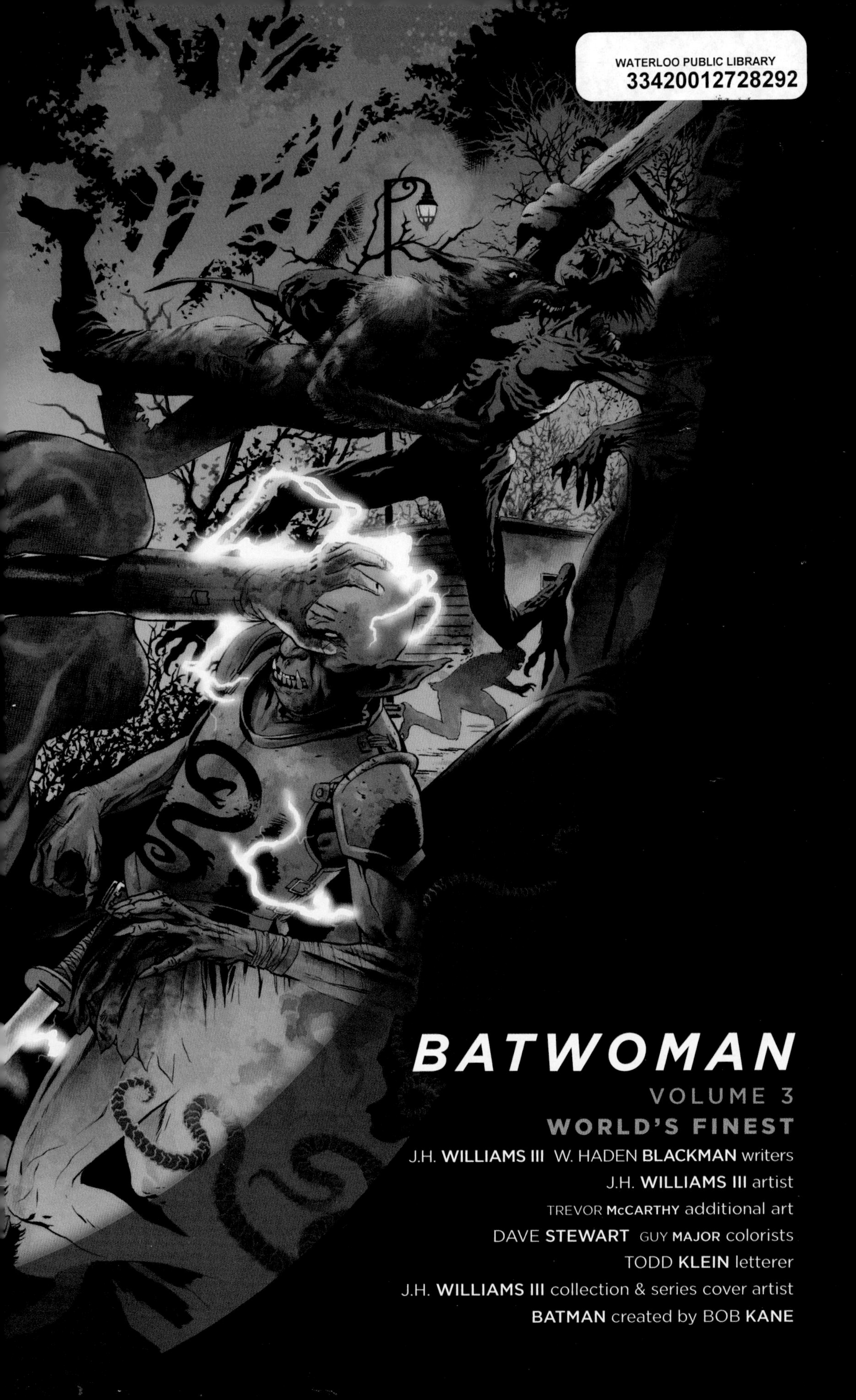

BATWOMAN

VOLUME 3

WORLD'S FINEST

J.H. **WILLIAMS III** W. HADEN **BLACKMAN** writers

J.H. **WILLIAMS III** artist

TREVOR **McCARTHY** additional art

DAVE **STEWART** GUY **MAJOR** colorists

TODD **KLEIN** letterer

J.H. **WILLIAMS III** collection & series cover artist

BATMAN created by BOB **KANE**

MIKE MARTS Editor - Original Series HARVEY RICHARDS Associate Editor - Original Series
RICKEY PURDIN Assistant Editor - Original Series PETER HAMBOUSSI Editor ROBIN WILDMAN Assistant Editor
ROBBIN BROSTERMAN Design Director - Books ROBBIE BIEDERMAN Publication Design

BOB HARRAS Senior VP - Editor-in-Chief

DIANE NELSON President DAN DIDIO and JIM LEE Co-Publishers
GEOFF JOHNS Chief Creative Officer
JOHN ROOD Executive VP - Sales, Marketing and Business Development
AMY GENKINS Senior VP - Business and Legal Affairs NAIRI GARDINER Senior VP - Finance
JEFF BOISON VP - Publishing Planning MARK CHIARELLO VP - Art Direction and Design
JOHN CUNNINGHAM VP - Marketing TERRI CUNNINGHAM VP - Editorial Administration
ALISON GILL Senior VP - Manufacturing and Operations HANK KANALZ Senior VP - Vertigo and Integrated Publishing
JAY KOGAN VP - Business and Legal Affairs, Publishing JACK MAHAN VP - Business Affairs, Talent
NICK NAPOLITANO VP - Manufacturing Administration SUE POHJA VP - Book Sales
COURTNEY SIMMONS Senior VP - Publicity BOB WAYNE Senior VP - Sales

BATWOMAN VOLUME 3: WORLD'S FINEST

DC Comics, 1700 Broadway, New York, NY 10019
A Warner Bros. Entertainment Company.
Printed by RR Donnelley, Willard, OH, USA. 8/16/13. First Printing.
HC ISBN: 978-1-4012-4246-6
SC ISBN: 978-1-4012-4610-5

 SUSTAINABLE FORESTRY INITIATIVE Certified Chain of Custody
At Least 20% Certified Forest Content
www.sfiprogram.org
SFI-01042
APPLIES TO TEXT STOCK ONLY

Library of Congress Cataloging-in-Publication Data

Williams, J. H. III.
Batwoman. Volume 3, World's finest / J.H. Williams III, W. Haden Blackman.
pages cm
"Originally published in single magazine form in Batwoman 0, 12-17."
ISBN 978-1-4012-4246-6
1. Graphic novels. I. Blackman, W. Haden. II. Title. III. Title: World's finest.
PN6728.B365W57 2013
741.5'973--dc23
2013016902

THE STORY SO FAR

Kate Kane survived a brutal kidnapping by terrorists that left her mother dead and her twin sister lost.

Following her father's example, she vowed to serve her country and attended West Point until she was expelled under "Don't Ask, Don't Tell."

Now she is many things: estranged daughter, grieving sister, proud lesbian, brave soldier, determined hero.

She is BATWOMAN.

And she is at war.

Gotham City has become a battleground, invaded by monsters torn from urban legends. Bloody Mary. Killer Croc. The Hook. The Weeping Woman. Strengthened by the sorcerer Maro and joined by one of Gotham's most vicious gangs as backup, these beasts have terrorized the city, kidnapping its children for unknown ends.

Meanwhile, Batwoman is closer than ever to her girlfriend, Maggie Sawyer of the G.C.P.D., but cannot tell her who she really is. She's still being forced to spy for Director Bones of the D.E.O., and her cousin, Bette Kane aka Flamebird, is still recovering from the brutal attack by The Hook.

The urban legends serve MEDUSA, an international criminal conspiracy. And though Batwoman and her allies defeated its local commander, the fanatic demigod called Falchion, the organization has sprouted a new head, just as determined to offer the children in sacrifice to an entity known only as the Mother of All Monsters.

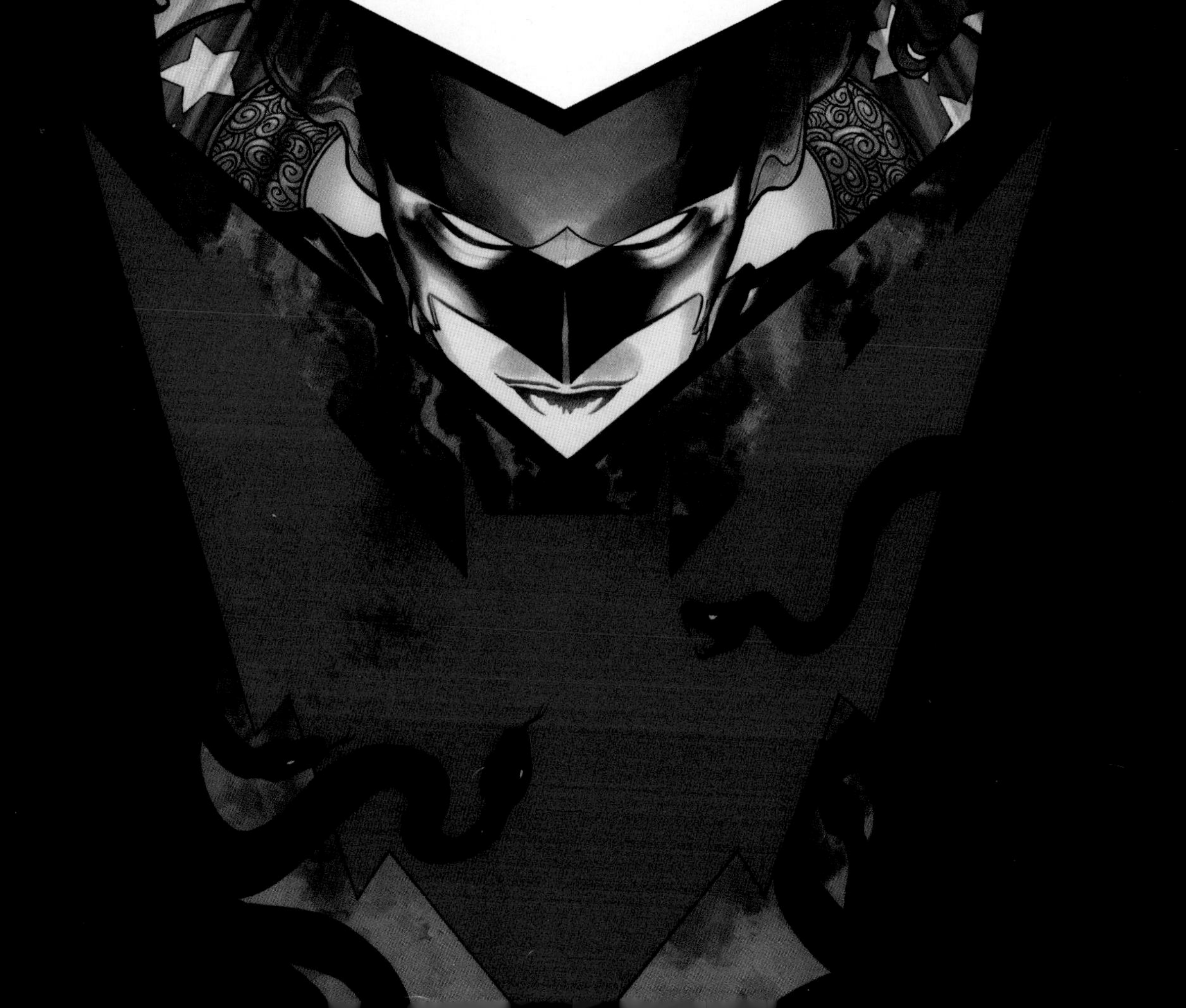

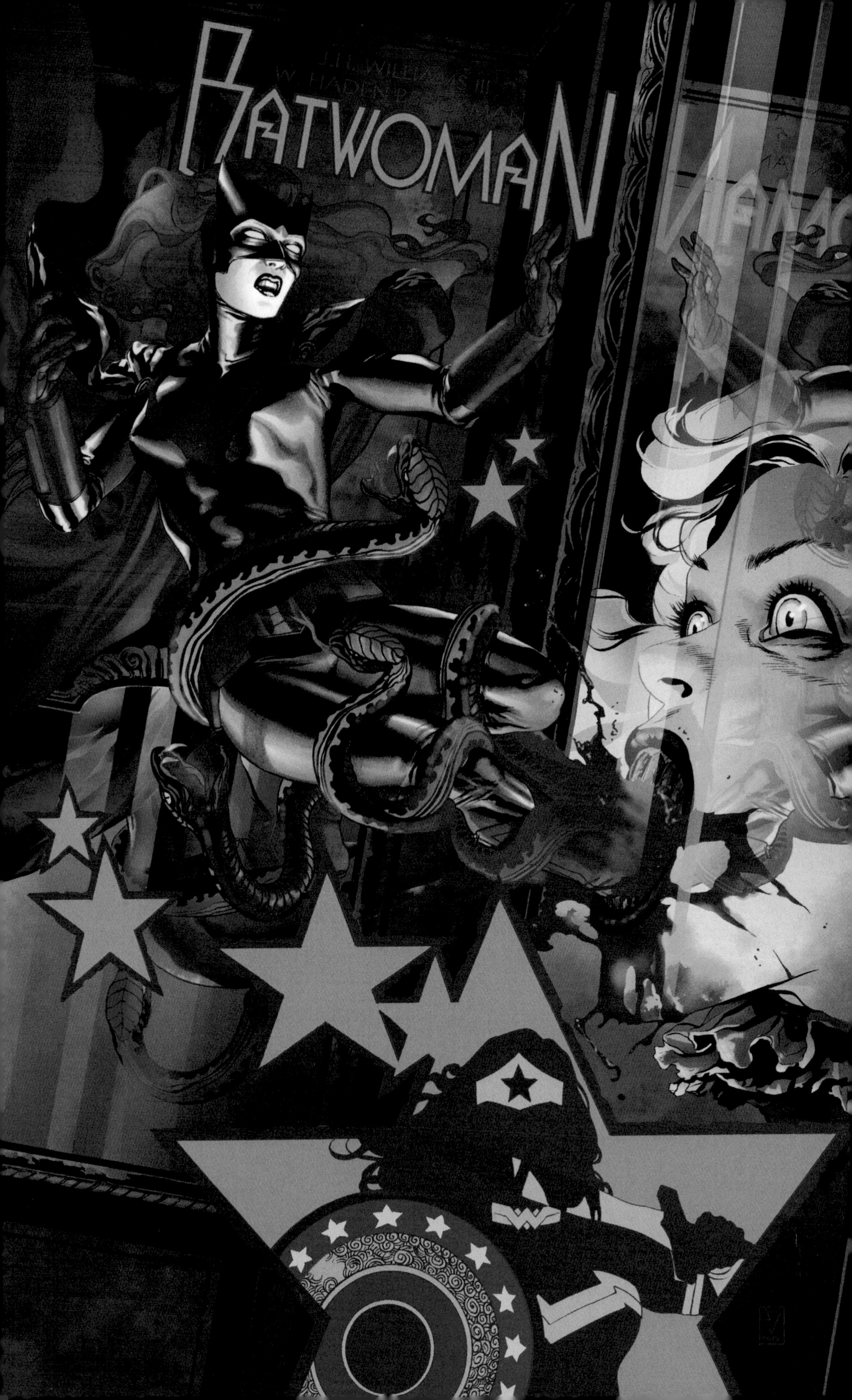
BATWOMAN

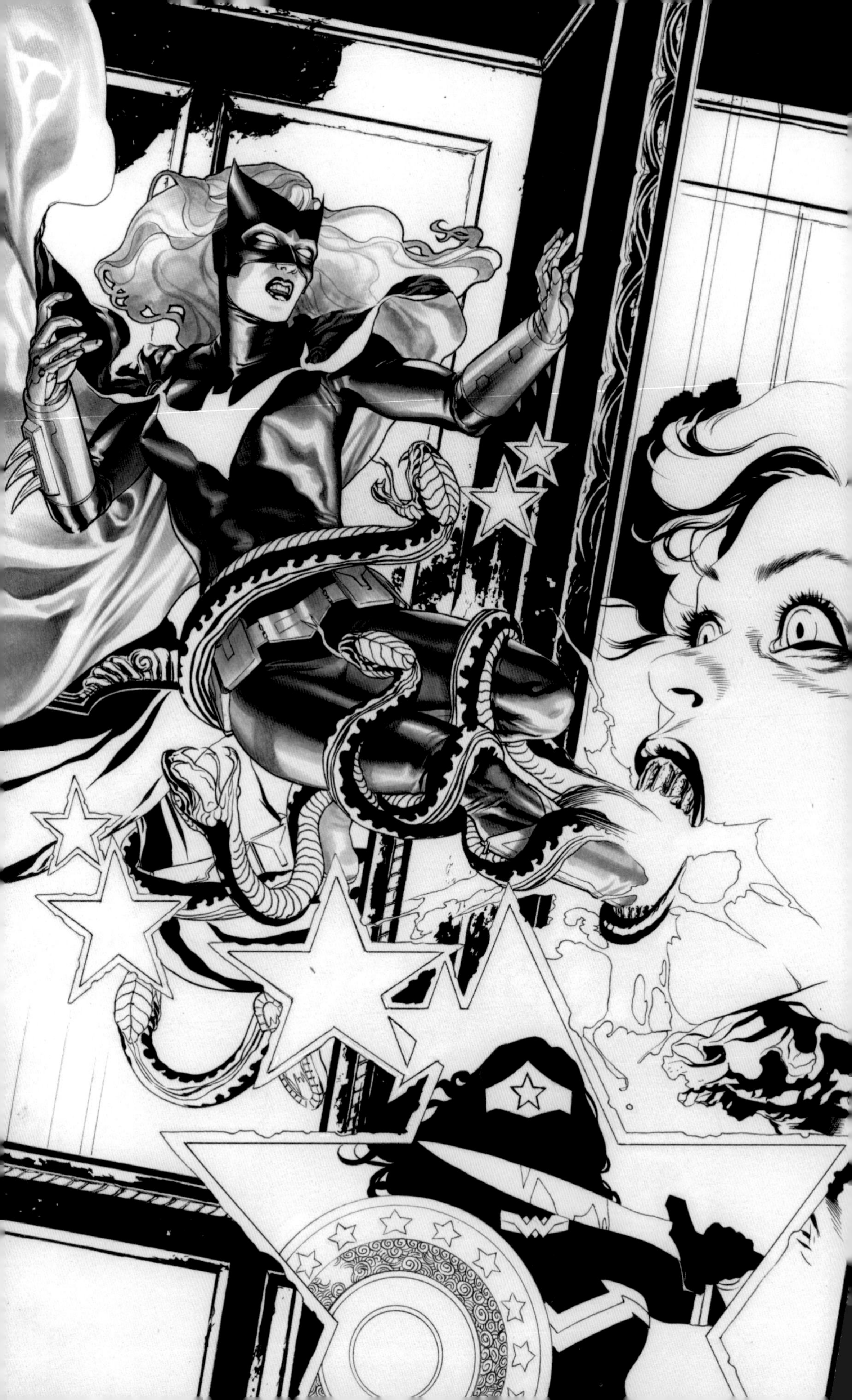

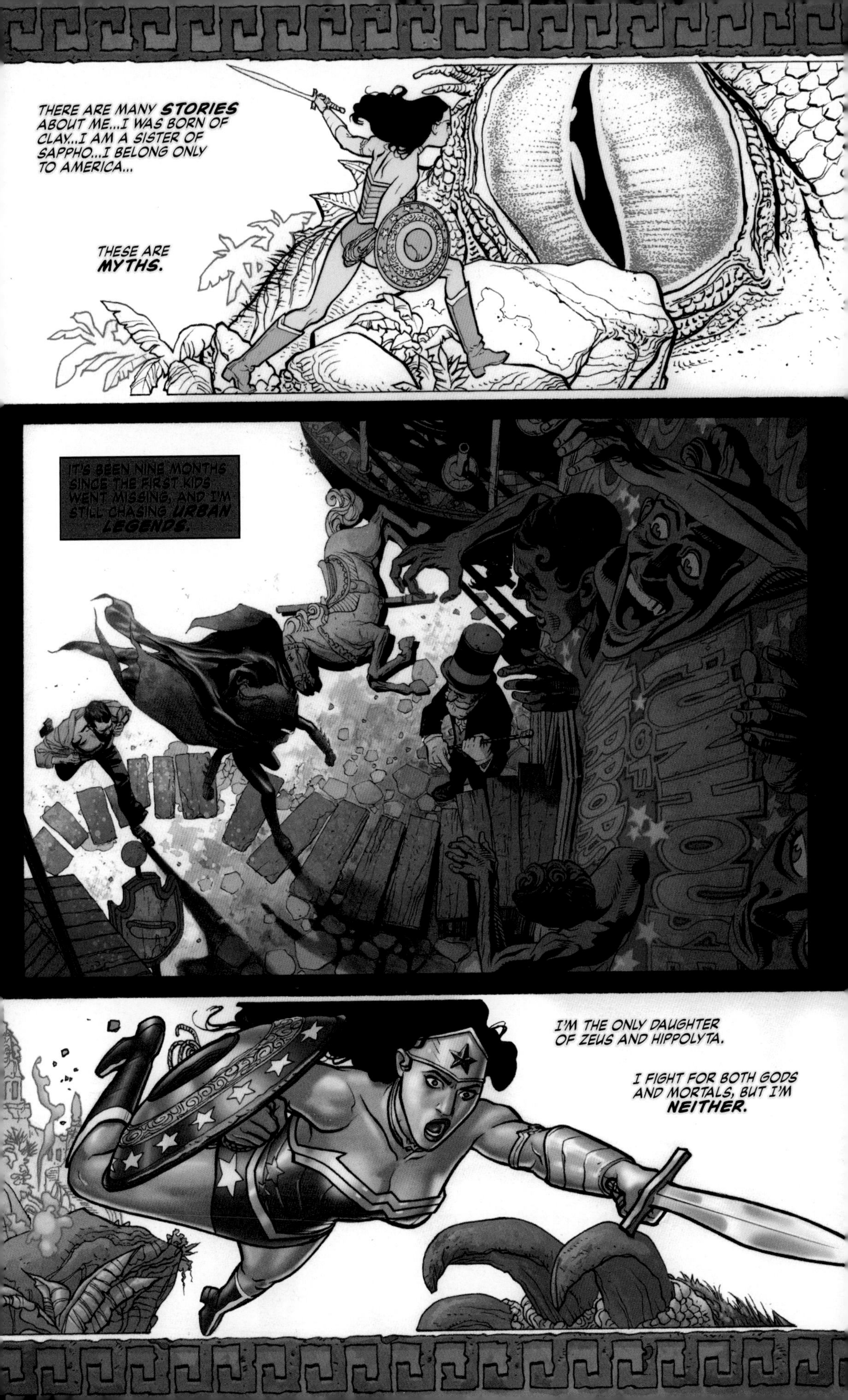
THERE ARE MANY STORIES ABOUT ME...I WAS BORN OF CLAY...I AM A SISTER OF SAPPHO...I BELONG ONLY TO AMERICA...
THESE ARE MYTHS.
IT'S BEEN NINE MONTHS SINCE THE FIRST KIDS WENT MISSING, AND I'M STILL CHASING URBAN LEGENDS.
I'M THE ONLY DAUGHTER OF ZEUS AND HIPPOLYTA.
I FIGHT FOR BOTH GODS AND MORTALS, BUT I'M NEITHER.

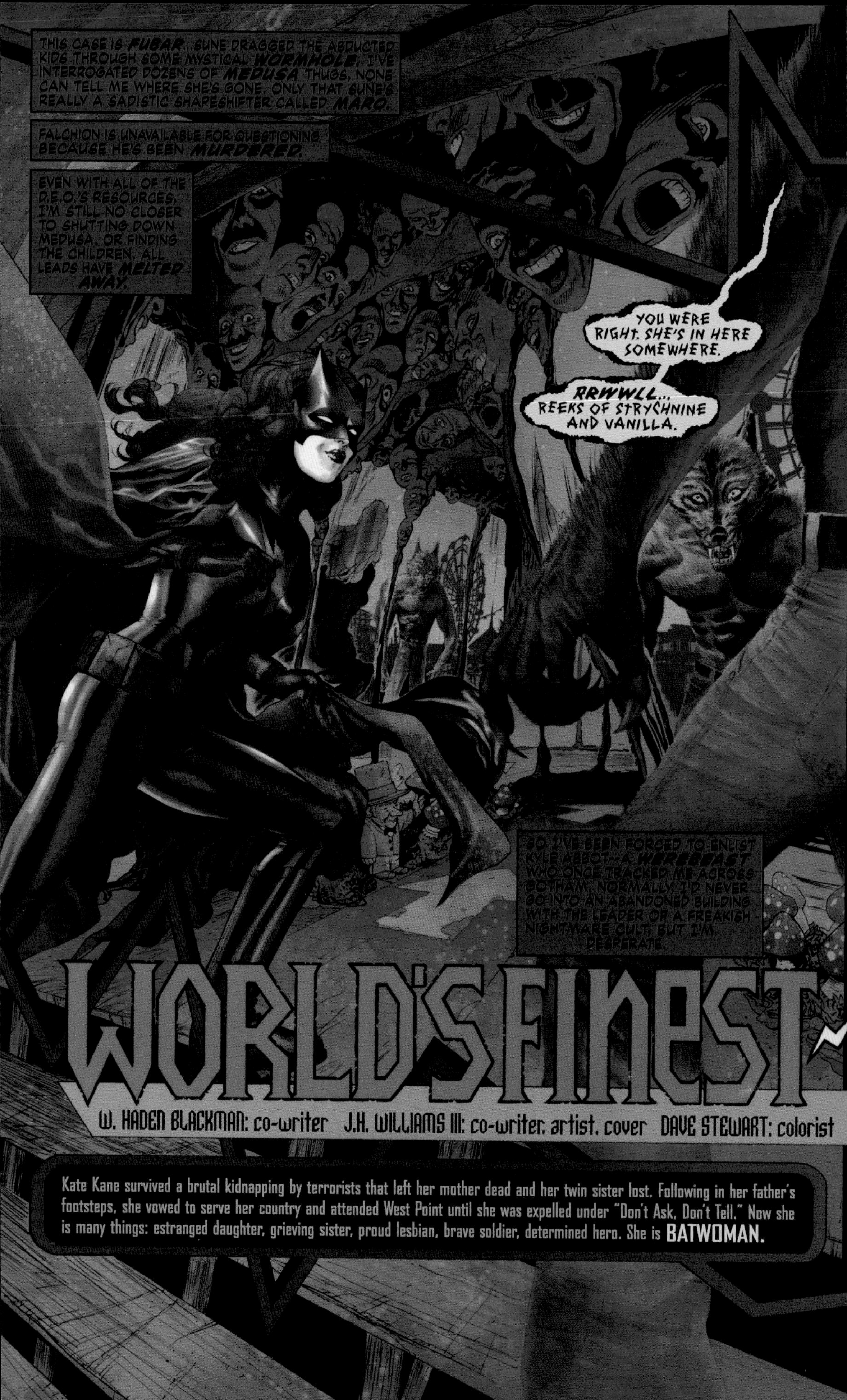
THIS CASE IS FUBAR...SUNE DRAGGED THE ABDUCTED KIDS THROUGH SOME MYSTICAL WORMHOLE. I'VE INTERROGATED DOZENS OF MEDUSA THUGS. NONE CAN TELL ME WHERE SHE'S GONE. ONLY THAT SUNE'S REALLY A SADISTIC SHAPESHIFTER CALLED MARO.
FALCHION IS UNAVAILABLE FOR QUESTIONING BECAUSE HE'S BEEN MURDERED.
EVEN WITH ALL OF THE D.E.O.'S RESOURCES, I'M STILL NO CLOSER TO SHUTTING DOWN MEDUSA, OR FINDING THE CHILDREN. ALL LEADS HAVE MELTED AWAY.
YOU WERE RIGHT. SHE'S IN HERE SOMEWHERE.
RRWWLL... REEKS OF STRYCHNINE AND VANILLA.
SO I'VE BEEN FORCED TO ENLIST KYLE ABBOT--A WEREBEAST WHO ONCE TRACKED ME ACROSS GOTHAM. NORMALLY, I'D NEVER GO INTO AN ABANDONED BUILDING WITH THE LEADER OF A FREAKISH NIGHTMARE CULT, BUT I'M DESPERATE.
WORLD'S FINEST
W. HADEN BLACKMAN: co-writer J.H. WILLIAMS III: co-writer, artist, cover DAVE STEWART: colorist
Kate Kane survived a brutal kidnapping by terrorists that left her mother dead and her twin sister lost. Following in her father's footsteps, she vowed to serve her country and attended West Point until she was expelled under "Don't Ask, Don't Tell." Now she is many things: estranged daughter, grieving sister, proud lesbian, brave soldier, determined hero. She is BATWOMAN.

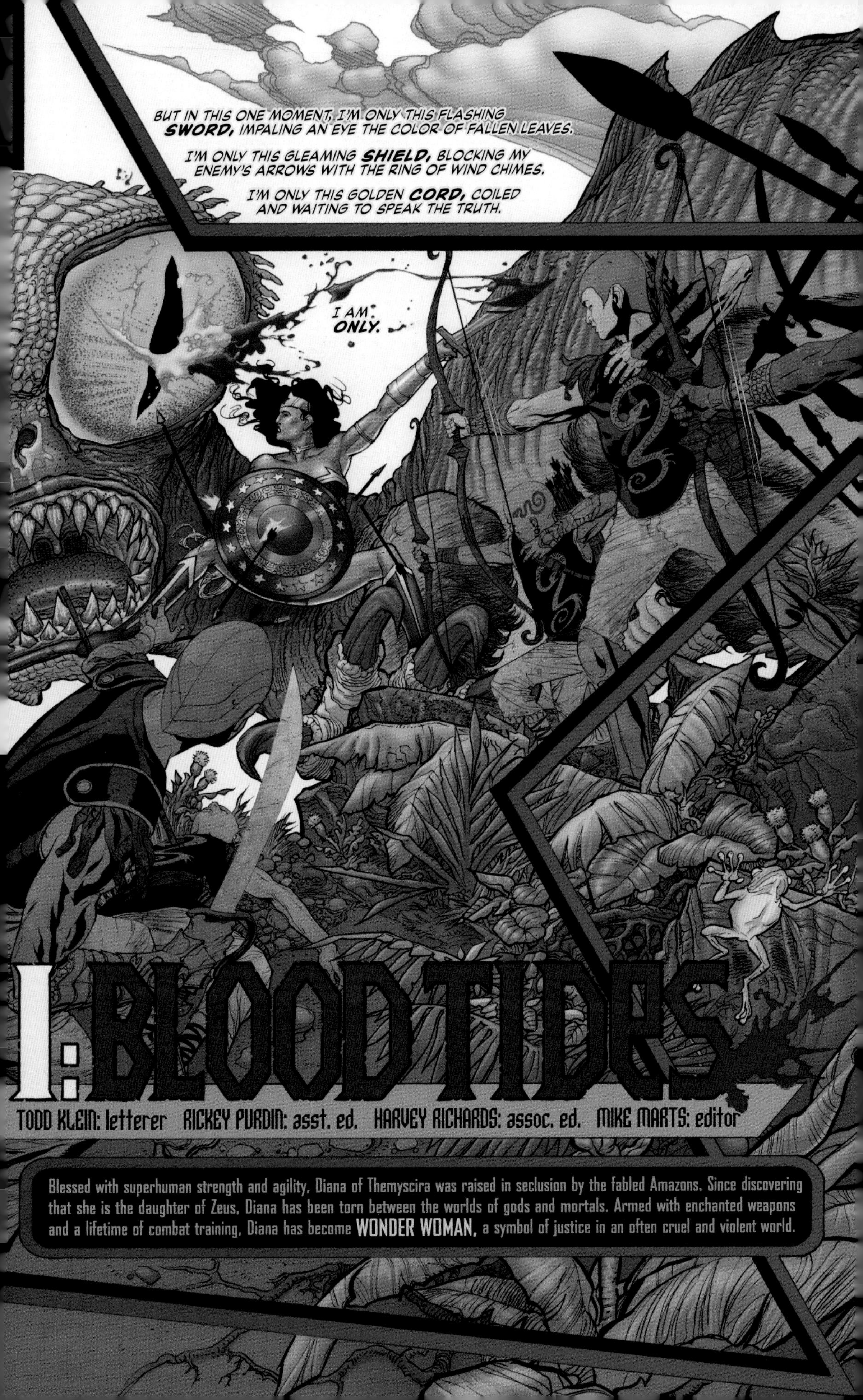
BUT IN THIS ONE MOMENT, I'M ONLY THIS FLASHING SWORD, IMPALING AN EYE THE COLOR OF FALLEN LEAVES.
I'M ONLY THIS GLEAMING SHIELD, BLOCKING MY ENEMY'S ARROWS WITH THE RING OF WIND CHIMES.
I'M ONLY THIS GOLDEN CORD, COILED AND WAITING TO SPEAK THE TRUTH.
I AM ONLY.
I: BLOOD TIDES
TODD KLEIN: letterer RICKEY PURDIN: asst. ed. HARVEY RICHARDS: assoc. ed. MIKE MARTS: editor
Blessed with superhuman strength and agility, Diana of Themyscira was raised in seclusion by the fabled Amazons. Since discovering that she is the daughter of Zeus, Diana has been torn between the worlds of gods and mortals. Armed with enchanted weapons and a lifetime of combat training, Diana has become WONDER WOMAN, a symbol of justice in an often cruel and violent world.

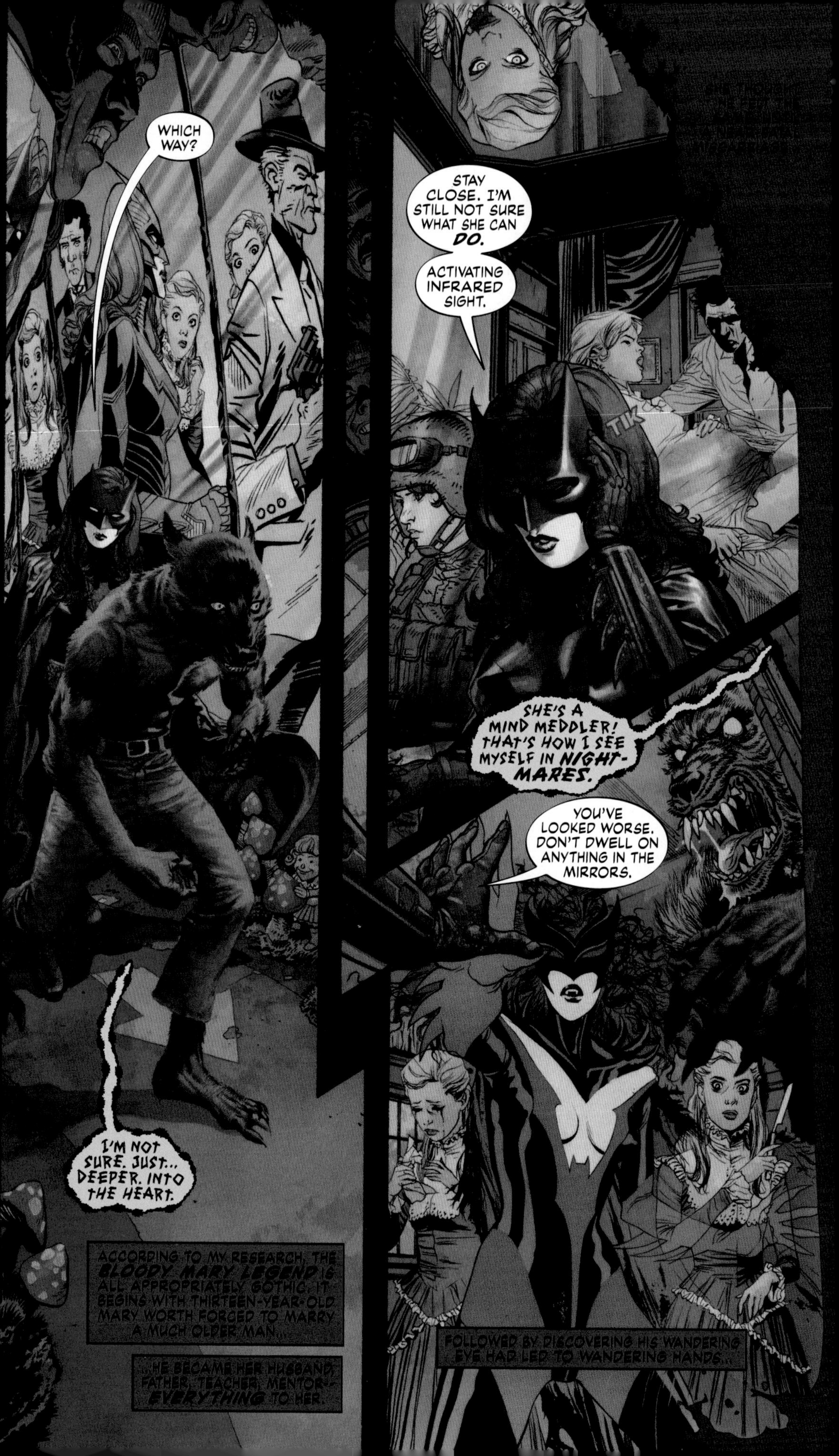
WHICH WAY?
I'M NOT SURE. JUST... DEEPER. INTO THE HEART.
ACCORDING TO MY RESEARCH, THE BLOODY MARY LEGEND IS ALL APPROPRIATELY GOTHIC. IT BEGINS WITH THIRTEEN-YEAR-OLD MARY WORTH FORCED TO MARRY A MUCH OLDER MAN...
...HE BECAME HER HUSBAND, FATHER, TEACHER, MENTOR--EVERYTHING TO HER.
STAY CLOSE. I'M STILL NOT SURE WHAT SHE CAN DO.
ACTIVATING INFRARED SIGHT.
TIK
SHE'S A MIND MEDDLER! THAT'S HOW I SEE MYSELF IN NIGHT-MARES.
YOU'VE LOOKED WORSE. DON'T DWELL ON ANYTHING IN THE MIRRORS.
FOLLOWED BY DISCOVERING HIS WANDERING EYE HAD LED TO WANDERING HANDS...

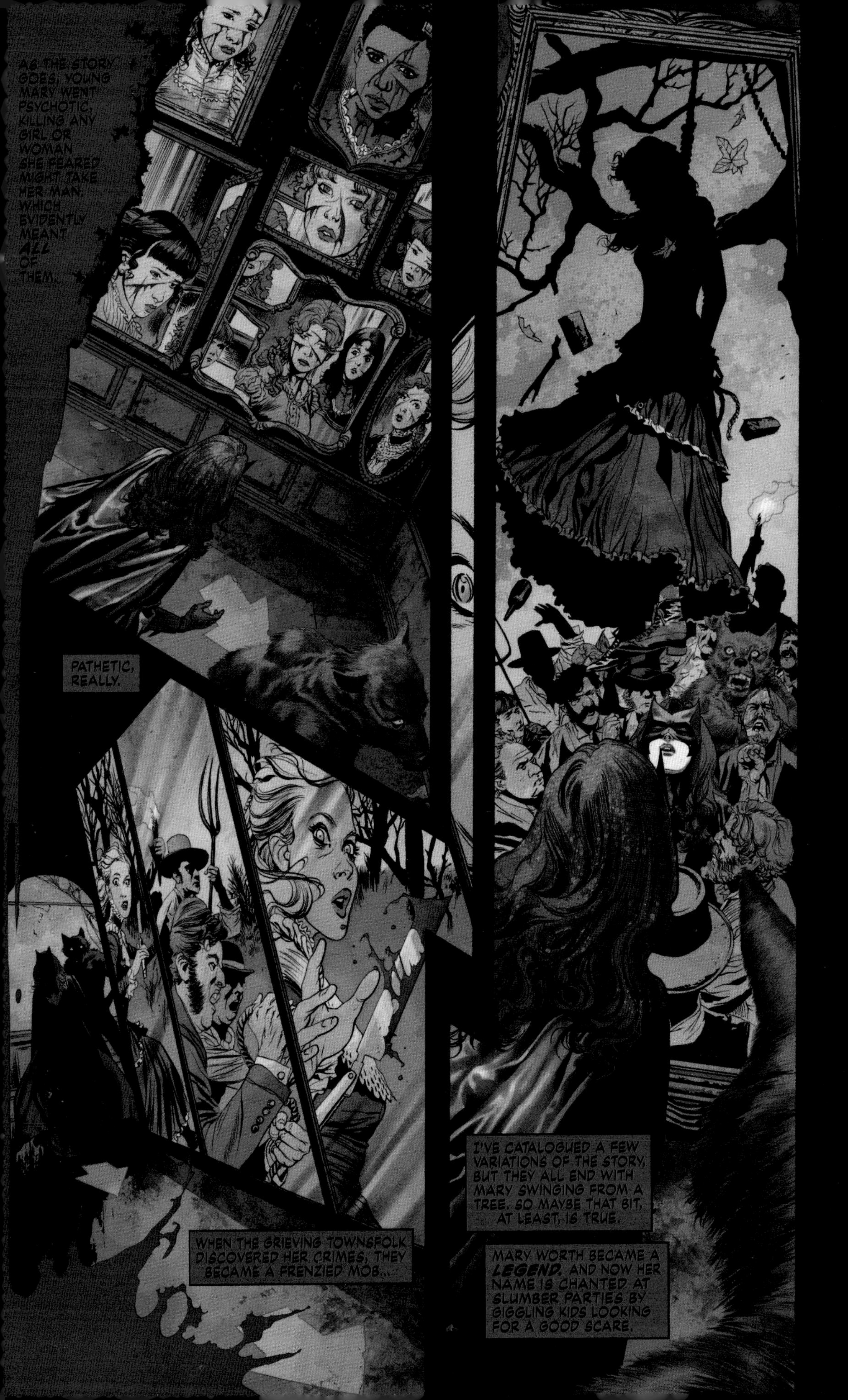
AS THE STORY GOES, YOUNG MARY WENT PSYCHOTIC, KILLING ANY GIRL OR WOMAN SHE FEARED MIGHT TAKE HER MAN. WHICH EVIDENTLY MEANT ALL OF THEM.
PATHETIC, REALLY.
WHEN THE GRIEVING TOWNSFOLK DISCOVERED HER CRIMES, THEY BECAME A FRENZIED MOB...
I'VE CATALOGUED A FEW VARIATIONS OF THE STORY, BUT THEY ALL END WITH MARY SWINGING FROM A TREE. SO MAYBE THAT BIT, AT LEAST, IS TRUE.
MARY WORTH BECAME A LEGEND, AND NOW HER NAME IS CHANTED AT SLUMBER PARTIES BY GIGGLING KIDS LOOKING FOR A GOOD SCARE.

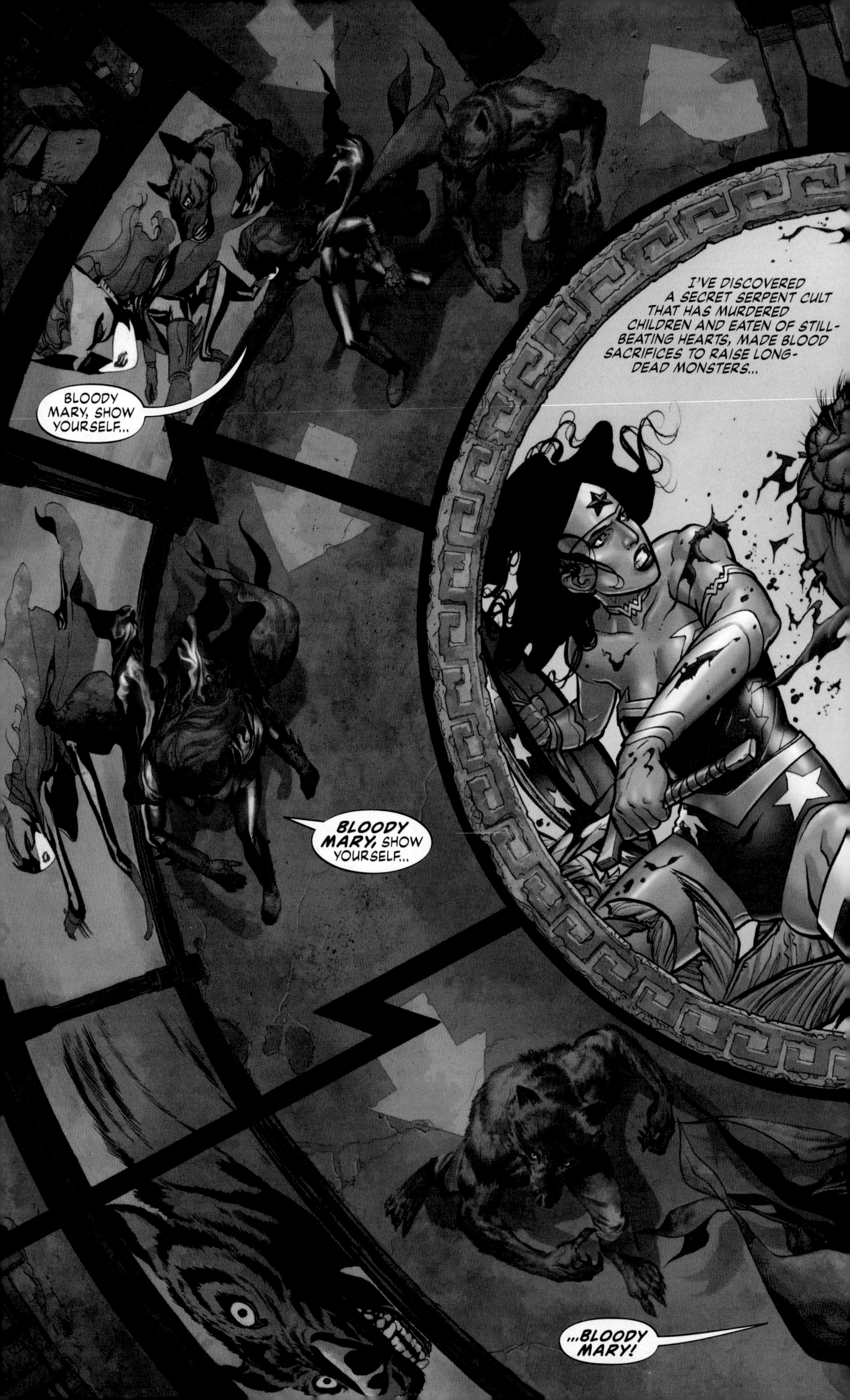
BLOODY MARY, SHOW YOURSELF...
I'VE DISCOVERED A SECRET SERPENT CULT THAT HAS MURDERED CHILDREN AND EATEN OF STILL-BEATING HEARTS, MADE BLOOD SACRIFICES TO RAISE LONG-DEAD MONSTERS...
BLOODY MARY, SHOW YOURSELF...
...BLOODY MARY!

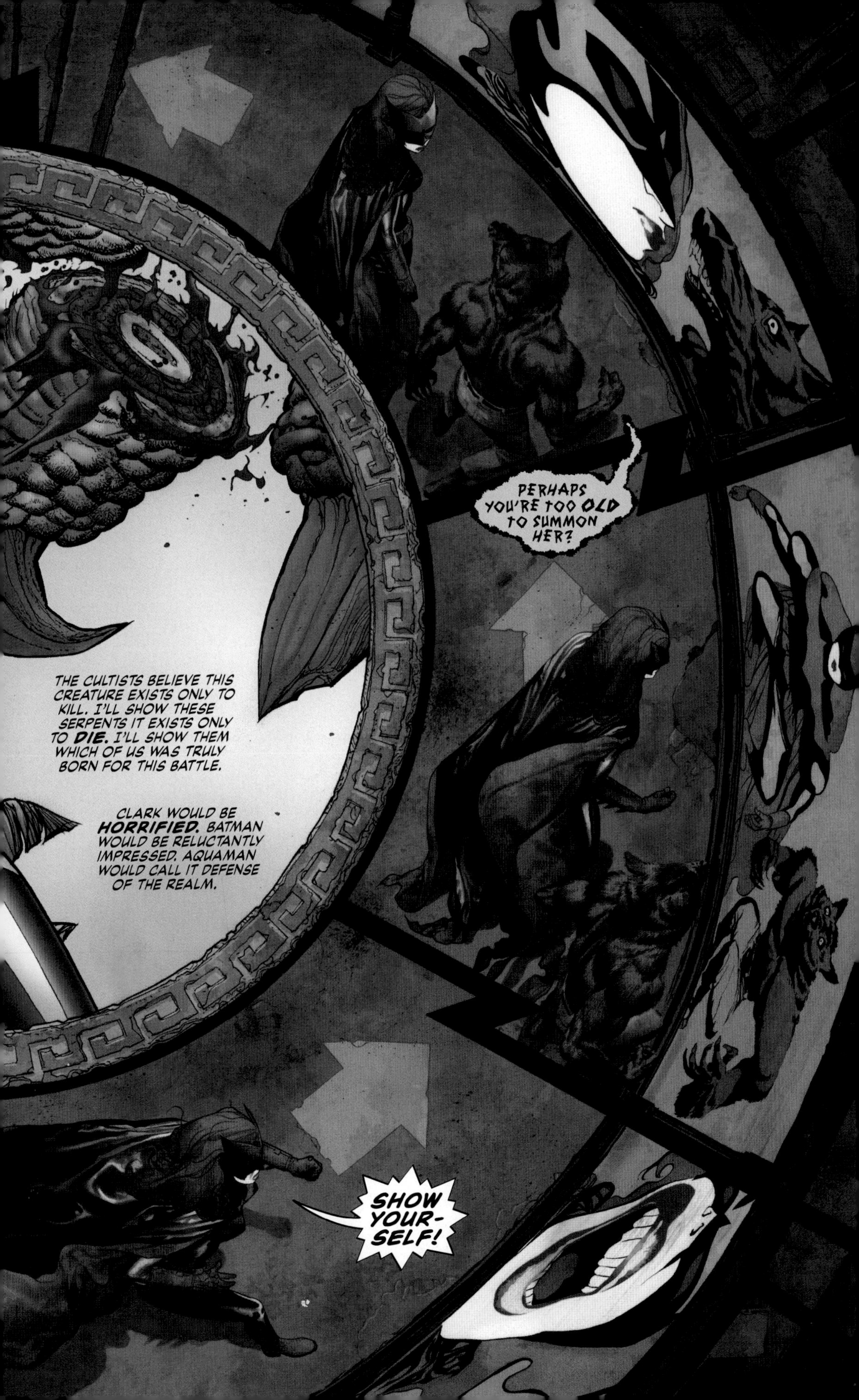
PERHAPS YOU'RE TOO OLD TO SUMMON HER?
THE CULTISTS BELIEVE THIS CREATURE EXISTS ONLY TO KILL. I'LL SHOW THESE SERPENTS IT EXISTS ONLY TO DIE. I'LL SHOW THEM WHICH OF US WAS TRULY BORN FOR THIS BATTLE.
CLARK WOULD BE HORRIFIED. BATMAN WOULD BE RELUCTANTLY IMPRESSED. AQUAMAN WOULD CALL IT DEFENSE OF THE REALM.
SHOW YOURSELF!

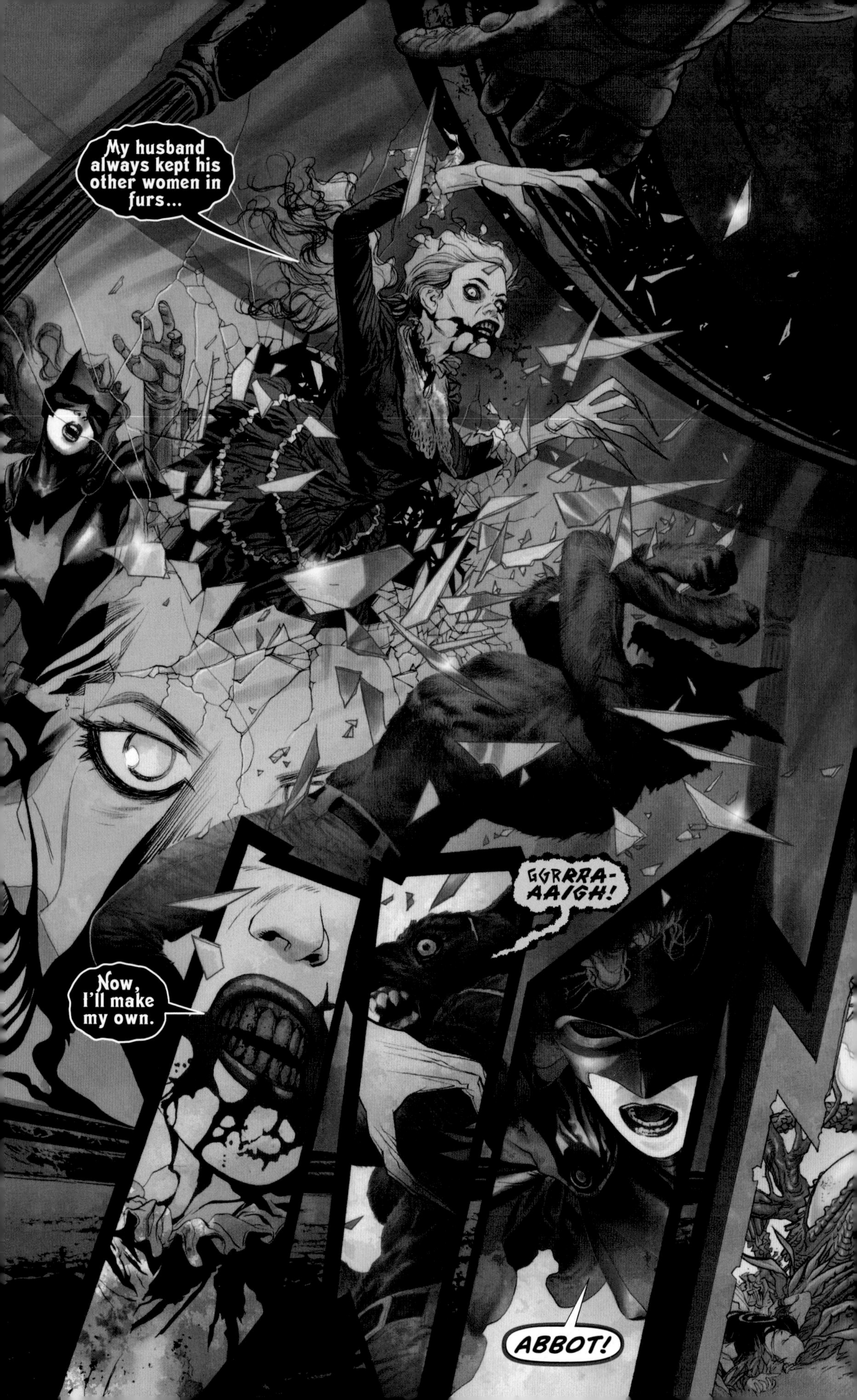
My husband always kept his other women in furs...
Now, I'll make my own.
GGRRRA-AAIGH!
ABBOT!

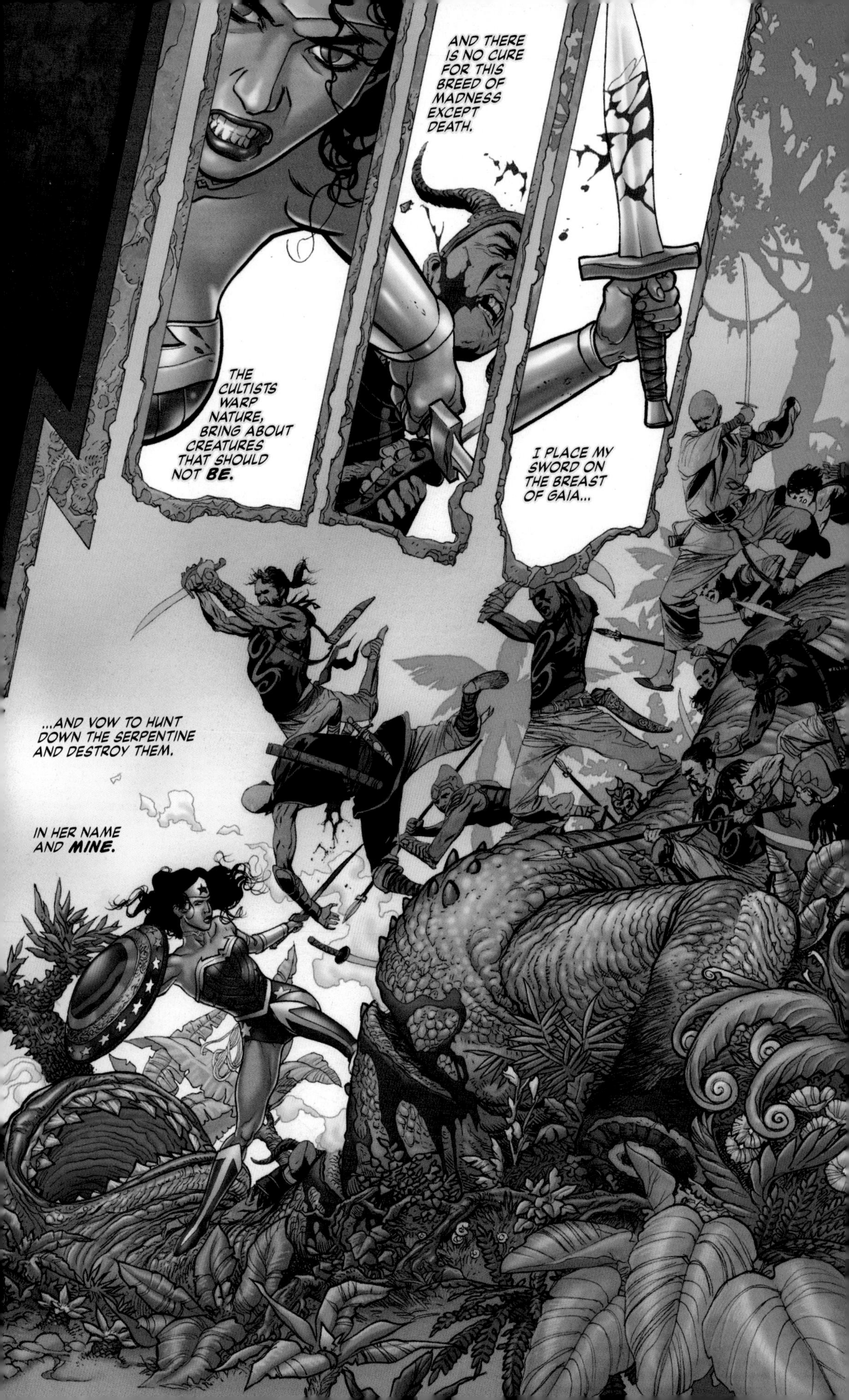
AND THERE IS NO CURE FOR THIS BREED OF MADNESS EXCEPT DEATH.
THE CULTISTS WARP NATURE, BRING ABOUT CREATURES THAT SHOULD NOT **BE.**
I PLACE MY SWORD ON THE BREAST OF GAIA...
...AND VOW TO HUNT DOWN THE SERPENTINE AND DESTROY THEM.
IN HER NAME AND **MINE.**

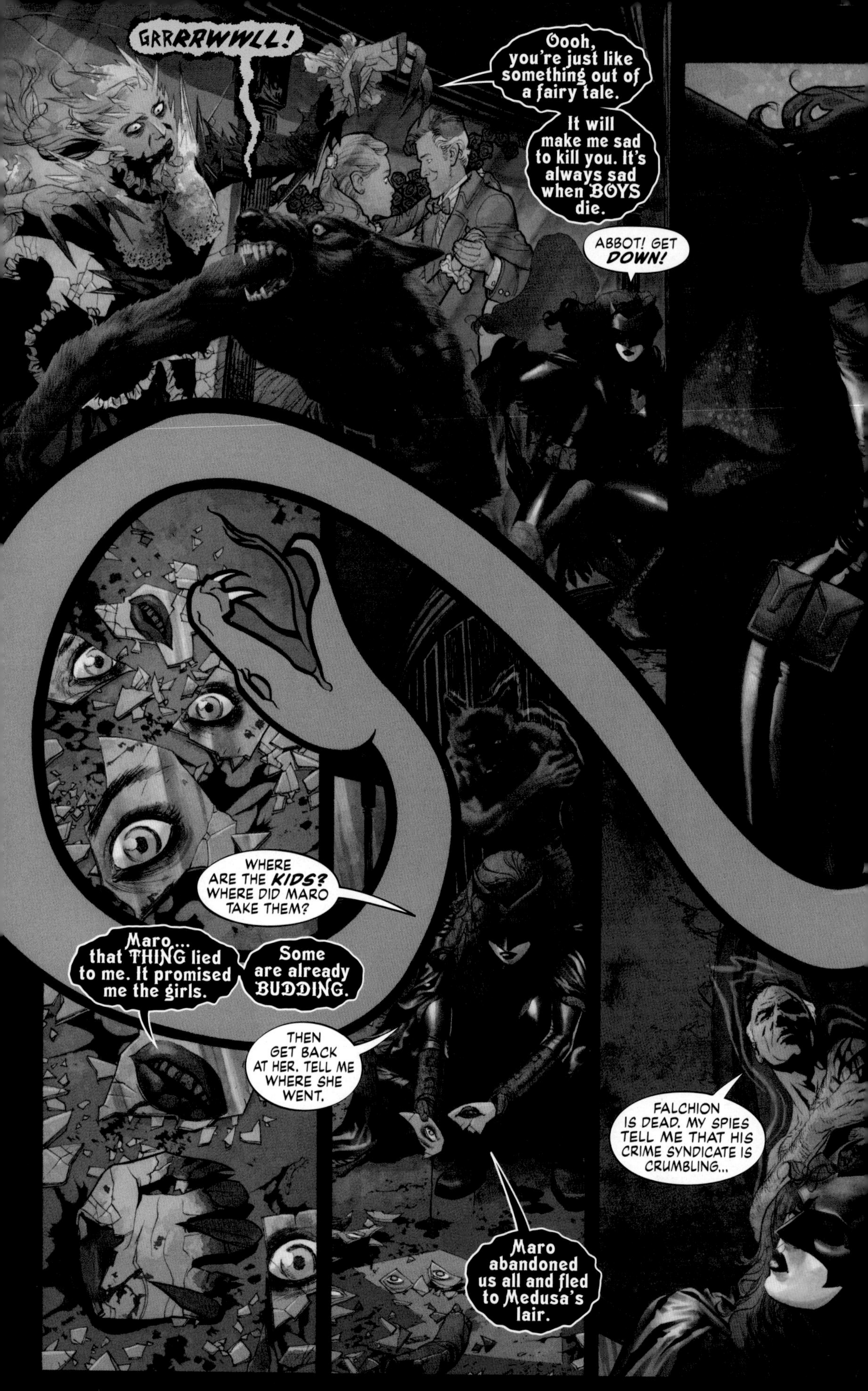

GRRRRWWLL!
Oooh, you're just like something out of a fairy tale.
It will make me sad to kill you. It's always sad when BOYS die.
ABBOT! GET DOWN!
WHERE ARE THE KIDS? WHERE DID MARO TAKE THEM?
Maro... that THING lied to me. It promised me the girls.
Some are already BUDDING.
THEN GET BACK AT HER. TELL ME WHERE SHE WENT.
Maro abandoned us all and fled to Medusa's lair.
FALCHION IS DEAD. MY SPIES TELL ME THAT HIS CRIME SYNDICATE IS CRUMBLING...

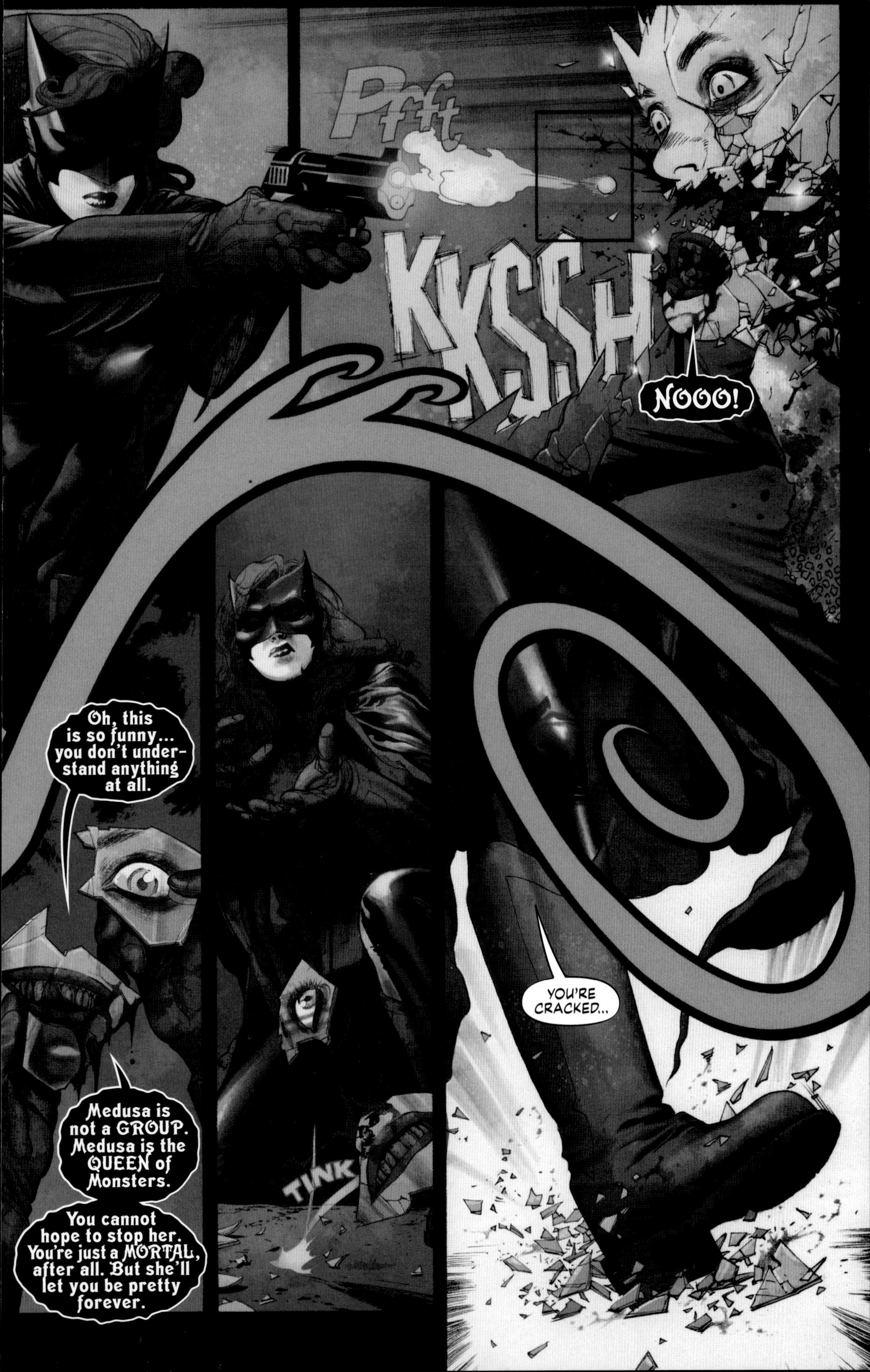
Pfft
KXSSH
NOOO!
Oh, this is so funny... you don't understand anything at all.
Medusa is not a GROUP. Medusa is the QUEEN of Monsters.
You cannot hope to stop her. You're just a MORTAL, after all. But she'll let you be pretty forever.
TINK
YOU'RE CRACKED...

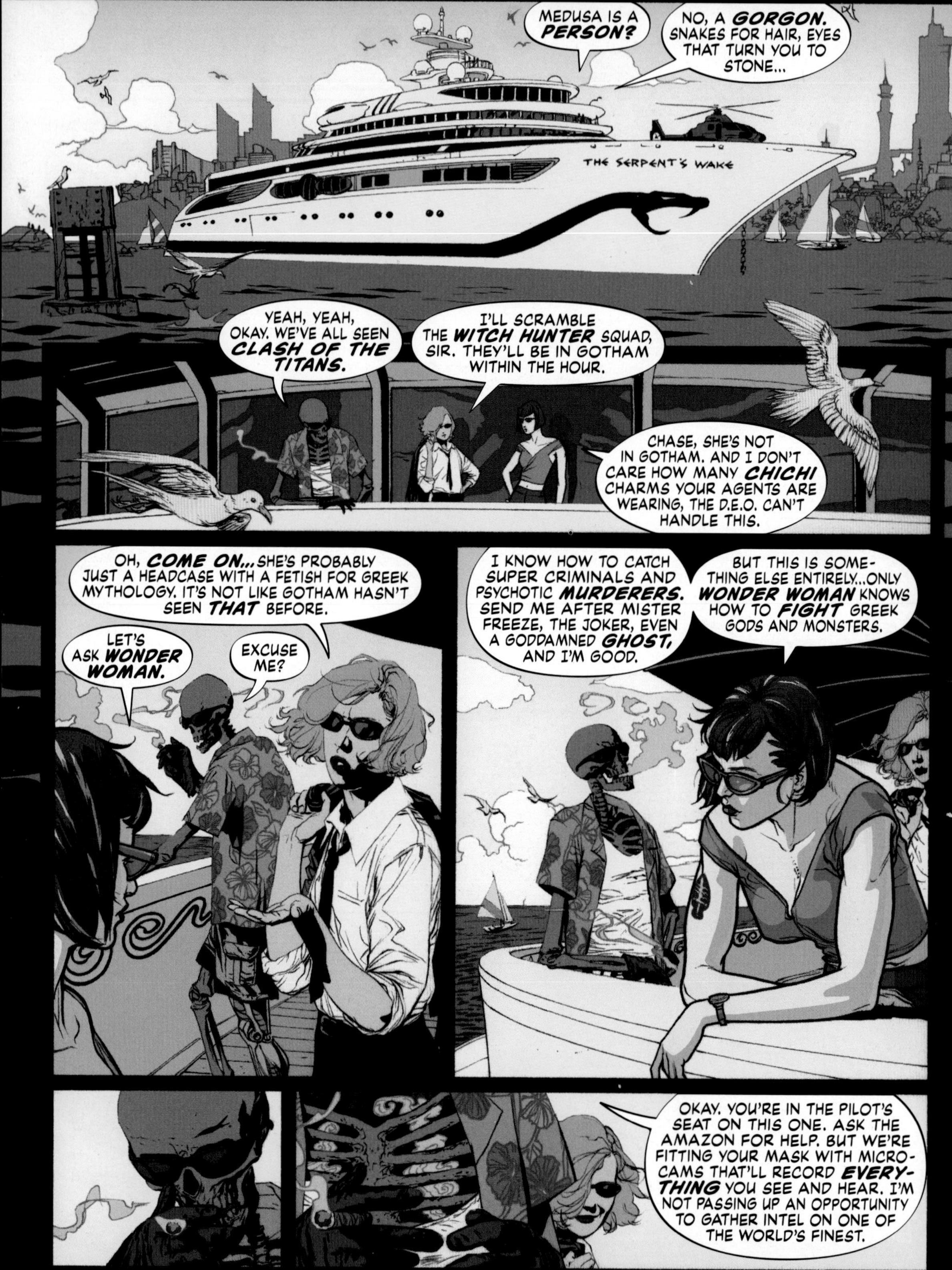
MEDUSA IS A PERSON?
NO, A GORGON. SNAKES FOR HAIR, EYES THAT TURN YOU TO STONE...
THE SERPENT'S WAKE
YEAH, YEAH, OKAY. WE'VE ALL SEEN CLASH OF THE TITANS.
I'LL SCRAMBLE THE WITCH HUNTER SQUAD, SIR. THEY'LL BE IN GOTHAM WITHIN THE HOUR.
CHASE, SHE'S NOT IN GOTHAM. AND I DON'T CARE HOW MANY CHICHI CHARMS YOUR AGENTS ARE WEARING, THE D.E.O. CAN'T HANDLE THIS.
OH, COME ON... SHE'S PROBABLY JUST A HEADCASE WITH A FETISH FOR GREEK MYTHOLOGY. IT'S NOT LIKE GOTHAM HASN'T SEEN THAT BEFORE.
LET'S ASK WONDER WOMAN.
EXCUSE ME?
I KNOW HOW TO CATCH SUPER CRIMINALS AND PSYCHOTIC MURDERERS. SEND ME AFTER MISTER FREEZE, THE JOKER, EVEN A GODDAMNED GHOST, AND I'M GOOD.
BUT THIS IS SOMETHING ELSE ENTIRELY...ONLY WONDER WOMAN KNOWS HOW TO FIGHT GREEK GODS AND MONSTERS.
OKAY. YOU'RE IN THE PILOT'S SEAT ON THIS ONE. ASK THE AMAZON FOR HELP. BUT WE'RE FITTING YOUR MASK WITH MICROCAMS THAT'LL RECORD EVERYTHING YOU SEE AND HEAR. I'M NOT PASSING UP AN OPPORTUNITY TO GATHER INTEL ON ONE OF THE WORLD'S FINEST.

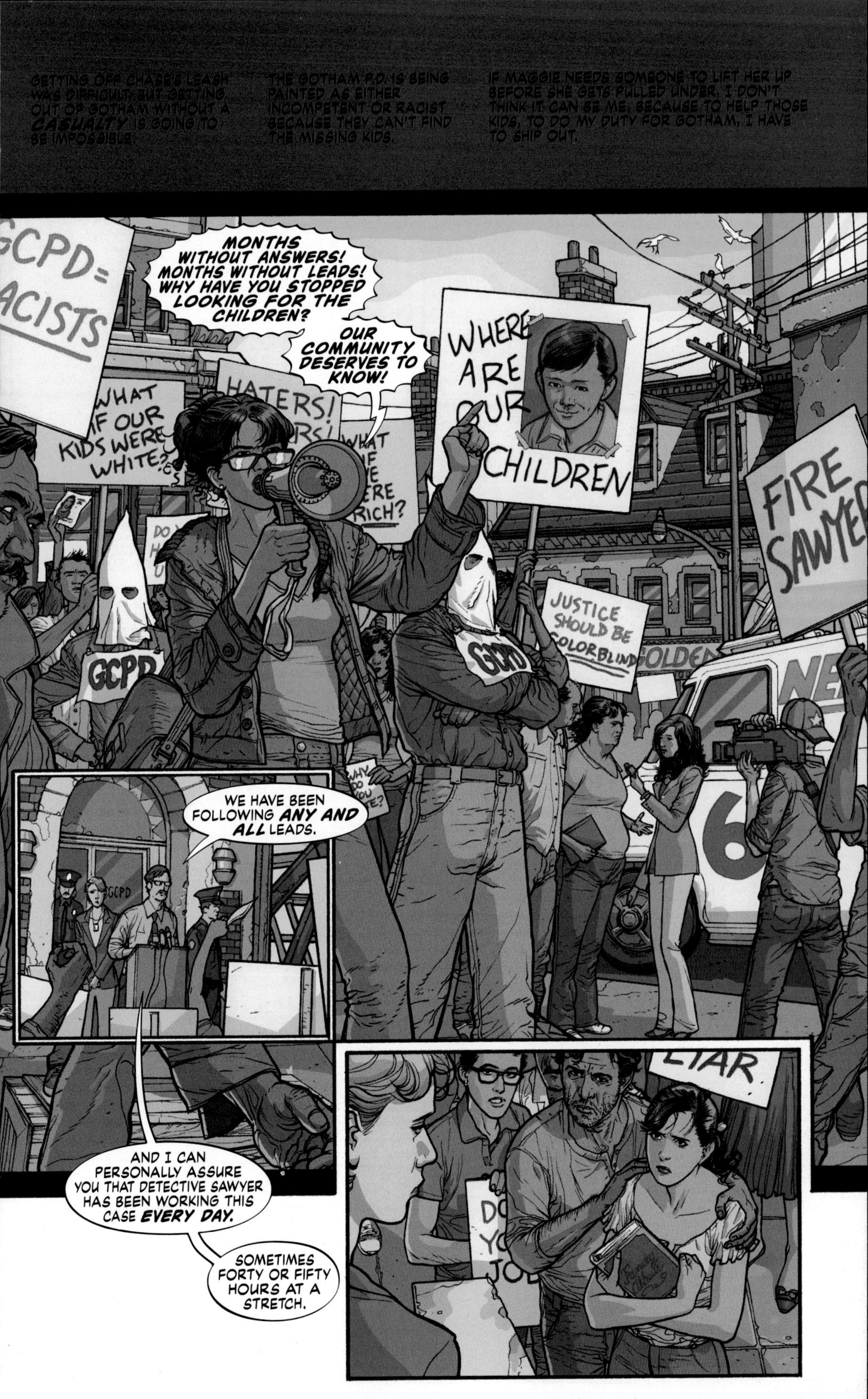
GETTING OFF CHASE'S LEASH WAS DIFFICULT, BUT GETTING OUT OF GOTHAM WITHOUT A CASUALTY IS GOING TO BE IMPOSSIBLE.
THE GOTHAM P.D. IS BEING PAINTED AS EITHER INCOMPETENT OR RACIST BECAUSE THEY CAN'T FIND THE MISSING KIDS.
IF MAGGIE NEEDS SOMEONE TO LIFT HER UP BEFORE SHE GETS PULLED UNDER, I DON'T THINK IT CAN BE ME. BECAUSE TO HELP THOSE KIDS, TO DO MY DUTY FOR GOTHAM, I HAVE TO SHIP OUT.
GCPD= RACISTS
MONTHS WITHOUT ANSWERS! MONTHS WITHOUT LEADS! WHY HAVE YOU STOPPED LOOKING FOR THE CHILDREN?
OUR COMMUNITY DESERVES TO KNOW!
WHERE ARE OUR CHILDREN
WHAT IF OUR KIDS WERE WHITE?
HATERS!
FIRE SAWYER
JUSTICE SHOULD BE COLORBLIND
GCPD
GCPD
WE HAVE BEEN FOLLOWING ANY AND ALL LEADS.
GCPD
LIAR.
AND I CAN PERSONALLY ASSURE YOU THAT DETECTIVE SAWYER HAS BEEN WORKING THIS CASE EVERY DAY.
SOMETIMES FORTY OR FIFTY HOURS AT A STRETCH.

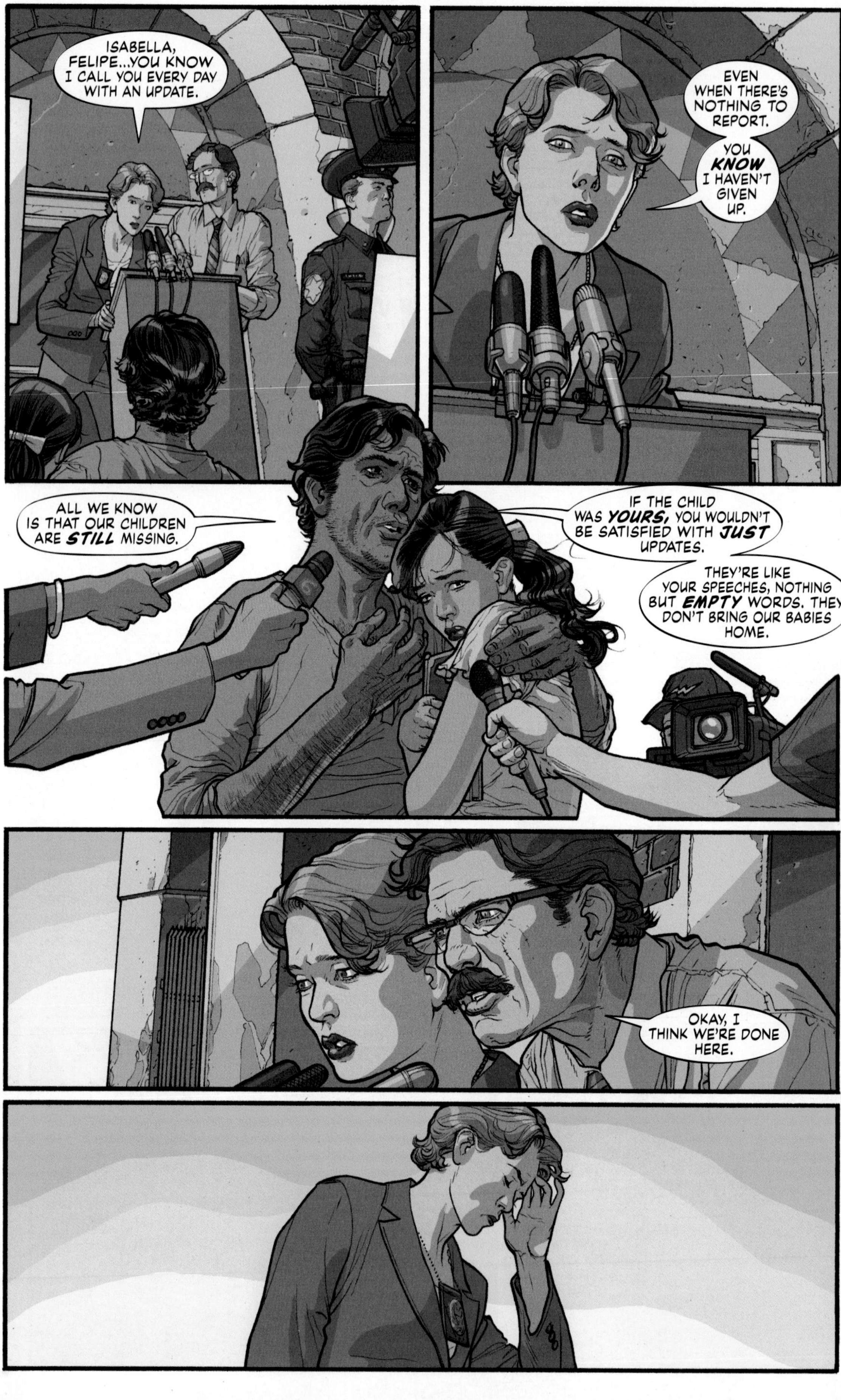
ISABELLA, FELIPE...YOU KNOW I CALL YOU EVERY DAY WITH AN UPDATE.
EVEN WHEN THERE'S NOTHING TO REPORT.
YOU KNOW I HAVEN'T GIVEN UP.
ALL WE KNOW IS THAT OUR CHILDREN ARE STILL MISSING.
IF THE CHILD WAS YOURS, YOU WOULDN'T BE SATISFIED WITH JUST UPDATES.
THEY'RE LIKE YOUR SPEECHES, NOTHING BUT EMPTY WORDS. THEY DON'T BRING OUR BABIES HOME.
OKAY, I THINK WE'RE DONE HERE.

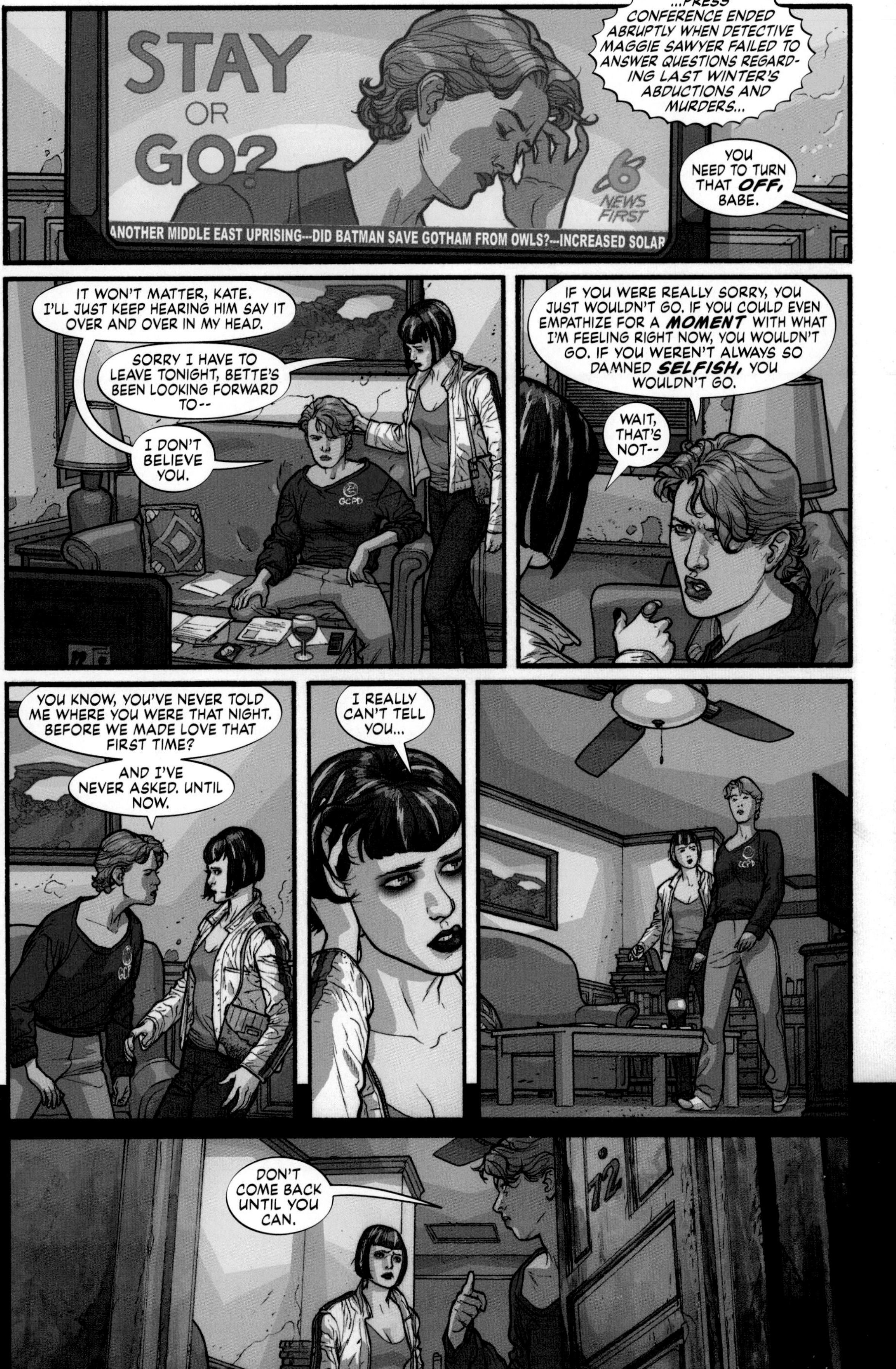

STAY OR GO?
6 NEWS FIRST
...PRESS CONFERENCE ENDED ABRUPTLY WHEN DETECTIVE MAGGIE SAWYER FAILED TO ANSWER QUESTIONS REGARDING LAST WINTER'S ABDUCTIONS AND MURDERS...
ANOTHER MIDDLE EAST UPRISING---DID BATMAN SAVE GOTHAM FROM OWLS?---INCREASED SOLAR
YOU NEED TO TURN THAT OFF, BABE.
IT WON'T MATTER, KATE. I'LL JUST KEEP HEARING HIM SAY IT OVER AND OVER IN MY HEAD.
SORRY I HAVE TO LEAVE TONIGHT, BETTE'S BEEN LOOKING FORWARD TO--
I DON'T BELIEVE YOU.
GCPD
IF YOU WERE REALLY SORRY, YOU JUST WOULDN'T GO. IF YOU COULD EVEN EMPATHIZE FOR A MOMENT WITH WHAT I'M FEELING RIGHT NOW, YOU WOULDN'T GO. IF YOU WEREN'T ALWAYS SO DAMNED SELFISH, YOU WOULDN'T GO.
WAIT, THAT'S NOT--
YOU KNOW, YOU'VE NEVER TOLD ME WHERE YOU WERE THAT NIGHT. BEFORE WE MADE LOVE THAT FIRST TIME?
AND I'VE NEVER ASKED. UNTIL NOW.
GCPD
I REALLY CAN'T TELL YOU...
GCPD
DON'T COME BACK UNTIL YOU CAN.
72

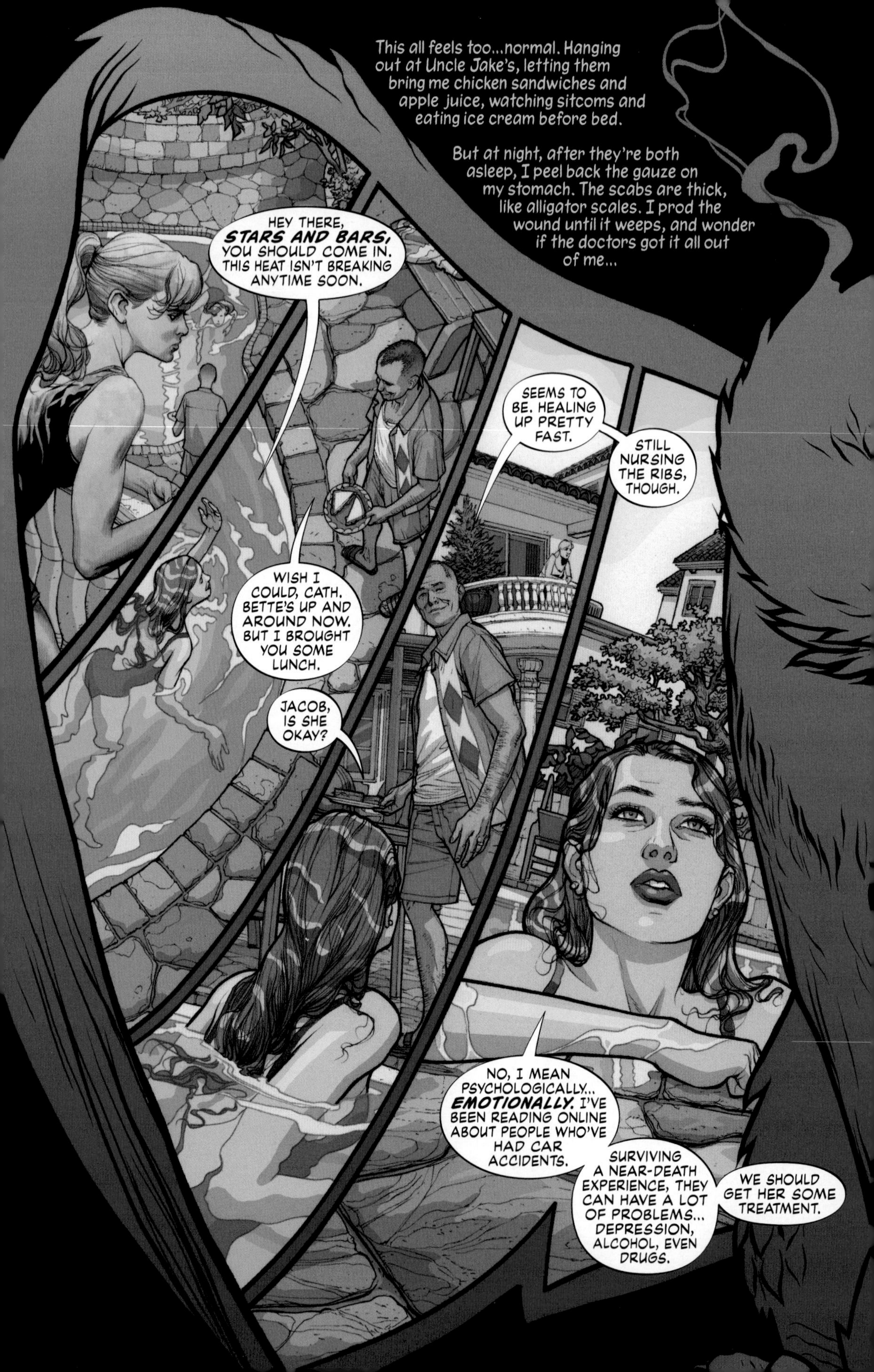
This all feels too...normal. Hanging out at Uncle Jake's, letting them bring me chicken sandwiches and apple juice, watching sitcoms and eating ice cream before bed.
But at night, after they're both asleep, I peel back the gauze on my stomach. The scabs are thick, like alligator scales. I prod the wound until it weeps, and wonder if the doctors got it all out of me...
HEY THERE, STARS AND BARS, YOU SHOULD COME IN. THIS HEAT ISN'T BREAKING ANYTIME SOON.
WISH I COULD, CATH. BETTE'S UP AND AROUND NOW. BUT I BROUGHT YOU SOME LUNCH.
JACOB, IS SHE OKAY?
SEEMS TO BE. HEALING UP PRETTY FAST.
STILL NURSING THE RIBS, THOUGH.
NO, I MEAN PSYCHOLOGICALLY... EMOTIONALLY. I'VE BEEN READING ONLINE ABOUT PEOPLE WHO'VE HAD CAR ACCIDENTS.
SURVIVING A NEAR-DEATH EXPERIENCE, THEY CAN HAVE A LOT OF PROBLEMS... DEPRESSION, ALCOHOL, EVEN DRUGS.
WE SHOULD GET HER SOME TREATMENT.

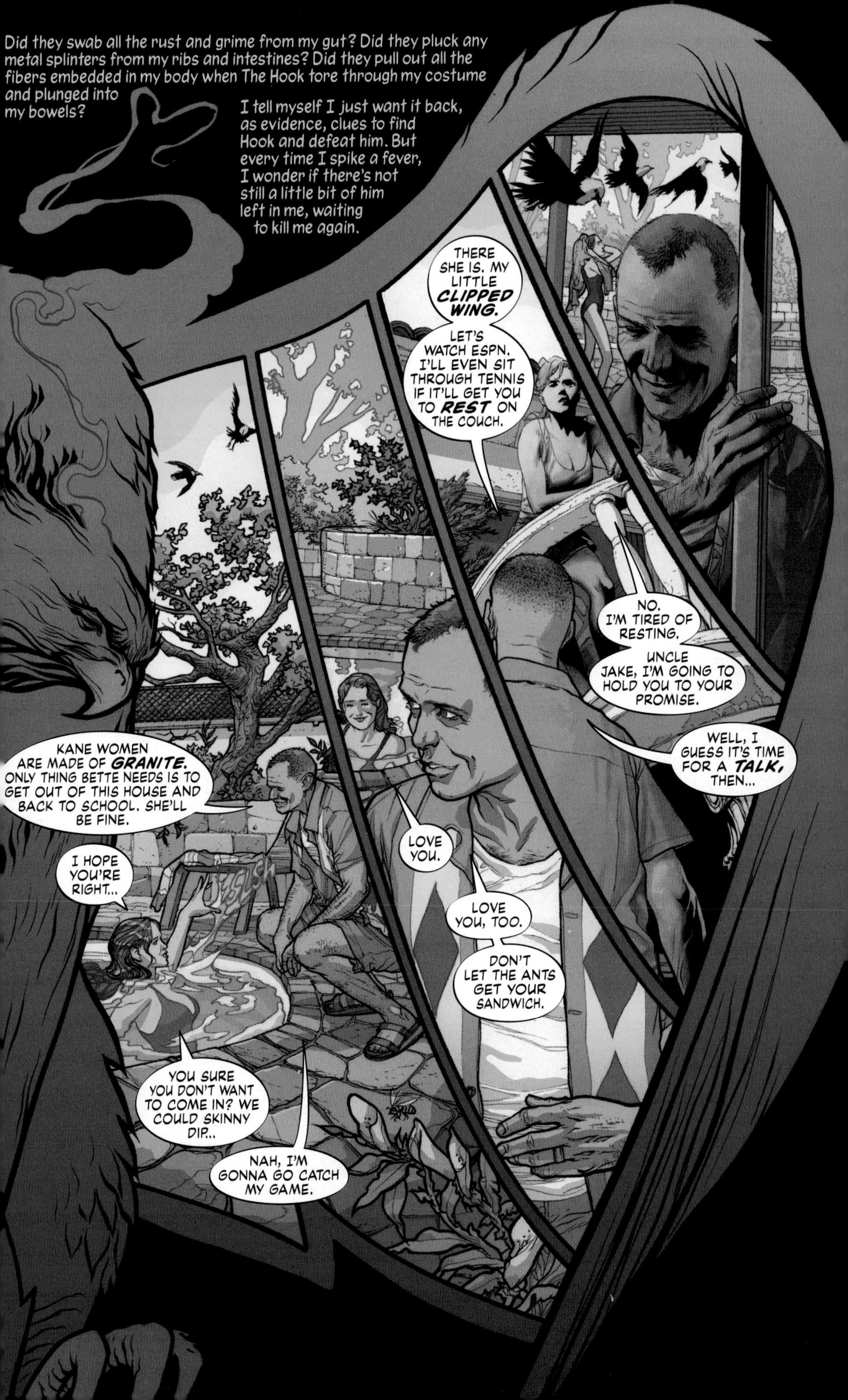
Did they swab all the rust and grime from my gut? Did they pluck any metal splinters from my ribs and intestines? Did they pull out all the fibers embedded in my body when The Hook tore through my costume and plunged into my bowels?
I tell myself I just want it back, as evidence, clues to find Hook and defeat him. But every time I spike a fever, I wonder if there's not still a little bit of him left in me, waiting to kill me again.
KANE WOMEN ARE MADE OF GRANITE. ONLY THING BETTE NEEDS IS TO GET OUT OF THIS HOUSE AND BACK TO SCHOOL. SHE'LL BE FINE.
I HOPE YOU'RE RIGHT...
SPLSH
YOU SURE YOU DON'T WANT TO COME IN? WE COULD SKINNY DIP...
NAH, I'M GONNA GO CATCH MY GAME.
LOVE YOU.
LOVE YOU, TOO.
DON'T LET THE ANTS GET YOUR SANDWICH.
THERE SHE IS. MY LITTLE CLIPPED WING.
LET'S WATCH ESPN. I'LL EVEN SIT THROUGH TENNIS IF IT'LL GET YOU TO REST ON THE COUCH.
NO. I'M TIRED OF RESTING.
UNCLE JAKE, I'M GOING TO HOLD YOU TO YOUR PROMISE.
WELL, I GUESS IT'S TIME FOR A TALK, THEN...

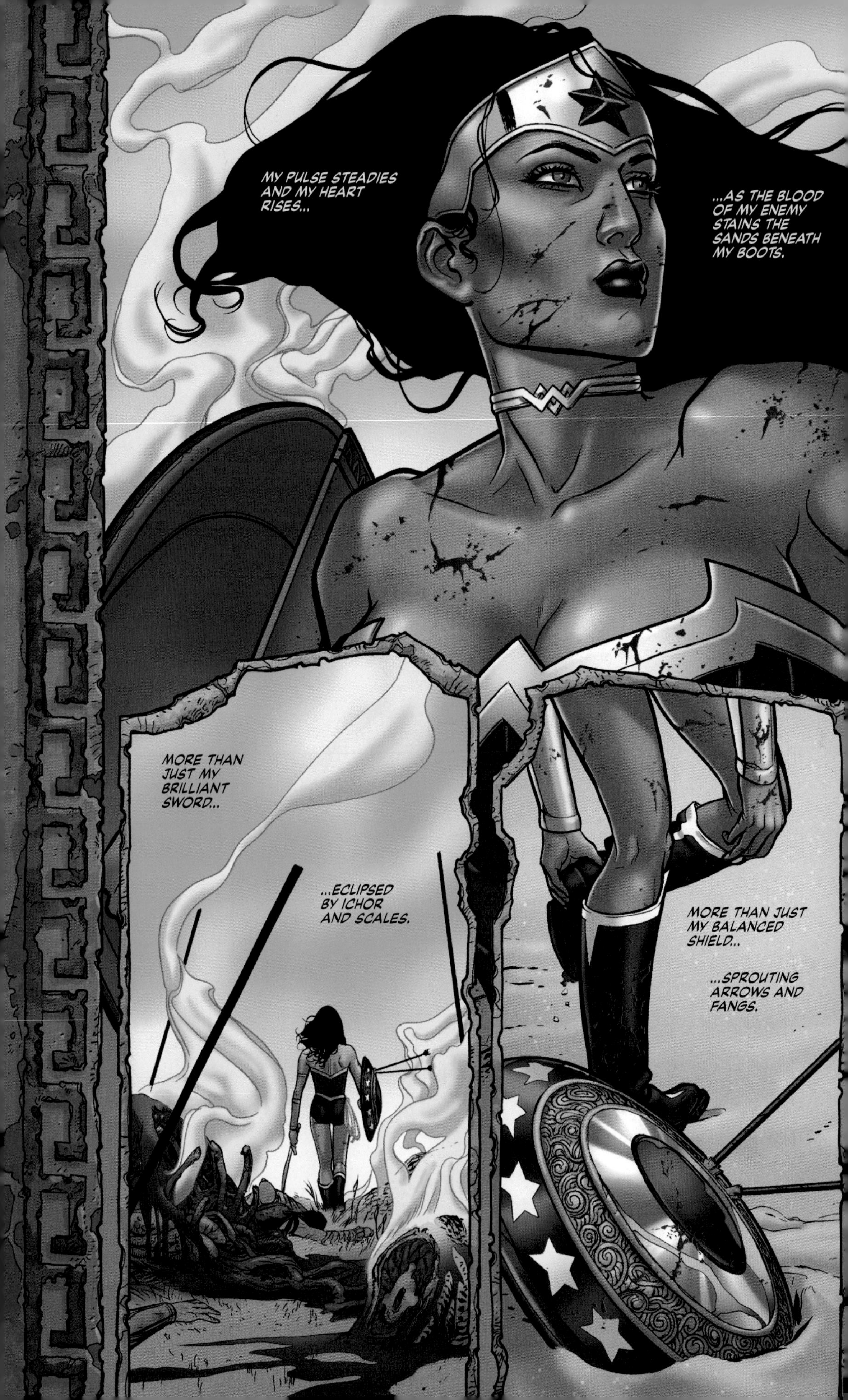
MY PULSE STEADIES AND MY HEART RISES...
...AS THE BLOOD OF MY ENEMY STAINS THE SANDS BENEATH MY BOOTS.
MORE THAN JUST MY BRILLIANT SWORD...
...ECLIPSED BY ICHOR AND SCALES.
MORE THAN JUST MY BALANCED SHIELD...
...SPROUTING ARROWS AND FANGS.

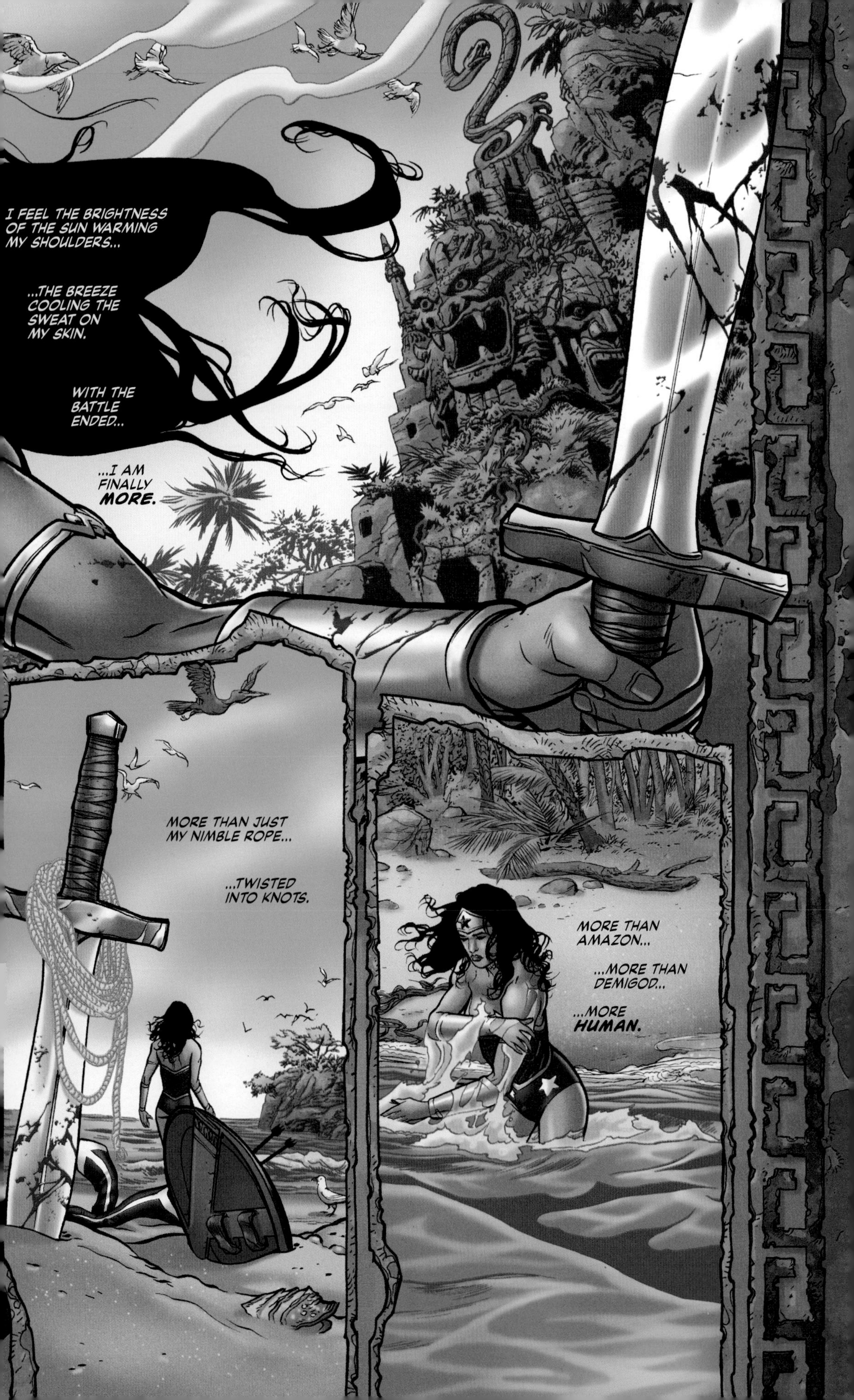
I FEEL THE BRIGHTNESS OF THE SUN WARMING MY SHOULDERS...
...THE BREEZE COOLING THE SWEAT ON MY SKIN.
WITH THE BATTLE ENDED...
...I AM FINALLY MORE.
MORE THAN JUST MY NIMBLE ROPE...
...TWISTED INTO KNOTS.
MORE THAN AMAZON...
...MORE THAN DEMIGOD...
...MORE HUMAN.

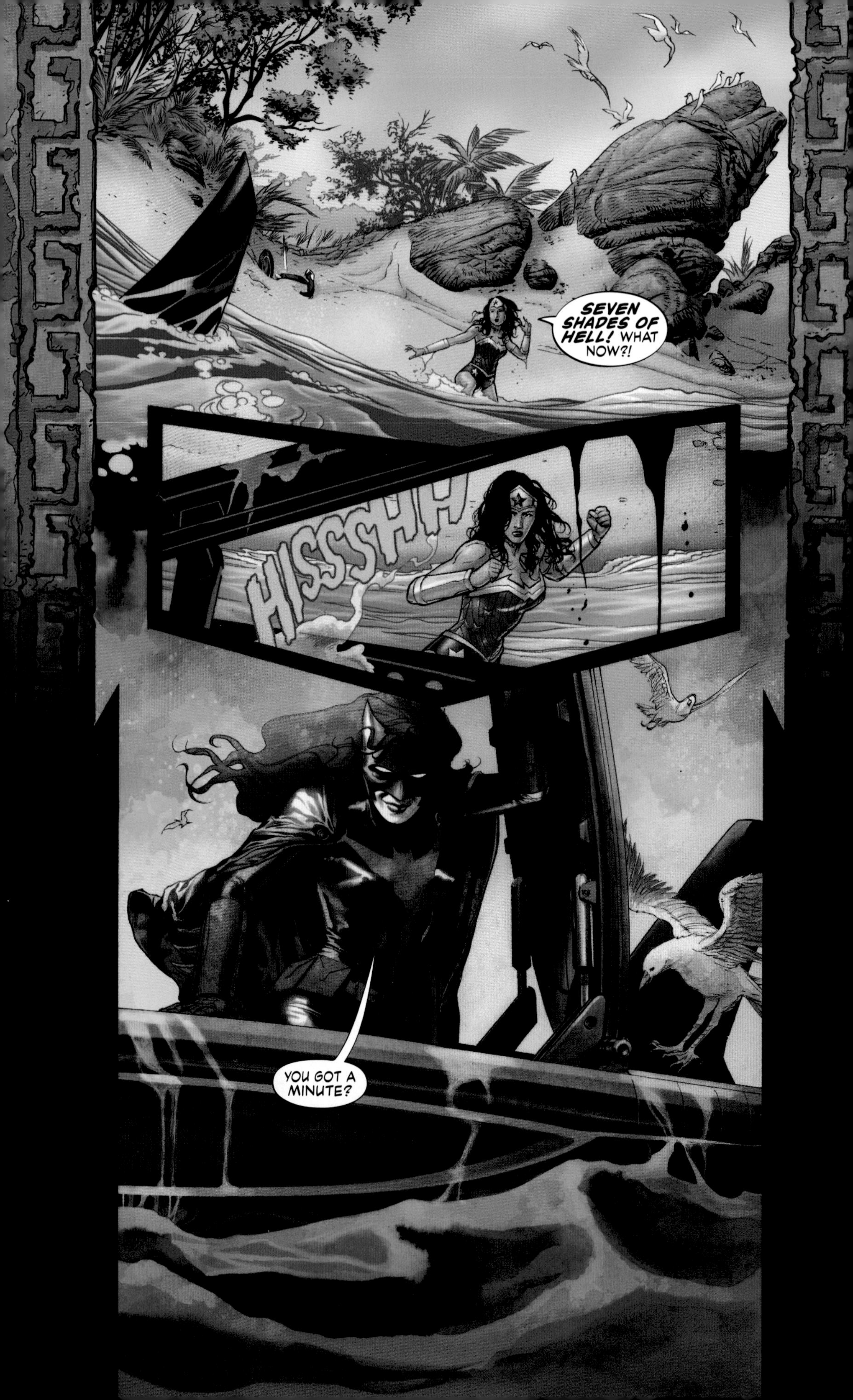
SEVEN SHADES OF HELL! WHAT NOW?!
HISSSHH
YOU GOT A MINUTE?

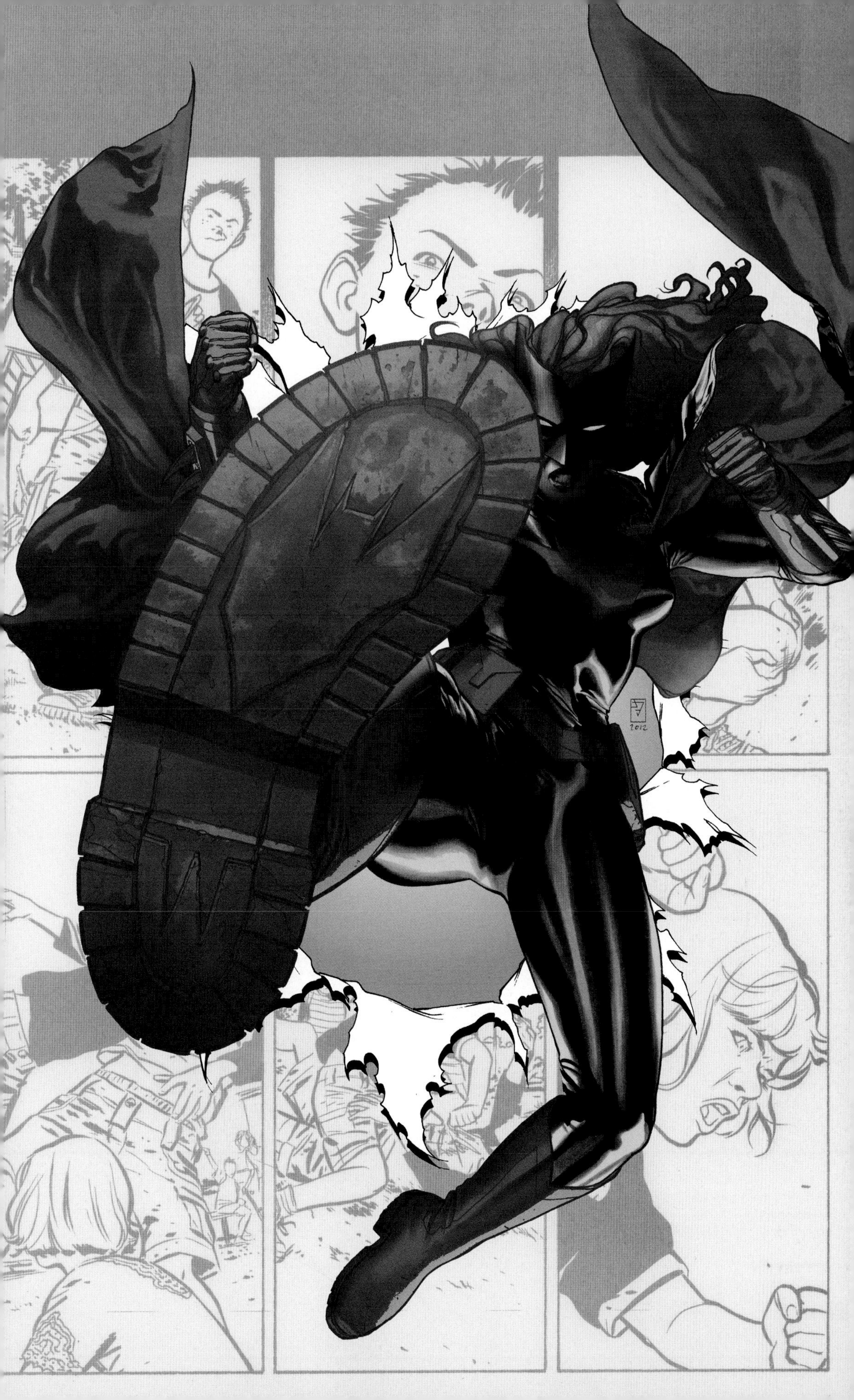

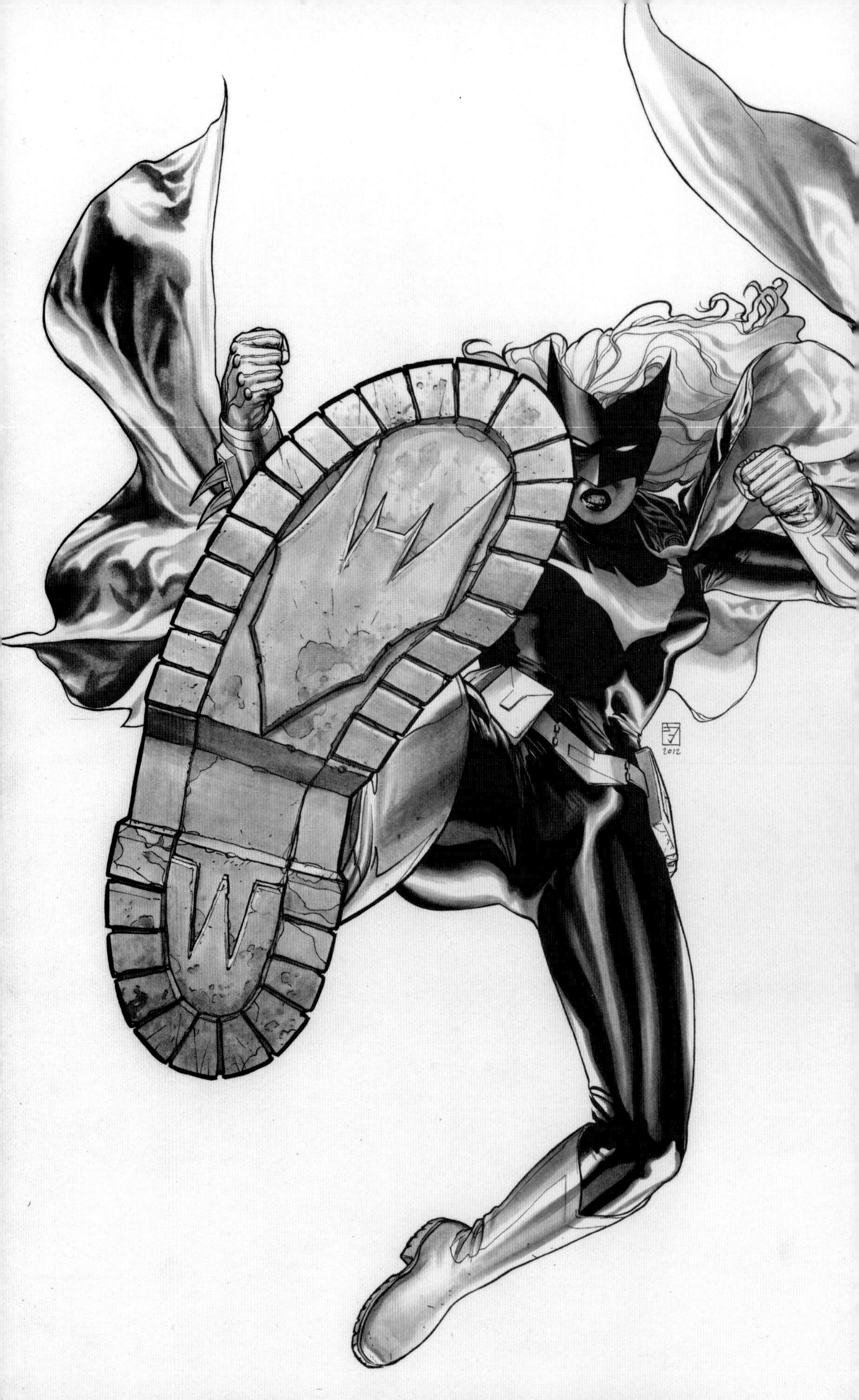
2012

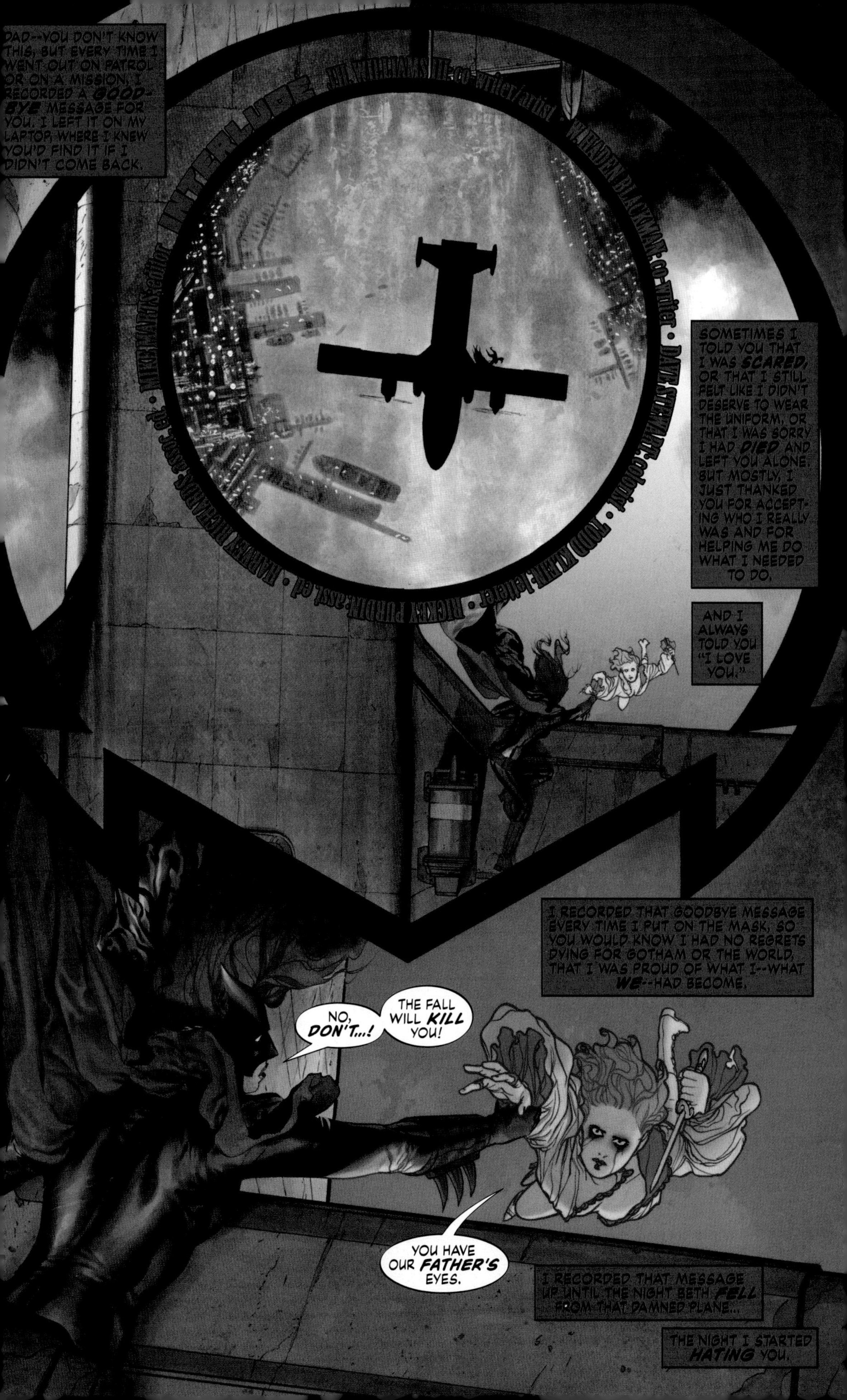
DAD--YOU DON'T KNOW THIS, BUT EVERY TIME I WENT OUT ON PATROL OR ON A MISSION, I RECORDED A GOOD-BYE MESSAGE FOR YOU. I LEFT IT ON MY LAPTOP, WHERE I KNEW YOU'D FIND IT IF I DIDN'T COME BACK.
INTERLUDE
J.H. WILLIAMS III co-writer/artist • W. HADEN BLACKMAN co-writer • DAVE STEWART colorist • TODD KLEIN letterer • RICKY PURDIN asst ed • HARVEY RICHARDS asst. ed. • MIKE MARTS editor •
SOMETIMES I TOLD YOU THAT I WAS SCARED, OR THAT I STILL FELT LIKE I DIDN'T DESERVE TO WEAR THE UNIFORM, OR THAT I WAS SORRY I HAD DIED AND LEFT YOU ALONE. BUT MOSTLY, I JUST THANKED YOU FOR ACCEPTING WHO I REALLY WAS AND FOR HELPING ME DO WHAT I NEEDED TO DO.
AND I ALWAYS TOLD YOU "I LOVE YOU."
I RECORDED THAT GOODBYE MESSAGE EVERY TIME I PUT ON THE MASK, SO YOU WOULD KNOW I HAD NO REGRETS DYING FOR GOTHAM OR THE WORLD, THAT I WAS PROUD OF WHAT I--WHAT WE--HAD BECOME.
NO, DON'T...!
THE FALL WILL KILL YOU!
YOU HAVE OUR FATHER'S EYES.
I RECORDED THAT MESSAGE UP UNTIL THE NIGHT BETH FELL FROM THAT DAMNED PLANE...
THE NIGHT I STARTED HATING YOU.

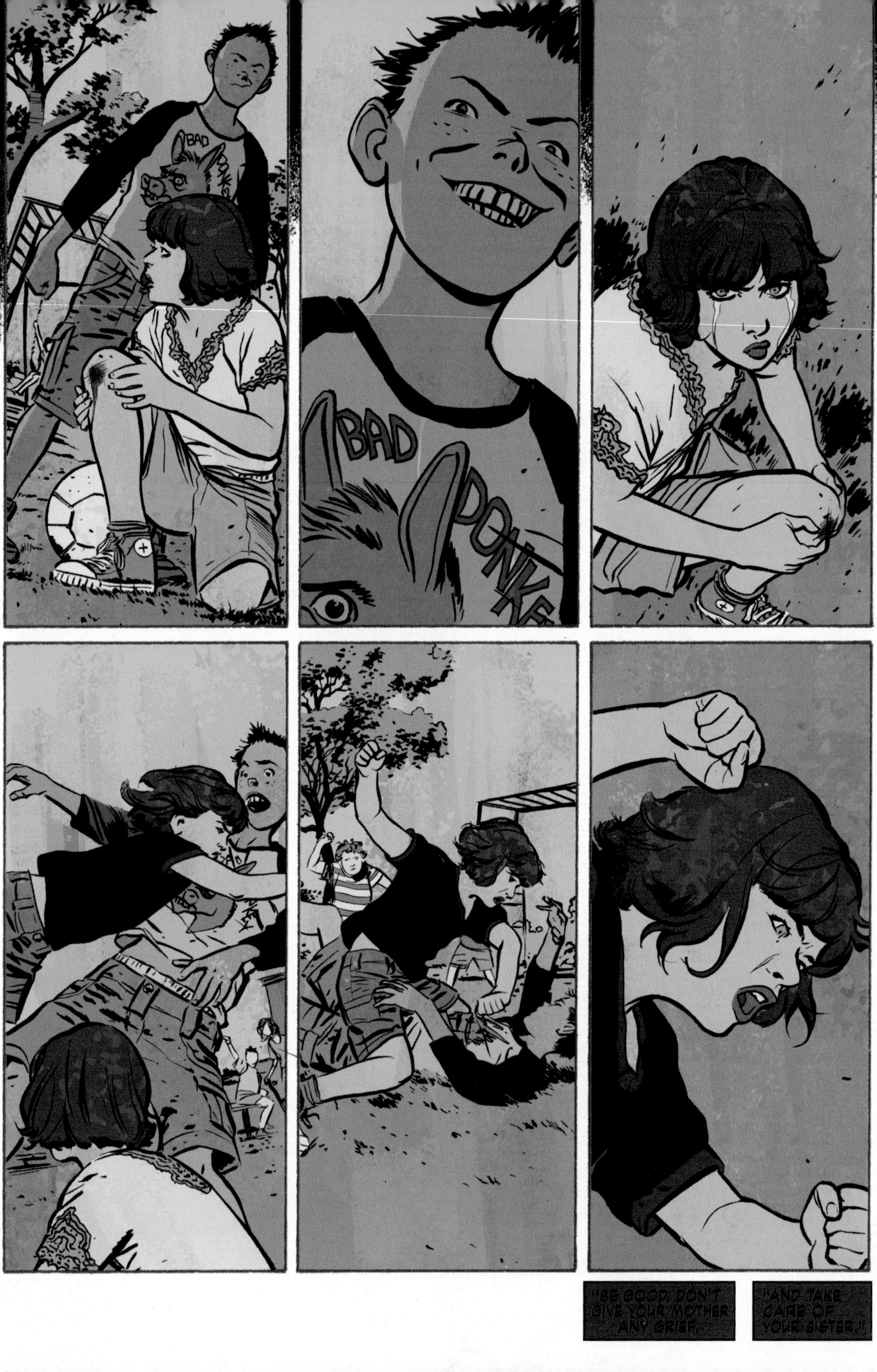
BAD
BAD
DONKE
"BE GOOD. DON'T GIVE YOUR MOTHER ANY GRIEF.
"AND TAKE CARE OF YOUR SISTER."

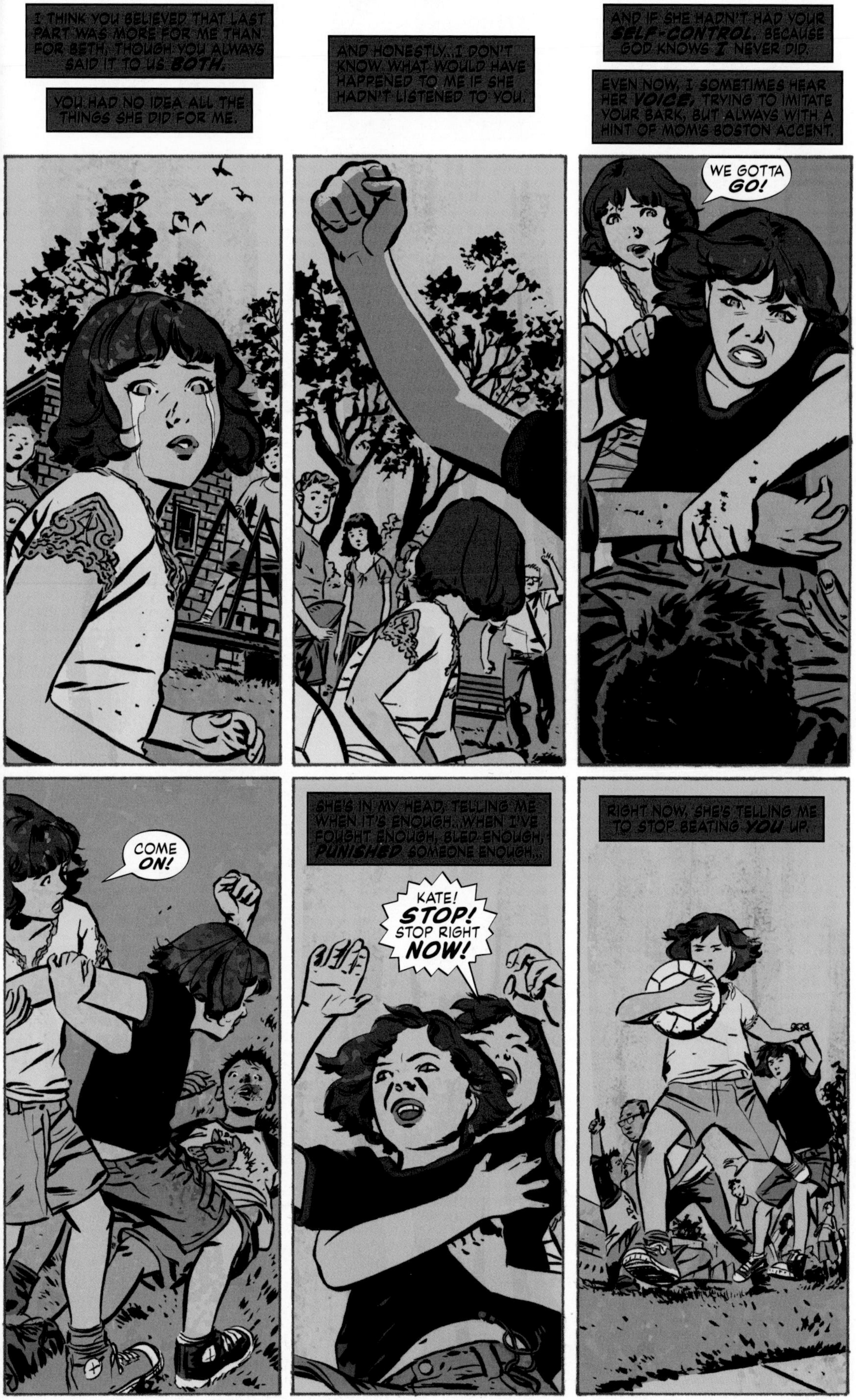
I THINK YOU BELIEVED THAT LAST PART WAS MORE FOR ME THAN FOR BETH, THOUGH YOU ALWAYS SAID IT TO US BOTH.
YOU HAD NO IDEA ALL THE THINGS SHE DID FOR ME.
AND HONESTLY...I DON'T KNOW WHAT WOULD HAVE HAPPENED TO ME IF SHE HADN'T LISTENED TO YOU.
AND IF SHE HADN'T HAD YOUR SELF-CONTROL, BECAUSE GOD KNOWS I NEVER DID.
EVEN NOW, I SOMETIMES HEAR HER VOICE, TRYING TO IMITATE YOUR BARK, BUT ALWAYS WITH A HINT OF MOM'S BOSTON ACCENT.
WE GOTTA GO!
COME ON!
SHE'S IN MY HEAD, TELLING ME WHEN IT'S ENOUGH...WHEN I'VE FOUGHT ENOUGH, BLED ENOUGH, PUNISHED SOMEONE ENOUGH...
KATE! STOP! STOP RIGHT NOW!
RIGHT NOW, SHE'S TELLING ME TO STOP BEATING YOU UP.

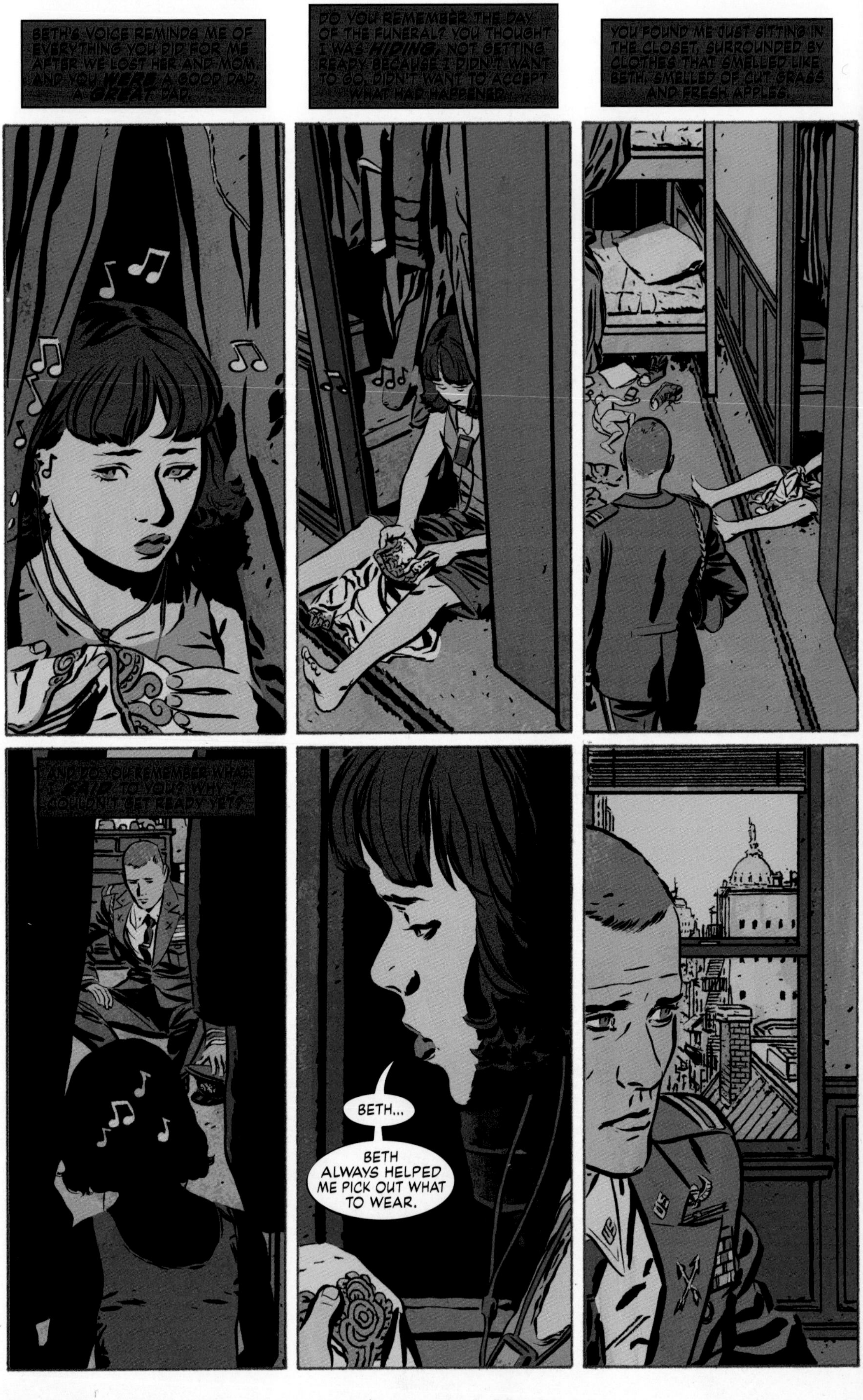
BETH'S VOICE REMINDS ME OF EVERYTHING YOU DID FOR ME AFTER WE LOST HER AND MOM. AND YOU *WERE* A GOOD DAD. A *GREAT* DAD.
DO YOU REMEMBER THE DAY OF THE FUNERAL? YOU THOUGHT I WAS *HIDING*, NOT GETTING READY BECAUSE I DIDN'T WANT TO GO, DIDN'T WANT TO ACCEPT WHAT HAD HAPPENED...
YOU FOUND ME JUST SITTING IN THE CLOSET, SURROUNDED BY CLOTHES THAT SMELLED LIKE BETH. SMELLED OF CUT GRASS AND FRESH APPLES.
AND DO YOU REMEMBER WHAT I *SAID* TO YOU? WHY I COULDN'T GET READY YET?
BETH...
BETH ALWAYS HELPED ME PICK OUT WHAT TO WEAR.

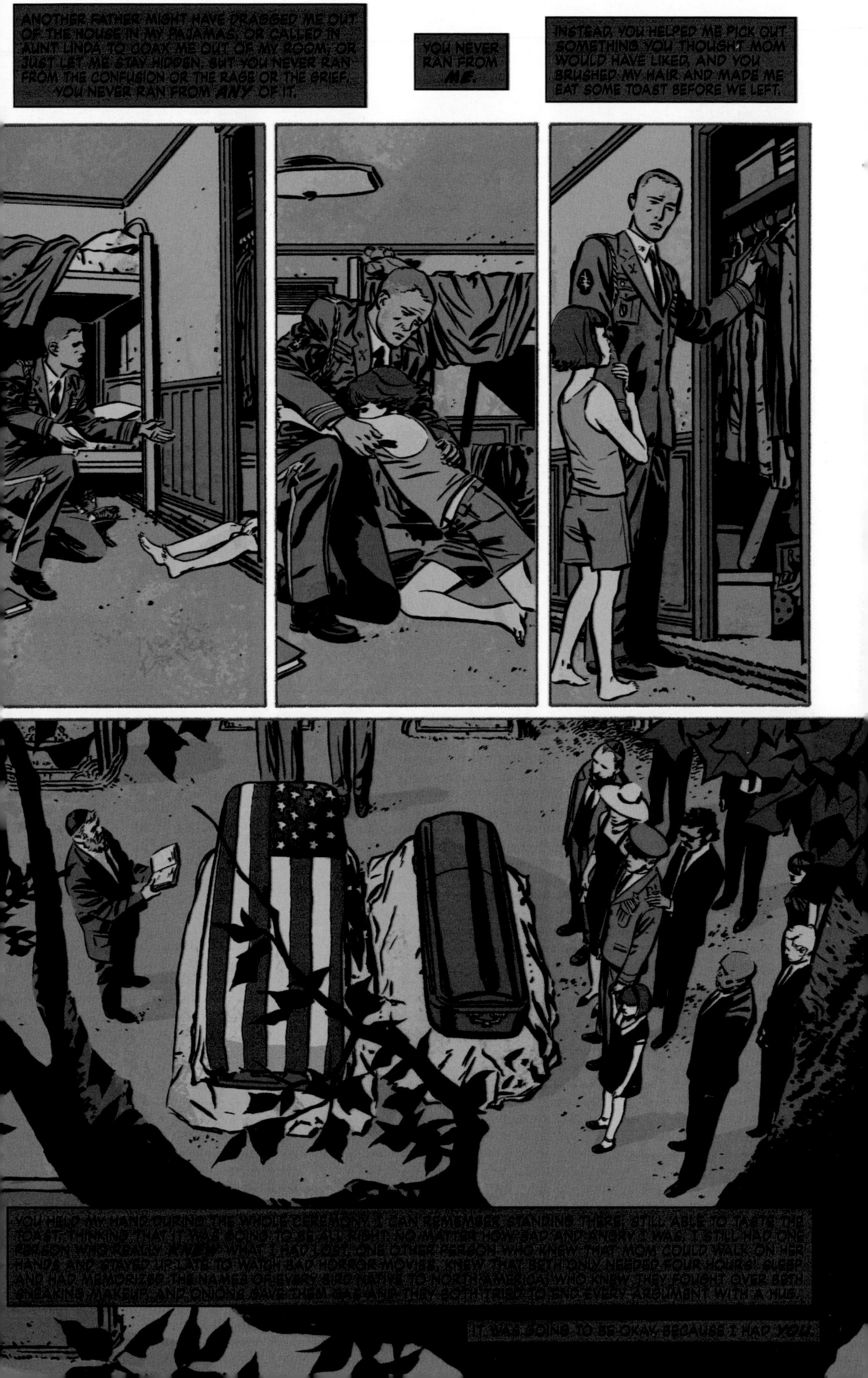
ANOTHER FATHER MIGHT HAVE DRAGGED ME OUT OF THE HOUSE IN MY PAJAMAS, OR CALLED IN AUNT LINDA TO COAX ME OUT OF MY ROOM, OR JUST LET ME STAY HIDDEN. BUT YOU NEVER RAN FROM THE CONFUSION OR THE RAGE OR THE GRIEF. YOU NEVER RAN FROM ANY OF IT.
YOU NEVER RAN FROM ME.
INSTEAD, YOU HELPED ME PICK OUT SOMETHING YOU THOUGHT MOM WOULD HAVE LIKED, AND YOU BRUSHED MY HAIR AND MADE ME EAT SOME TOAST BEFORE WE LEFT.
YOU HELD MY HAND DURING THE WHOLE CEREMONY. I CAN REMEMBER STANDING THERE, STILL ABLE TO TASTE THE TOAST, THINKING THAT IT WAS GOING TO BE ALL RIGHT. NO MATTER HOW SAD AND ANGRY I WAS, I STILL HAD ONE PERSON WHO REALLY KNEW WHAT I HAD LOST. ONE OTHER PERSON WHO KNEW THAT MOM COULD WALK ON HER HANDS AND STAYED UP LATE TO WATCH BAD HORROR MOVIES, KNEW THAT BETH ONLY NEEDED FOUR HOURS' SLEEP AND HAD MEMORIZED THE NAMES OF EVERY BIRD NATIVE TO NORTH AMERICA. WHO KNEW THEY FOUGHT OVER BETH SNEAKING MAKEUP AND ONIONS GAVE THEM GAS AND THEY BOTH TRIED TO END EVERY ARGUMENT WITH A HUG.
IT WAS GOING TO BE OKAY BECAUSE I HAD YOU.

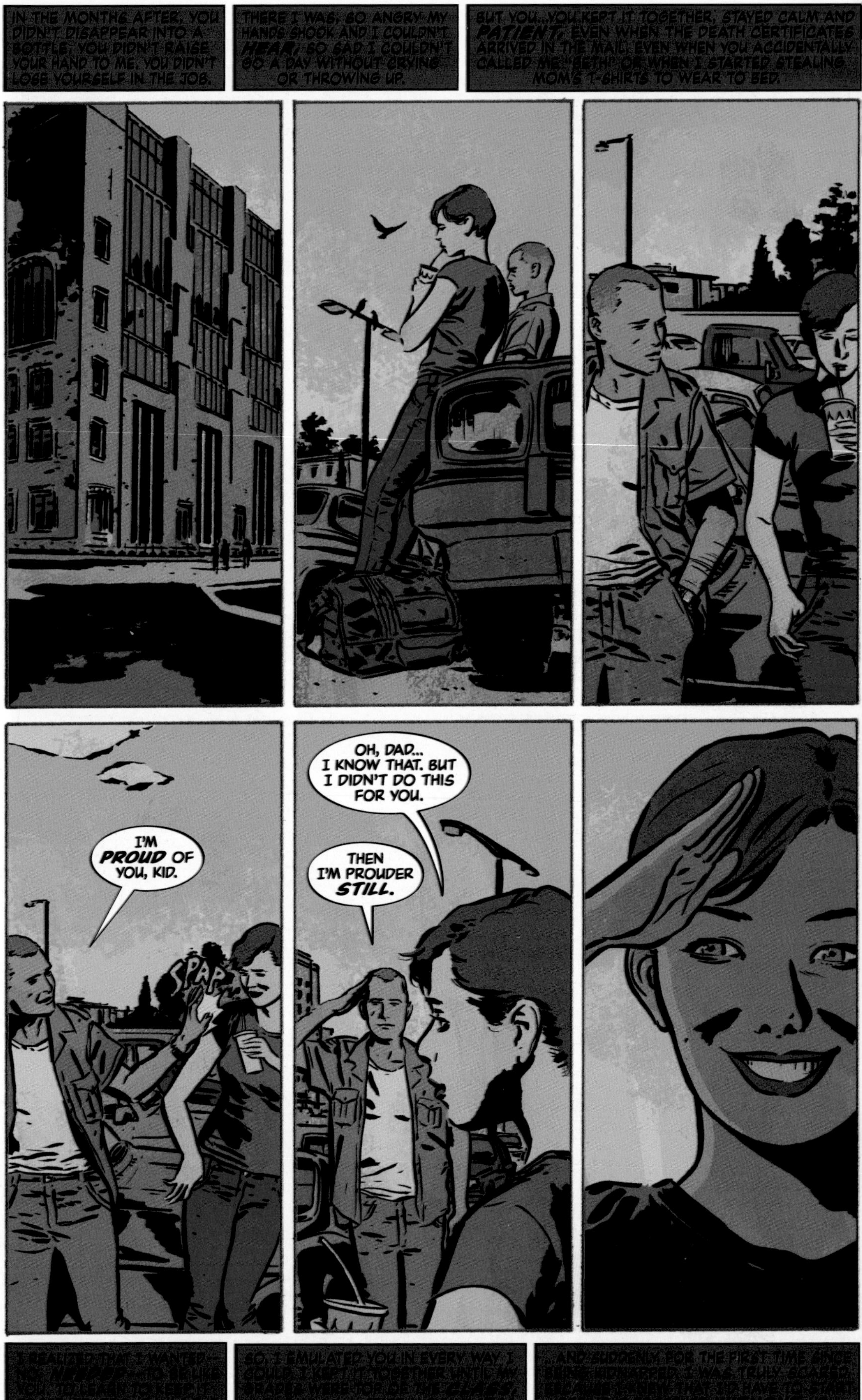
IN THE MONTHS AFTER, YOU DIDN'T DISAPPEAR INTO A BOTTLE. YOU DIDN'T RAISE YOUR HAND TO ME. YOU DIDN'T LOSE YOURSELF IN THE JOB.
THERE I WAS, SO ANGRY MY HANDS SHOOK AND I COULDN'T *HEAR*, SO SAD I COULDN'T GO A DAY WITHOUT CRYING OR THROWING UP.
BUT YOU...YOU KEPT IT TOGETHER, STAYED CALM AND *PATIENT*, EVEN WHEN THE DEATH CERTIFICATES ARRIVED IN THE MAIL, EVEN WHEN YOU ACCIDENTALLY CALLED ME "BETH" OR WHEN I STARTED STEALING MOM'S T-SHIRTS TO WEAR TO BED.
I'M *PROUD* OF YOU, KID.
SPAP
OH, DAD... I KNOW THAT. BUT I DIDN'T DO THIS FOR YOU.
THEN I'M PROUDER *STILL*.
I REALIZED THAT I WANTED—NO, *NEEDED*—TO BE LIKE YOU. TO LEARN TO KEEP IT TOGETHER, TOO. IT WAS THE ONLY WAY I'D SURVIVE.
SO, I EMULATED YOU IN EVERY WAY I COULD. I KEPT IT TOGETHER UNTIL MY GRADES WERE TOP OF THE *CLASS*, UNTIL I WAS ALL-STATE IN GYMNASTICS, UNTIL I MADE IT INTO WEST POINT...
...AND SUDDENLY, FOR THE FIRST TIME SINCE BEING KIDNAPPED, I WAS TRULY SCARED. BECAUSE I KNEW THAT I'D HAVE TO START KEEPING IT TOGETHER *WITHOUT* YOU...

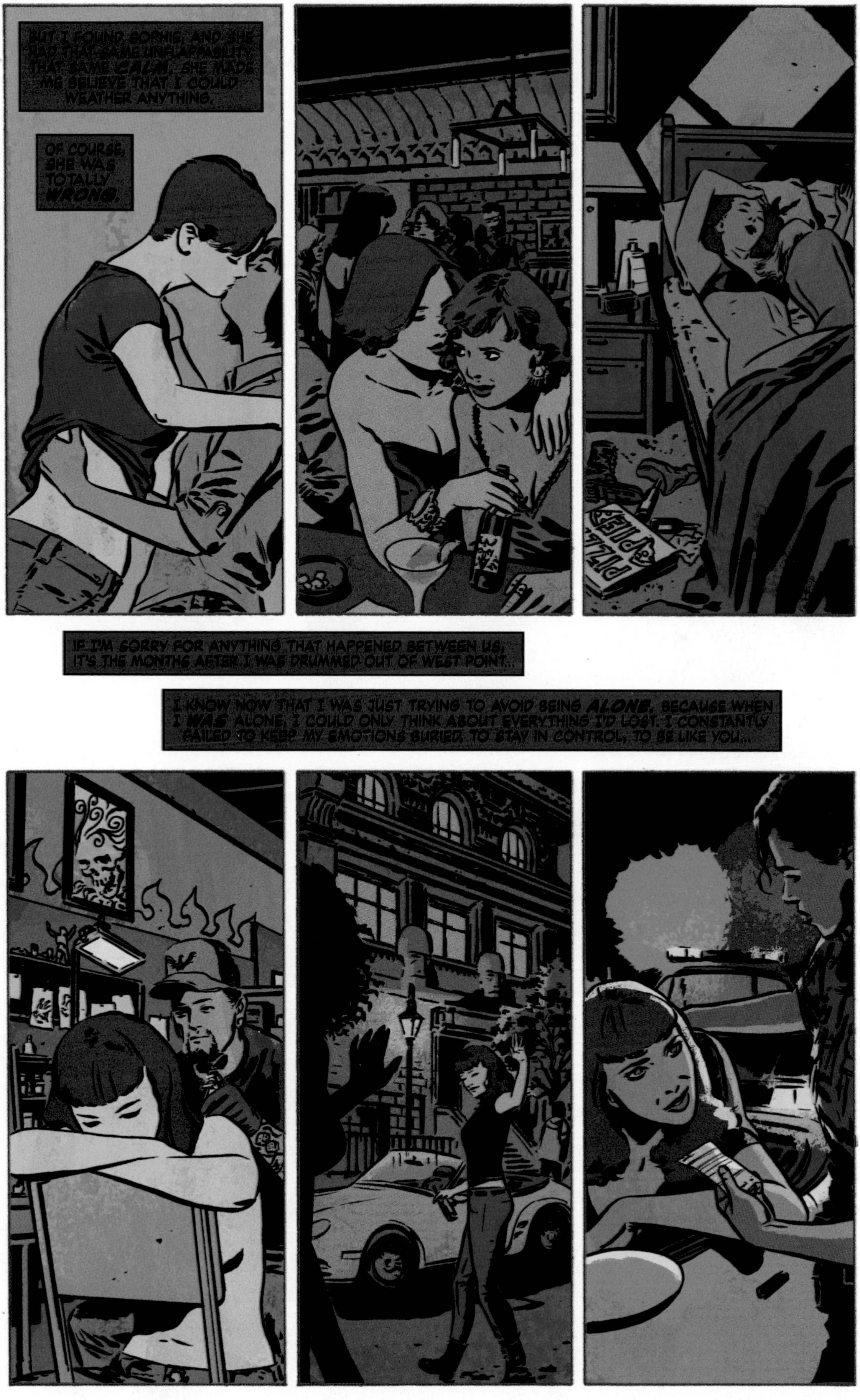
BUT I FOUND SOPHIE, AND SHE HAD THAT SAME UNFLAPPABILITY, THAT SAME *CALM*. SHE MADE ME BELIEVE THAT I COULD WEATHER ANYTHING.
OF COURSE, SHE WAS TOTALLY *WRONG.*
PIZZA
IF I'M SORRY FOR ANYTHING THAT HAPPENED BETWEEN US, IT'S THE MONTHS AFTER I WAS DRUMMED OUT OF WEST POINT...
I KNOW NOW THAT I WAS JUST TRYING TO AVOID BEING *ALONE*. BECAUSE WHEN I *WAS* ALONE, I COULD ONLY THINK ABOUT EVERYTHING I'D LOST. I CONSTANTLY FAILED TO KEEP MY EMOTIONS BURIED, TO STAY IN CONTROL, TO BE LIKE YOU...

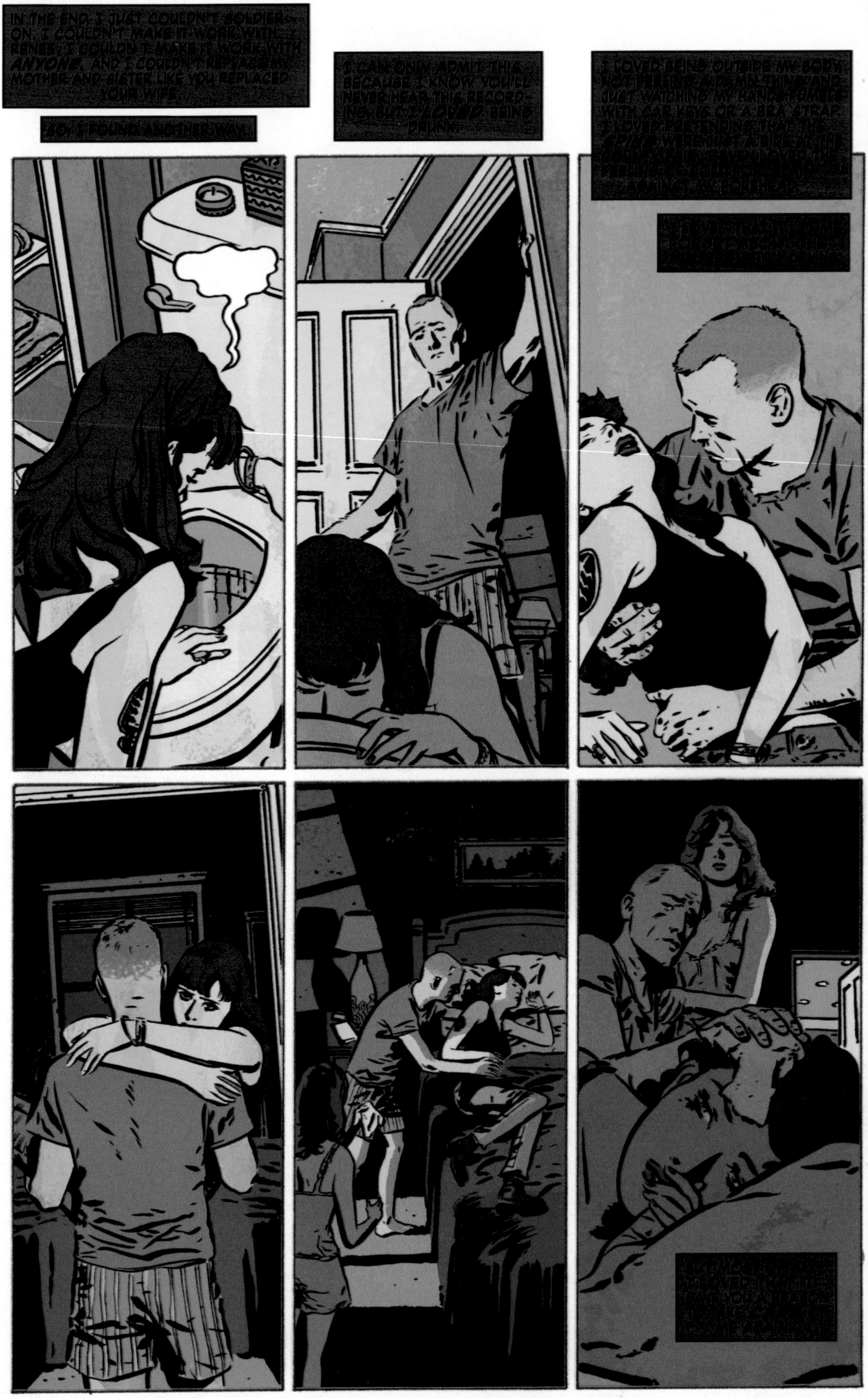
IN THE END, I JUST COULDN'T SOLDIER ON. I COULDN'T MAKE IT WORK WITH RENEE, I COULDN'T MAKE IT WORK WITH ANYONE, AND I COULDN'T REPLACE MY MOTHER AND SISTER LIKE YOU REPLACED YOUR WIFE.
SO, I FOUND ANOTHER WAY.
I CAN ONLY ADMIT THIS BECAUSE I KNOW YOU'LL NEVER HEAR THIS RECORDING, BUT I LOVED BEING DRUNK.
I LOVED BEING OUTSIDE MY BODY, NOT FEELING A DAMN THING AND JUST WATCHING MY HANDS FUMBLE WITH CAR KEYS OR A BRA STRAP.

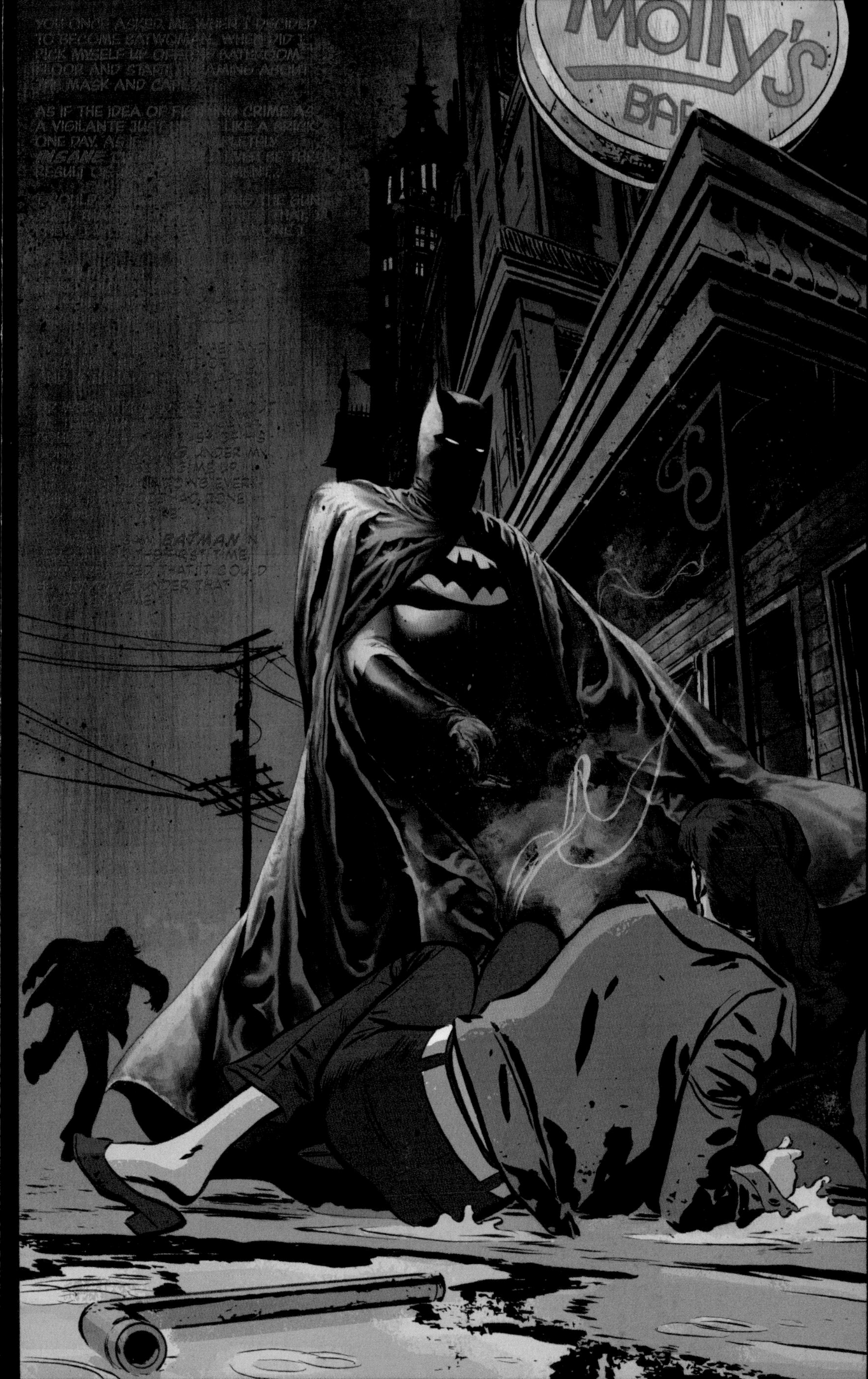

Molly's
YOU ONCE ASKED ME WHEN I DECIDED
TO BECOME BATWOMAN. WHEN DID I
PICK MYSELF UP OFF THE BATHROOM
FLOOR AND START DREAMING ABOUT
THE MASK AND CAPE.
AS IF THE IDEA OF FIGHTING CRIME AS
A VIGILANTE JUST
LIKE A BRICK
ONE DAY.
INSANE
BATMAN

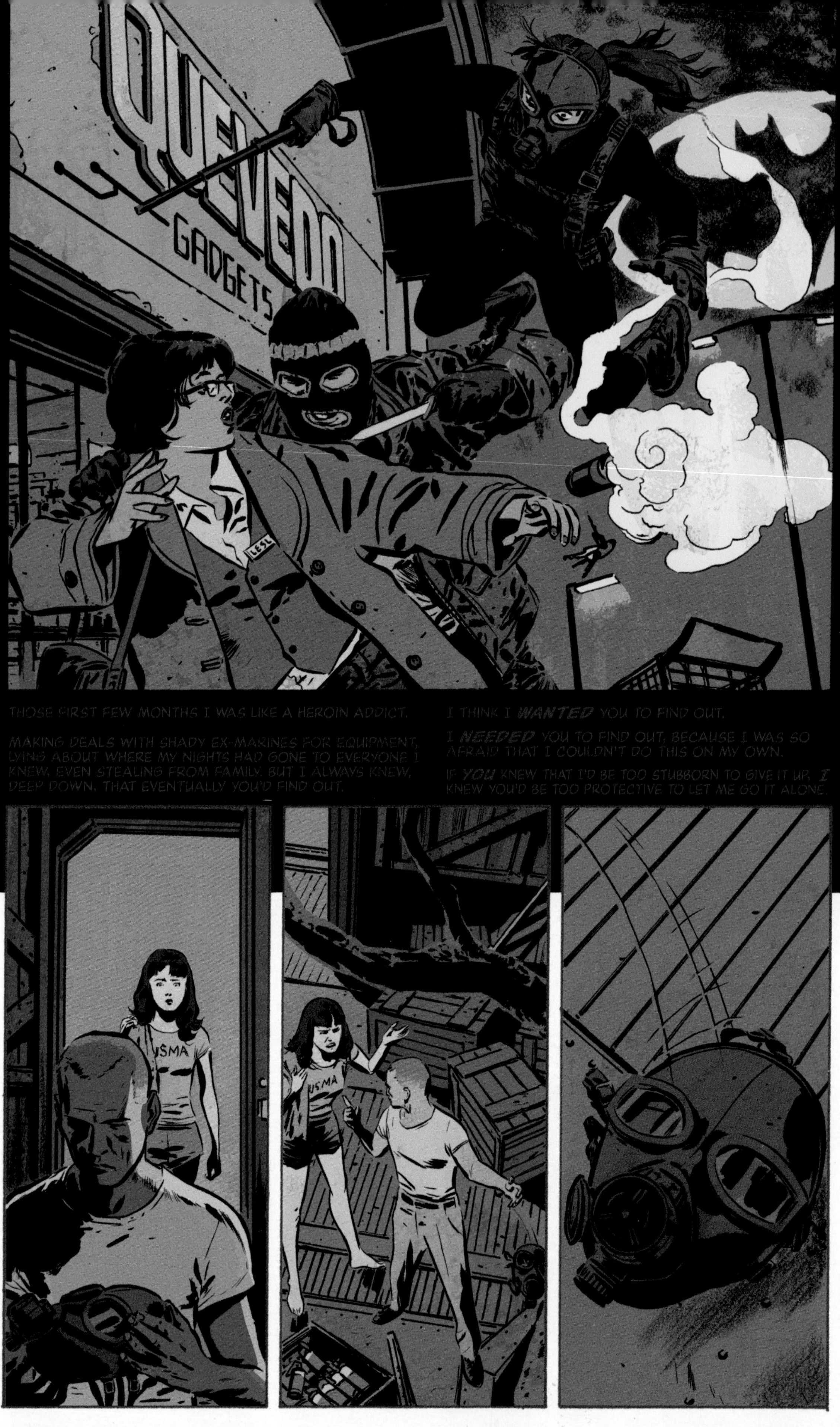
QUEVEDO
GADGETS
LESL
THOSE FIRST FEW MONTHS I WAS LIKE A HEROIN ADDICT.
MAKING DEALS WITH SHADY EX-MARINES FOR EQUIPMENT, LYING ABOUT WHERE MY NIGHTS HAD GONE TO EVERYONE I KNEW, EVEN STEALING FROM FAMILY. BUT I ALWAYS KNEW, DEEP DOWN, THAT EVENTUALLY YOU'D FIND OUT.
I THINK I ***WANTED*** YOU TO FIND OUT.
I ***NEEDED*** YOU TO FIND OUT, BECAUSE I WAS SO AFRAID THAT I COULDN'T DO THIS ON MY OWN.
IF ***YOU*** KNEW THAT I'D BE TOO STUBBORN TO GIVE IT UP, ***I*** KNEW YOU'D BE TOO PROTECTIVE TO LET ME GO IT ALONE.
USMA
USMA

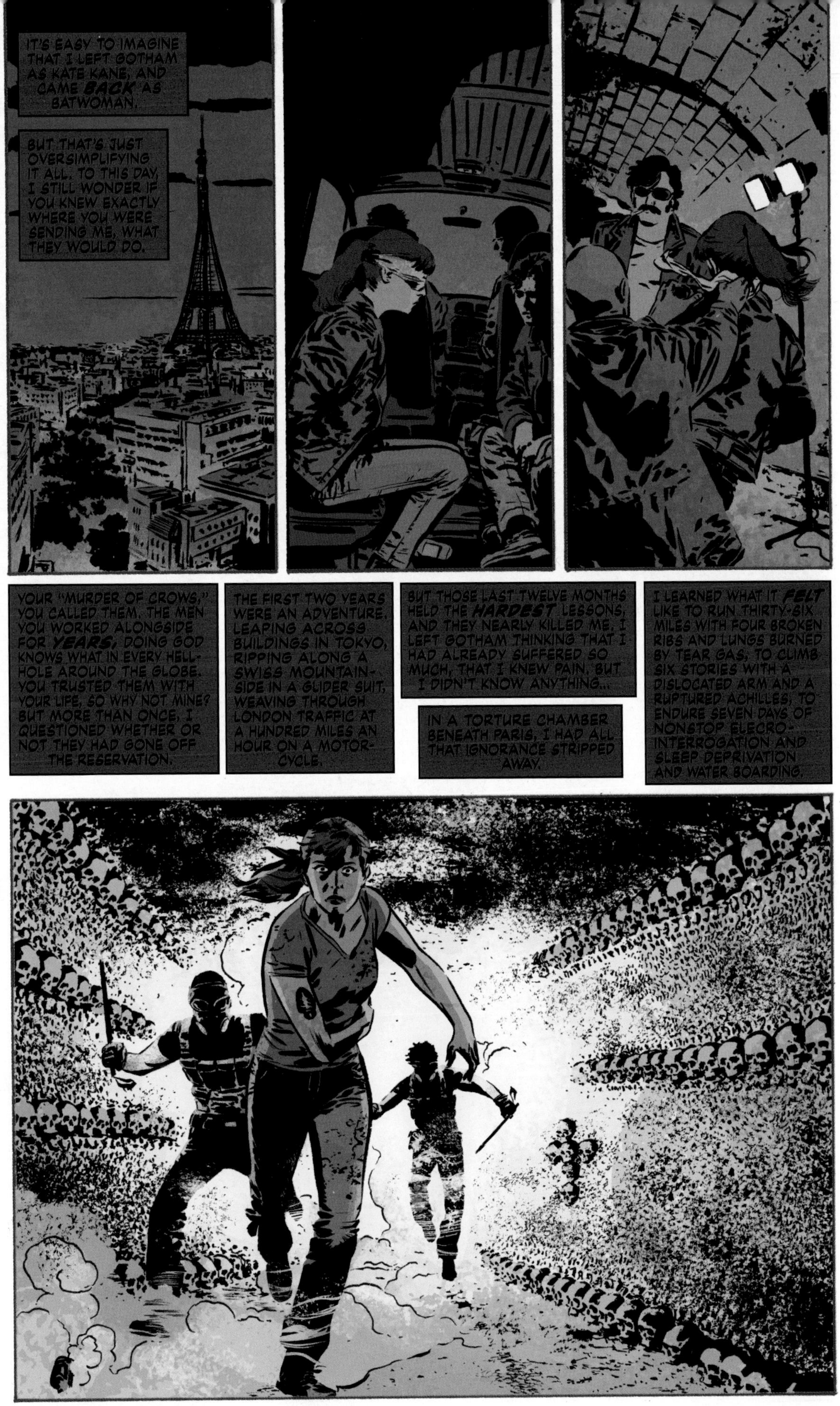
IT'S EASY TO IMAGINE THAT I LEFT GOTHAM AS KATE KANE, AND CAME BACK AS BATWOMAN.
BUT THAT'S JUST OVERSIMPLIFYING IT ALL. TO THIS DAY, I STILL WONDER IF YOU KNEW EXACTLY WHERE YOU WERE SENDING ME, WHAT THEY WOULD DO.
YOUR "MURDER OF CROWS," YOU CALLED THEM. THE MEN YOU WORKED ALONGSIDE FOR YEARS, DOING GOD KNOWS WHAT IN EVERY HELL-HOLE AROUND THE GLOBE. YOU TRUSTED THEM WITH YOUR LIFE, SO WHY NOT MINE? BUT MORE THAN ONCE, I QUESTIONED WHETHER OR NOT THEY HAD GONE OFF THE RESERVATION.
THE FIRST TWO YEARS WERE AN ADVENTURE. LEAPING ACROSS BUILDINGS IN TOKYO, RIPPING ALONG A SWISS MOUNTAIN-SIDE IN A GLIDER SUIT, WEAVING THROUGH LONDON TRAFFIC AT A HUNDRED MILES AN HOUR ON A MOTOR-CYCLE.
BUT THOSE LAST TWELVE MONTHS HELD THE HARDEST LESSONS, AND THEY NEARLY KILLED ME. I LEFT GOTHAM THINKING THAT I HAD ALREADY SUFFERED SO MUCH, THAT I KNEW PAIN. BUT I DIDN'T KNOW ANYTHING...
IN A TORTURE CHAMBER BENEATH PARIS, I HAD ALL THAT IGNORANCE STRIPPED AWAY.
I LEARNED WHAT IT FELT LIKE TO RUN THIRTY-SIX MILES WITH FOUR BROKEN RIBS AND LUNGS BURNED BY TEAR GAS, TO CLIMB SIX STORIES WITH A DISLOCATED ARM AND A RUPTURED ACHILLES, TO ENDURE SEVEN DAYS OF NONSTOP ELECRO-INTERROGATION AND SLEEP DEPRIVATION AND WATER BOARDING.

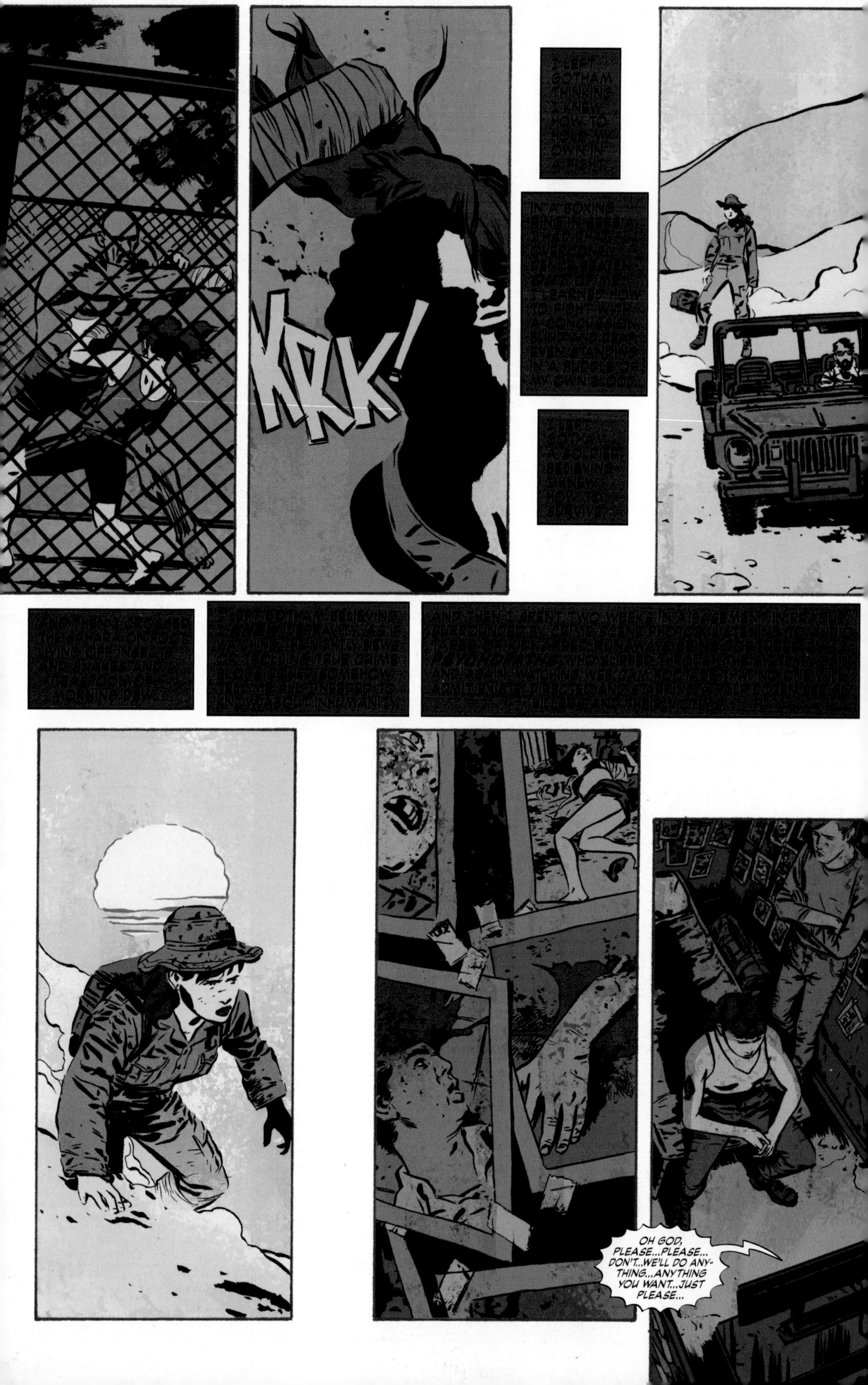
KRK!
[redacted]
[redacted]
[redacted]
[redacted]
[redacted]
[redacted]
OH GOD, PLEASE...PLEASE... DON'T...WE'LL DO ANYTHING...ANYTHING YOU WANT...JUST PLEASE...

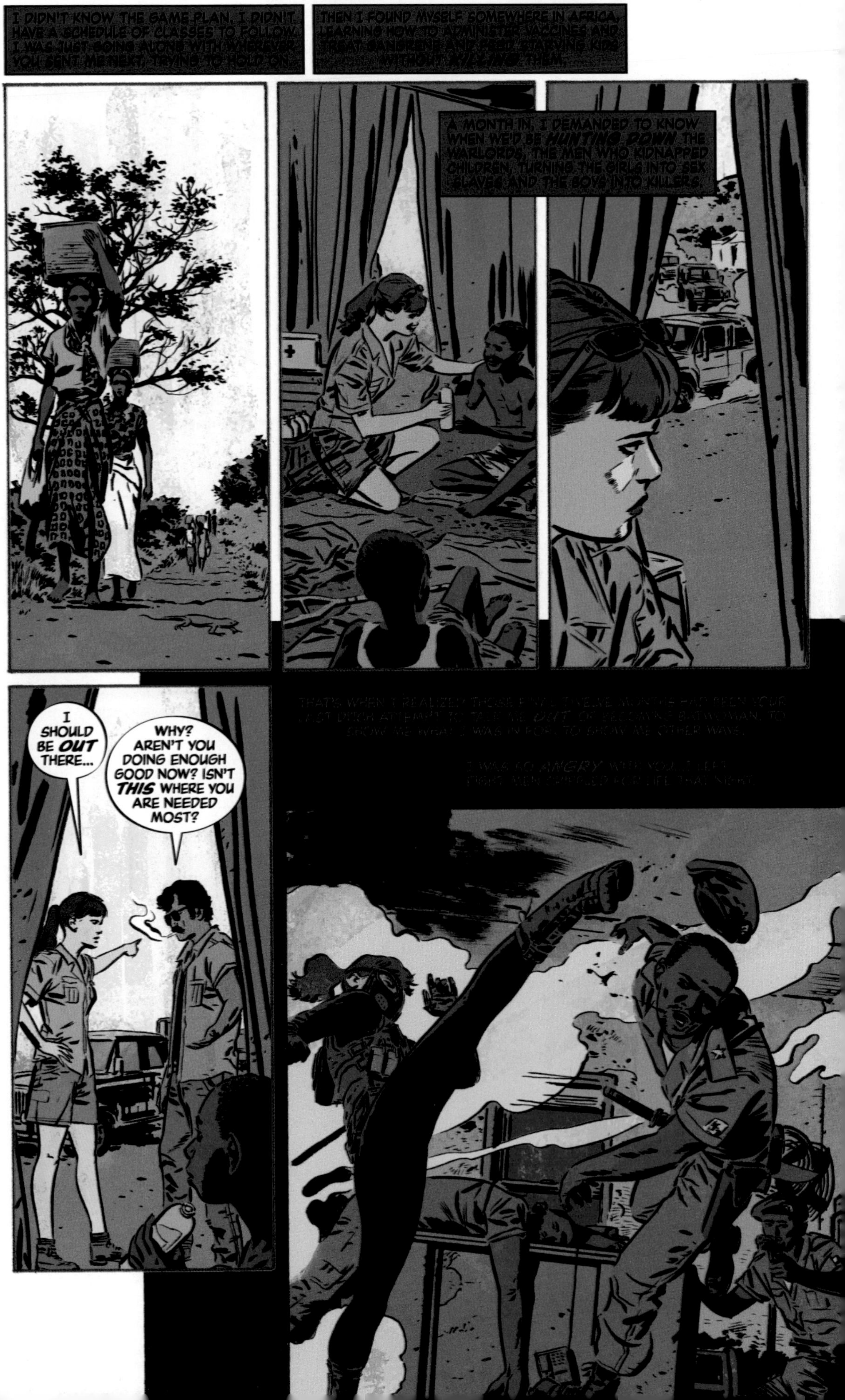
I DIDN'T KNOW THE GAME PLAN. I DIDN'T HAVE A SCHEDULE OF CLASSES TO FOLLOW. I WAS JUST GOING ALONG WITH WHEREVER YOU SENT ME NEXT, TRYING TO HOLD ON.
THEN I FOUND MYSELF SOMEWHERE IN AFRICA, LEARNING HOW TO ADMINISTER VACCINES AND TREAT GANGRENE AND FEED STARVING KIDS WITHOUT *KILLING* THEM.
A MONTH IN, I DEMANDED TO KNOW WHEN WE'D BE *HUNTING DOWN* THE WARLORDS, THE MEN WHO KIDNAPPED CHILDREN, TURNING THE GIRLS INTO SEX SLAVES AND THE BOYS INTO KILLERS.
I SHOULD BE *OUT* THERE...
WHY? AREN'T YOU DOING ENOUGH GOOD NOW? ISN'T *THIS* WHERE YOU ARE NEEDED MOST?
THAT'S WHEN I REALIZED THOSE FINAL TWELVE MONTHS HAD BEEN YOUR LAST DITCH ATTEMPT TO TALK ME *OUT* OF BECOMING BATWOMAN. TO SHOW ME WHAT I WAS IN FOR. TO SHOW ME OTHER WAYS.
I WAS SO *ANGRY* WITH YOU, I LEFT EIGHT MEN CRIPPLED FOR LIFE THAT NIGHT.

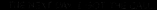

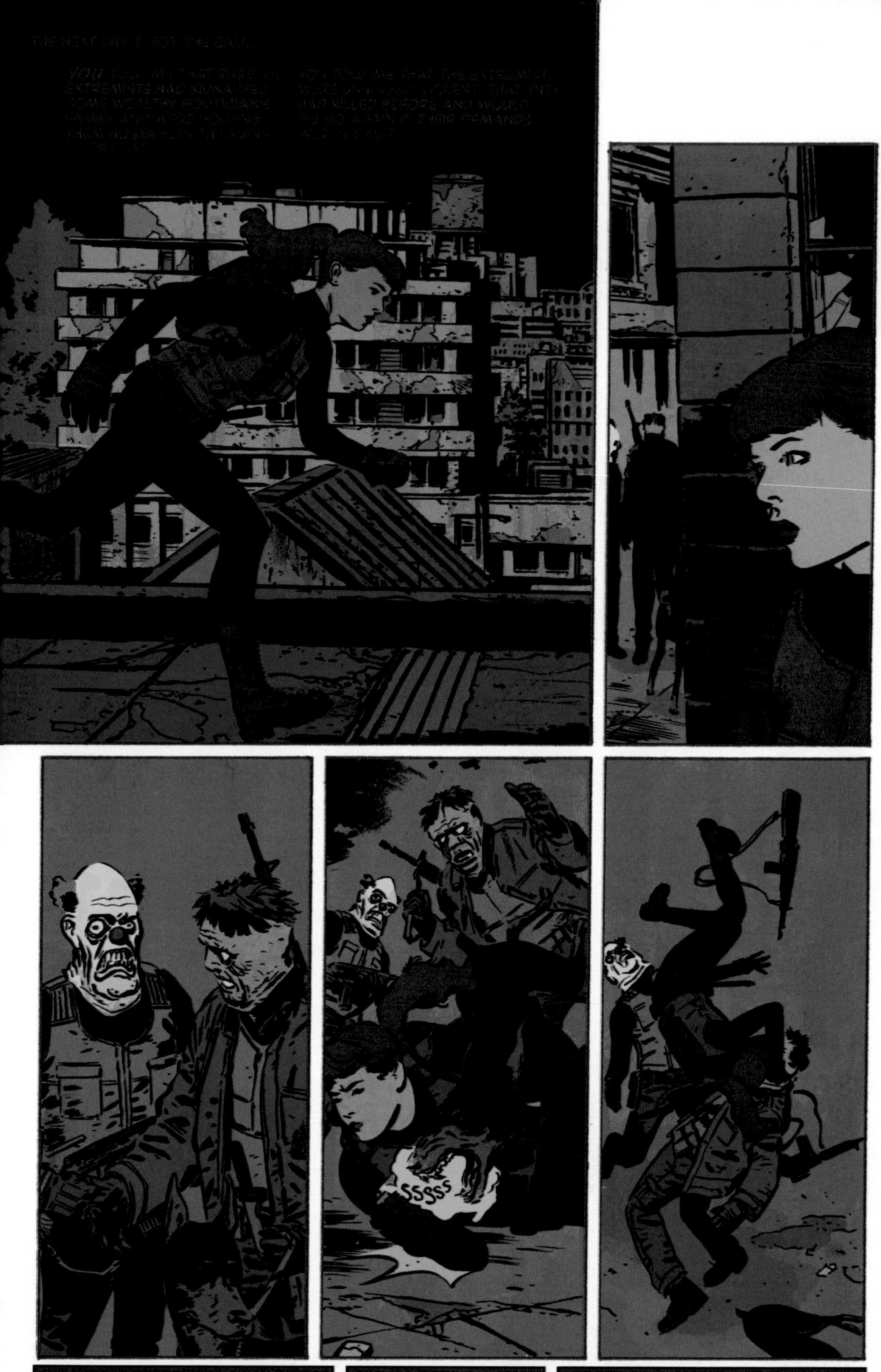
THE NEXT DAY, I GOT THE CALL.
YOU TOLD ME THAT RUSSIAN EXTREMISTS HAD KIDNAPPED SOME WEALTHY POLITICIAN'S FAMILY AND WERE HOLDING THEM HOSTAGE IN THE RUINS OF PRYPIAT.
YOU TOLD ME THAT THE EXTREMISTS WERE UNHINGED. VIOLENT. THAT THEY HAD KILLED BEFORE AND WOULD DO SO AGAIN IF THEIR DEMANDS WEREN'T MET.
SSSSS
YOU TOLD ME THAT THE RUSSIAN GOVERNMENT WAS IGNORING THE SITUATION, AND I WAS THE ONLY ONE WHO COULD SAVE THAT FAMILY. A FAMILY, DAD.
YOU TOLD ME THAT THIS WAS MY FINAL TEST, AND THEN I'D BE ABLE TO COME HOME TO GOTHAM.
PRYPIAT. THAT HAUNTED CITY, ABANDONED IN THE WAKE OF CHERNOBYL,

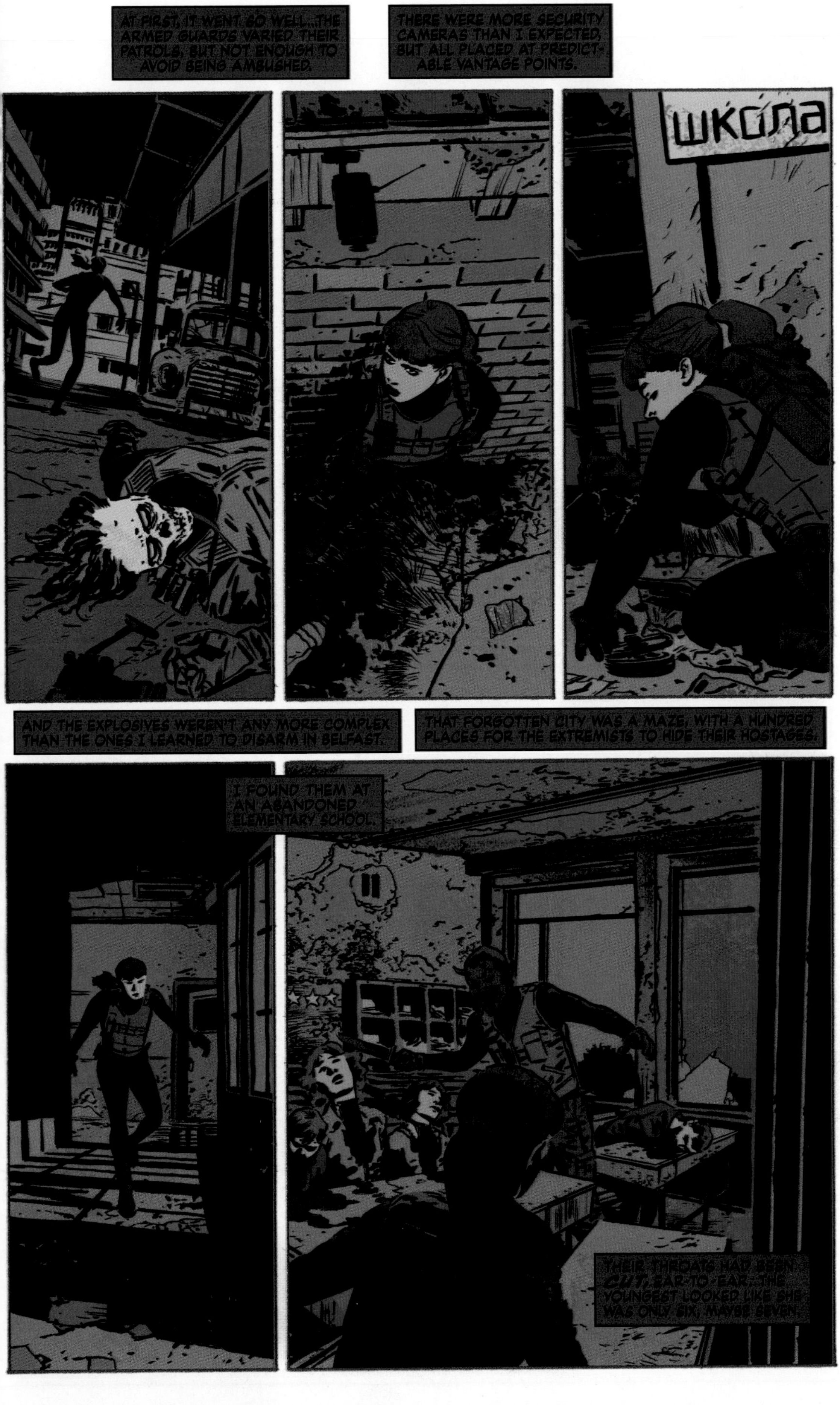
AT FIRST, IT WENT SO WELL...THE ARMED GUARDS VARIED THEIR PATROLS, BUT NOT ENOUGH TO AVOID BEING AMBUSHED.
THERE WERE MORE SECURITY CAMERAS THAN I EXPECTED, BUT ALL PLACED AT PREDICTABLE VANTAGE POINTS.
ШКОЛА
AND THE EXPLOSIVES WEREN'T ANY MORE COMPLEX THAN THE ONES I LEARNED TO DISARM IN BELFAST.
THAT FORGOTTEN CITY WAS A MAZE, WITH A HUNDRED PLACES FOR THE EXTREMISTS TO HIDE THEIR HOSTAGES.
I FOUND THEM AT AN ABANDONED ELEMENTARY SCHOOL.
THEIR THROATS HAD BEEN CUT, EAR-TO-EAR... THE YOUNGEST LOOKED LIKE SHE WAS ONLY SIX, MAYBE SEVEN.

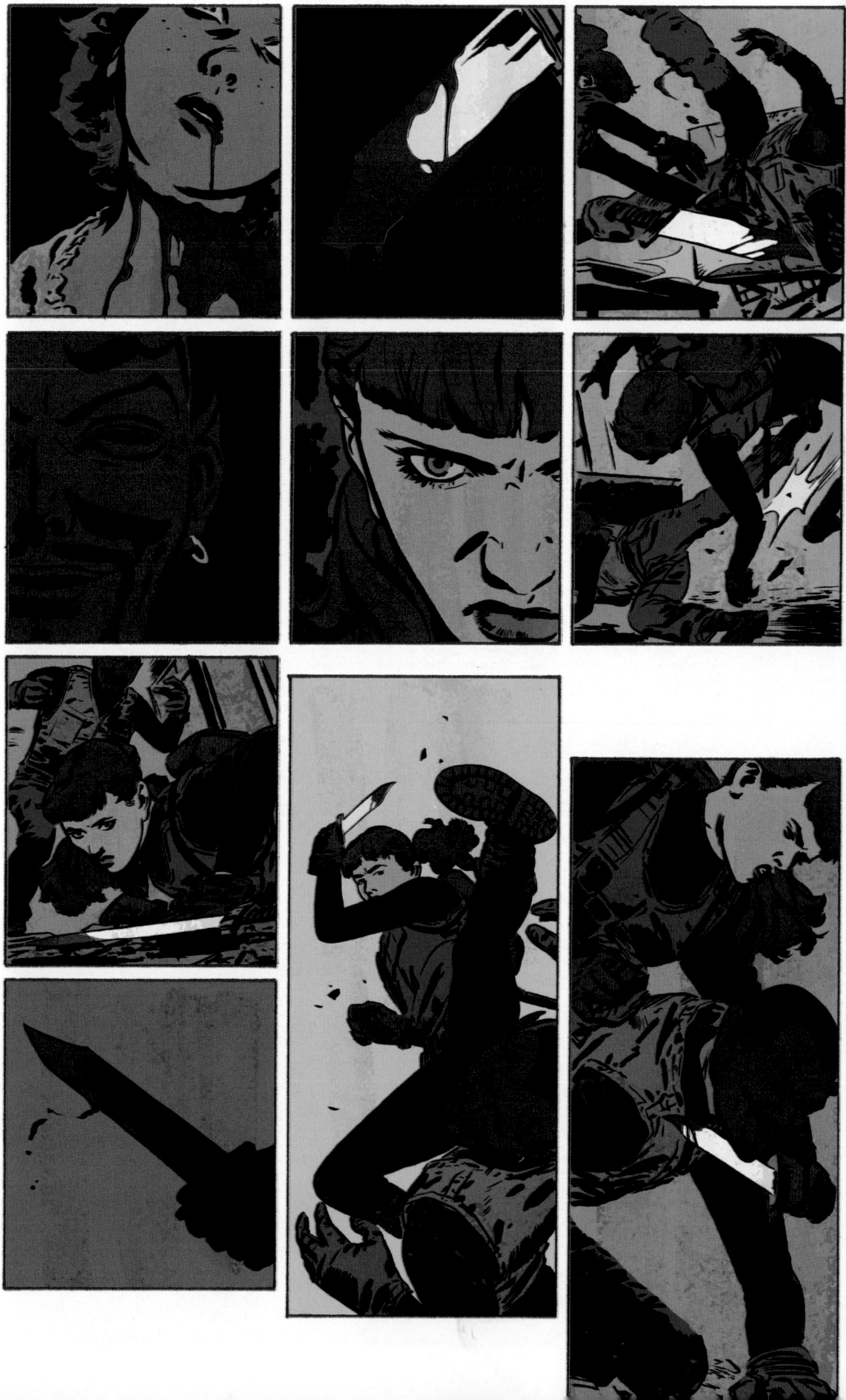

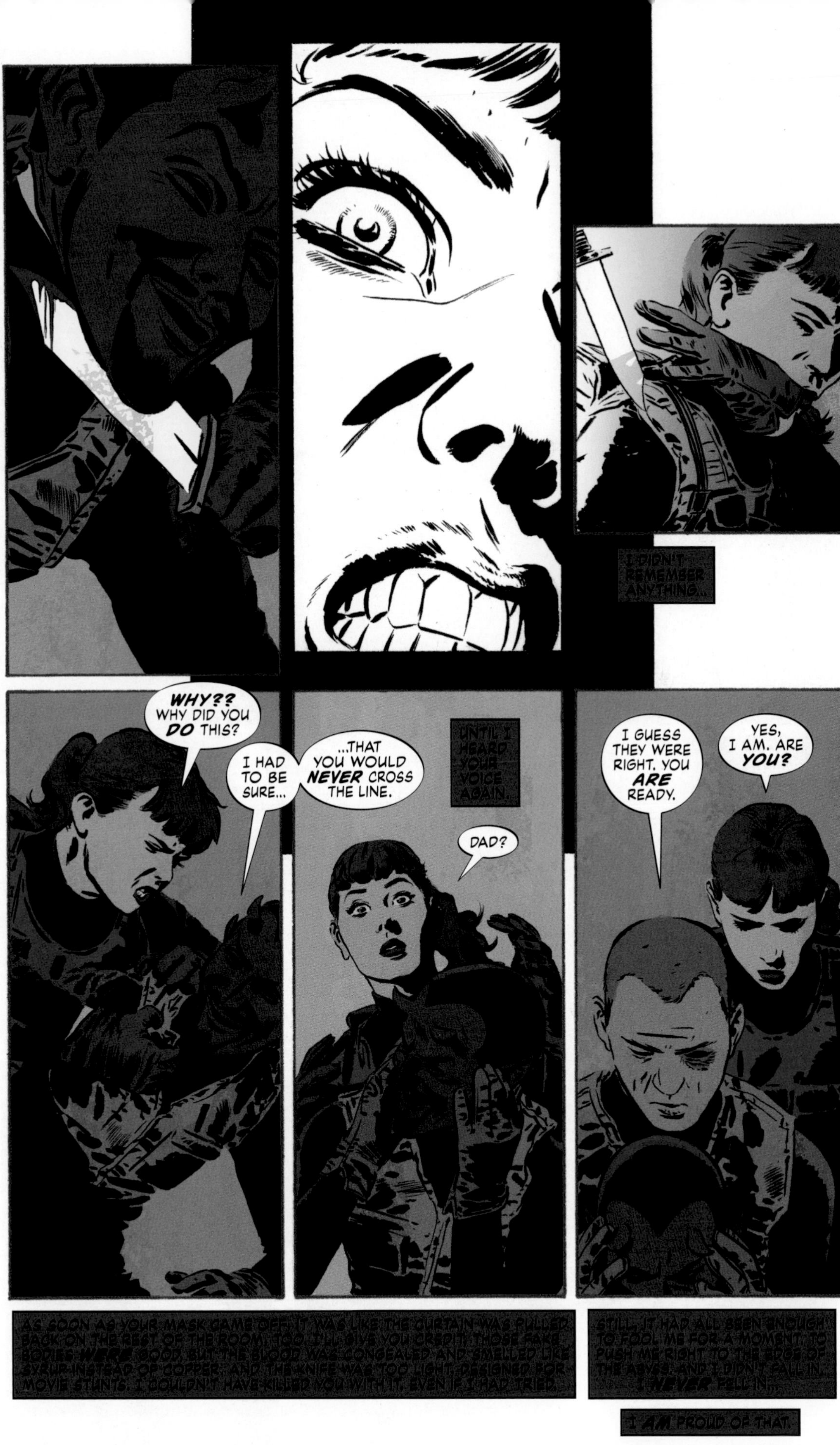
I DIDN'T REMEMBER ANYTHING...
WHY?? WHY DID YOU DO THIS?
I HAD TO BE SURE...
...THAT YOU WOULD NEVER CROSS THE LINE.
UNTIL I HEARD YOUR VOICE AGAIN.
DAD?
I GUESS THEY WERE RIGHT. YOU ARE READY.
YES, I AM. ARE YOU?
AS SOON AS YOUR MASK CAME OFF, IT WAS LIKE THE CURTAIN WAS PULLED BACK ON THE REST OF THE ROOM, TOO. I'LL GIVE YOU CREDIT, THOSE FAKE BODIES WERE GOOD, BUT THE BLOOD WAS CONGEALED AND SMELLED LIKE SYRUP INSTEAD OF COPPER. AND THE KNIFE WAS TOO LIGHT, DESIGNED FOR MOVIE STUNTS. I COULDN'T HAVE KILLED YOU WITH IT, EVEN IF I HAD TRIED.
STILL, IT HAD ALL BEEN ENOUGH TO FOOL ME FOR A MOMENT. TO PUSH ME RIGHT TO THE EDGE OF THE ABYSS. AND I DIDN'T FALL IN. I NEVER FELL IN...
I AM PROUD OF THAT.

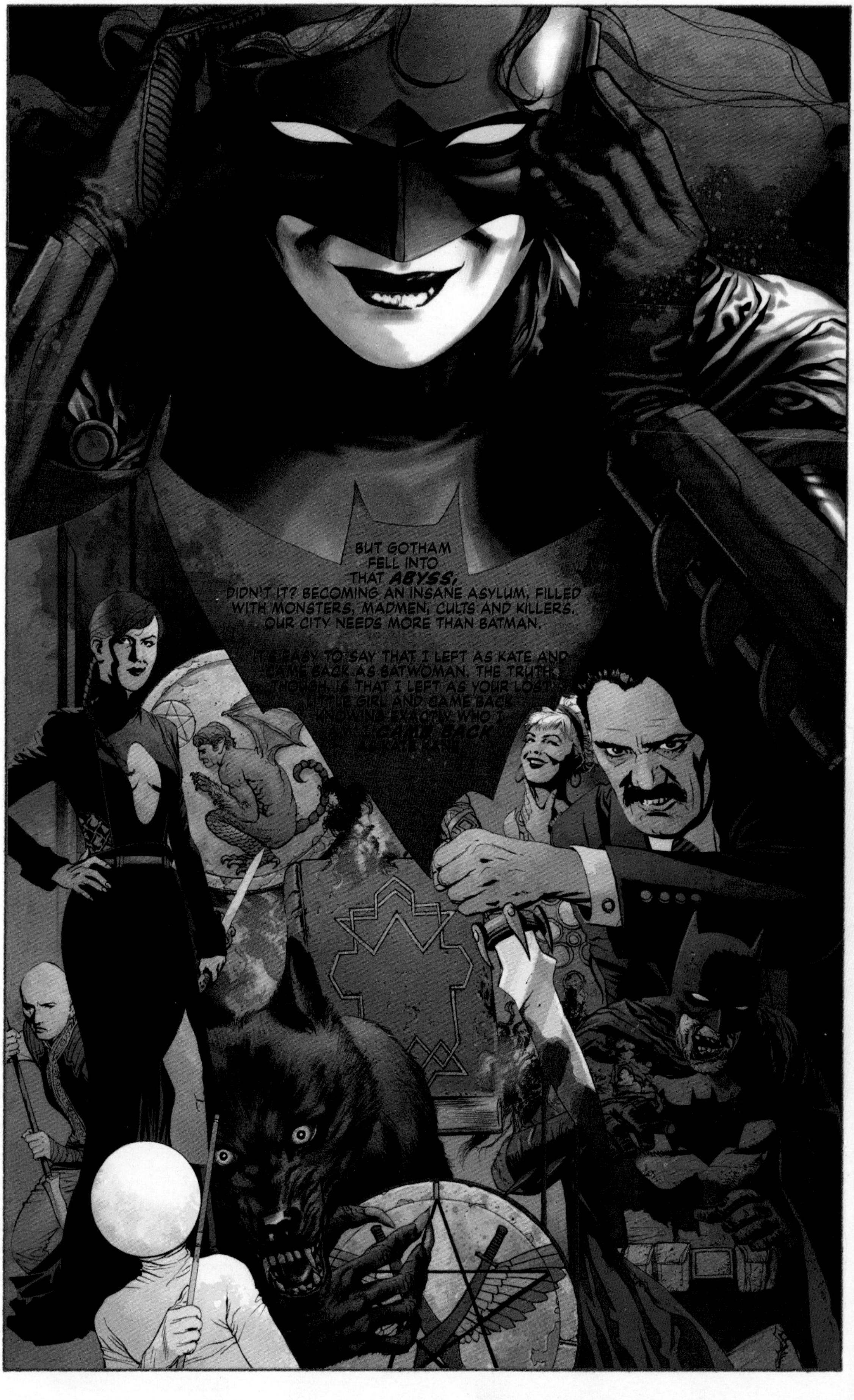
BUT GOTHAM FELL INTO THAT ***ABYSS,*** DIDN'T IT? BECOMING AN INSANE ASYLUM, FILLED WITH MONSTERS, MADMEN, CULTS AND KILLERS. OUR CITY NEEDS MORE THAN BATMAN.
IT'S EASY TO SAY THAT I LEFT AS KATE AND CAME BACK AS BATWOMAN. THE TRUTH, THOUGH, IS THAT I LEFT AS YOUR LOST LITTLE GIRL AND CAME BACK KNOWING EXACTLY WHO I AM. I ***CAME BACK*** AS KATE KANE.

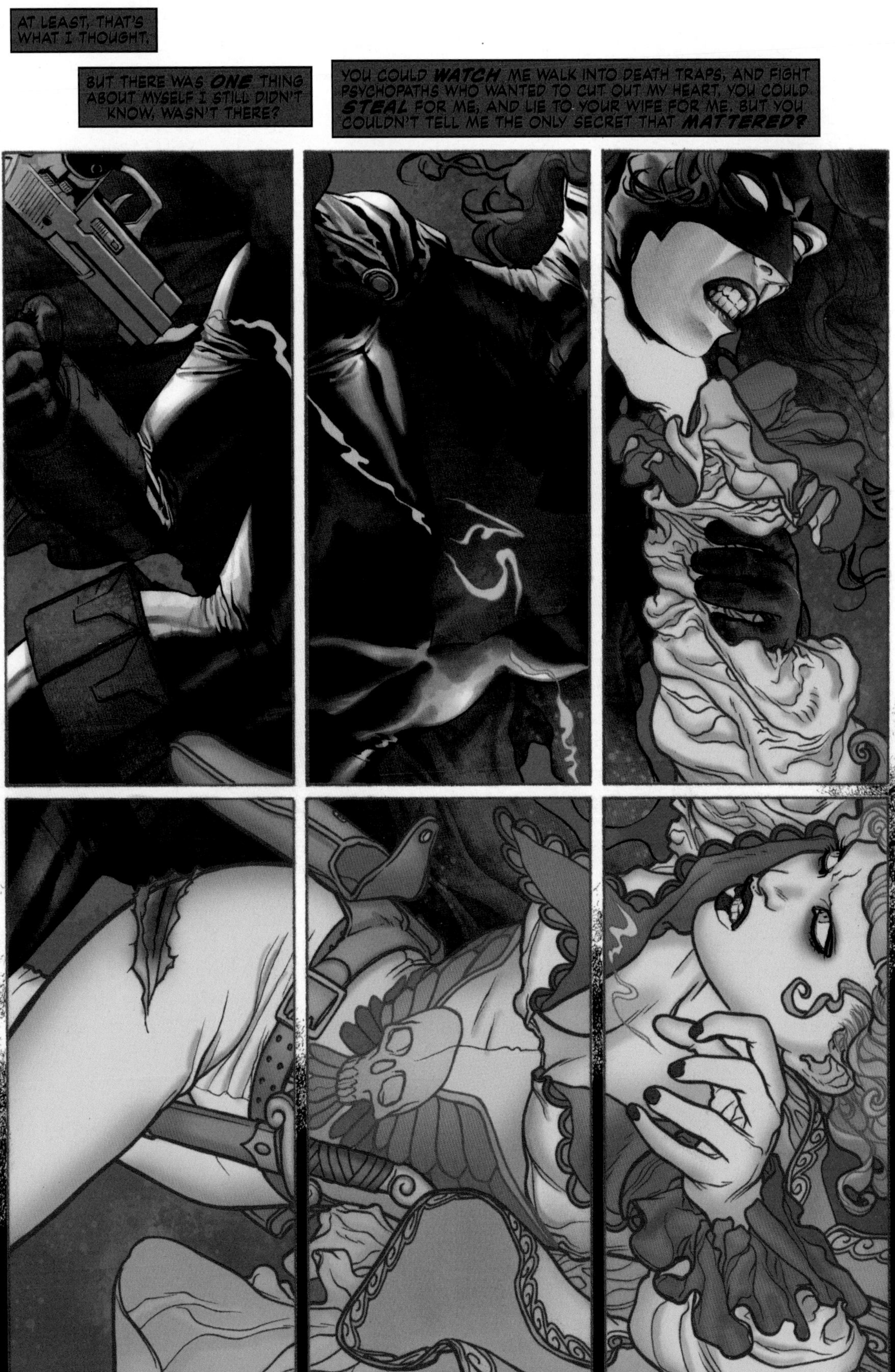
AT LEAST, THAT'S WHAT I THOUGHT.
BUT THERE WAS ONE THING ABOUT MYSELF I STILL DIDN'T KNOW, WASN'T THERE?
YOU COULD WATCH ME WALK INTO DEATH TRAPS, AND FIGHT PSYCHOPATHS WHO WANTED TO CUT OUT MY HEART. YOU COULD STEAL FOR ME, AND LIE TO YOUR WIFE FOR ME. BUT YOU COULDN'T TELL ME THE ONLY SECRET THAT MATTERED?
YOU COULDN'T TELL ME MY SISTER HAD REALLY

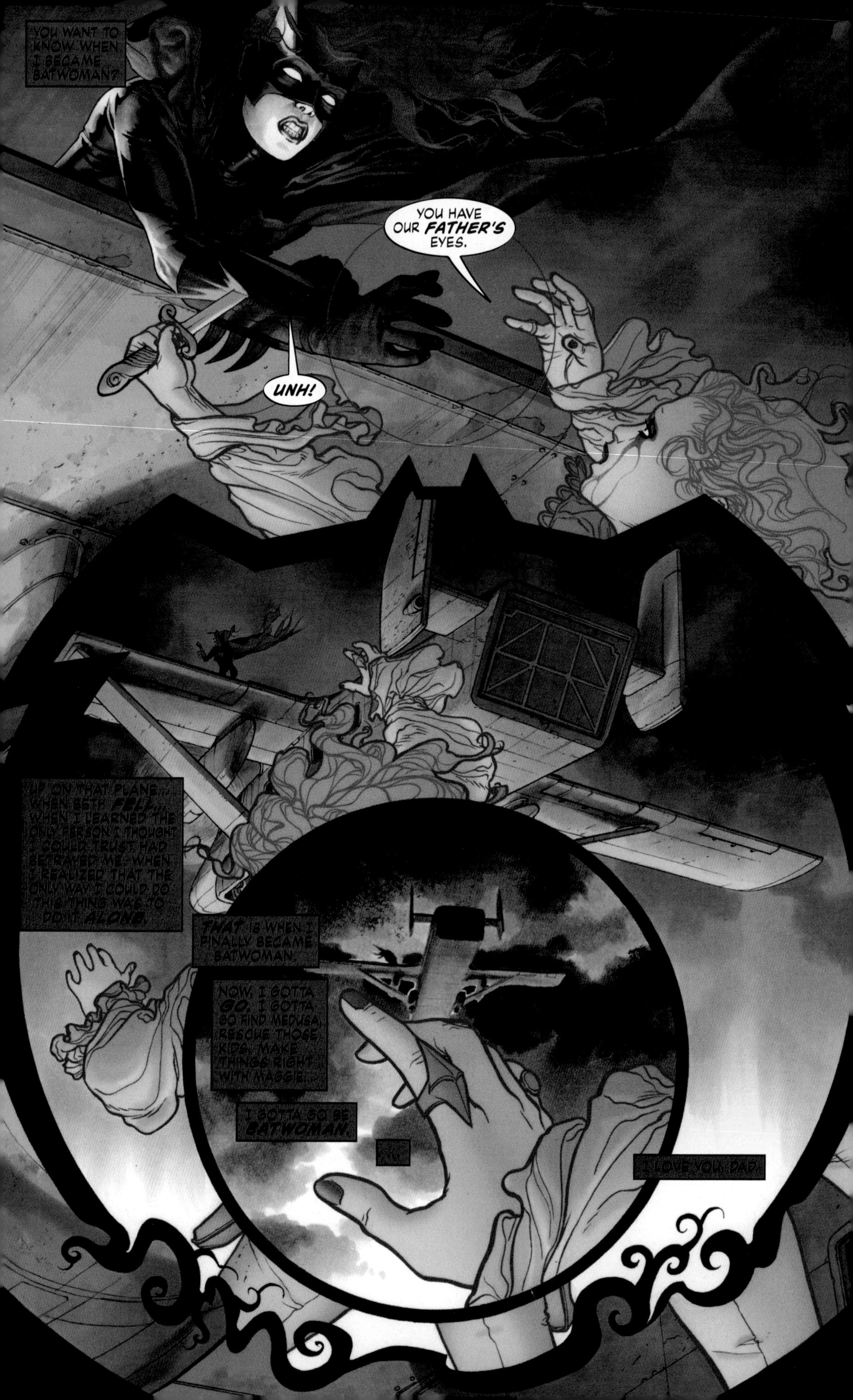
YOU WANT TO KNOW WHEN I BECAME BATWOMAN?
YOU HAVE OUR FATHER'S EYES.
UNH!
UP ON THAT PLANE... WHEN BETH FELL... WHEN I LEARNED THE ONLY PERSON I THOUGHT I COULD TRUST HAD BETRAYED ME. WHEN I REALIZED THAT THE ONLY WAY I COULD DO THIS THING WAS TO DO IT ALONE.
THAT IS WHEN I FINALLY BECAME BATWOMAN.
NOW, I GOTTA GO. I GOTTA GO FIND MEDUSA, RESCUE THOSE KIDS, MAKE THINGS RIGHT WITH MAGGIE...
I GOTTA GO BE BATWOMAN.
I LOVE YOU, DAD.

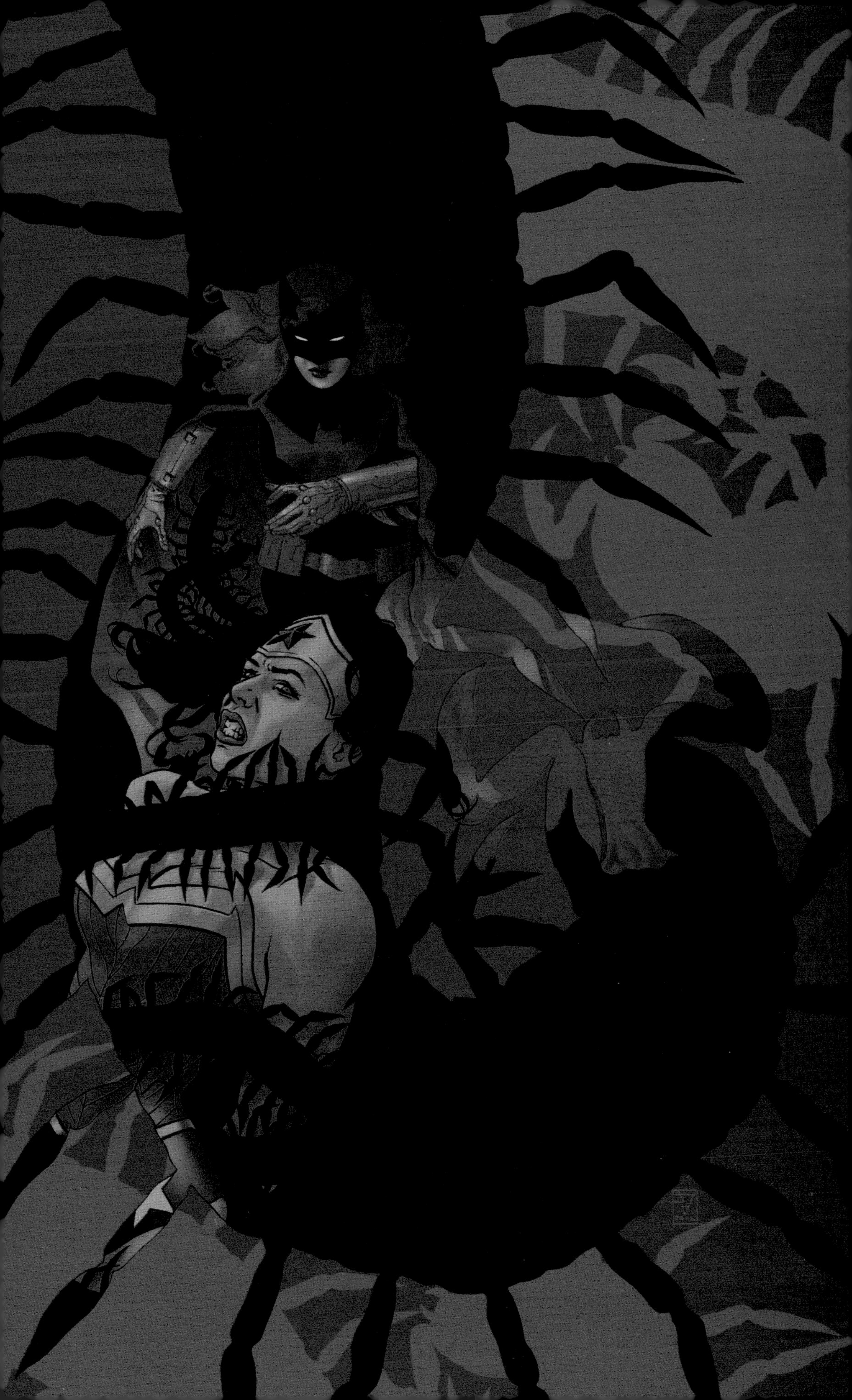

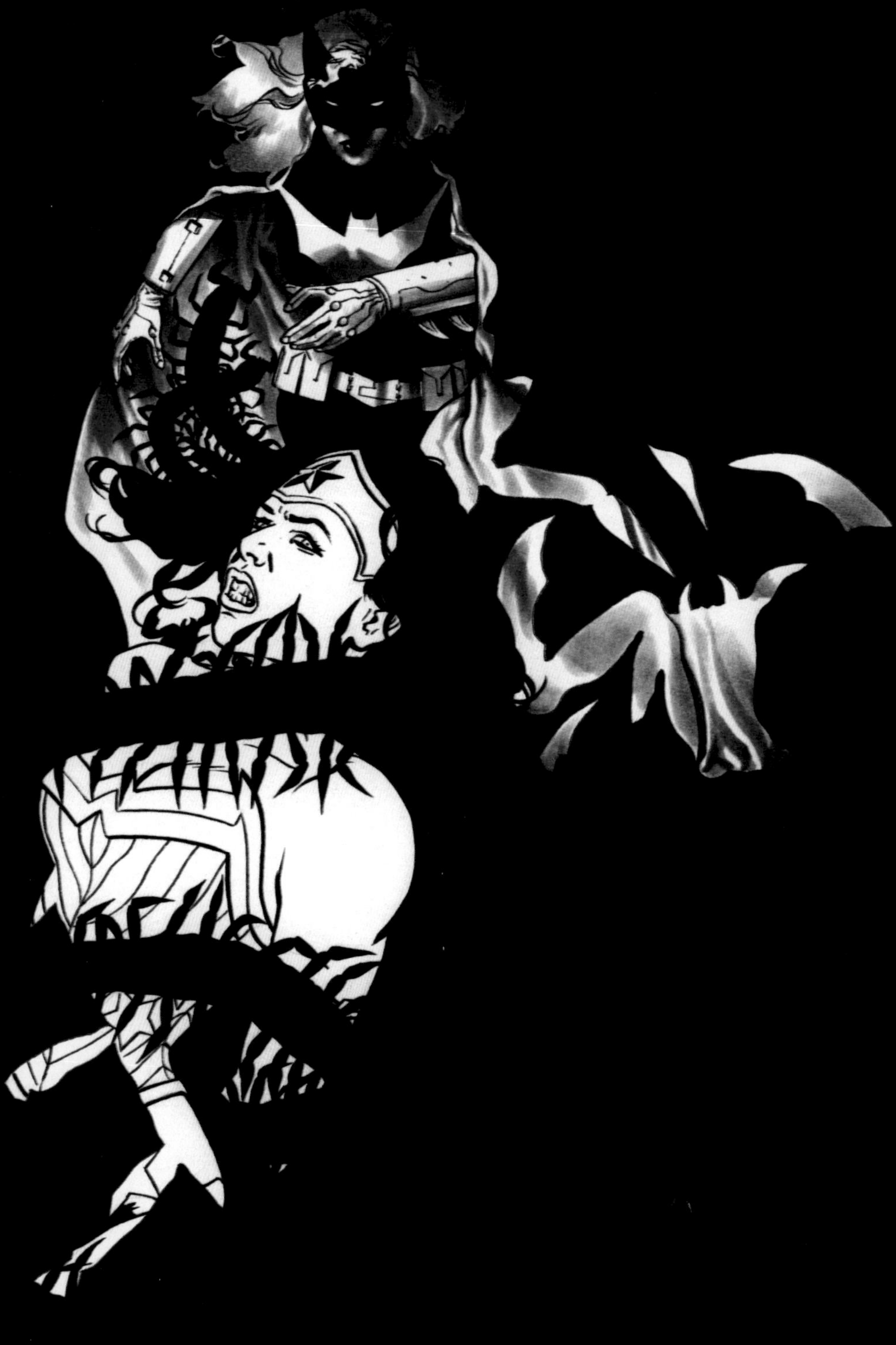

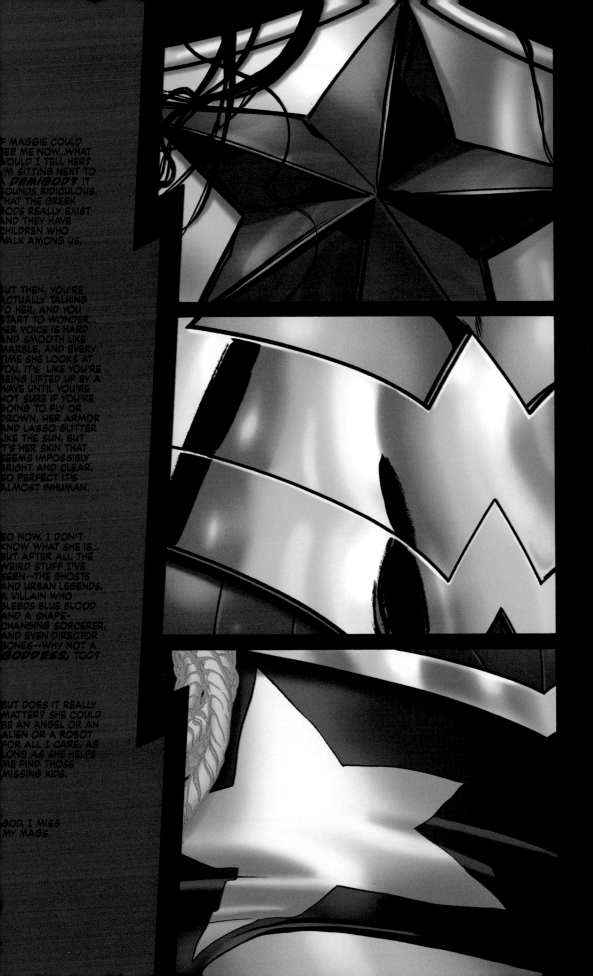

IF MAGGIE COULD
SEE ME NOW...WHAT
WOULD I TELL HER?
I'M SITTING NEXT TO
A *DEMIGOD?* IT
SOUNDS RIDICULOUS,
THAT THE GREEK
GODS REALLY EXIST
AND THEY HAVE
CHILDREN WHO
WALK AMONG US.

BUT THEN, YOU'RE
ACTUALLY TALKING
TO HER, AND YOU
START TO WONDER...
HER VOICE IS HARD
AND SMOOTH LIKE
MARBLE, AND EVERY
TIME SHE LOOKS AT
YOU, IT'S LIKE YOU'RE
BEING LIFTED UP BY A
WAVE UNTIL YOU'RE
NOT SURE IF YOU'RE
GOING TO FLY OR
DROWN. HER ARMOR
AND LASSO GLITTER
LIKE THE SUN, BUT
IT'S HER SKIN THAT
SEEMS IMPOSSIBLY
BRIGHT AND CLEAR,
SO PERFECT IT'S
ALMOST INHUMAN.

SO NOW, I DON'T
KNOW WHAT SHE IS...
BUT AFTER ALL THE
WEIRD STUFF I'VE
SEEN--THE GHOSTS
AND URBAN LEGENDS,
A VILLAIN WHO
BLEEDS BLUE BLOOD
AND A SHAPE-
CHANGING SORCERER,
AND EVEN DIRECTOR
BONES--WHY NOT A
GODDESS, TOO?

BUT DOES IT REALLY
MATTER? SHE COULD
BE AN ANGEL OR AN
ALIEN OR A ROBOT
FOR ALL I CARE, AS
LONG AS SHE HELPS
ME FIND THOSE
MISSING KIDS.

GOD, I MISS
MY MAGS.

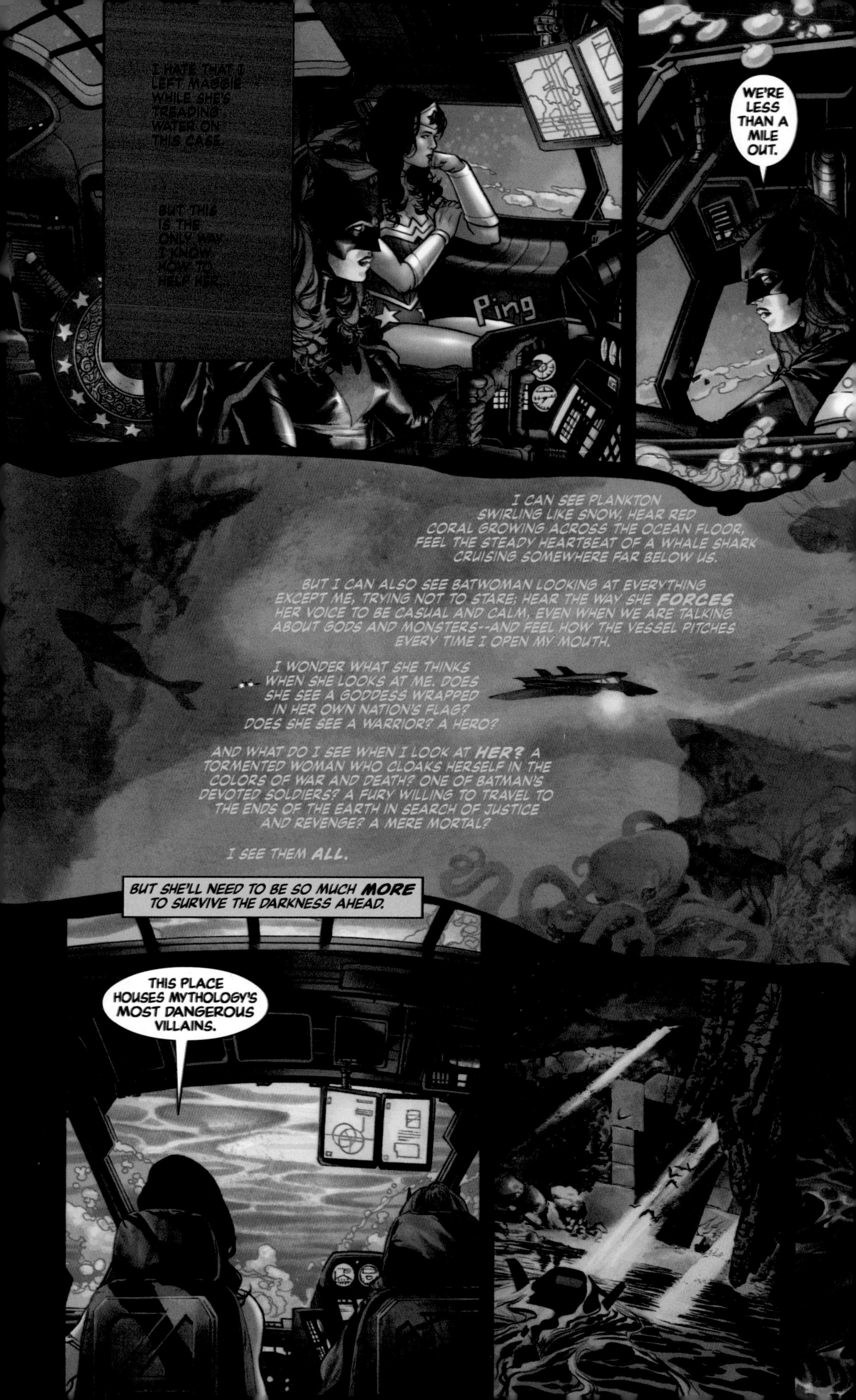

I HATE THAT I LEFT MAGGIE WHILE SHE'S TREADING WATER ON THIS CASE.
BUT THIS IS THE ONLY WAY I KNOW HOW TO HELP HER...
PING
WE'RE LESS THAN A MILE OUT.
I CAN SEE PLANKTON SWIRLING LIKE SNOW, HEAR RED CORAL GROWING ACROSS THE OCEAN FLOOR, FEEL THE STEADY HEARTBEAT OF A WHALE SHARK CRUISING SOMEWHERE FAR BELOW US.
BUT I CAN ALSO SEE BATWOMAN LOOKING AT EVERYTHING EXCEPT ME, TRYING NOT TO STARE; HEAR THE WAY SHE FORCES HER VOICE TO BE CASUAL AND CALM, EVEN WHEN WE ARE TALKING ABOUT GODS AND MONSTERS--AND FEEL HOW THE VESSEL PITCHES EVERY TIME I OPEN MY MOUTH.
I WONDER WHAT SHE THINKS WHEN SHE LOOKS AT ME. DOES SHE SEE A GODDESS WRAPPED IN HER OWN NATION'S FLAG? DOES SHE SEE A WARRIOR? A HERO?
AND WHAT DO I SEE WHEN I LOOK AT HER? A TORMENTED WOMAN WHO CLOAKS HERSELF IN THE COLORS OF WAR AND DEATH? ONE OF BATMAN'S DEVOTED SOLDIERS? A FURY WILLING TO TRAVEL TO THE ENDS OF THE EARTH IN SEARCH OF JUSTICE AND REVENGE? A MERE MORTAL?
I SEE THEM ALL.
BUT SHE'LL NEED TO BE SO MUCH MORE TO SURVIVE THE DARKNESS AHEAD.
THIS PLACE HOUSES MYTHOLOGY'S MOST DANGEROUS VILLAINS.

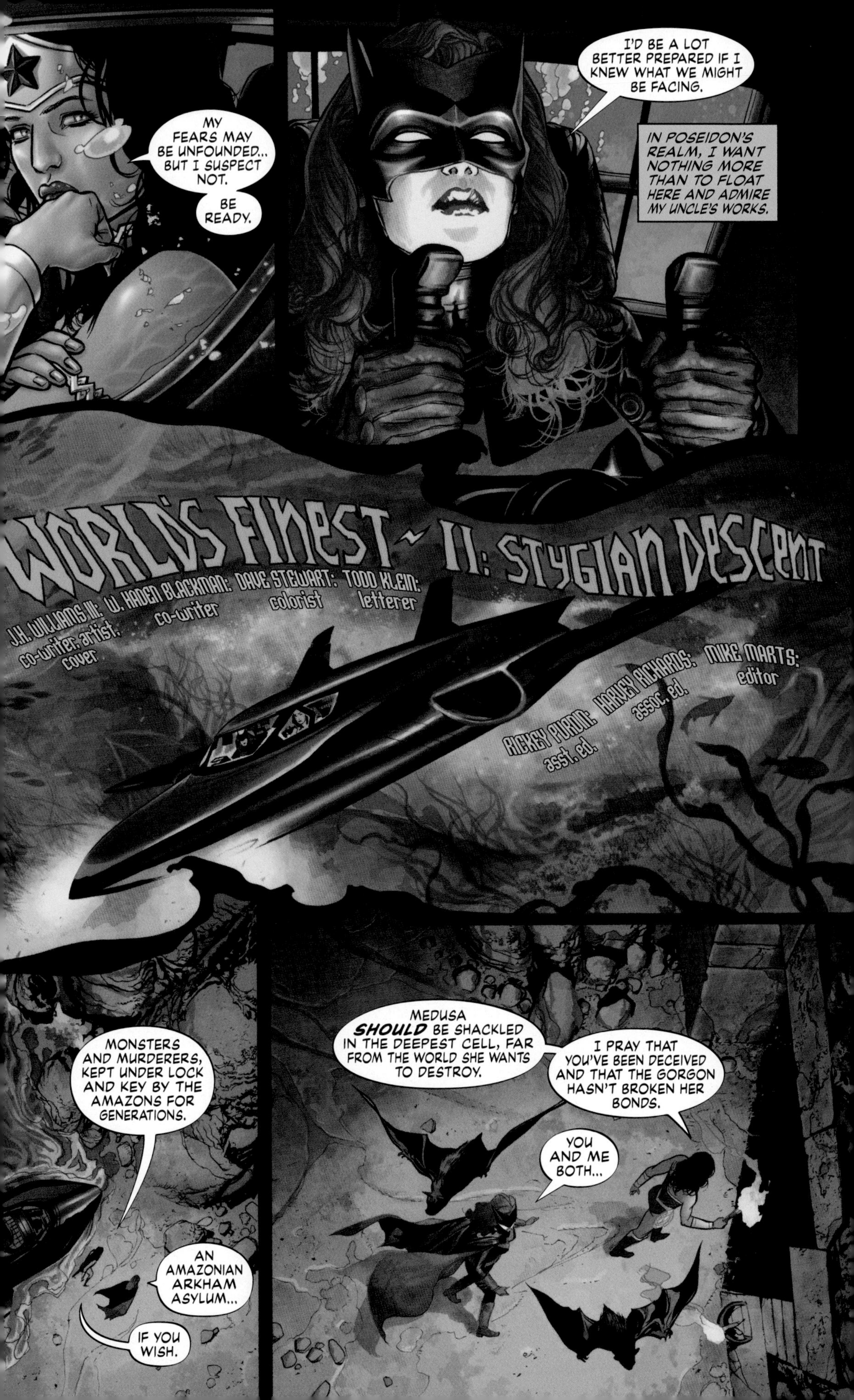
MY FEARS MAY BE UNFOUNDED... BUT I SUSPECT NOT.
BE READY.
I'D BE A LOT BETTER PREPARED IF I KNEW WHAT WE MIGHT BE FACING.
IN POSEIDON'S REALM, I WANT NOTHING MORE THAN TO FLOAT HERE AND ADMIRE MY UNCLE'S WORKS.
WORLD'S FINEST ~ II: STYGIAN DESCENT
J.H. WILLIAMS III: co-writer, artist, cover
W. HADEN BLACKMAN: co-writer
DAVE STEWART: colorist
TODD KLEIN: letterer
RICKEY PURDIN: asst. ed.
HARVEY RICHARDS: assoc. ed.
MIKE MARTS: editor
MONSTERS AND MURDERERS, KEPT UNDER LOCK AND KEY BY THE AMAZONS FOR GENERATIONS.
AN AMAZONIAN ARKHAM ASYLUM...
IF YOU WISH.
MEDUSA SHOULD BE SHACKLED IN THE DEEPEST CELL, FAR FROM THE WORLD SHE WANTS TO DESTROY.
I PRAY THAT YOU'VE BEEN DECEIVED AND THAT THE GORGON HASN'T BROKEN HER BONDS.
YOU AND ME BOTH...

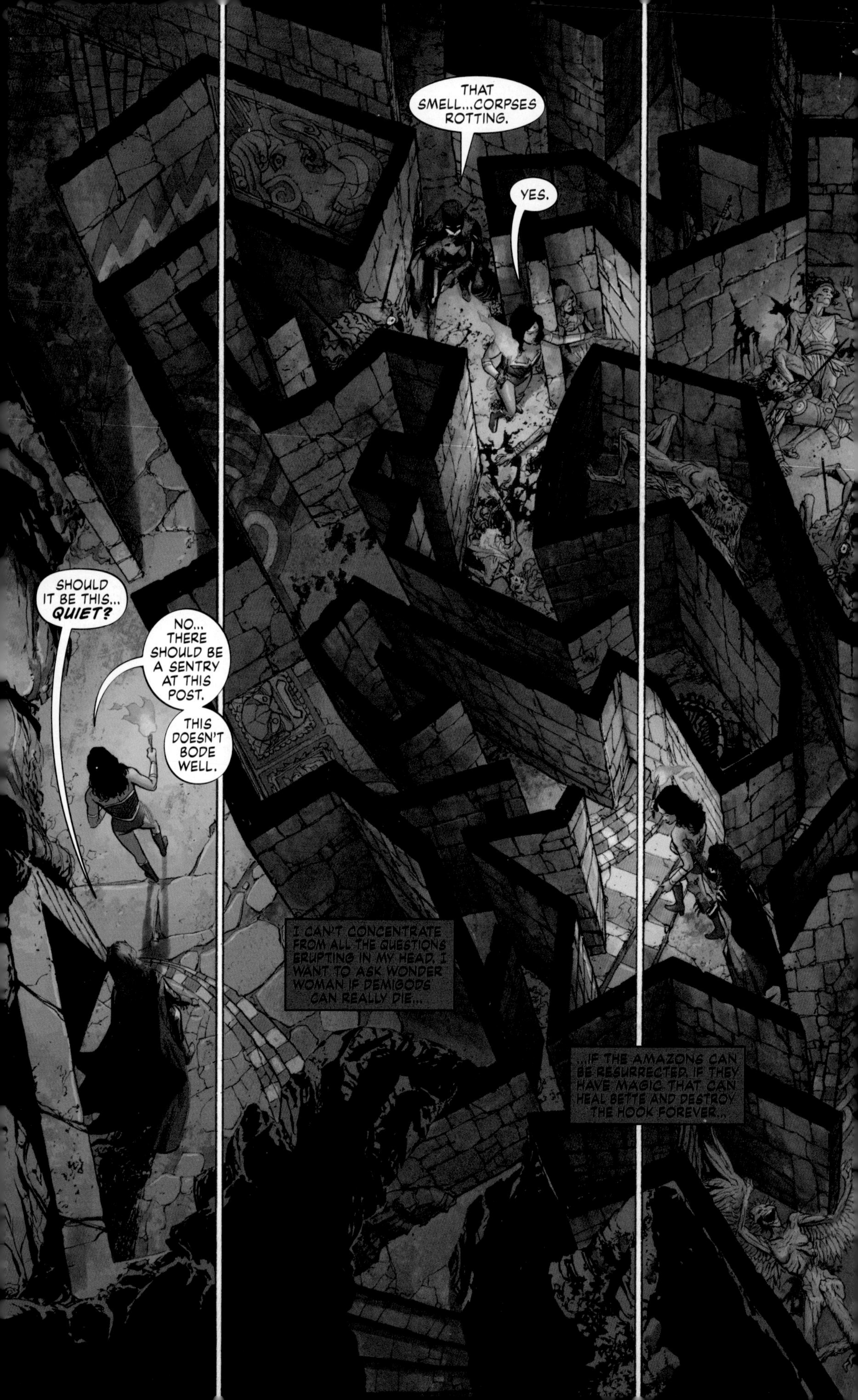
THAT SMELL...CORPSES ROTTING.
YES.
SHOULD IT BE THIS... ***QUIET?***
NO... THERE SHOULD BE A SENTRY AT THIS POST.
THIS DOESN'T BODE WELL.
I CAN'T CONCENTRATE FROM ALL THE QUESTIONS ERUPTING IN MY HEAD. I WANT TO ASK WONDER WOMAN IF DEMIGODS CAN REALLY DIE...
...IF THE AMAZONS CAN BE RESURRECTED, IF THEY HAVE MAGIC THAT CAN HEAL BETTE AND DESTROY THE HOOK FOREVER...

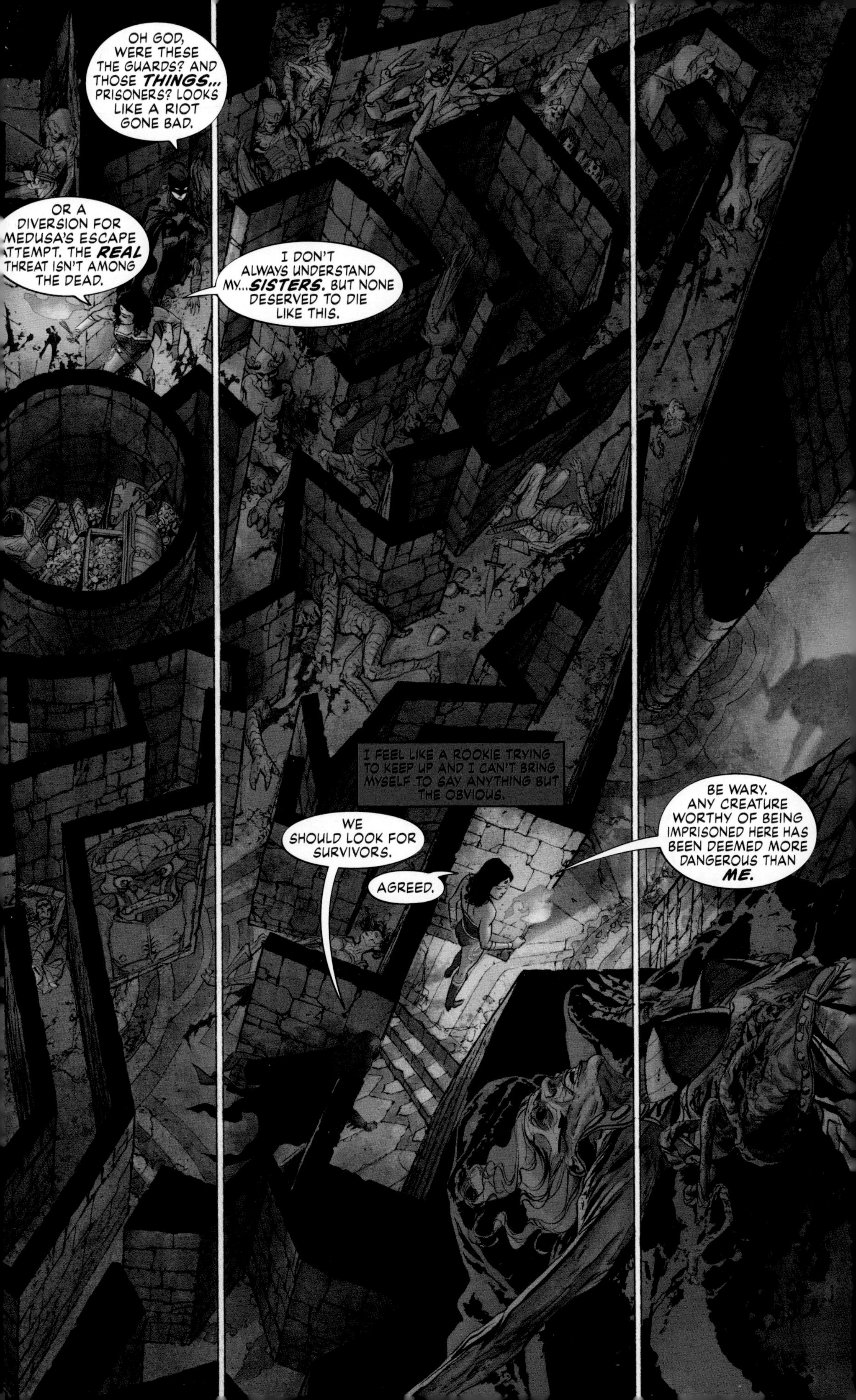
OH GOD, WERE THESE THE GUARDS? AND THOSE THINGS... PRISONERS? LOOKS LIKE A RIOT GONE BAD.
OR A DIVERSION FOR MEDUSA'S ESCAPE ATTEMPT. THE REAL THREAT ISN'T AMONG THE DEAD.
I DON'T ALWAYS UNDERSTAND MY...SISTERS. BUT NONE DESERVED TO DIE LIKE THIS.
I FEEL LIKE A ROOKIE TRYING TO KEEP UP AND I CAN'T BRING MYSELF TO SAY ANYTHING BUT THE OBVIOUS.
WE SHOULD LOOK FOR SURVIVORS.
AGREED.
BE WARY. ANY CREATURE WORTHY OF BEING IMPRISONED HERE HAS BEEN DEEMED MORE DANGEROUS THAN ME.

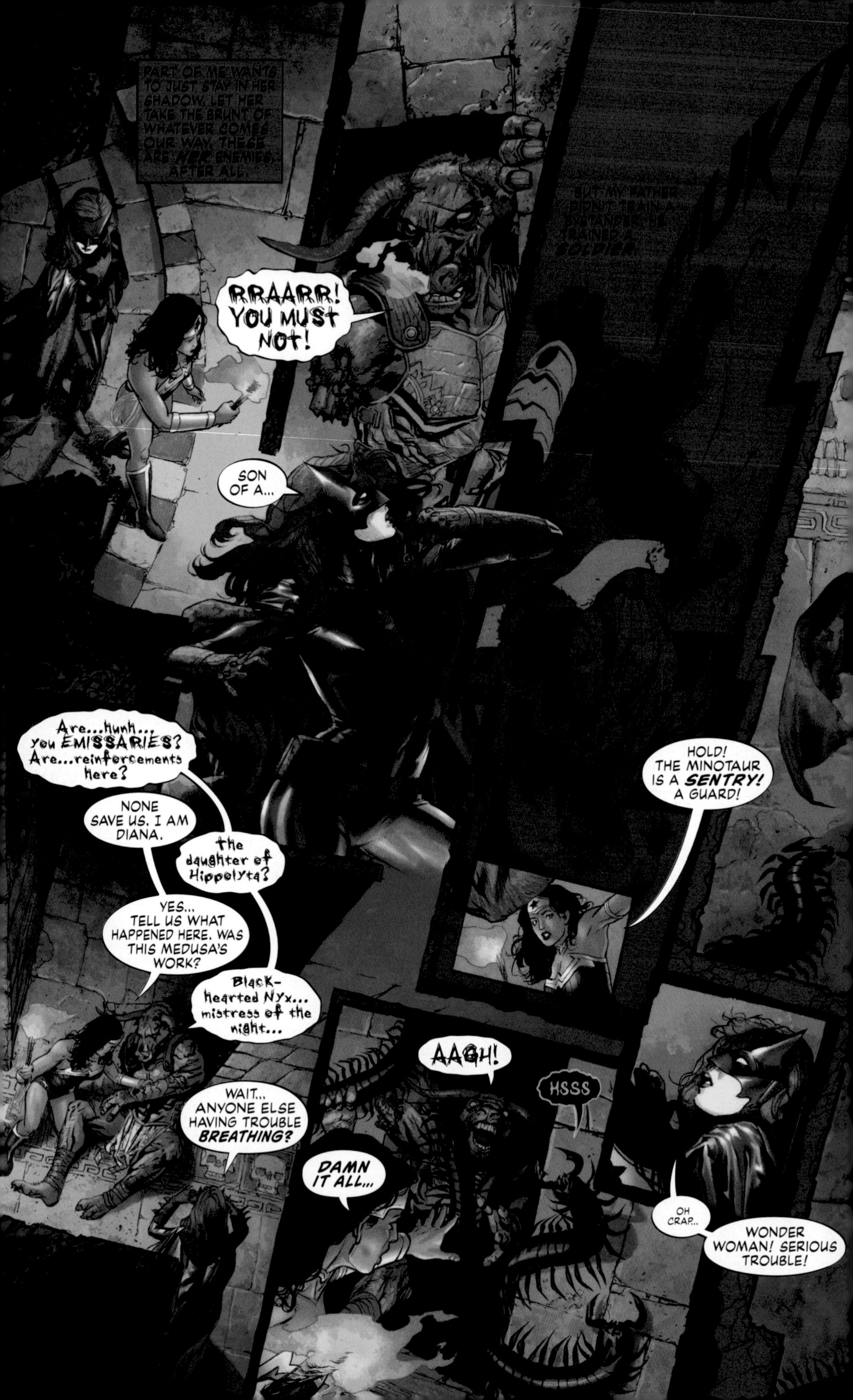

PART OF ME WANTS TO JUST STAY IN HER SHADOW. LET HER TAKE THE BRUNT OF WHATEVER COMES OUR WAY. THESE ARE HER ENEMIES, AFTER ALL.
BUT MY FATHER DIDN'T TRAIN A BYSTANDER. HE TRAINED A SOLDIER.
RRAARR! YOU MUST NOT!
SON OF A...
HOLD! THE MINOTAUR IS A SENTRY! A GUARD!
Are...hunh... you EMISSARIES? Are...reinforcements here?
NONE SAVE US. I AM DIANA.
the daughter of Hippolyta?
YES... TELL US WHAT HAPPENED HERE. WAS THIS MEDUSA'S WORK?
Black-hearted Nyx... mistress of the night...
WAIT... ANYONE ELSE HAVING TROUBLE BREATHING?
AAGH!
HSSS
DAMN IT ALL...
OH CRAP...
WONDER WOMAN! SERIOUS TROUBLE!

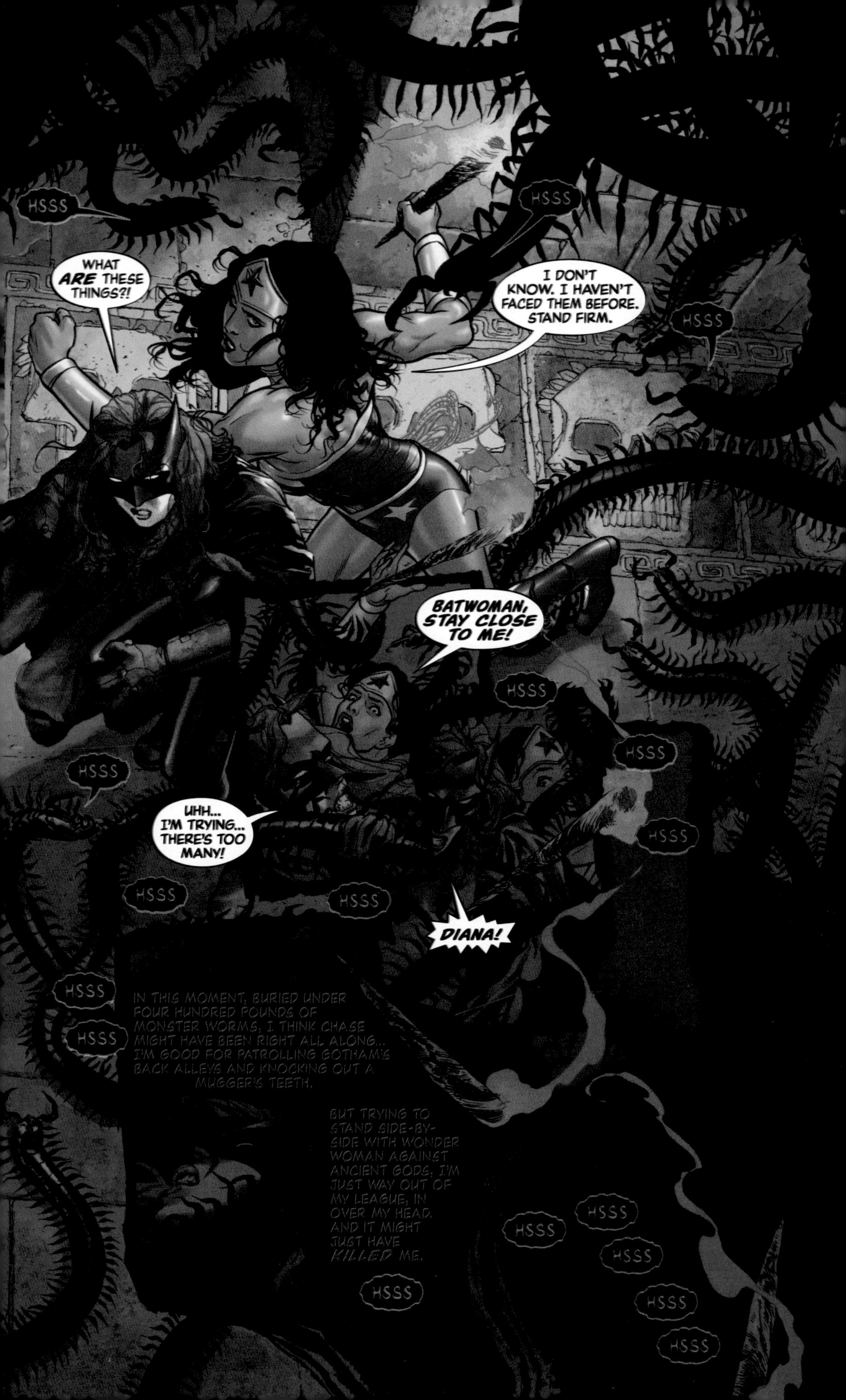
HSSS
HSSS
WHAT *ARE* THESE THINGS?!
I DON'T KNOW. I HAVEN'T FACED THEM BEFORE. STAND FIRM.
HSSS
BATWOMAN, STAY CLOSE TO ME!
HSSS
HSSS
HSSS
UHH... I'M TRYING... THERE'S TOO MANY!
HSSS
HSSS
HSSS
DIANA!
HSSS
HSSS
IN THIS MOMENT, BURIED UNDER FOUR HUNDRED POUNDS OF MONSTER WORMS, I THINK CHASE MIGHT HAVE BEEN RIGHT ALL ALONG... I'M GOOD FOR PATROLLING GOTHAM'S BACK ALLEYS AND KNOCKING OUT A MUGGER'S TEETH.
BUT TRYING TO STAND SIDE-BY-SIDE WITH WONDER WOMAN AGAINST ANCIENT GODS, I'M JUST WAY OUT OF MY LEAGUE, IN OVER MY HEAD. AND IT MIGHT JUST HAVE *KILLED* ME.
HSSS
HSSS
HSSS
HSSS
HSSS
HSSS

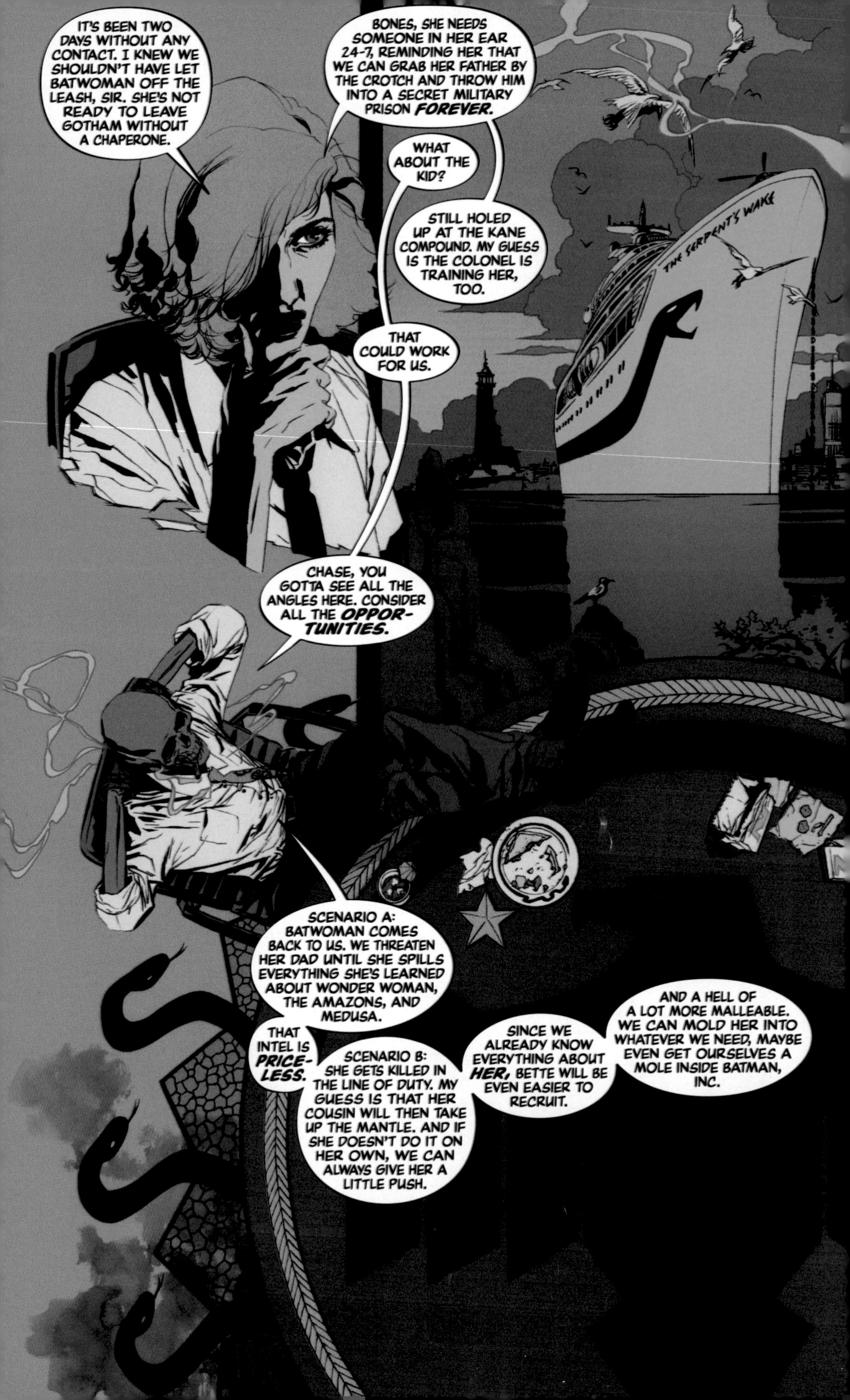
IT'S BEEN TWO DAYS WITHOUT ANY CONTACT. I KNEW WE SHOULDN'T HAVE LET BATWOMAN OFF THE LEASH, SIR. SHE'S NOT READY TO LEAVE GOTHAM WITHOUT A CHAPERONE.
BONES, SHE NEEDS SOMEONE IN HER EAR 24-7, REMINDING HER THAT WE CAN GRAB HER FATHER BY THE CROTCH AND THROW HIM INTO A SECRET MILITARY PRISON FOREVER.
WHAT ABOUT THE KID?
STILL HOLED UP AT THE KANE COMPOUND. MY GUESS IS THE COLONEL IS TRAINING HER, TOO.
THAT COULD WORK FOR US.
THE SERPENT'S WAKE
CHASE, YOU GOTTA SEE ALL THE ANGLES HERE. CONSIDER ALL THE OPPORTUNITIES.
SCENARIO A: BATWOMAN COMES BACK TO US. WE THREATEN HER DAD UNTIL SHE SPILLS EVERYTHING SHE'S LEARNED ABOUT WONDER WOMAN, THE AMAZONS, AND MEDUSA.
THAT INTEL IS PRICELESS.
SCENARIO B: SHE GETS KILLED IN THE LINE OF DUTY. MY GUESS IS THAT HER COUSIN WILL THEN TAKE UP THE MANTLE. AND IF SHE DOESN'T DO IT ON HER OWN, WE CAN ALWAYS GIVE HER A LITTLE PUSH.
SINCE WE ALREADY KNOW EVERYTHING ABOUT HER, BETTE WILL BE EVEN EASIER TO RECRUIT.
AND A HELL OF A LOT MORE MALLEABLE. WE CAN MOLD HER INTO WHATEVER WE NEED, MAYBE EVEN GET OURSELVES A MOLE INSIDE BATMAN, INC.

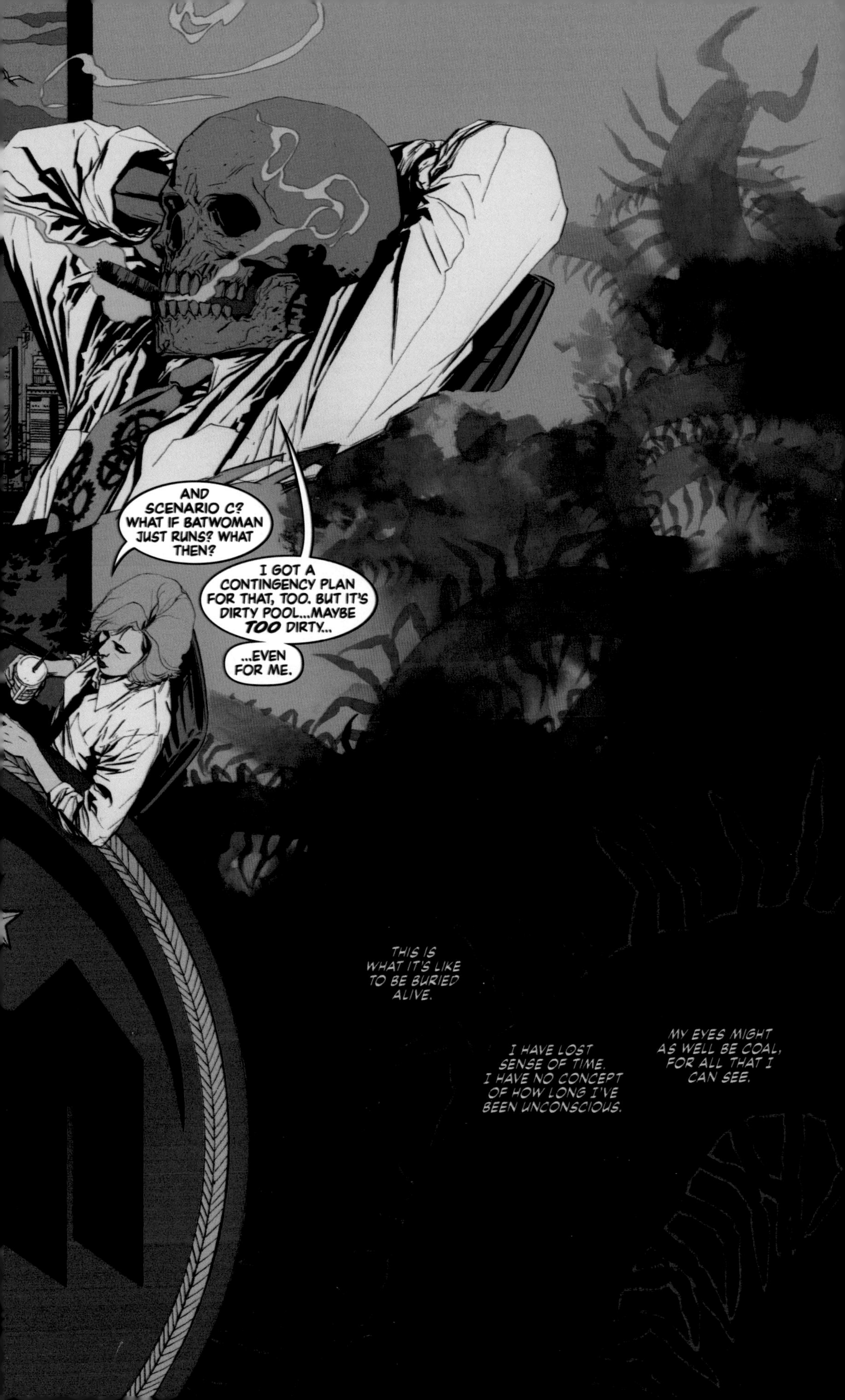
AND SCENARIO C? WHAT IF BATWOMAN JUST RUNS? WHAT THEN?
I GOT A CONTINGENCY PLAN FOR THAT, TOO. BUT IT'S DIRTY POOL...MAYBE TOO DIRTY...
...EVEN FOR ME.
THIS IS WHAT IT'S LIKE TO BE BURIED ALIVE.
I HAVE LOST SENSE OF TIME. I HAVE NO CONCEPT OF HOW LONG I'VE BEEN UNCONSCIOUS.
MY EYES MIGHT AS WELL BE COAL, FOR ALL THAT I CAN SEE.

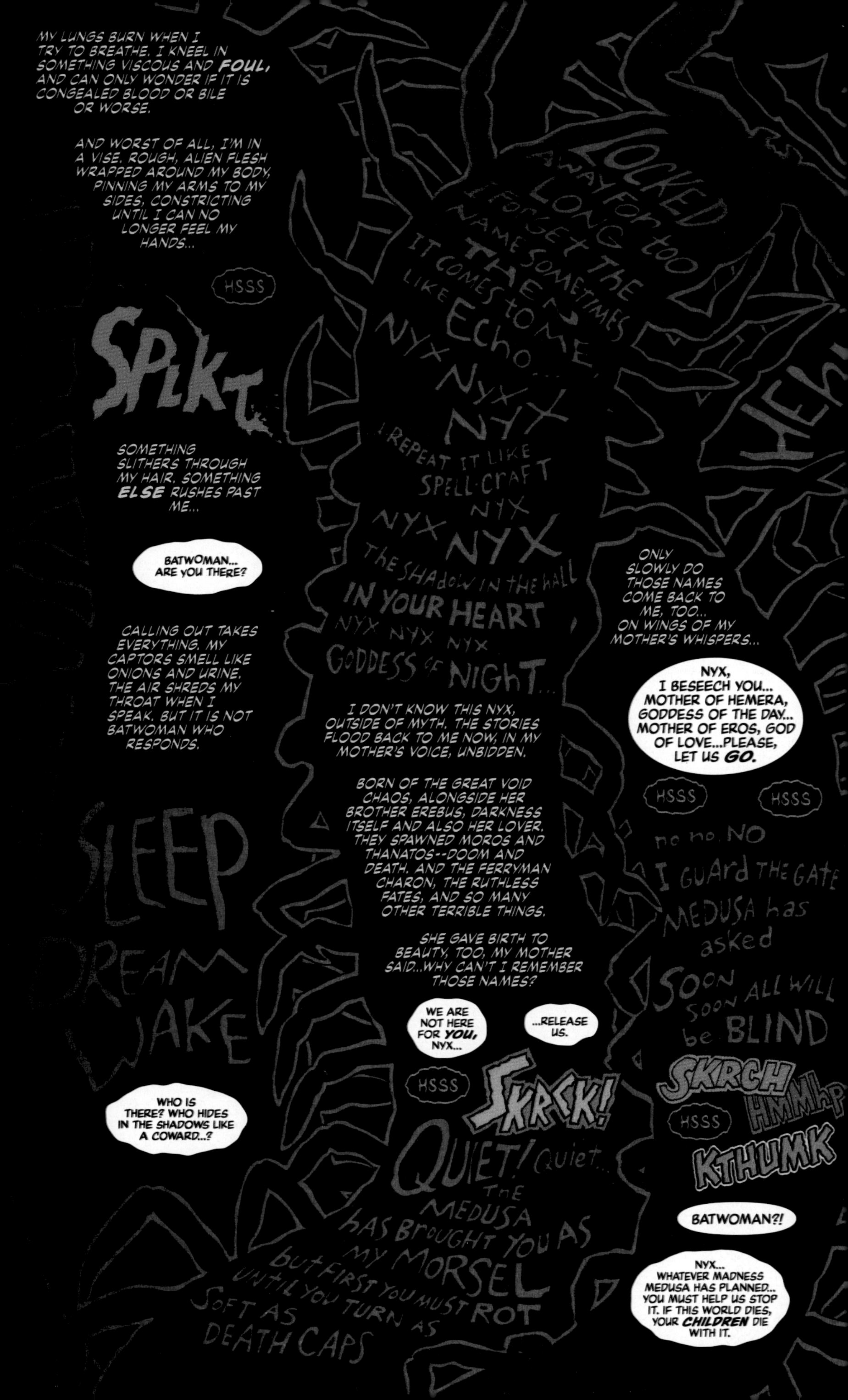
MY LUNGS BURN WHEN I TRY TO BREATHE. I KNEEL IN SOMETHING VISCOUS AND **FOUL,** AND CAN ONLY WONDER IF IT IS CONGEALED BLOOD OR BILE OR WORSE.
AND WORST OF ALL, I'M IN A VISE. ROUGH, ALIEN FLESH WRAPPED AROUND MY BODY, PINNING MY ARMS TO MY SIDES, CONSTRICTING UNTIL I CAN NO LONGER FEEL MY HANDS...
HSSS
SPLKT
SOMETHING SLITHERS THROUGH MY HAIR. SOMETHING **ELSE** RUSHES PAST ME...
BATWOMAN... ARE YOU THERE?
CALLING OUT TAKES EVERYTHING. MY CAPTORS SMELL LIKE ONIONS AND URINE. THE AIR SHREDS MY THROAT WHEN I SPEAK. BUT IT IS NOT BATWOMAN WHO RESPONDS.
WHO IS THERE? WHO HIDES IN THE SHADOWS LIKE A COWARD...?
LOCKED AWAY FOR TOO LONG FORGET THE NAME SOMETIMES THE NAMES IT COMES TO ME LIKE ECHO...
NYX NYX NYX
I REPEAT IT LIKE SPELL-CRAFT
NYX NYX NYX
THE SHADOW IN THE HALL IN YOUR HEART
NYX NYX NYX
GODDESS OF NIGHT...
I DON'T KNOW THIS NYX, OUTSIDE OF MYTH. THE STORIES FLOOD BACK TO ME NOW, IN MY MOTHER'S VOICE, UNBIDDEN.
BORN OF THE GREAT VOID CHAOS, ALONGSIDE HER BROTHER EREBUS, DARKNESS ITSELF AND ALSO HER LOVER. THEY SPAWNED MOROS AND THANATOS--DOOM AND DEATH. AND THE FERRYMAN CHARON, THE RUTHLESS FATES, AND SO MANY OTHER TERRIBLE THINGS.
SHE GAVE BIRTH TO BEAUTY, TOO, MY MOTHER SAID...WHY CAN'T I REMEMBER THOSE NAMES?
ONLY SLOWLY DO THOSE NAMES COME BACK TO ME, TOO... ON WINGS OF MY MOTHER'S WHISPERS...
NYX, I BESEECH YOU... MOTHER OF HEMERA, GODDESS OF THE DAY... MOTHER OF EROS, GOD OF LOVE...PLEASE, LET US **GO.**
HSSS
HSSS
no no NO
I GUARD THE GATE
MEDUSA has asked
SOON SOON ALL WILL be BLIND
WE ARE NOT HERE FOR ***YOU,*** NYX...
...RELEASE US.
HSSS
SKRCK!
QUIET! Quiet...
ThE MEDUSA has Brought YOU AS MY MORSEL but FIRST YOU MUST ROT UNTIL YOU TURN AS SOFT AS DEATH CAPS
SKRCH
HMMhP
HSSS
KTHUMK
BATWOMAN?!
NYX... WHATEVER MADNESS MEDUSA HAS PLANNED... YOU MUST HELP US STOP IT. IF THIS WORLD DIES, YOUR ***CHILDREN*** DIE WITH IT.

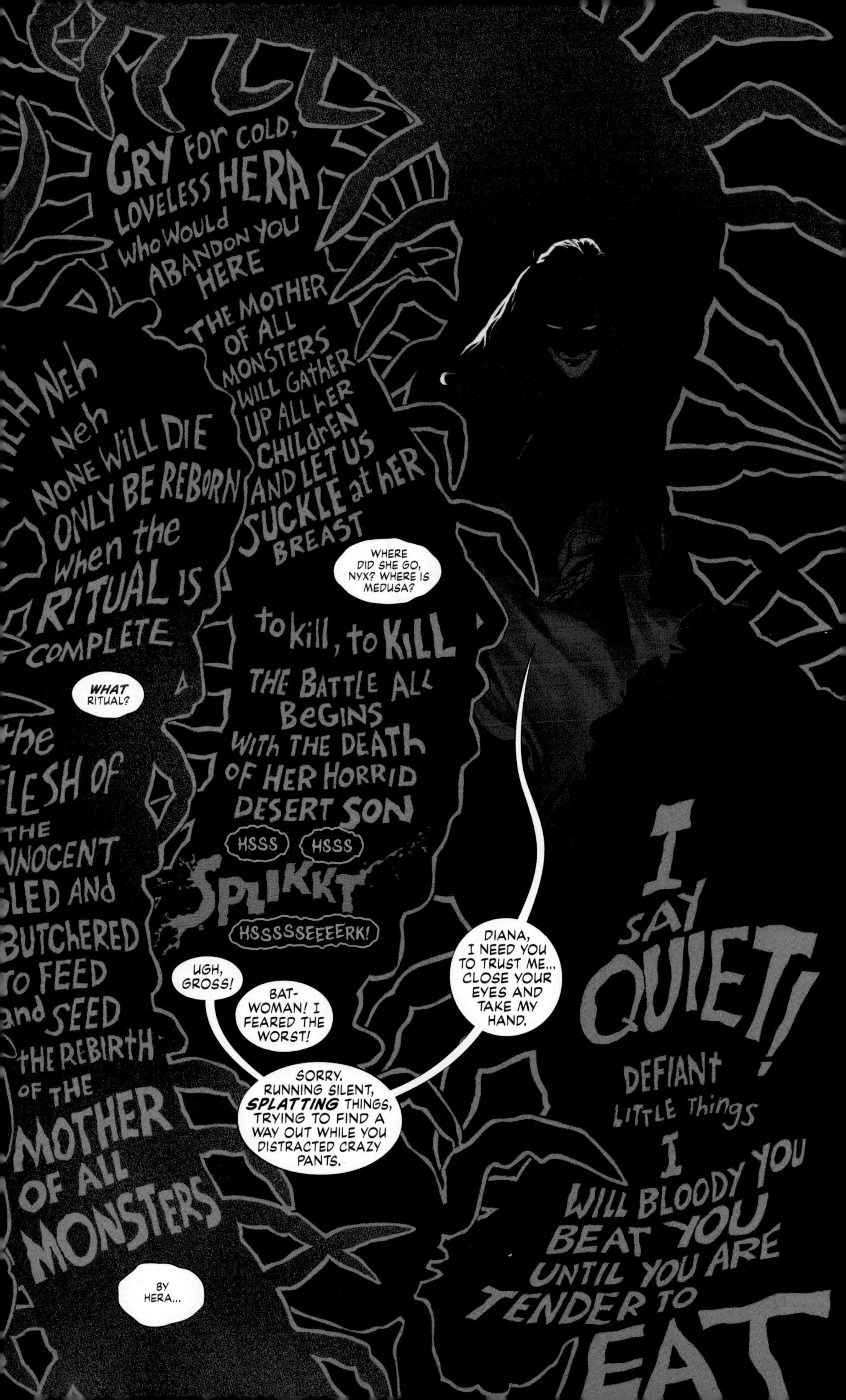
CRY FOR COLD, LOVELESS HERA WHO WOULD ABANDON YOU HERE
THE MOTHER OF ALL MONSTERS WILL GATHER UP ALL HER CHILDREN AND LET US SUCKLE AT HER BREAST
Neh Neh NONE WILL DIE ONLY BE REBORN WHEN THE RITUAL IS COMPLETE
WHERE DID SHE GO, NYX? WHERE IS MEDUSA?
WHAT RITUAL?
TO KILL, TO KILL THE BATTLE ALL BEGINS WITH THE DEATH OF HER HORRID DESERT SON
THE LESH OF THE NNOCENT LED AND BUTCHERED TO FEED AND SEED THE REBIRTH OF THE MOTHER OF ALL MONSTERS
HSSS
HSSS
SPLIKKT
HSSSSSEEEERK!
UGH, GROSS!
BAT-WOMAN! I FEARED THE WORST!
SORRY. RUNNING SILENT, SPLATTING THINGS, TRYING TO FIND A WAY OUT WHILE YOU DISTRACTED CRAZY PANTS.
DIANA, I NEED YOU TO TRUST ME... CLOSE YOUR EYES AND TAKE MY HAND.
I SAY QUIET! DEFIANT LITTLE THINGS I WILL BLOODY YOU BEAT YOU UNTIL YOU ARE TENDER TO EAT
BY HERA...

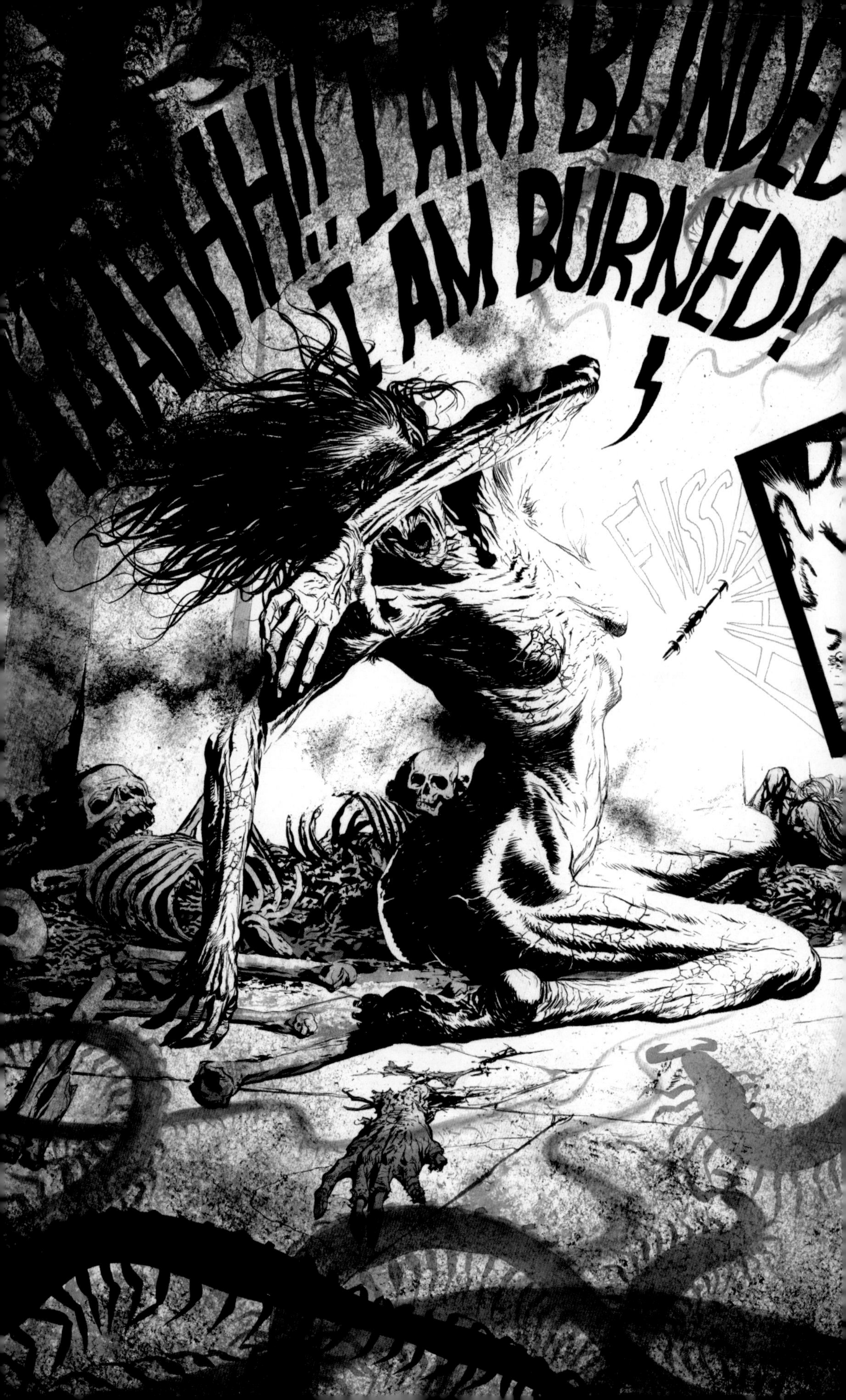
AAAHHH!! I AM BLINDE
I AM BURNED!

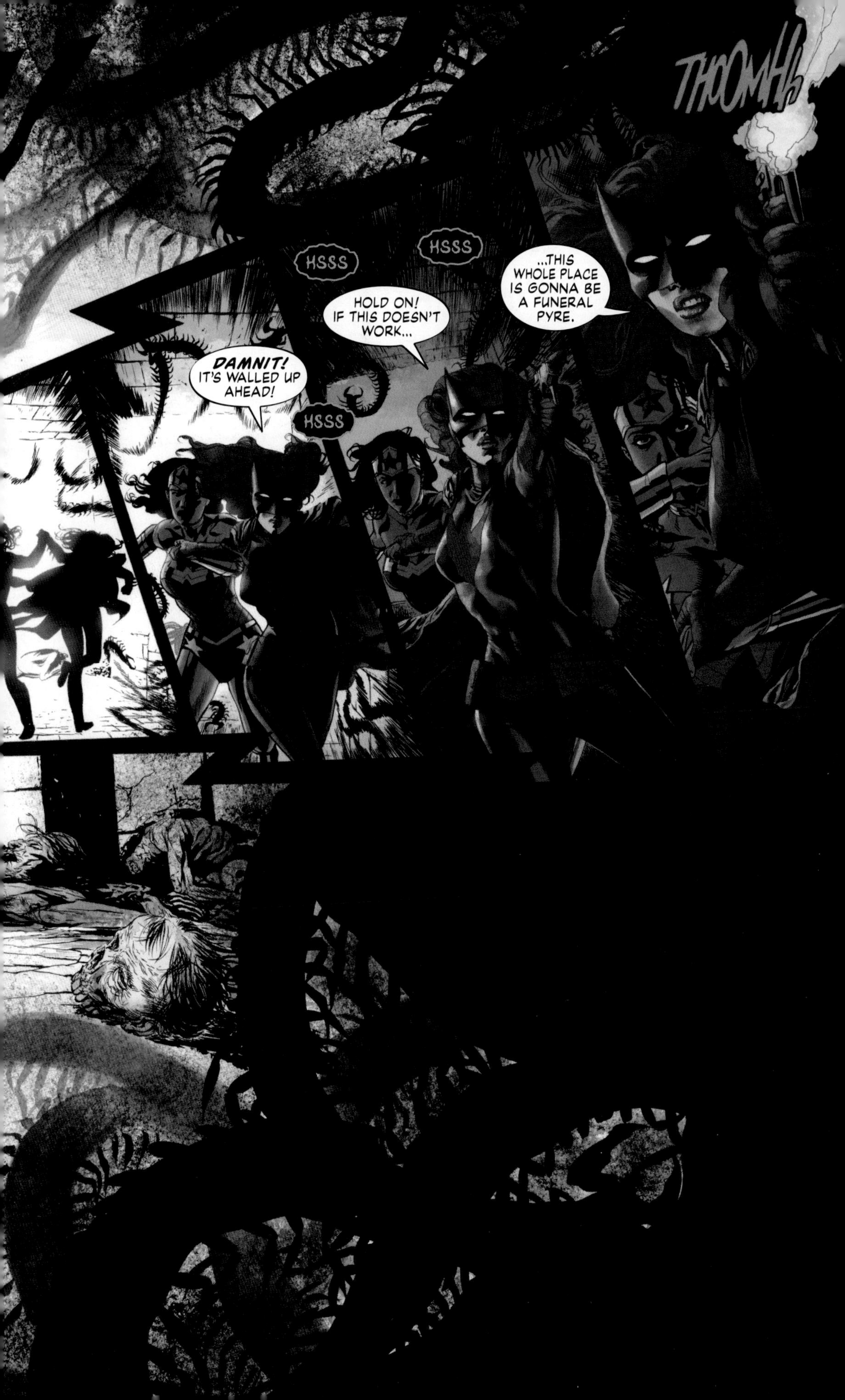
THOOMHh
HSSS
HSSS
HOLD ON! IF THIS DOESN'T WORK...
...THIS WHOLE PLACE IS GONNA BE A FUNERAL PYRE.
DAMNIT! IT'S WALLED UP AHEAD!
HSSS

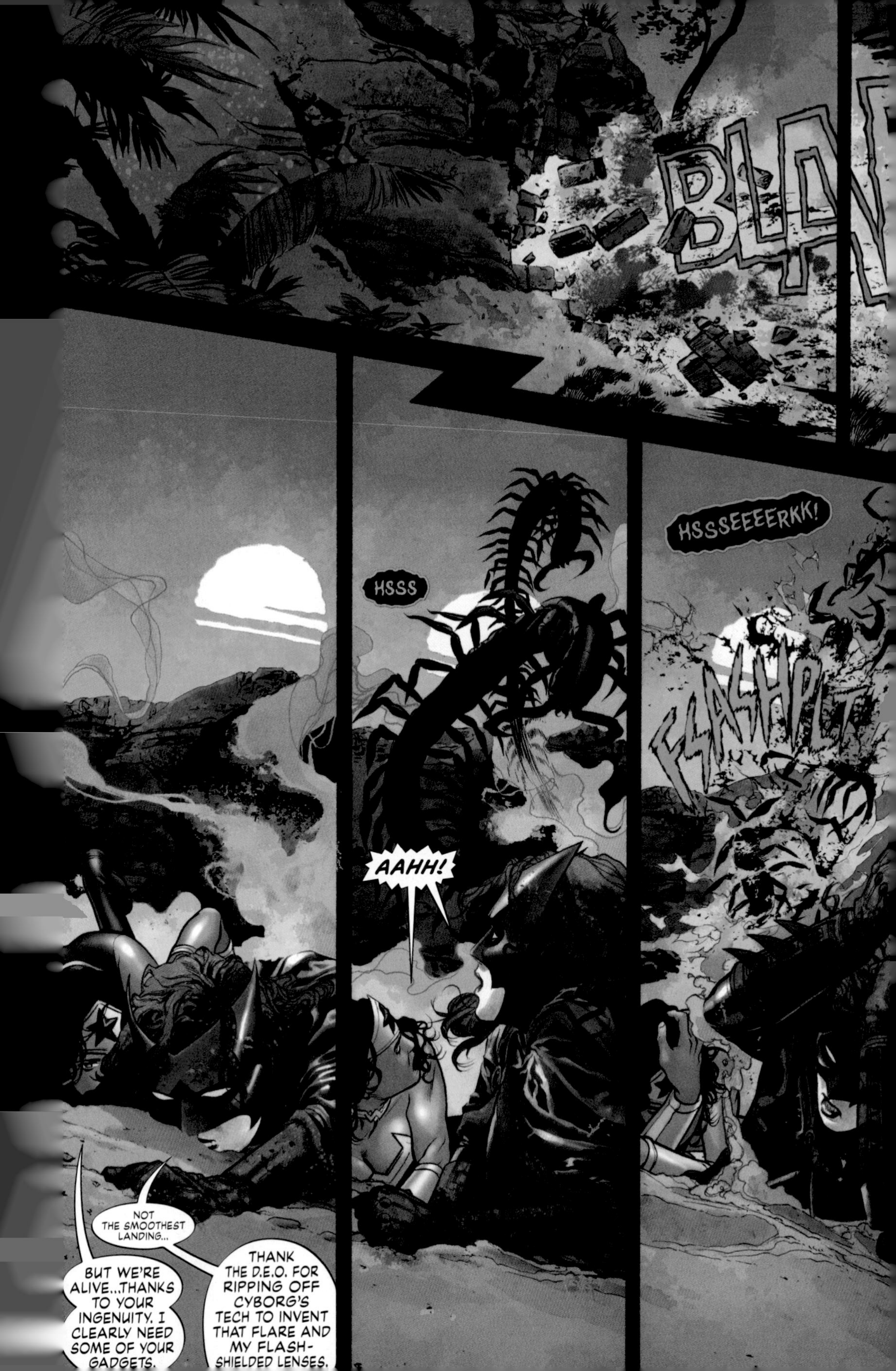
BLA
HSSS
AAHH!
HSSSEEEERKK!
FSSSHPLT
NOT THE SMOOTHEST LANDING...
BUT WE'RE ALIVE...THANKS TO YOUR INGENUITY. I CLEARLY NEED SOME OF YOUR GADGETS.
THANK THE D.E.O. FOR RIPPING OFF CYBORG'S TECH TO INVENT THAT FLARE AND MY FLASH-SHIELDED LENSES.

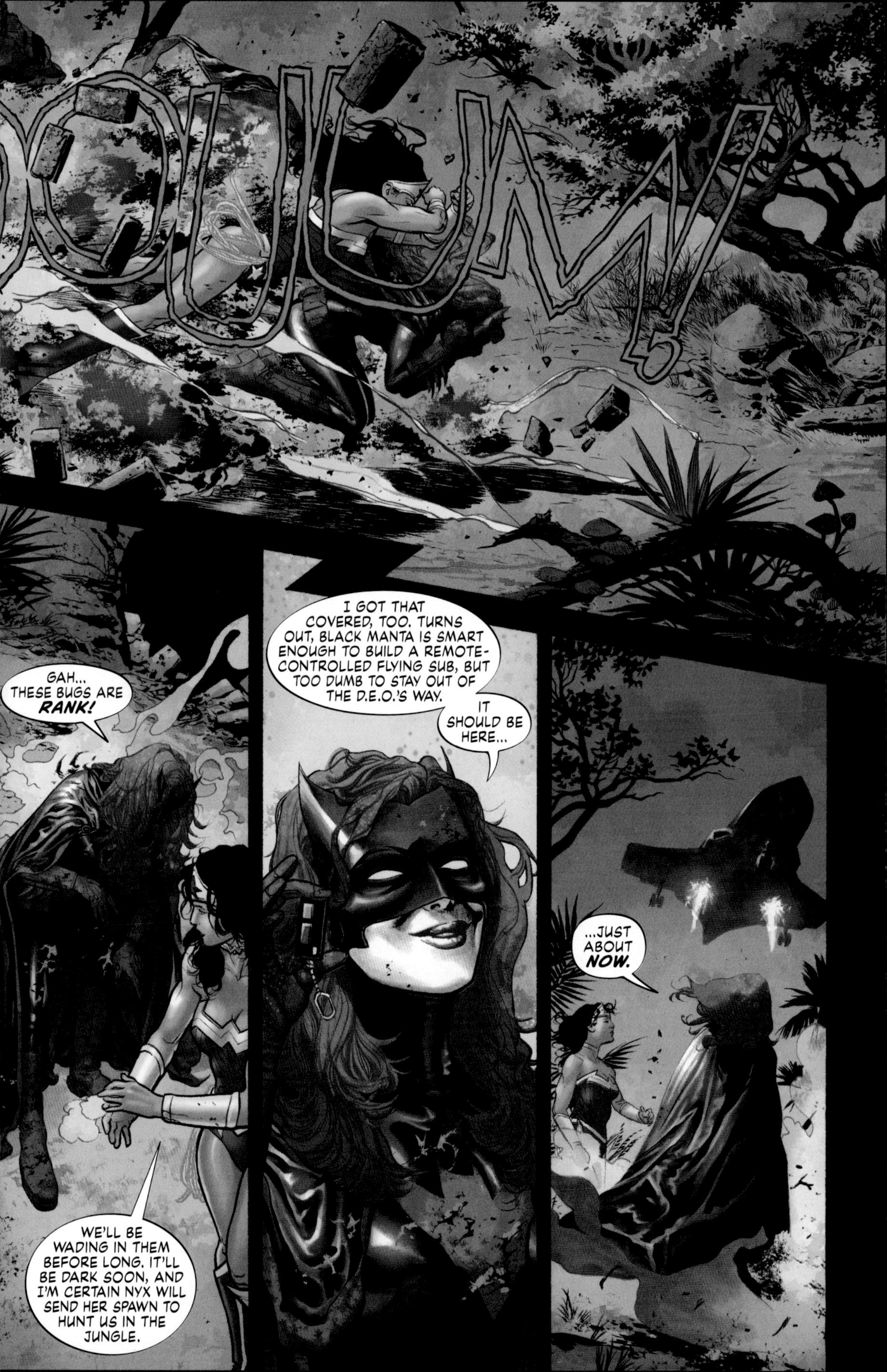

GAH... THESE BUGS ARE RANK!
WE'LL BE WADING IN THEM BEFORE LONG. IT'LL BE DARK SOON, AND I'M CERTAIN NYX WILL SEND HER SPAWN TO HUNT US IN THE JUNGLE.
I GOT THAT COVERED, TOO. TURNS OUT, BLACK MANTA IS SMART ENOUGH TO BUILD A REMOTE-CONTROLLED FLYING SUB, BUT TOO DUMB TO STAY OUT OF THE D.E.O.'S WAY.
IT SHOULD BE HERE...
...JUST ABOUT NOW.

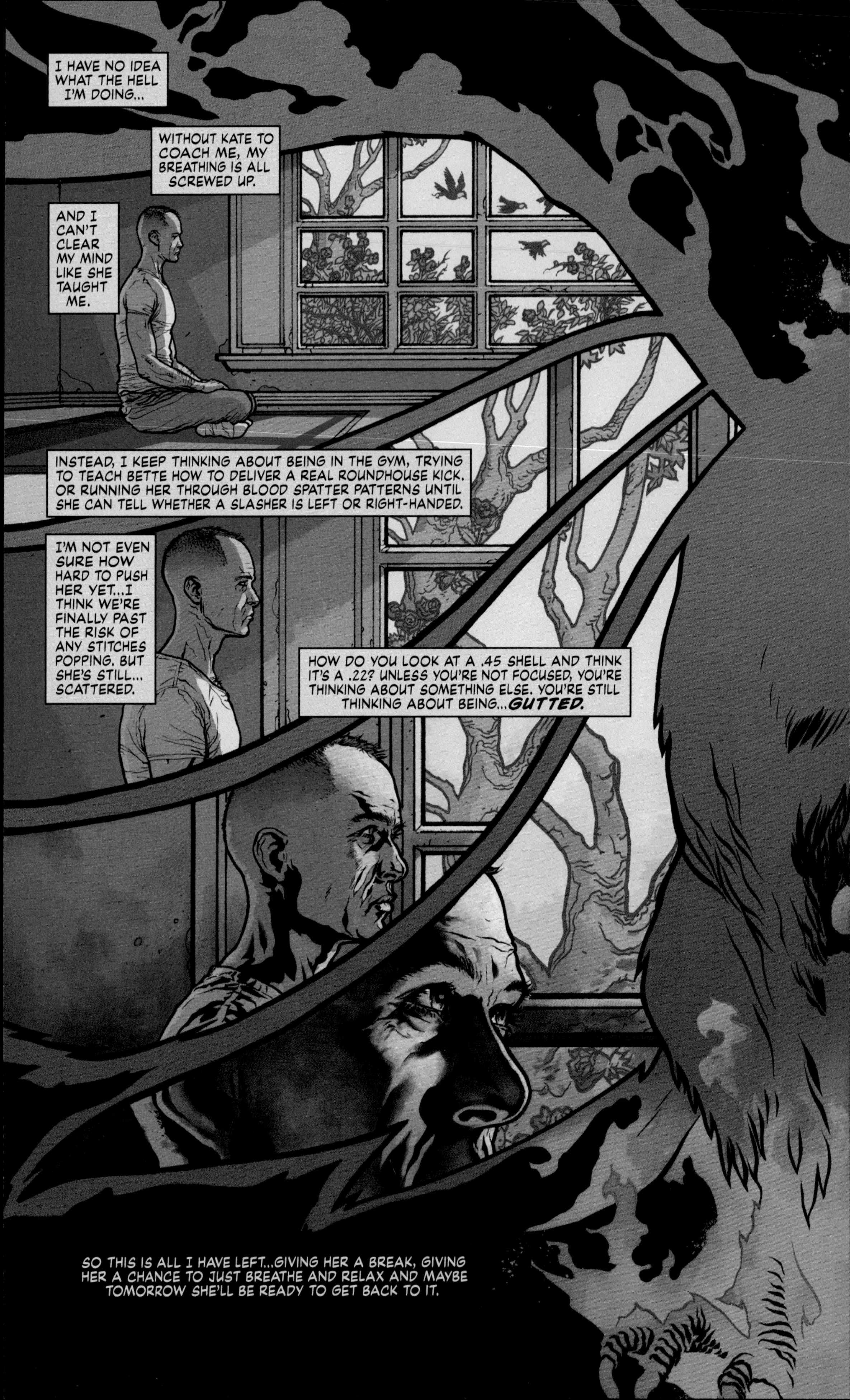
I HAVE NO IDEA WHAT THE HELL I'M DOING...
WITHOUT KATE TO COACH ME, MY BREATHING IS ALL SCREWED UP.
AND I CAN'T CLEAR MY MIND LIKE SHE TAUGHT ME.
INSTEAD, I KEEP THINKING ABOUT BEING IN THE GYM, TRYING TO TEACH BETTE HOW TO DELIVER A REAL ROUNDHOUSE KICK. OR RUNNING HER THROUGH BLOOD SPATTER PATTERNS UNTIL SHE CAN TELL WHETHER A SLASHER IS LEFT OR RIGHT-HANDED.
I'M NOT EVEN SURE HOW HARD TO PUSH HER YET...I THINK WE'RE FINALLY PAST THE RISK OF ANY STITCHES POPPING. BUT SHE'S STILL... SCATTERED.
HOW DO YOU LOOK AT A .45 SHELL AND THINK IT'S A .22? UNLESS YOU'RE NOT FOCUSED, YOU'RE THINKING ABOUT SOMETHING ELSE. YOU'RE STILL THINKING ABOUT BEING...GUTTED.
SO THIS IS ALL I HAVE LEFT...GIVING HER A BREAK, GIVING HER A CHANCE TO JUST BREATHE AND RELAX AND MAYBE TOMORROW SHE'LL BE READY TO GET BACK TO IT.

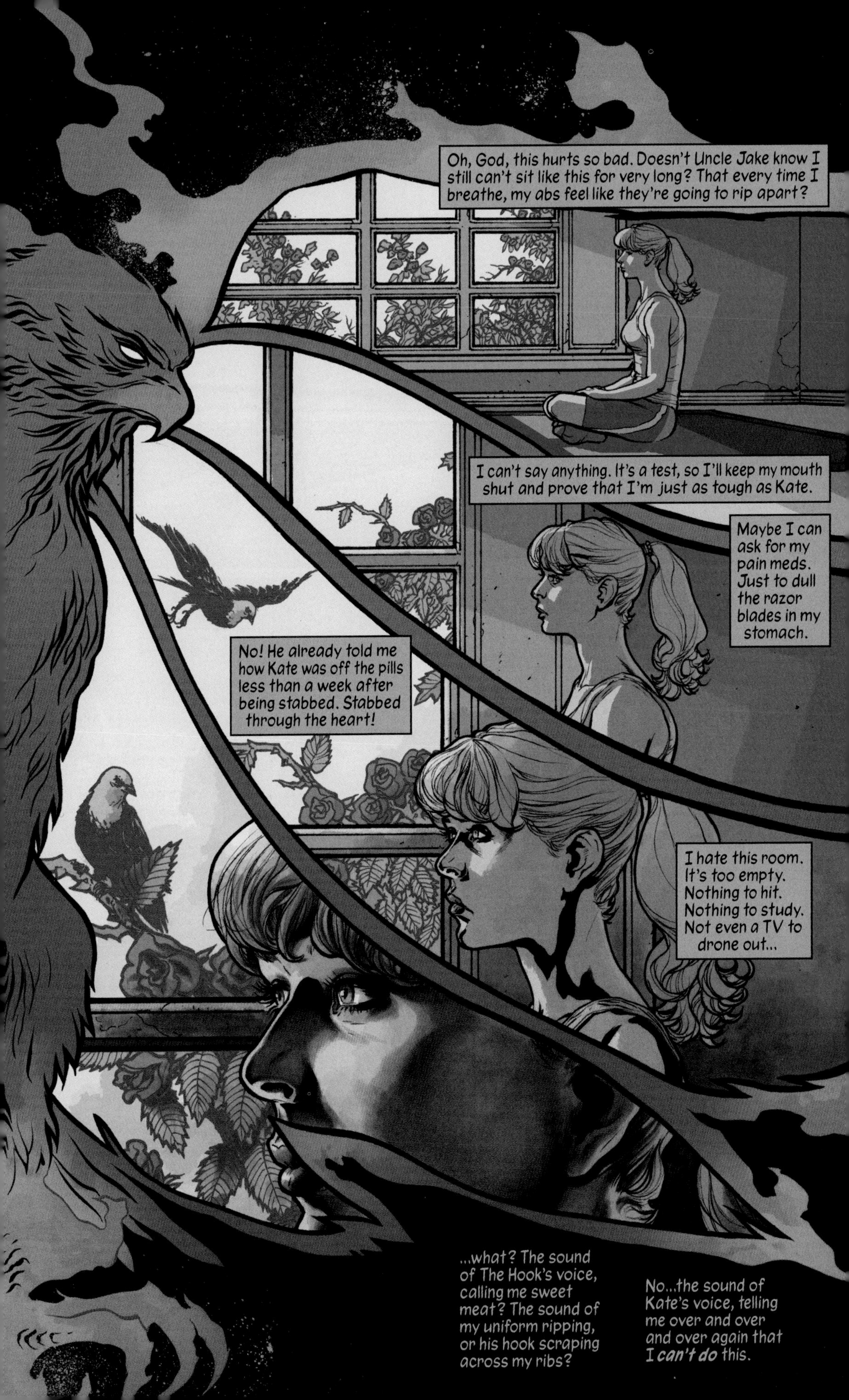
Oh, God, this hurts so bad. Doesn't Uncle Jake know I still can't sit like this for very long? That every time I breathe, my abs feel like they're going to rip apart?
I can't say anything. It's a test, so I'll keep my mouth shut and prove that I'm just as tough as Kate.
Maybe I can ask for my pain meds. Just to dull the razor blades in my stomach.
No! He already told me how Kate was off the pills less than a week after being stabbed. Stabbed through the heart!
I hate this room. It's too empty. Nothing to hit. Nothing to study. Not even a TV to drone out...
...what? The sound of The Hook's voice, calling me sweet meat? The sound of my uniform ripping, or his hook scraping across my ribs?
No...the sound of Kate's voice, telling me over and over and over again that I *can't do* this.

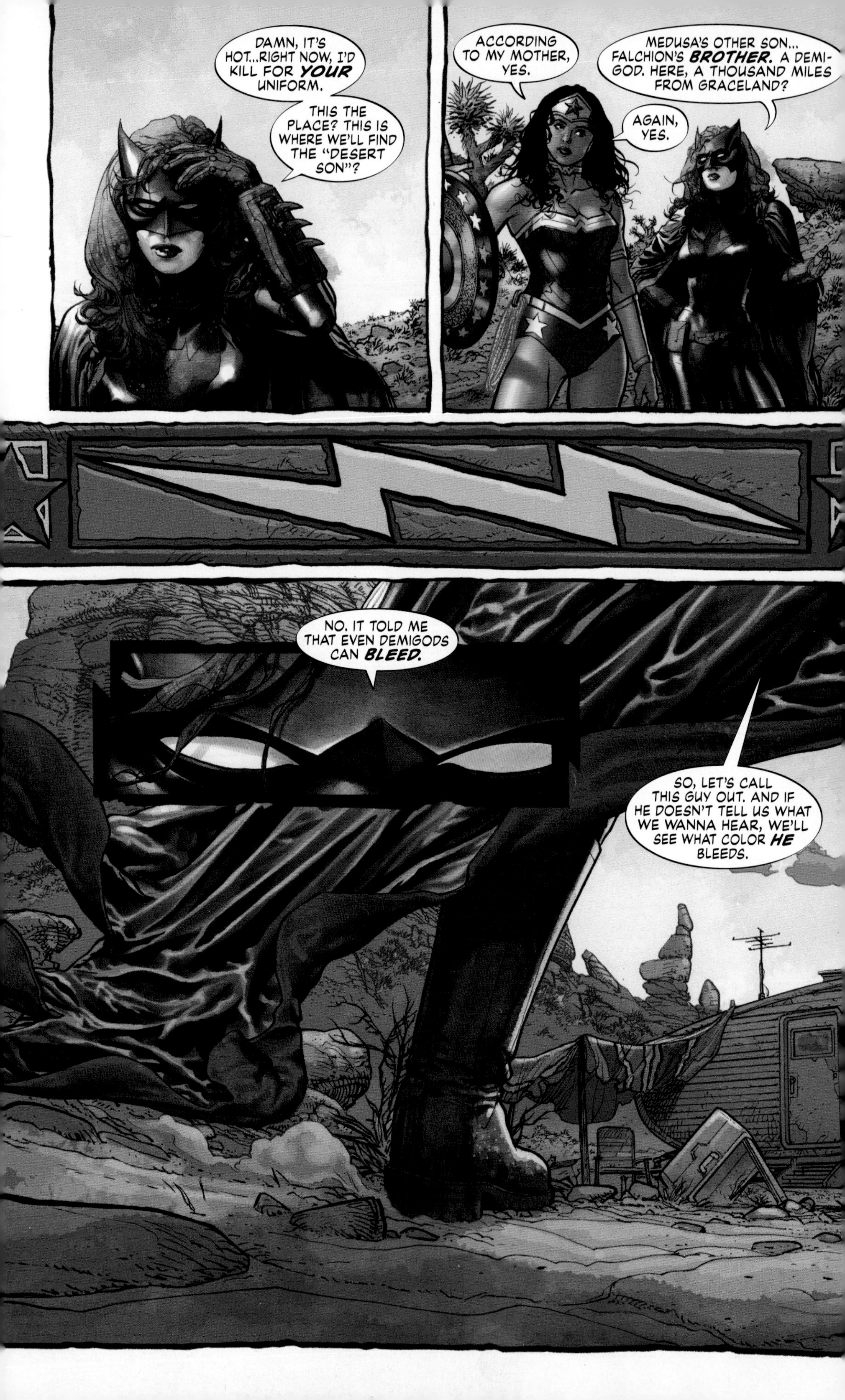
DAMN, IT'S HOT...RIGHT NOW, I'D KILL FOR **YOUR** UNIFORM.
THIS THE PLACE? THIS IS WHERE WE'LL FIND THE "DESERT SON"?
ACCORDING TO MY MOTHER, YES.
MEDUSA'S OTHER SON... FALCHION'S **BROTHER.** A DEMI-GOD. HERE, A THOUSAND MILES FROM GRACELAND?
AGAIN, YES.
NO. IT TOLD ME THAT EVEN DEMIGODS CAN **BLEED.**
SO, LET'S CALL THIS GUY OUT. AND IF HE DOESN'T TELL US WHAT WE WANNA HEAR, WE'LL SEE WHAT COLOR **HE** BLEEDS.

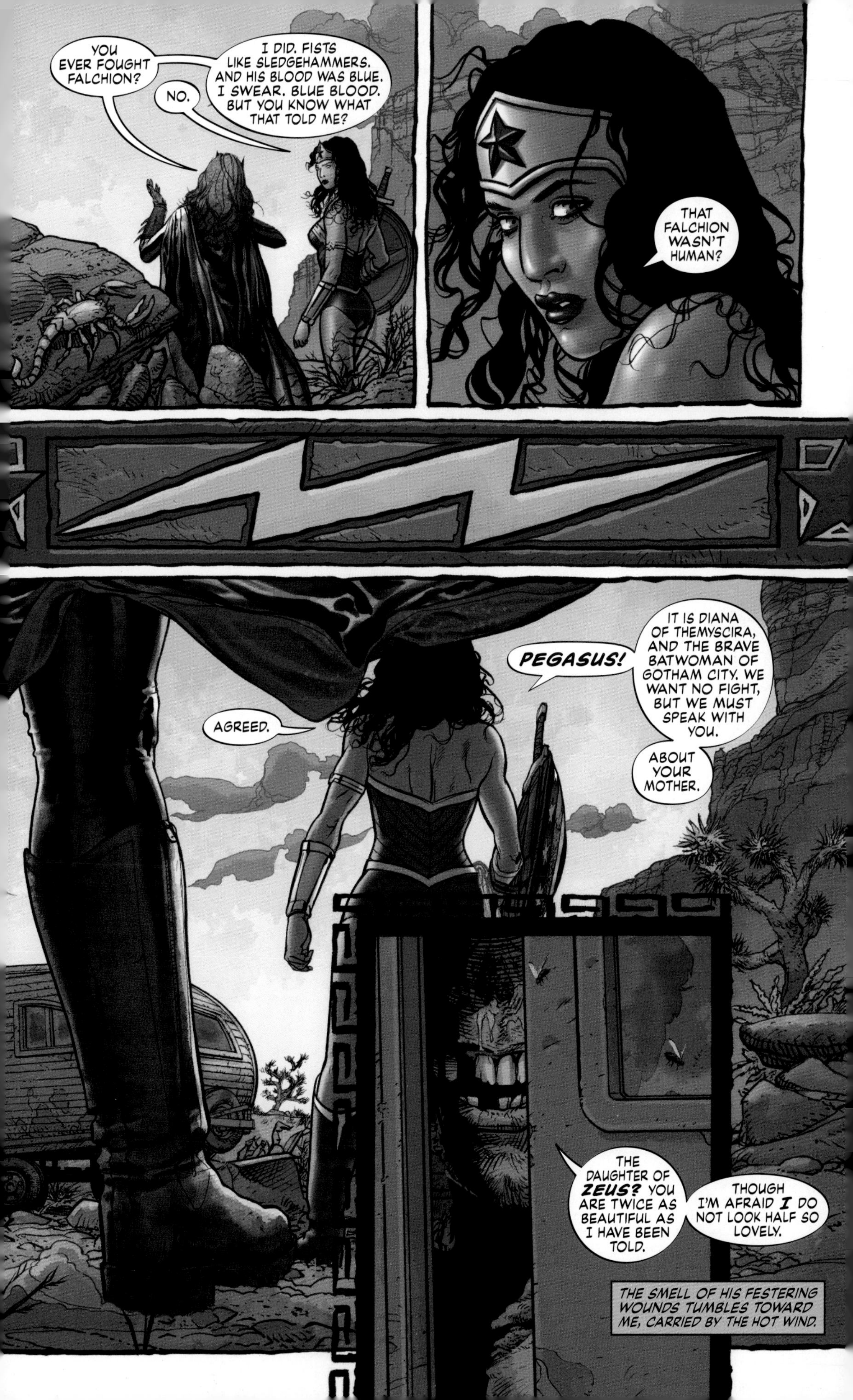
YOU EVER FOUGHT FALCHION?
NO.
I DID. FISTS LIKE SLEDGEHAMMERS. AND HIS BLOOD WAS BLUE. I SWEAR. BLUE BLOOD. BUT YOU KNOW WHAT THAT TOLD ME?
THAT FALCHION WASN'T HUMAN?
AGREED.
PEGASUS!
IT IS DIANA OF THEMYSCIRA, AND THE BRAVE BATWOMAN OF GOTHAM CITY. WE WANT NO FIGHT, BUT WE MUST SPEAK WITH YOU.
ABOUT YOUR MOTHER.
THE DAUGHTER OF ZEUS? YOU ARE TWICE AS BEAUTIFUL AS I HAVE BEEN TOLD.
THOUGH I'M AFRAID I DO NOT LOOK HALF SO LOVELY.
THE SMELL OF HIS FESTERING WOUNDS TUMBLES TOWARD ME, CARRIED BY THE HOT WIND.

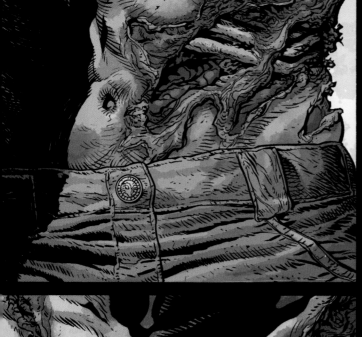

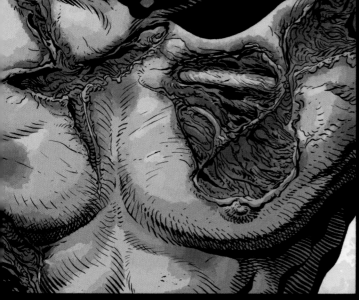

HE LIMPS TO THE DOOR, HIS BROKEN, HOLLOW BONES BANG TOGETHER LIKE REEDS.

IS THIS WHERE WE IMMORTALS ULTIMATELY FIND OURSELVES? HIDING FROM ONE ANOTHER IN EARTH'S MOST DESOLATE PLACES? WILL I, TOO, RETREAT ONE DAY TO A FORTRESS IN THE ARCTIC, OR A CASTLE UNDERSEA, OR PERHAPS EVEN A TOWER FLOATING IN THE HEAVENS?

AND WHEN MY TIME COMES, WILL IT BE ZEUS OR ARES OR HERA WHO FINALLY KILLS ME? OR ONE OF THE MANY ARCH-VILLAINS WHO WISH TO BECOME IMMORTAL? OR ONE OF MY ALLIES, ONE OF THE MANY HEROES THAT THE MORTALS TREAT AS GODS? OR PERHAPS AN AMAZON? OR MY OWN MOTHER?

WHATEVER MY FATE, I CANNOT ESCAPE IT. ALL I CAN DO IS STEEL MYSELF TO FACE PEGASUS AND ASK HIM ALL HE KNOWS ABOUT MEDUSA AND HER PLOT. AND IF WE MUST FIGHT, SO BE IT. BUT WHEN WE ARE DONE, ONE WAY OR ANOTHER, I WILL GIVE HIM MY HAND SO THAT NEITHER OF US WILL DIE ALONE.

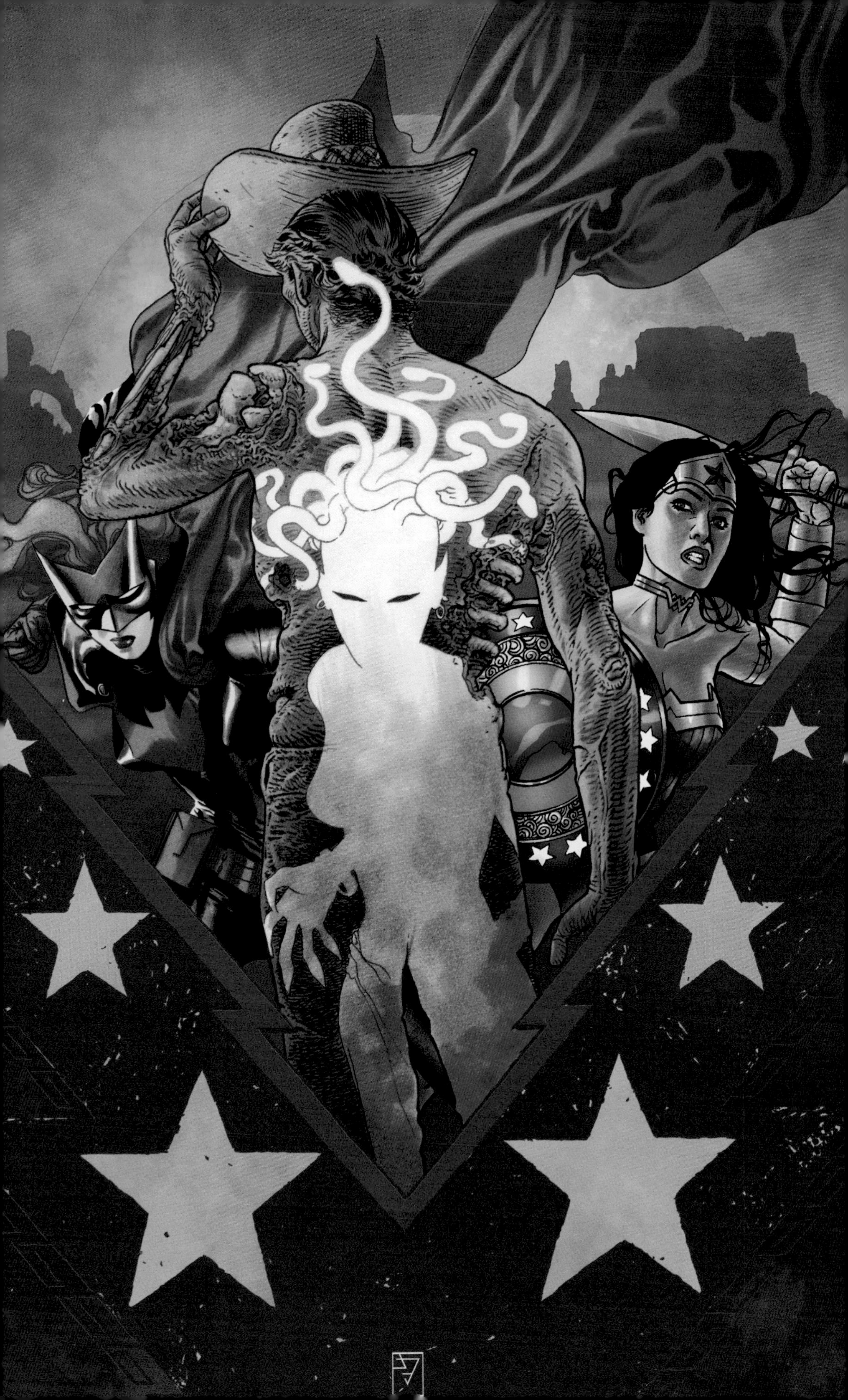

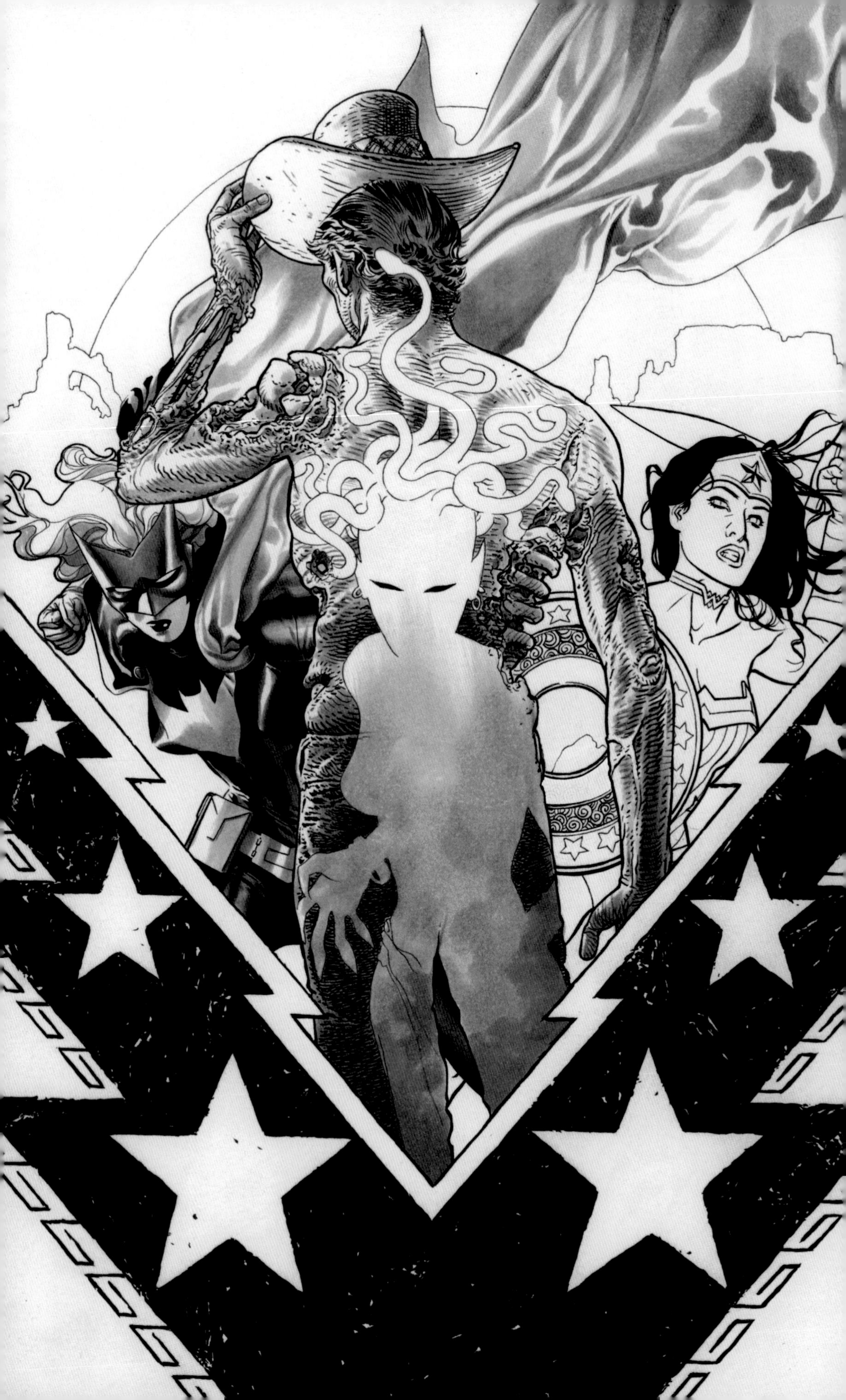

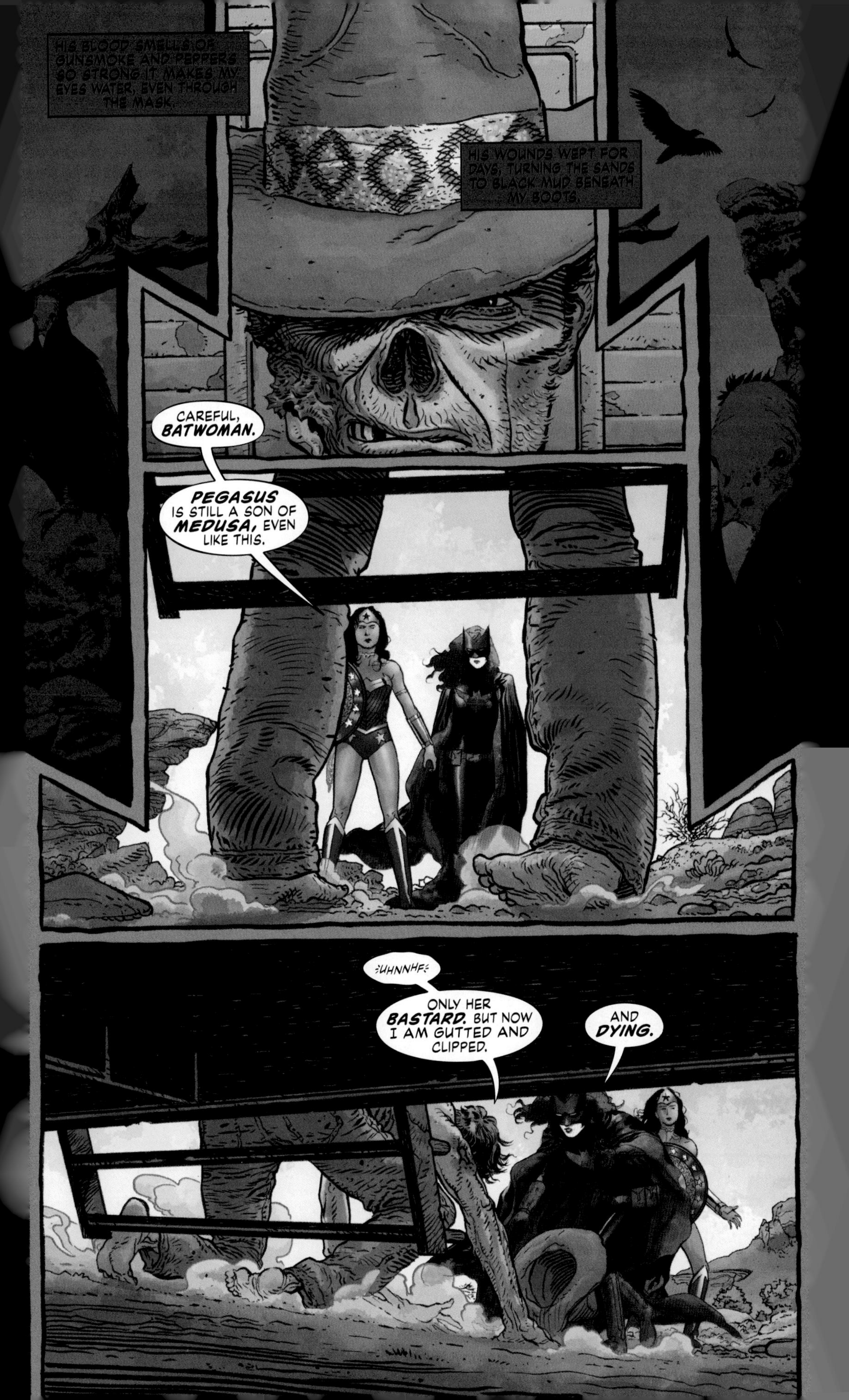
HIS BLOOD SMELLS OF GUNSMOKE AND PEPPERS SO STRONG IT MAKES MY EYES WATER, EVEN THROUGH THE MASK.
HIS WOUNDS WEPT FOR DAYS, TURNING THE SANDS TO BLACK MUD BENEATH MY BOOTS.
CAREFUL, BATWOMAN.
PEGASUS IS STILL A SON OF MEDUSA, EVEN LIKE THIS.
UHNNHF
ONLY HER BASTARD. BUT NOW I AM GUTTED AND CLIPPED.
AND DYING.

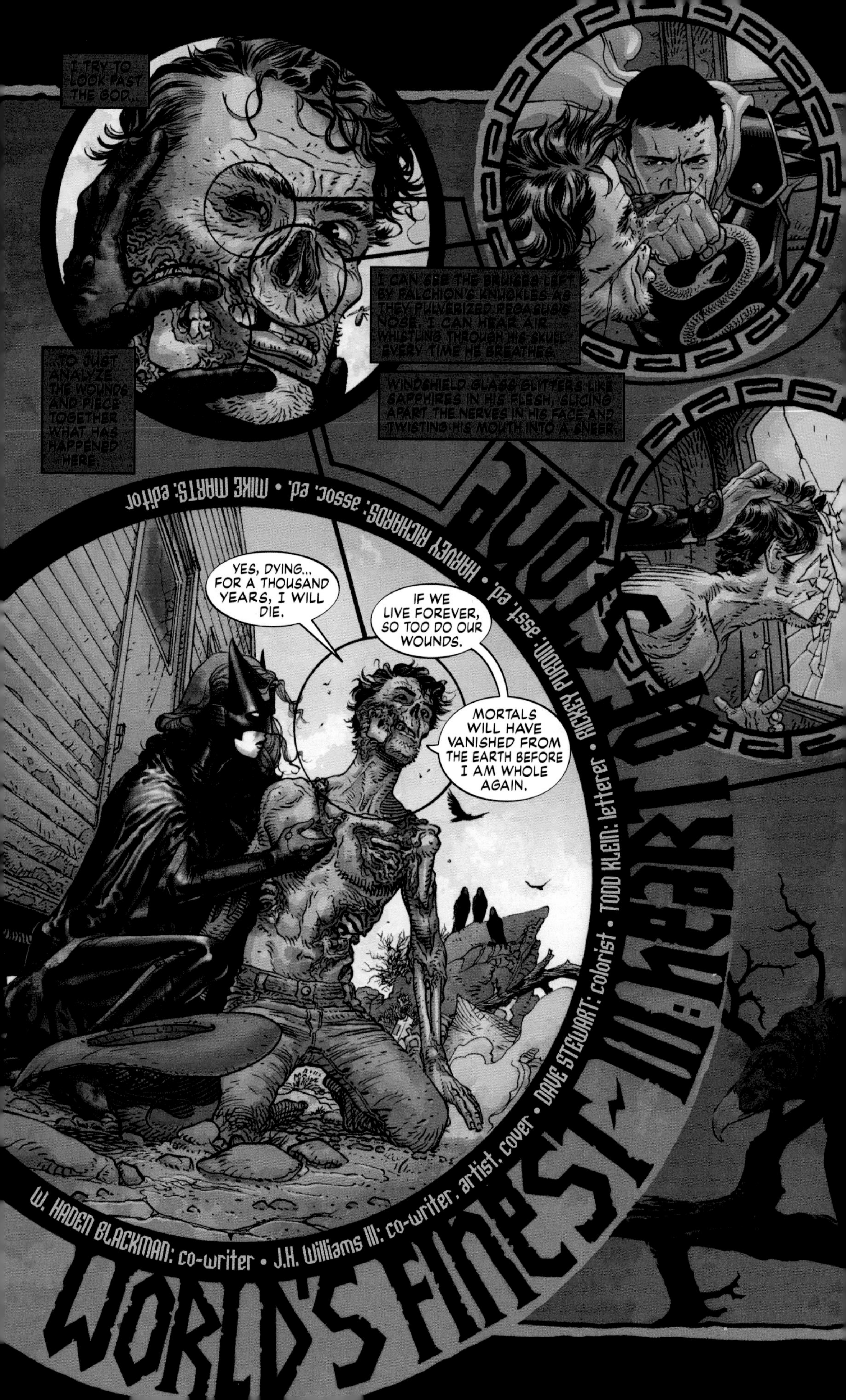
I TRY TO LOOK PAST THE GOD...
I CAN SEE THE BRUISES LEFT BY FALCHION'S KNUCKLES AS THEY PULVERIZED PEGASUS'S NOSE. I CAN HEAR AIR WHISTLING THROUGH HIS SKULL EVERY TIME HE BREATHES.
...TO JUST ANALYZE THE WOUNDS AND PIECE TOGETHER WHAT HAS HAPPENED HERE.
WINDSHIELD GLASS GLITTERS LIKE SAPPHIRES IN HIS FLESH, SLICING APART THE NERVES IN HIS FACE AND TWISTING HIS MOUTH INTO A SNEER.
YES, DYING... FOR A THOUSAND YEARS, I WILL DIE.
IF WE LIVE FOREVER, SO TOO DO OUR WOUNDS.
MORTALS WILL HAVE VANISHED FROM THE EARTH BEFORE I AM WHOLE AGAIN.
W. HADEN BLACKMAN: co-writer • J.H. Williams III: co-writer, artist, cover • DAVE STEWART: colorist • TODD KLEIN: letterer • RICKEY PURDIN: asst. ed. • HARVEY RICHARDS: assoc. ed. • MIKE MARTS: editor
WORLD'S FINEST

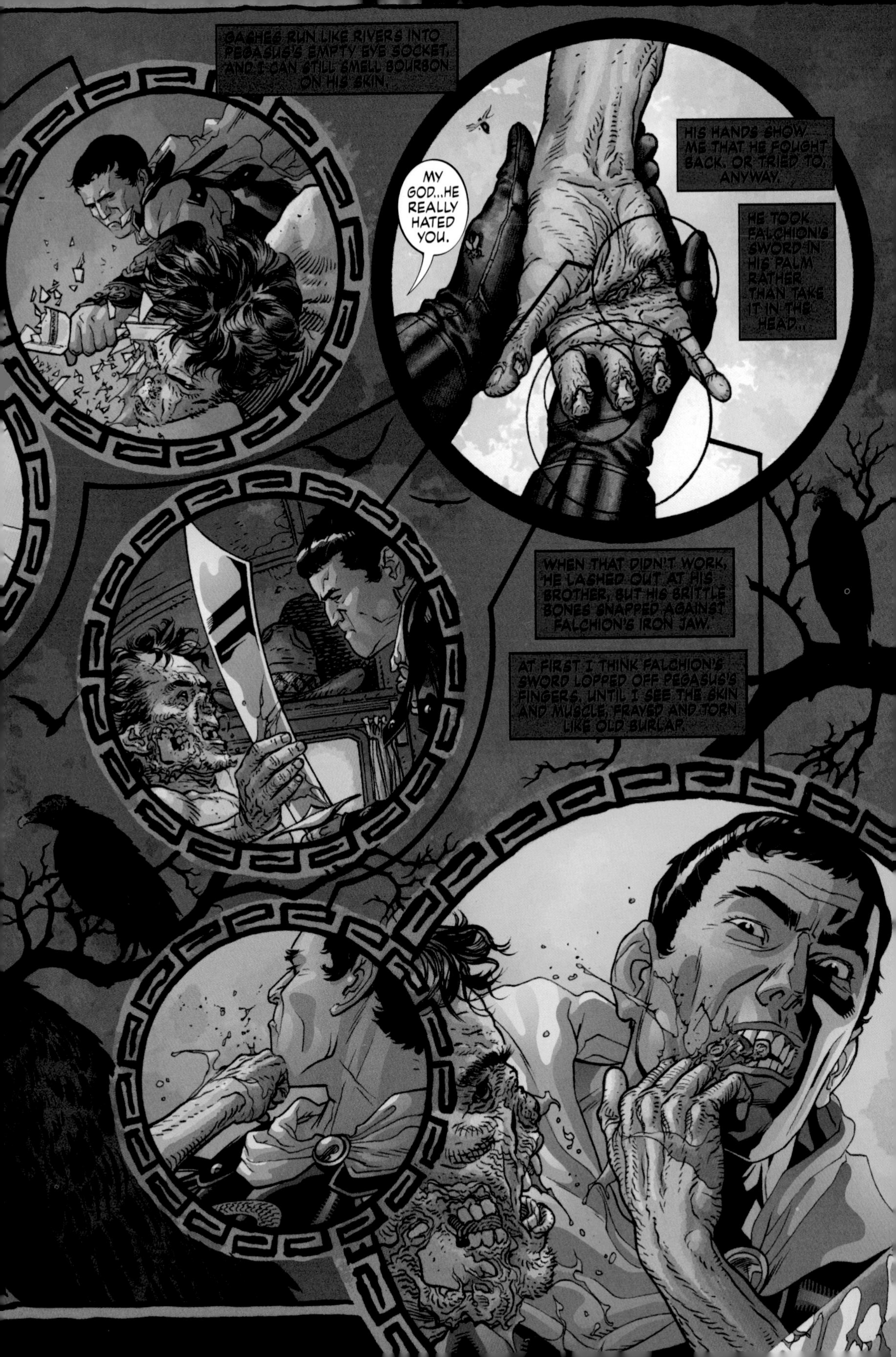
GASHES RUN LIKE RIVERS INTO PEGASUS'S EMPTY EYE SOCKET, AND I CAN STILL SMELL BOURBON ON HIS SKIN.
MY GOD...HE REALLY HATED YOU.
HIS HANDS SHOW ME THAT HE FOUGHT BACK, OR TRIED TO, ANYWAY.
HE TOOK FALCHION'S SWORD IN HIS PALM RATHER THAN TAKE IT IN THE HEAD...
WHEN THAT DIDN'T WORK, HE LASHED OUT AT HIS BROTHER, BUT HIS BRITTLE BONES SNAPPED AGAINST FALCHION'S IRON JAW.
AT FIRST I THINK FALCHION'S SWORD LOPPED OFF PEGASUS'S FINGERS, UNTIL I SEE THE SKIN AND MUSCLE, FRAYED AND TORN LIKE OLD BURLAP.

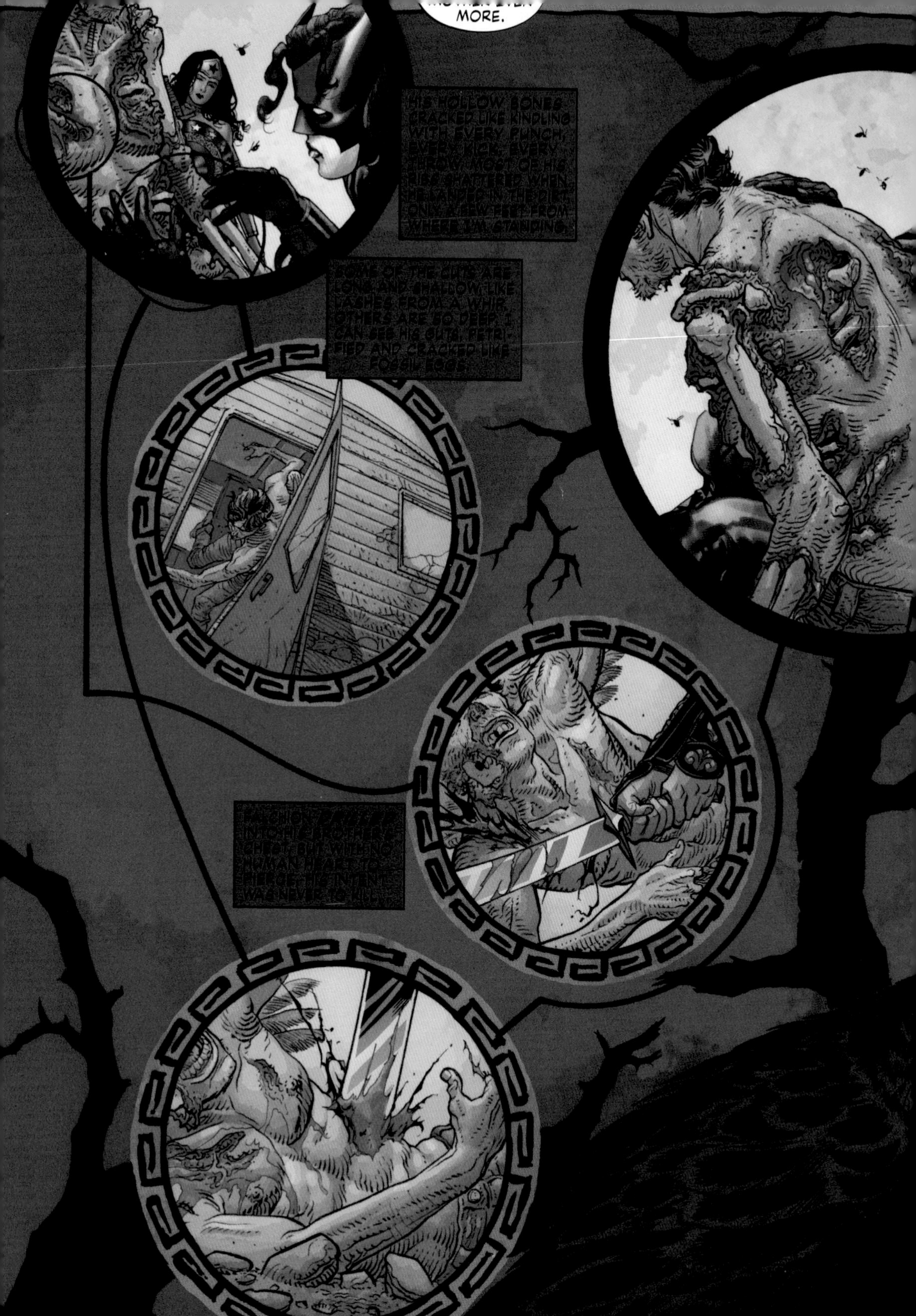
MORE.
HIS HOLLOW BONES CRACKED LIKE KINDLING WITH EVERY PUNCH, EVERY KICK, EVERY THROW. MOST OF HIS RIBS SHATTERED WHEN HE LANDED IN THE DIRT, ONLY A FEW FEET FROM WHERE I'M STANDING.
SOME OF THE CUTS ARE LONG AND SHALLOW LIKE LASHES FROM A WHIP. OTHERS ARE SO DEEP, I CAN SEE HIS GUTS, PETRIFIED AND CRACKED LIKE FOSSIL EGGS.
FALCHION INTO HIS BROTHER'S CHEST, BUT WITH NO HUMAN HEART TO PIERCE, HIS INTENT WAS NEVER TO KILL.

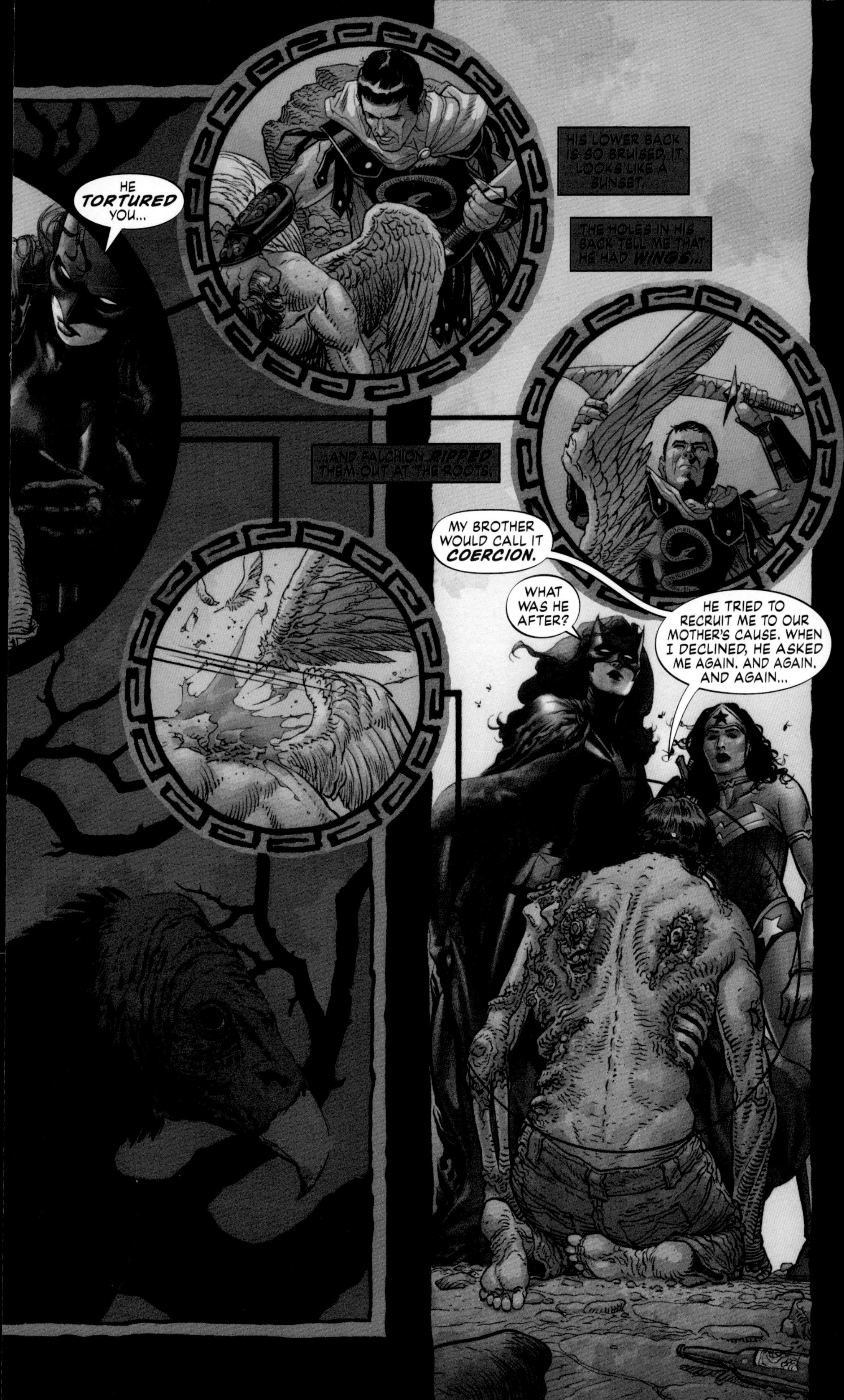
HE TORTURED YOU...
HIS LOWER BACK IS SO BRUISED, IT LOOKS LIKE A SUNSET.
THE HOLES IN HIS BACK TELL ME THAT HE HAD WINGS...
...AND FALCHION RIPPED THEM OUT AT THE ROOTS.
MY BROTHER WOULD CALL IT COERCION.
WHAT WAS HE AFTER?
HE TRIED TO RECRUIT ME TO OUR MOTHER'S CAUSE. WHEN I DECLINED, HE ASKED ME AGAIN. AND AGAIN. AND AGAIN...

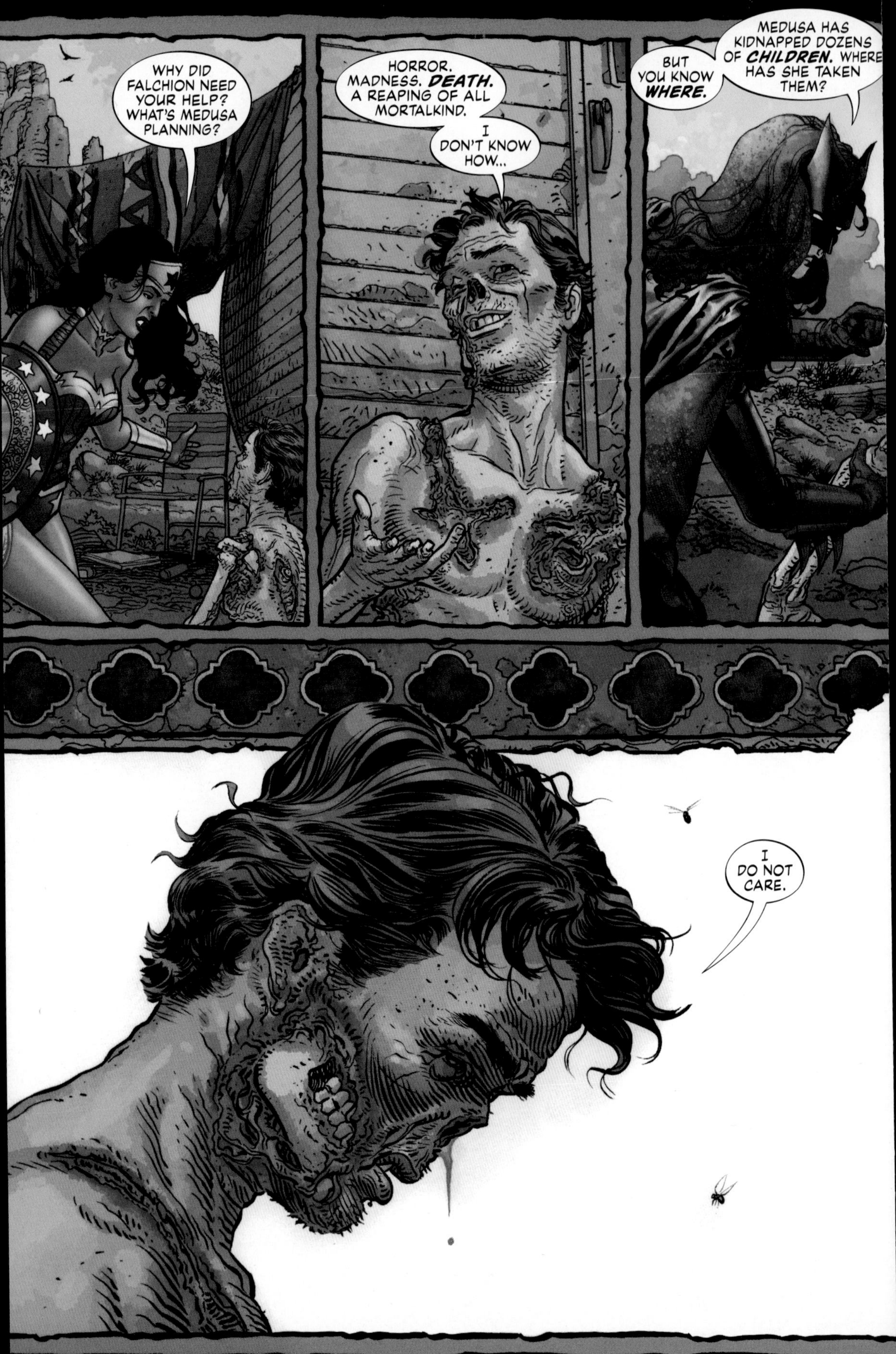
WHY DID FALCHION NEED YOUR HELP? WHAT'S MEDUSA PLANNING?
HORROR. MADNESS. **DEATH.** A REAPING OF ALL MORTALKIND.
I DON'T KNOW HOW...
BUT YOU KNOW **WHERE.**
MEDUSA HAS KIDNAPPED DOZENS OF **CHILDREN.** WHERE HAS SHE TAKEN THEM?
I DO NOT CARE.

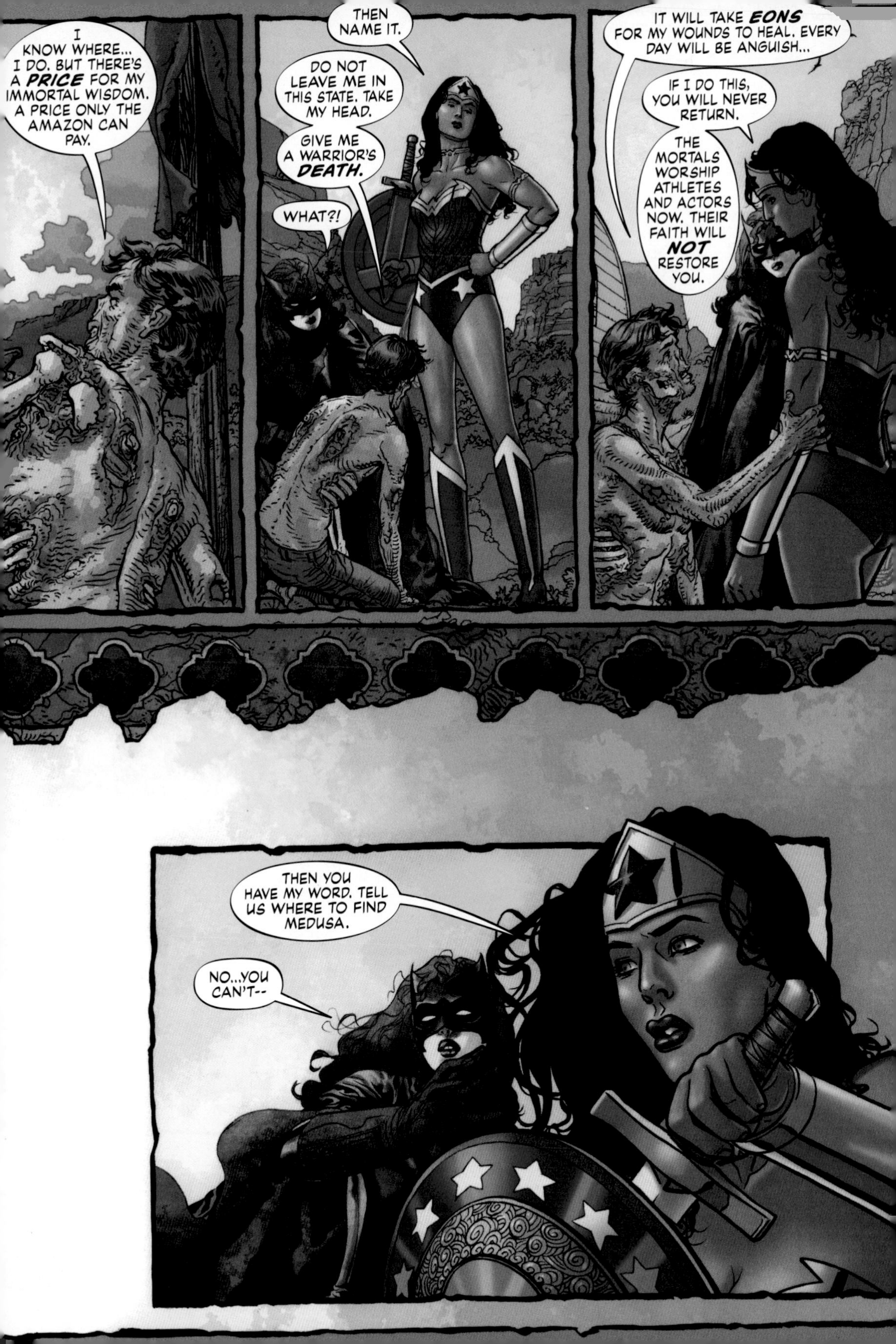
I KNOW WHERE... I DO. BUT THERE'S A **PRICE** FOR MY IMMORTAL WISDOM. A PRICE ONLY THE AMAZON CAN PAY.
THEN NAME IT.
DO NOT LEAVE ME IN THIS STATE. TAKE MY HEAD.
GIVE ME A WARRIOR'S **DEATH.**
WHAT?!
IT WILL TAKE **EONS** FOR MY WOUNDS TO HEAL. EVERY DAY WILL BE ANGUISH...
IF I DO THIS, YOU WILL NEVER RETURN.
THE MORTALS WORSHIP ATHLETES AND ACTORS NOW. THEIR FAITH WILL **NOT** RESTORE YOU.
THEN YOU HAVE MY WORD. TELL US WHERE TO FIND MEDUSA.
NO...YOU CAN'T--

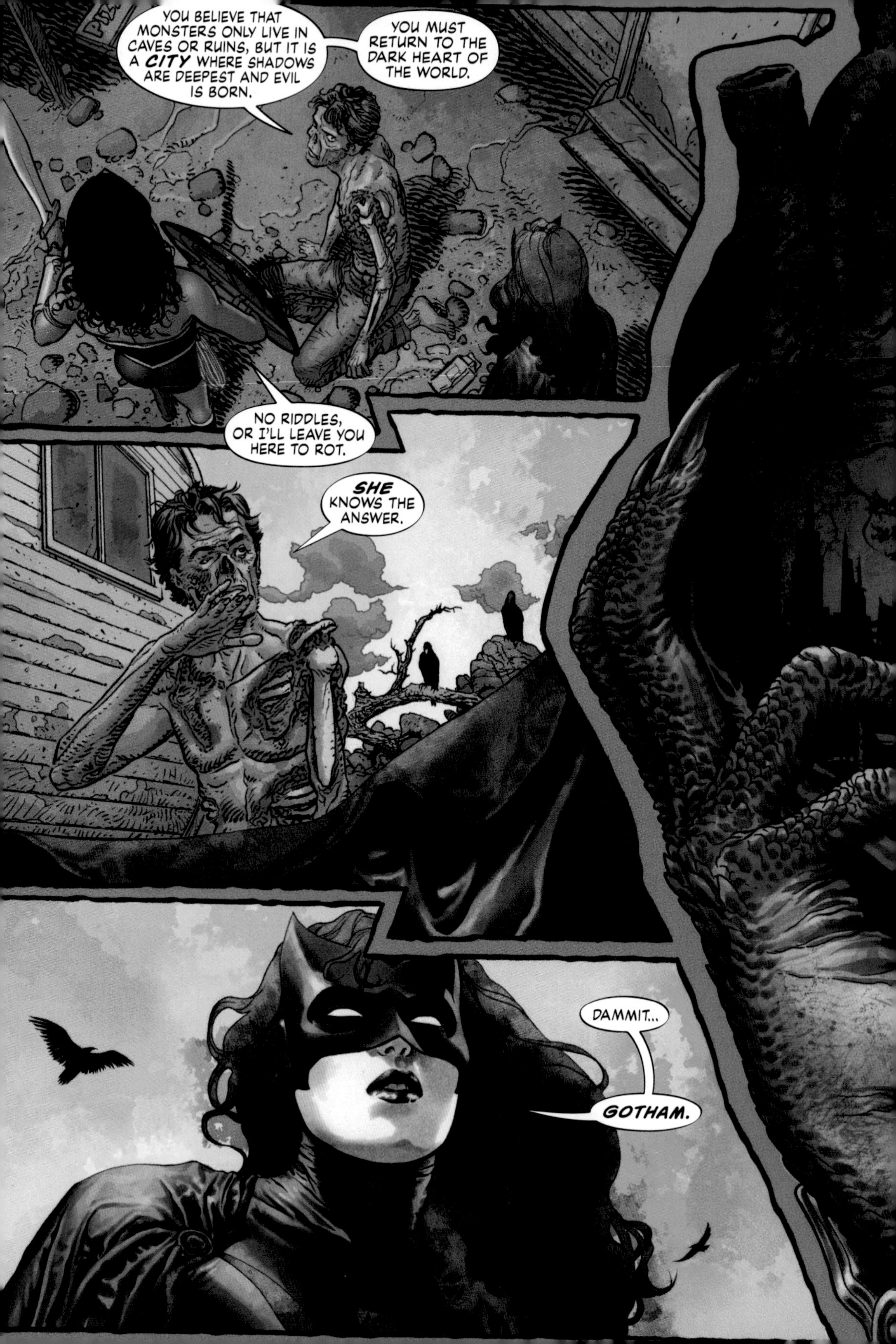
YOU BELIEVE THAT MONSTERS ONLY LIVE IN CAVES OR RUINS, BUT IT IS A CITY WHERE SHADOWS ARE DEEPEST AND EVIL IS BORN.
YOU MUST RETURN TO THE DARK HEART OF THE WORLD.
NO RIDDLES, OR I'LL LEAVE YOU HERE TO ROT.
SHE KNOWS THE ANSWER.
DAMMIT...
GOTHAM.

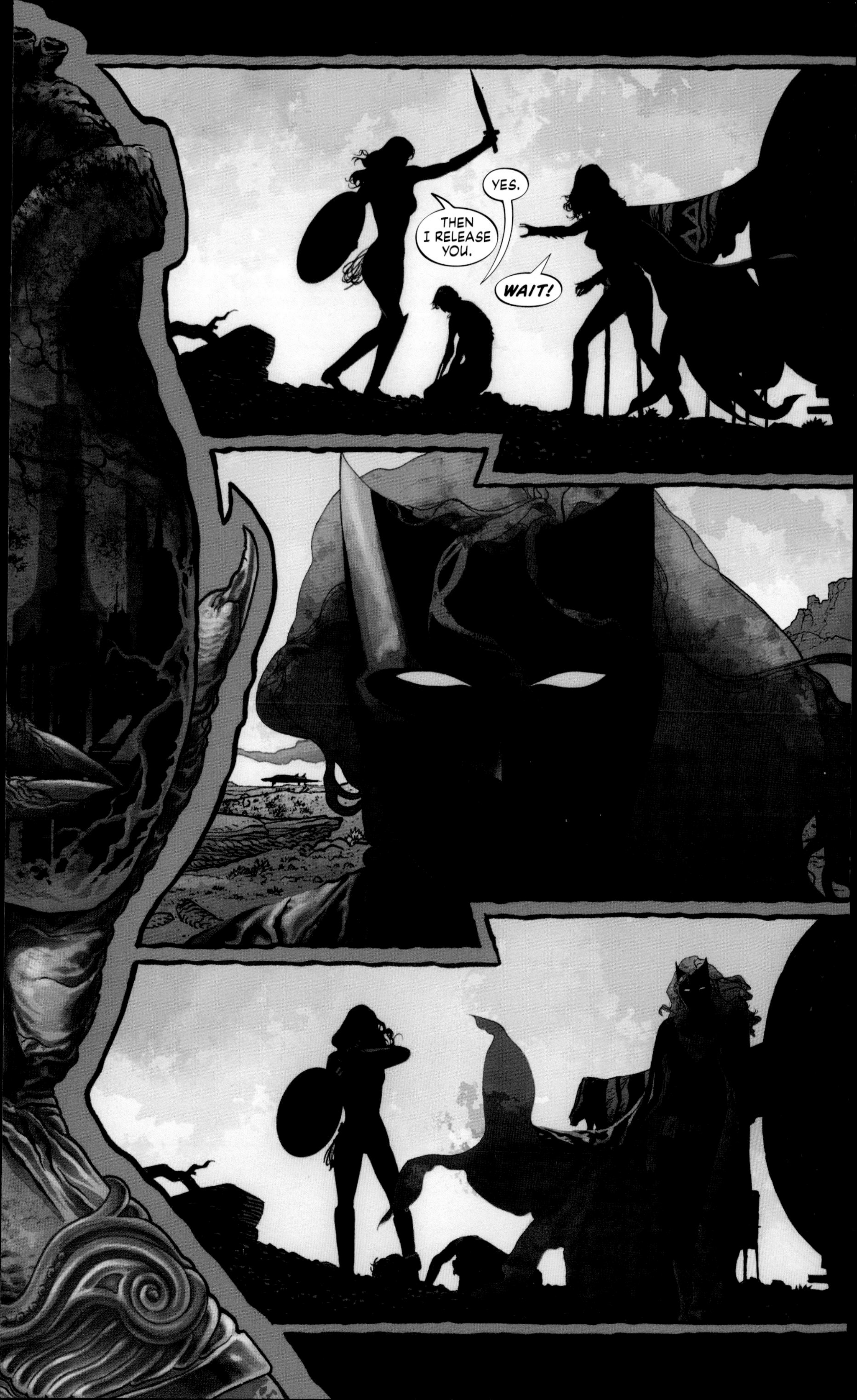
YES.
THEN I RELEASE YOU.
WAIT!

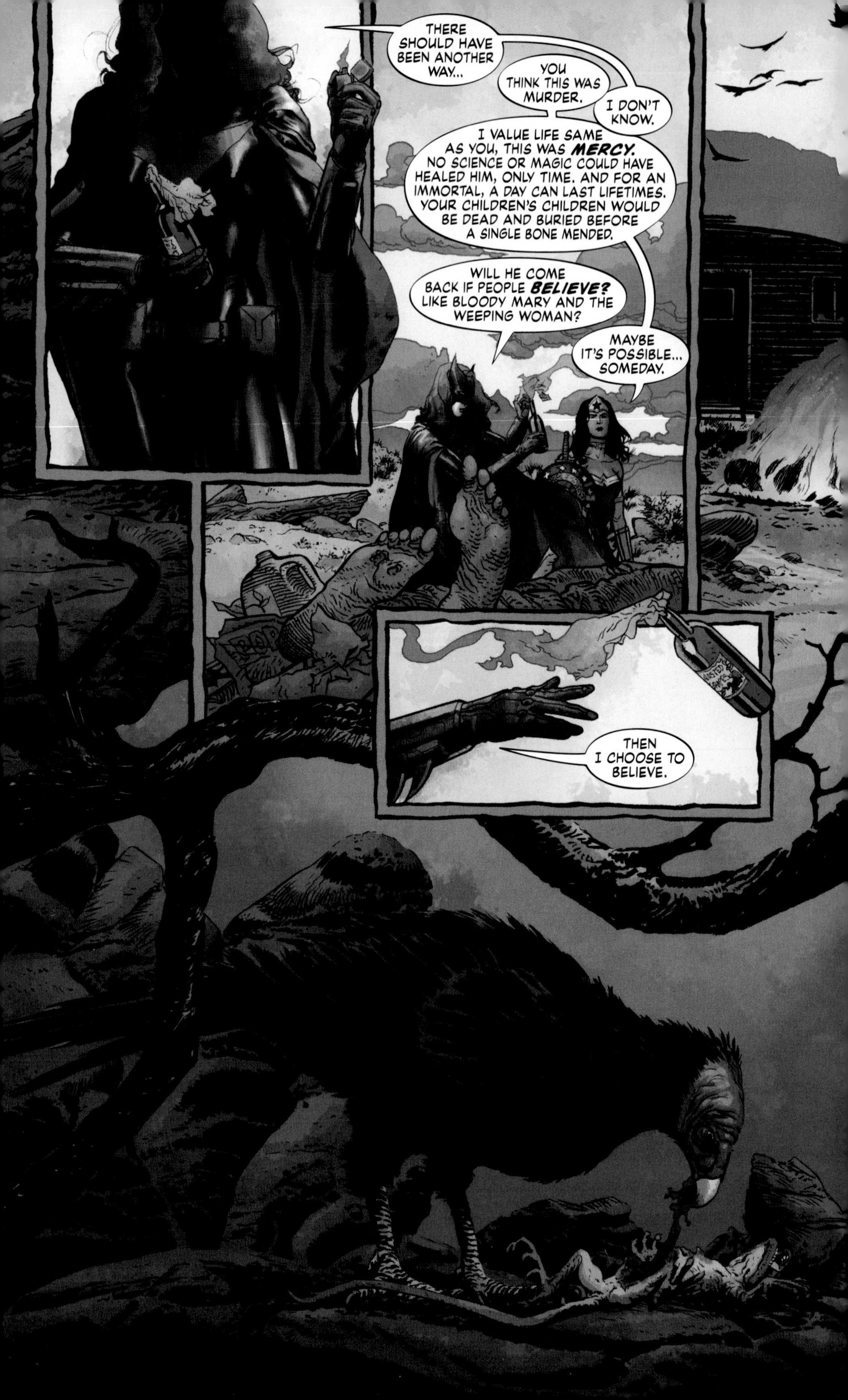
THERE SHOULD HAVE BEEN ANOTHER WAY...
YOU THINK THIS WAS MURDER.
I DON'T KNOW.
I VALUE LIFE SAME AS YOU, THIS WAS **MERCY.** NO SCIENCE OR MAGIC COULD HAVE HEALED HIM, ONLY TIME. AND FOR AN IMMORTAL, A DAY CAN LAST LIFETIMES. YOUR CHILDREN'S CHILDREN WOULD BE DEAD AND BURIED BEFORE A SINGLE BONE MENDED.
WILL HE COME BACK IF PEOPLE **BELIEVE?** LIKE BLOODY MARY AND THE WEEPING WOMAN?
MAYBE IT'S POSSIBLE... SOMEDAY.
THEN I CHOOSE TO BELIEVE.

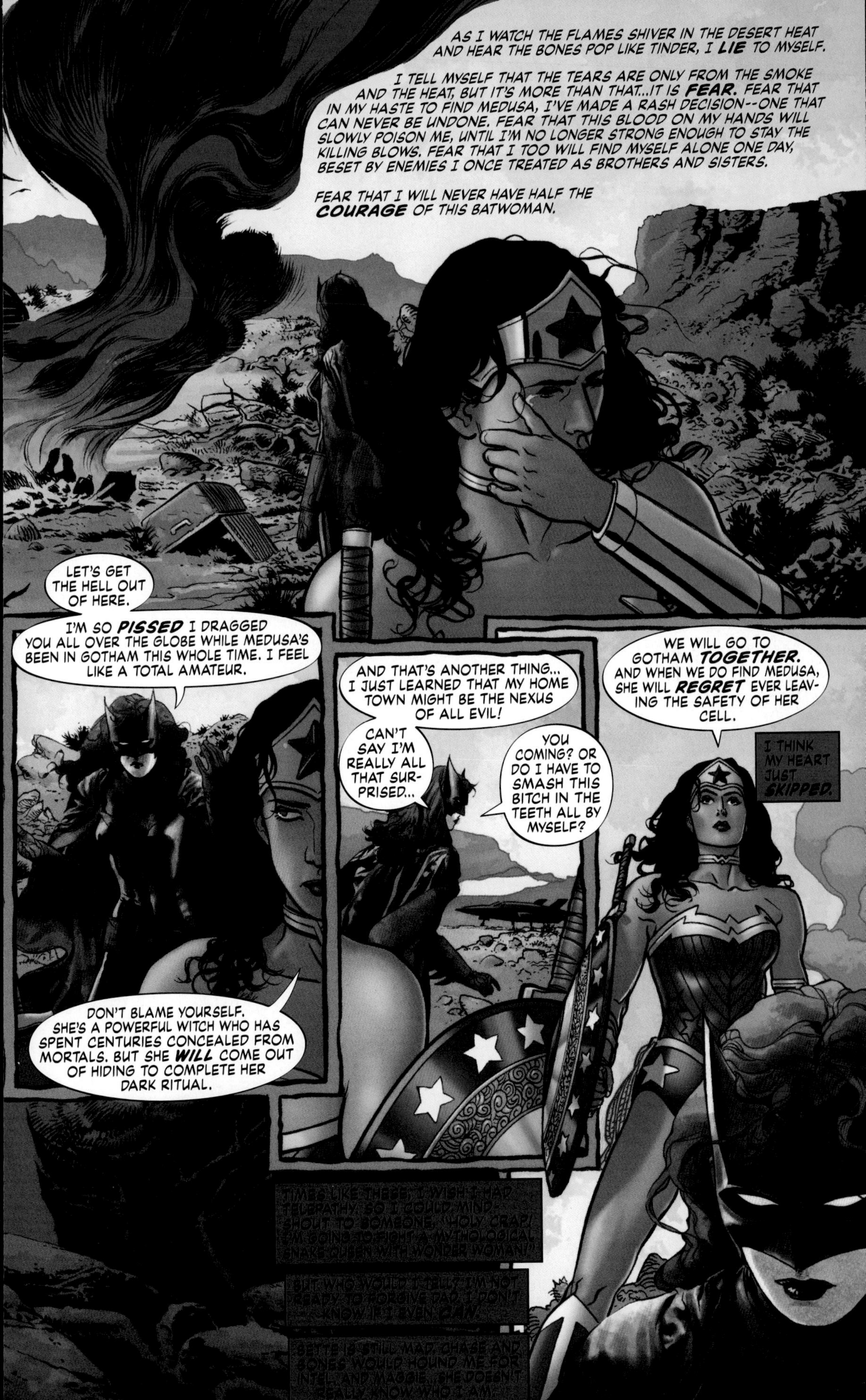

AS I WATCH THE FLAMES SHIVER IN THE DESERT HEAT AND HEAR THE BONES POP LIKE TINDER, I **LIE** TO MYSELF.
I TELL MYSELF THAT THE TEARS ARE ONLY FROM THE SMOKE AND THE HEAT, BUT IT'S MORE THAN THAT...IT IS **FEAR.** FEAR THAT IN MY HASTE TO FIND MEDUSA, I'VE MADE A RASH DECISION--ONE THAT CAN NEVER BE UNDONE. FEAR THAT THIS BLOOD ON MY HANDS WILL SLOWLY POISON ME, UNTIL I'M NO LONGER STRONG ENOUGH TO STAY THE KILLING BLOWS. FEAR THAT I TOO WILL FIND MYSELF ALONE ONE DAY, BESET BY ENEMIES I ONCE TREATED AS BROTHERS AND SISTERS.
FEAR THAT I WILL NEVER HAVE HALF THE **COURAGE** OF THIS BATWOMAN.
LET'S GET THE HELL OUT OF HERE.
I'M SO **PISSED** I DRAGGED YOU ALL OVER THE GLOBE WHILE MEDUSA'S BEEN IN GOTHAM THIS WHOLE TIME. I FEEL LIKE A TOTAL AMATEUR.
DON'T BLAME YOURSELF. SHE'S A POWERFUL WITCH WHO HAS SPENT CENTURIES CONCEALED FROM MORTALS. BUT SHE **WILL** COME OUT OF HIDING TO COMPLETE HER DARK RITUAL.
AND THAT'S ANOTHER THING... I JUST LEARNED THAT MY HOME TOWN MIGHT BE THE NEXUS OF ALL EVIL!
CAN'T SAY I'M REALLY ALL THAT SURPRISED...
YOU COMING? OR DO I HAVE TO SMASH THIS BITCH IN THE TEETH ALL BY MYSELF?
WE WILL GO TO GOTHAM **TOGETHER.** AND WHEN WE DO FIND MEDUSA, SHE WILL **REGRET** EVER LEAVING THE SAFETY OF HER CELL.
I THINK MY HEART JUST **SKIPPED.**
TIMES LIKE THESE, I WISH I HAD TELEPATHY SO I COULD MIND-SHOUT TO SOMEONE, "HOLY CRAP! I'M GOING TO FIGHT A MYTHOLOGICAL SNAKE QUEEN WITH WONDER WOMAN!"
BUT WHO WOULD I TELL? I'M NOT READY TO FORGIVE DAD. I DON'T KNOW IF I EVEN **CAN.**
BETTE IS STILL MAD. CHASE AND BONES WOULD HOUND ME FOR INTEL. AND MAGGIE...SHE DOESN'T REALLY KNOW WHO I AM.

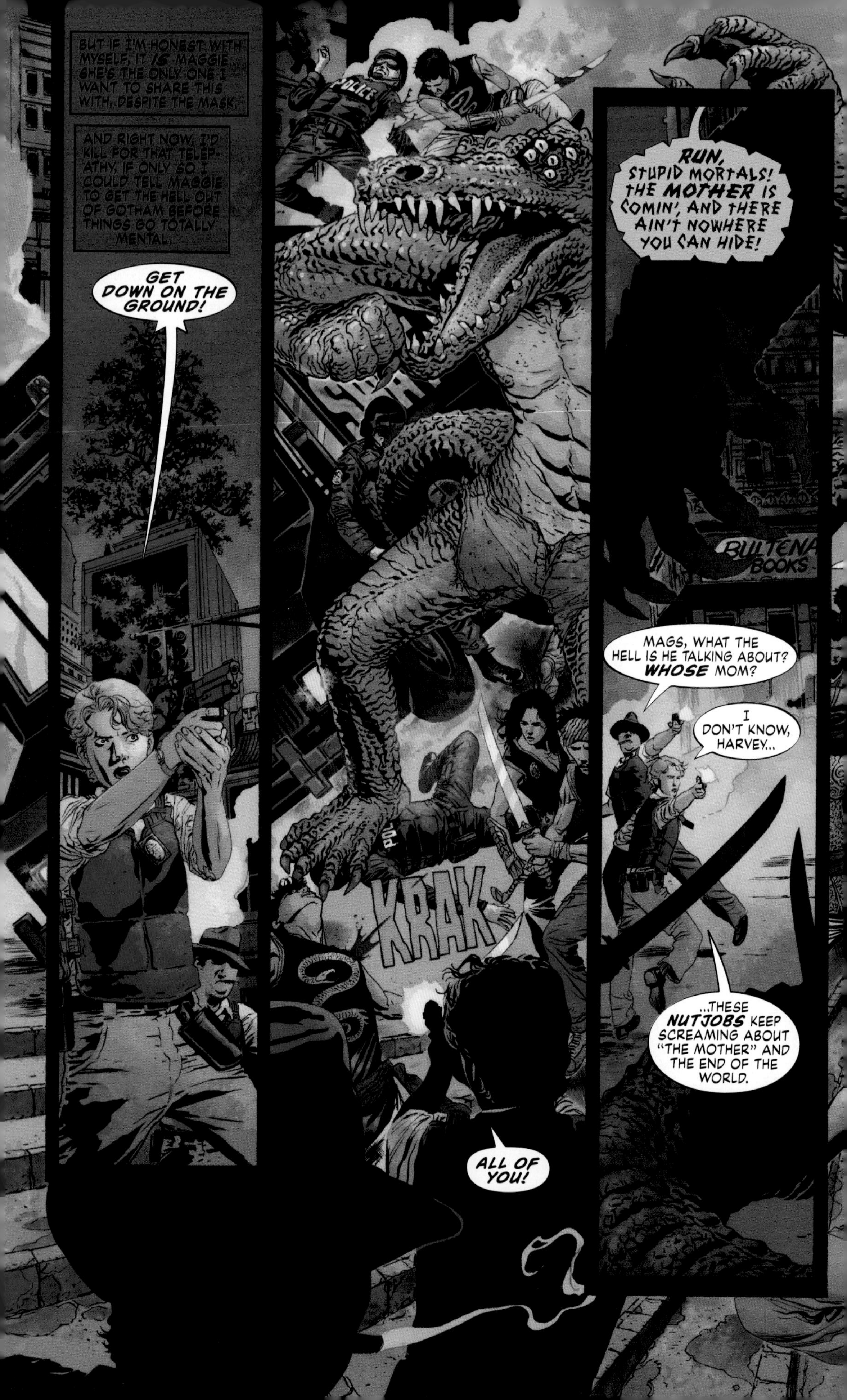

BUT IF I'M HONEST WITH MYSELF, IT IS MAGGIE... SHE'S THE ONLY ONE I WANT TO SHARE THIS WITH, DESPITE THE MASK.
AND RIGHT NOW, I'D KILL FOR THAT TELEPATHY, IF ONLY SO I COULD TELL MAGGIE TO GET THE HELL OUT OF GOTHAM BEFORE THINGS GO TOTALLY MENTAL.
GET DOWN ON THE GROUND!
POLICE
KRAK
ALL OF YOU!
RUN, STUPID MORTALS! THE MOTHER IS COMIN', AND THERE AIN'T NOWHERE YOU CAN HIDE!
BULTENA BOOKS
MAGS, WHAT THE HELL IS HE TALKING ABOUT? WHOSE MOM?
I DON'T KNOW, HARVEY...
...THESE NUTJOBS KEEP SCREAMING ABOUT "THE MOTHER" AND THE END OF THE WORLD.

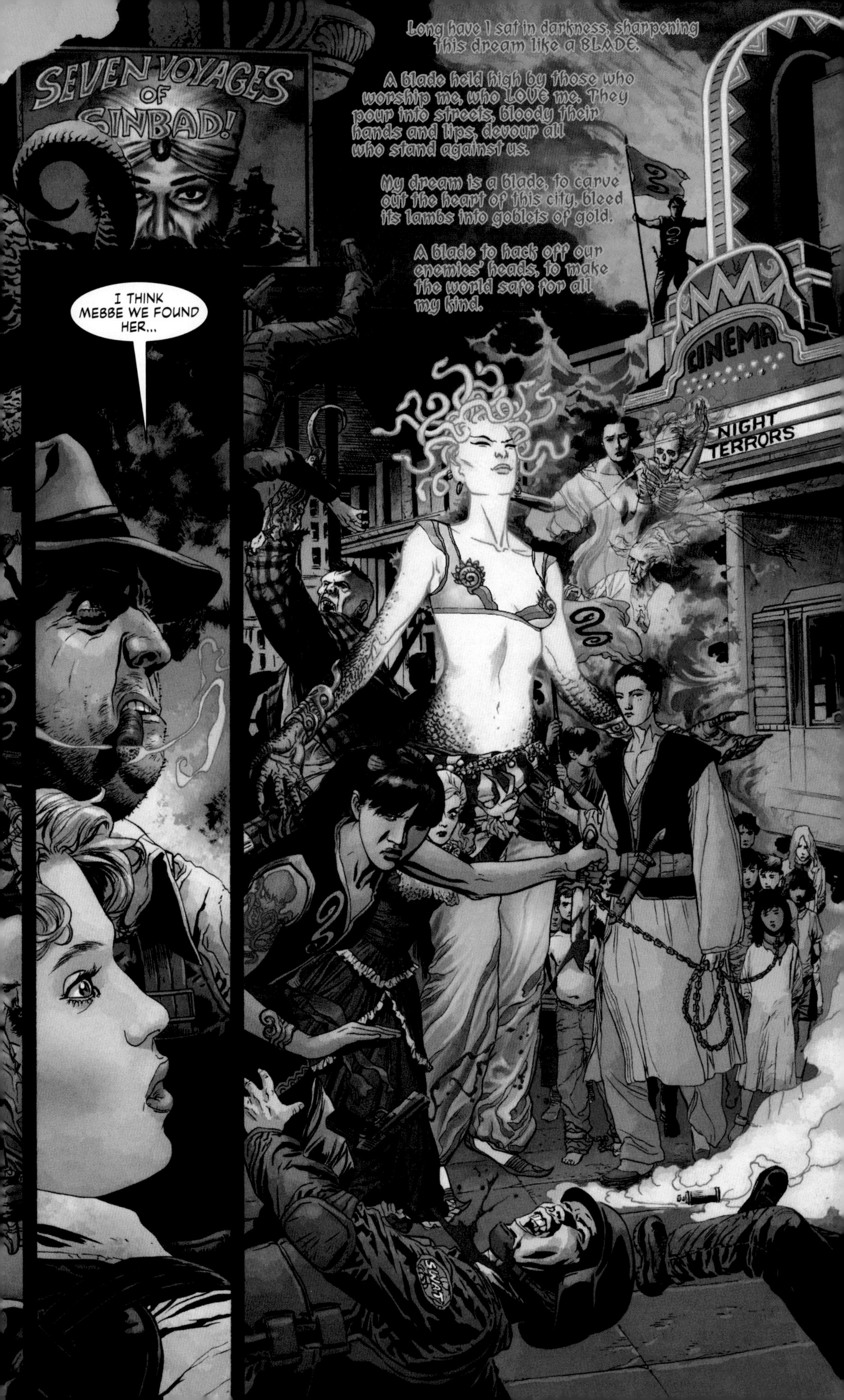
Long have I sat in darkness, sharpening this dream like a BLADE.
A blade held high by those who worship me, who LOVE me. They pour into streets, bloody their hands and lips, devour all who stand against us.
My dream is a blade, to carve out the heart of this city, bleed its lambs into goblets of gold.
A blade to hack off our enemies' heads, to make the world safe for all my kind.
SEVEN VOYAGES OF SINBAD!
CINEMA
NIGHT TERRORS
I THINK MEBBE WE FOUND HER...
SWAT

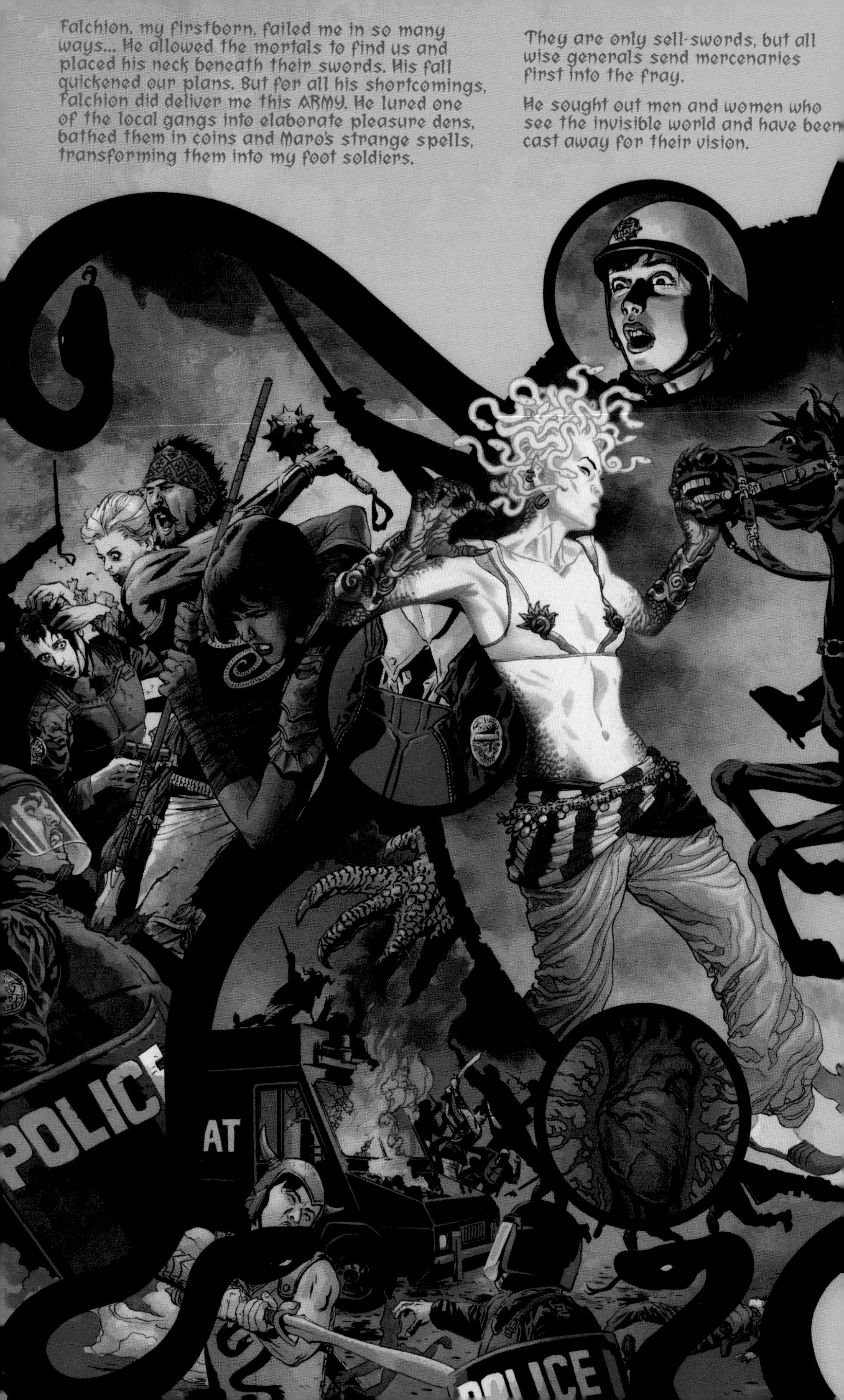
Falchion, my firstborn, failed me in so many ways... He allowed the mortals to find us and placed his neck beneath their swords. His fall quickened our plans. But for all his shortcomings, Falchion did deliver me this ARMY. He lured one of the local gangs into elaborate pleasure dens, bathed them in coins and Maro's strange spells, transforming them into my foot soldiers.
They are only sell-swords, but all wise generals send mercenaries first into the fray.
He sought out men and women who see the invisible world and have been cast away for their vision.

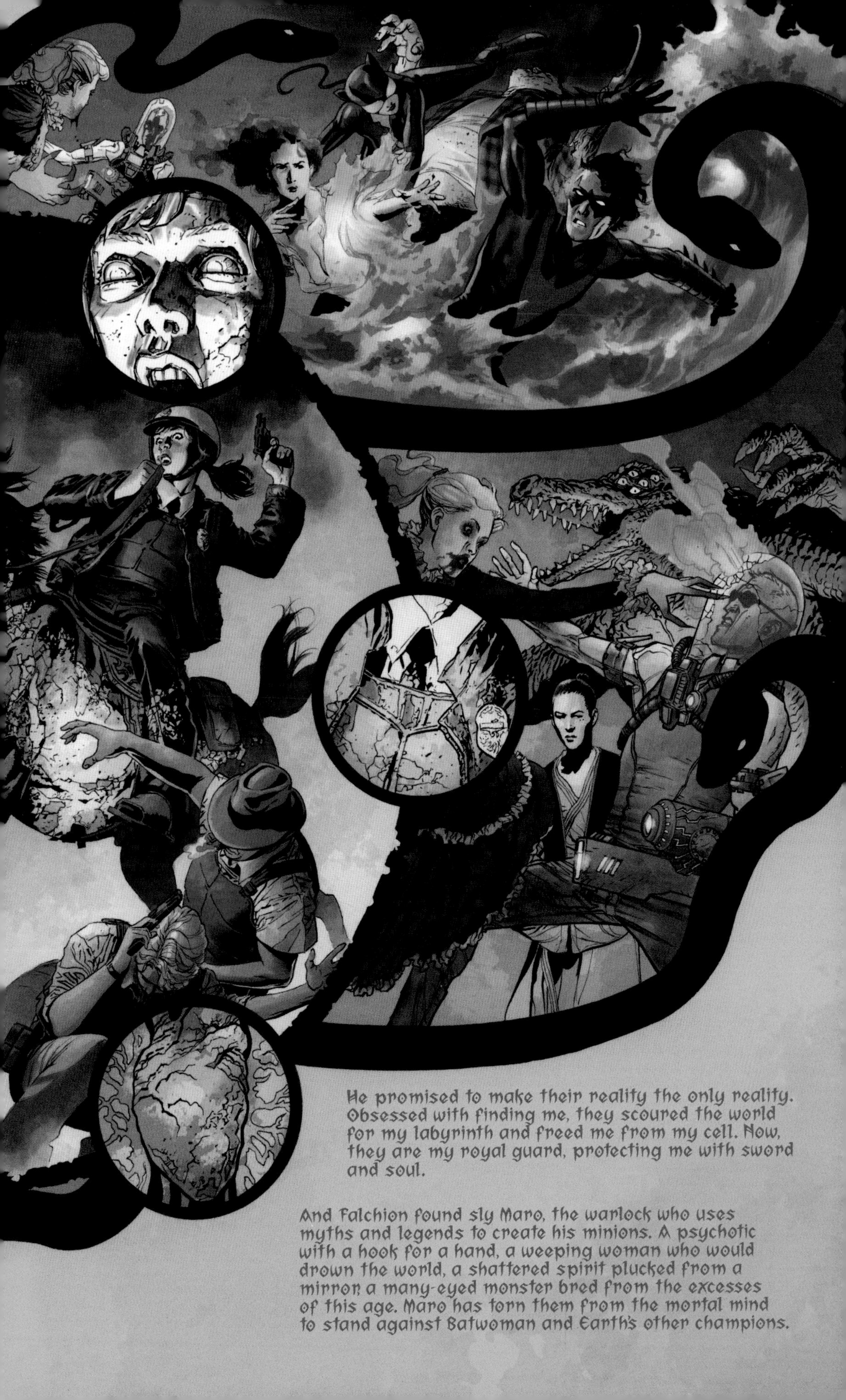
He promised to make their reality the only reality. Obsessed with finding me, they scoured the world for my labyrinth and freed me from my cell. Now, they are my royal guard, protecting me with sword and soul.
And Falchion found sly Maro, the warlock who uses myths and legends to create his minions. A psychotic with a hook for a hand, a weeping woman who would drown the world, a shattered spirit plucked from a mirror, a many-eyed monster bred from the excesses of this age. Maro has torn them from the mortal mind to stand against Batwoman and Earth's other champions.

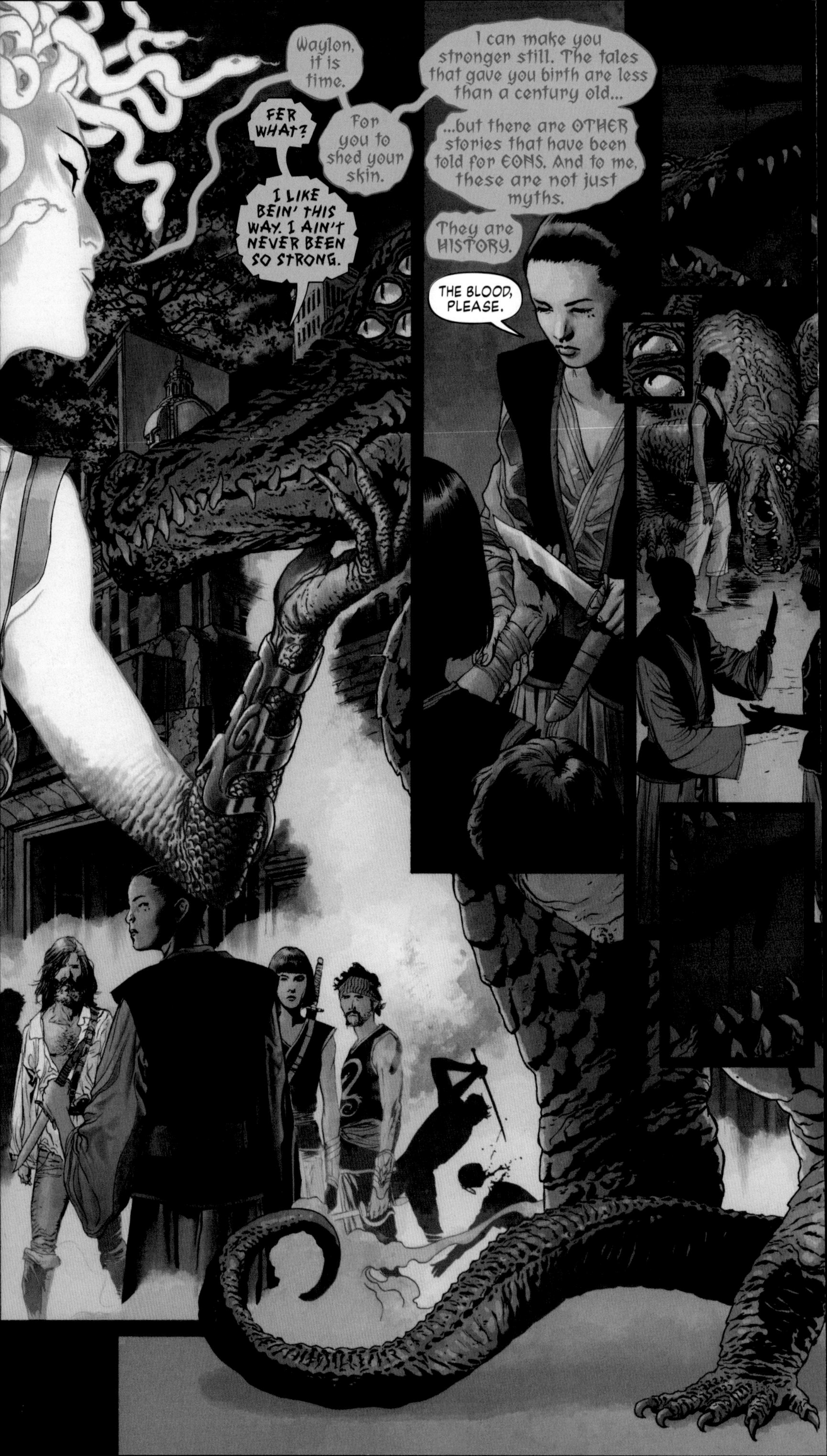

Waylon, it is time.
FER WHAT?
For you to shed your skin.
I LIKE BEIN' THIS WAY. I AIN'T NEVER BEEN SO STRONG.
I can make you stronger still. The tales that gave you birth are less than a century old...
...but there are OTHER stories that have been told for EONS. And to me, these are not just myths.
They are HISTORY.
THE BLOOD, PLEASE.

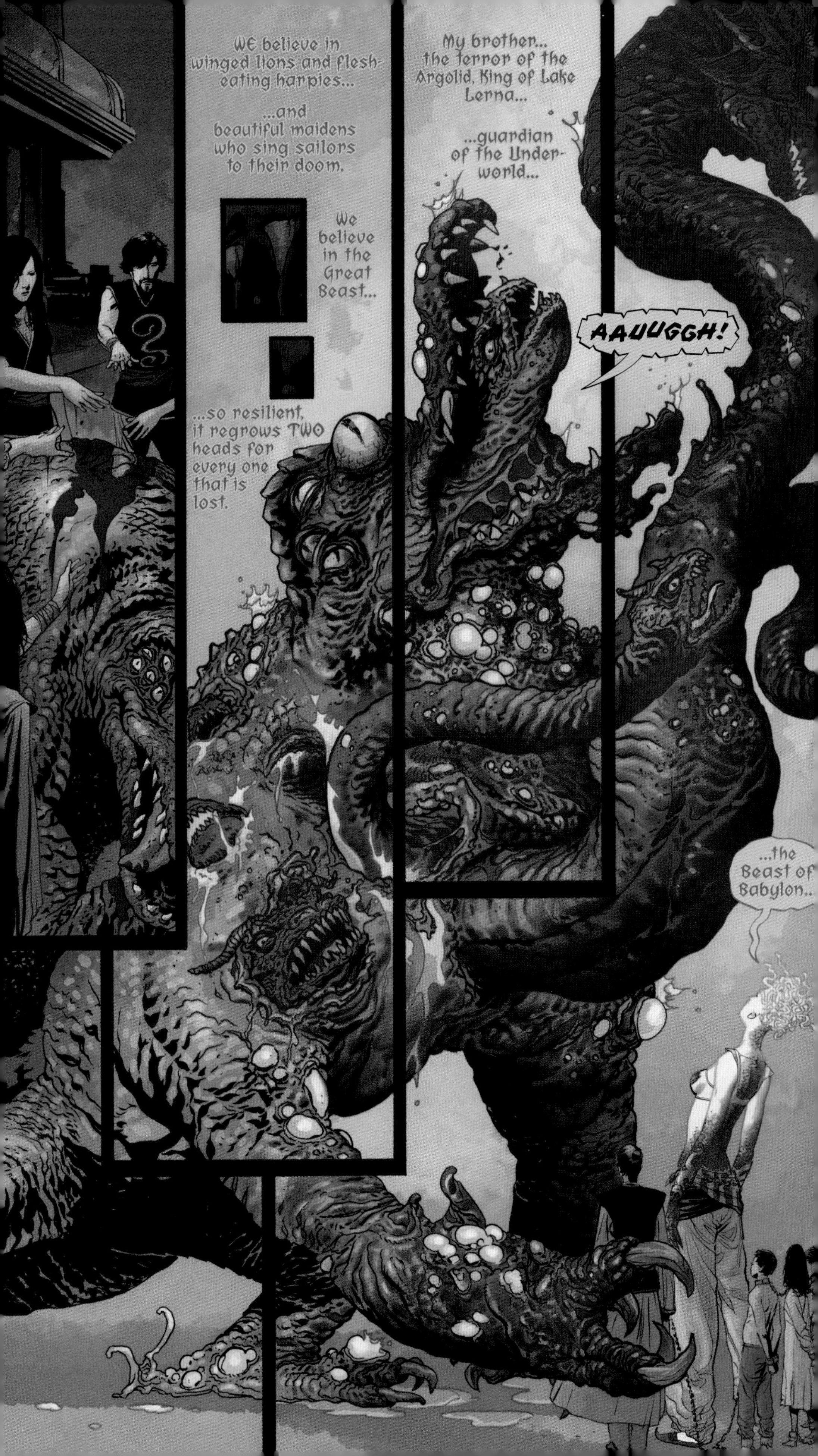
WE believe in winged lions and flesh-eating harpies...
...and beautiful maidens who sing sailors to their doom.
We believe in the Great Beast...
...so resilient, it regrows TWO heads for every one that is lost.
My brother... the terror of the Argolid, King of Lake Lerna...
...guardian of the Underworld...
AAUUGGH!
...the Beast of Babylon...

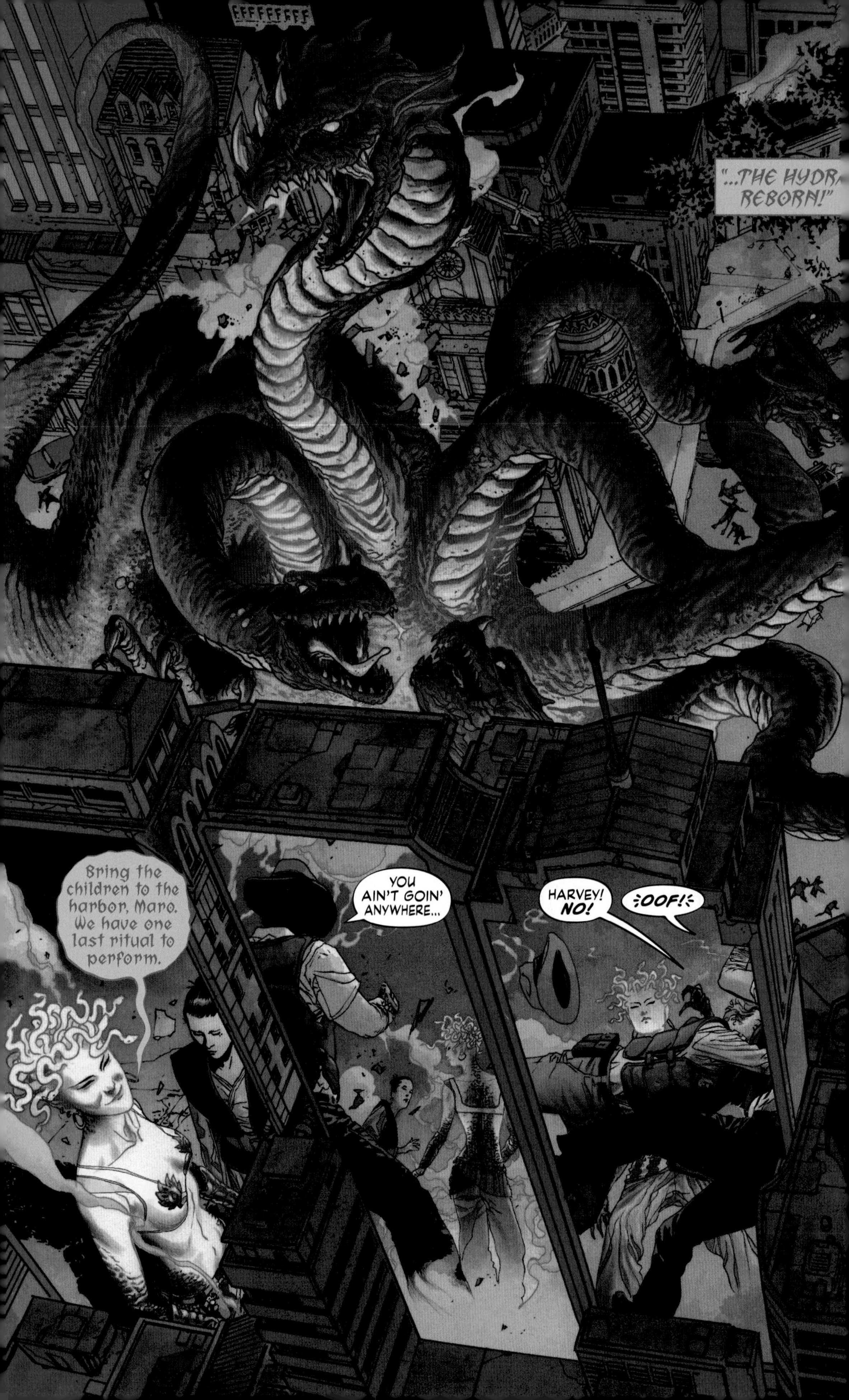
FFFFFFFFF
"...THE HYDR REBORN!"
Bring the children to the harbor, Maro. We have one last ritual to perform.
YOU AIN'T GOIN' ANYWHERE...
HARVEY! NO!
OOF!

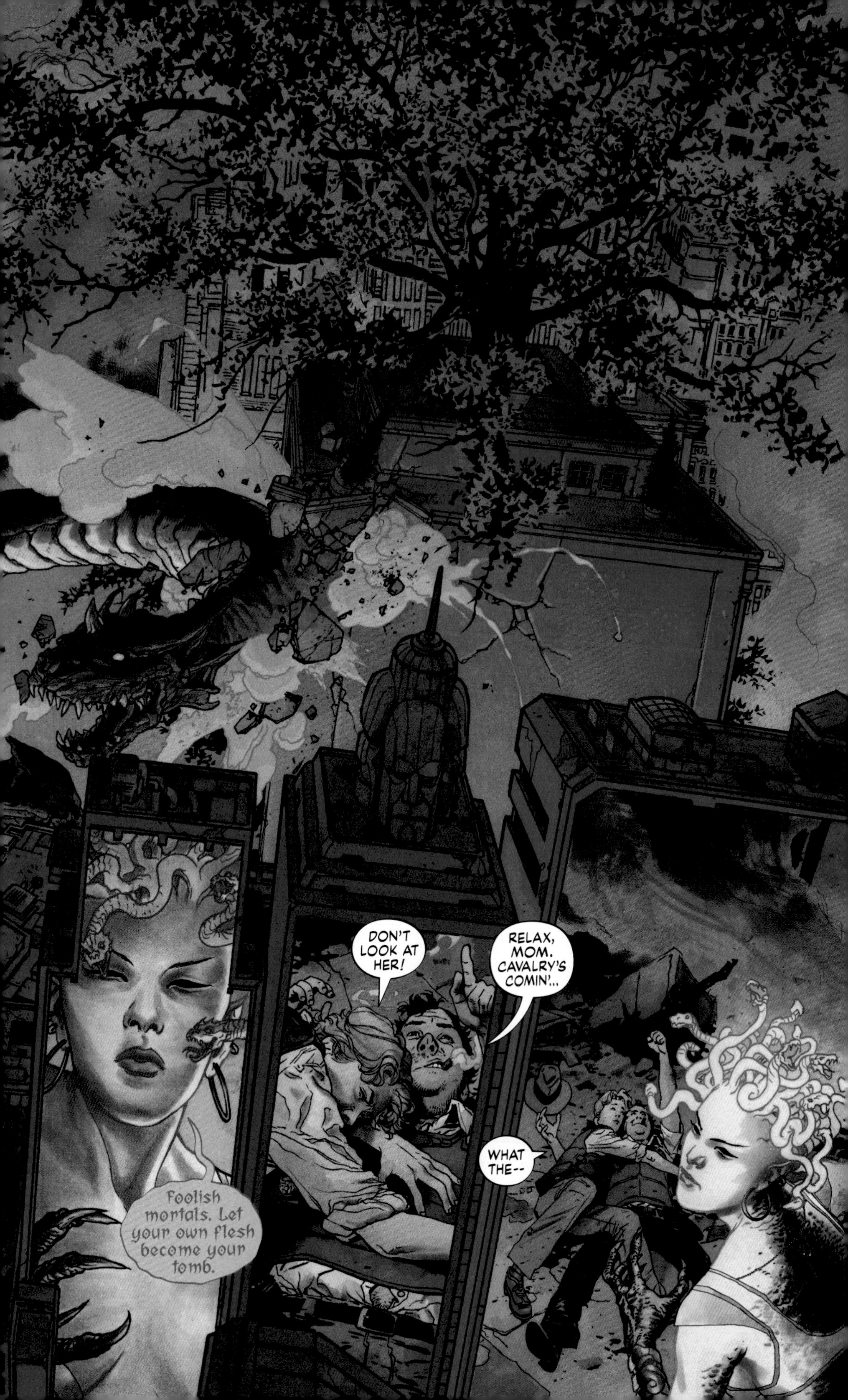
Foolish mortals. Let your own flesh become your tomb.
DON'T LOOK AT HER!
RELAX, MOM. CAVALRY'S COMIN'...
WHAT THE--

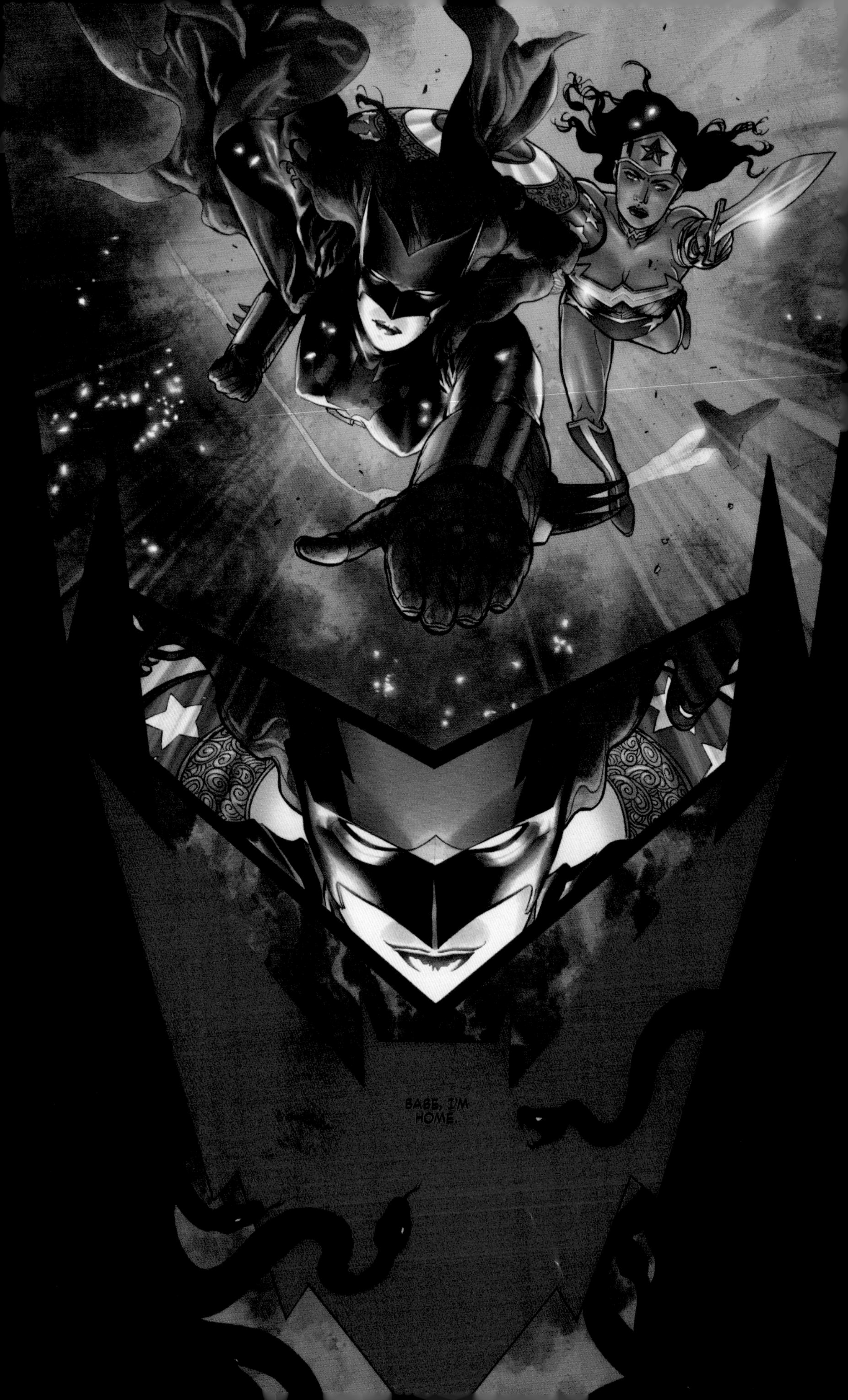
BABE, I'M HOME.

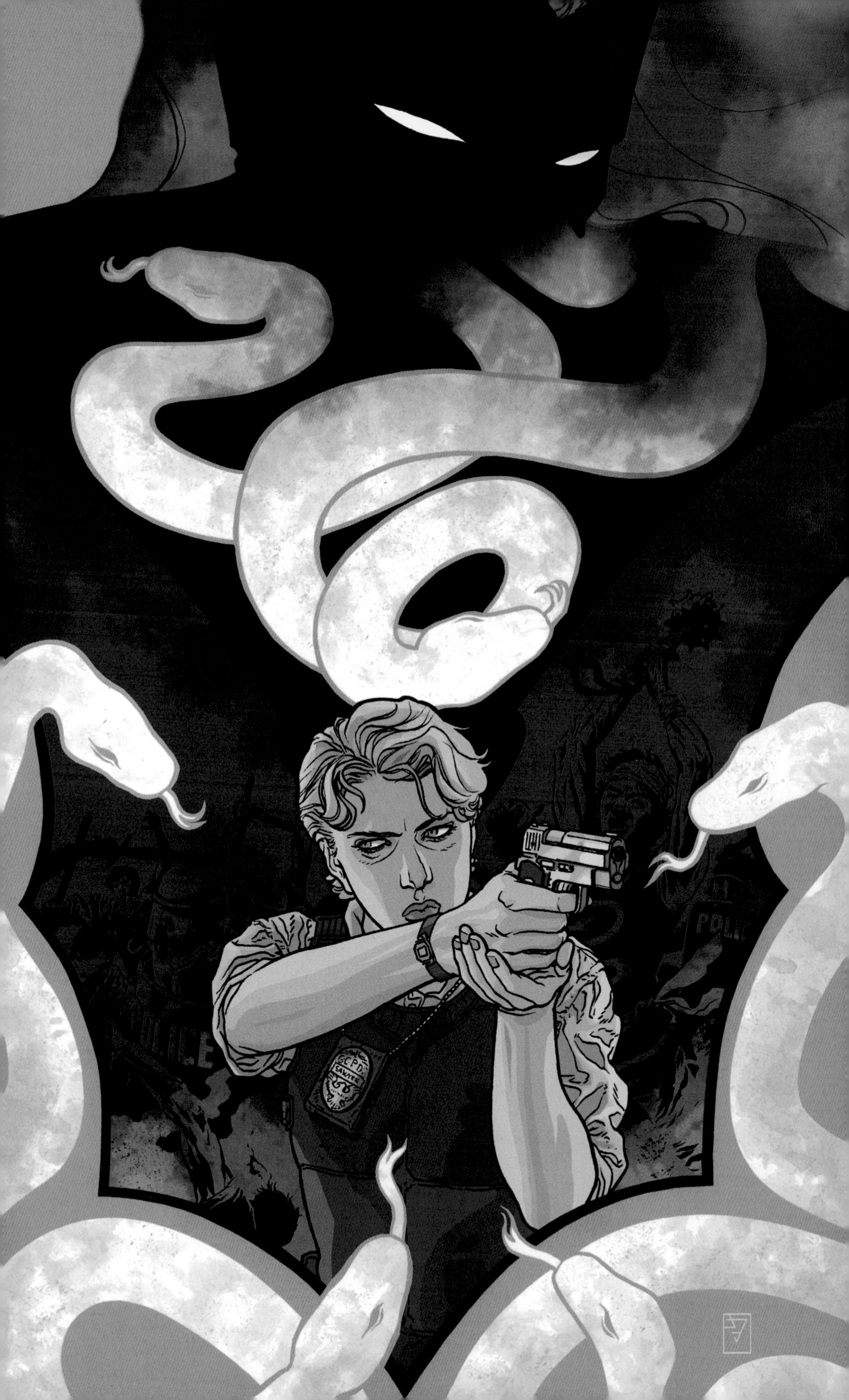
GCPD
SAWYER

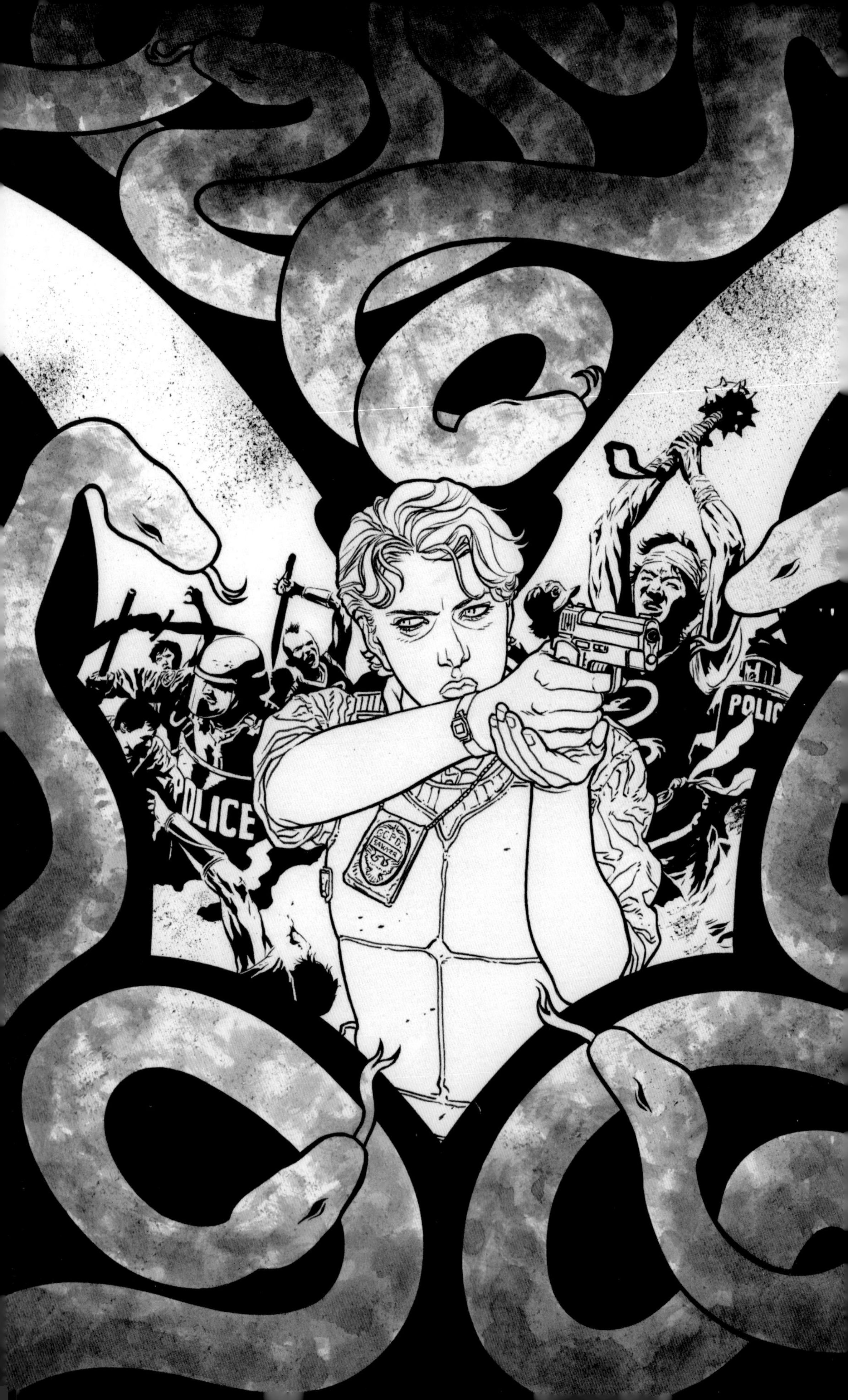
POLICE

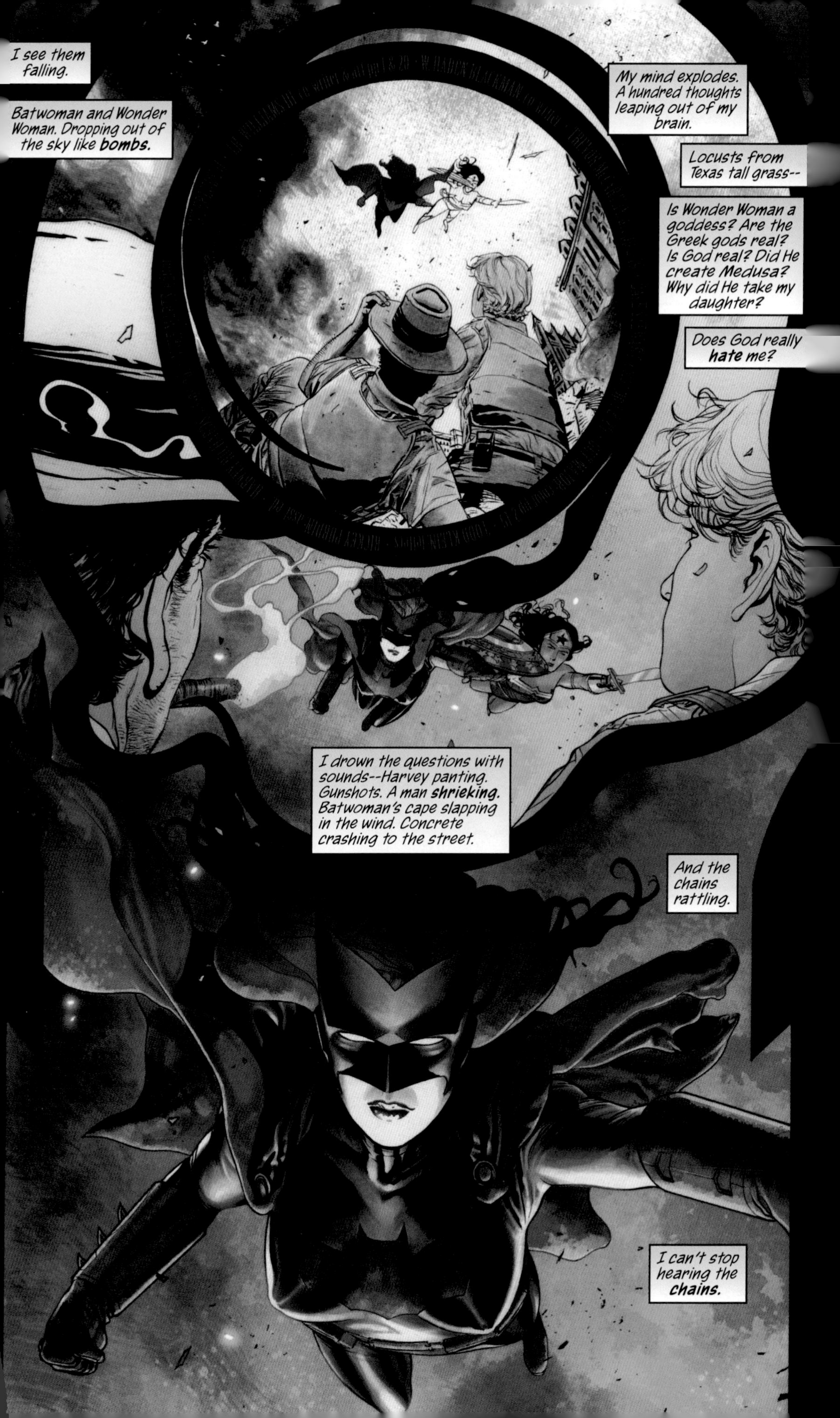
I see them falling.
Batwoman and Wonder Woman. Dropping out of the sky like **bombs.**
My mind explodes. A hundred thoughts leaping out of my brain.
Locusts from Texas tall grass--
Is Wonder Woman a goddess? Are the Greek gods real? Is God real? Did He create Medusa? Why did He take my daughter?
Does God really **hate** me?
I drown the questions with sounds--Harvey panting. Gunshots. A man **shrieking.** Batwoman's cape slapping in the wind. Concrete crashing to the street.
And the chains rattling.
I can't stop hearing the **chains.**

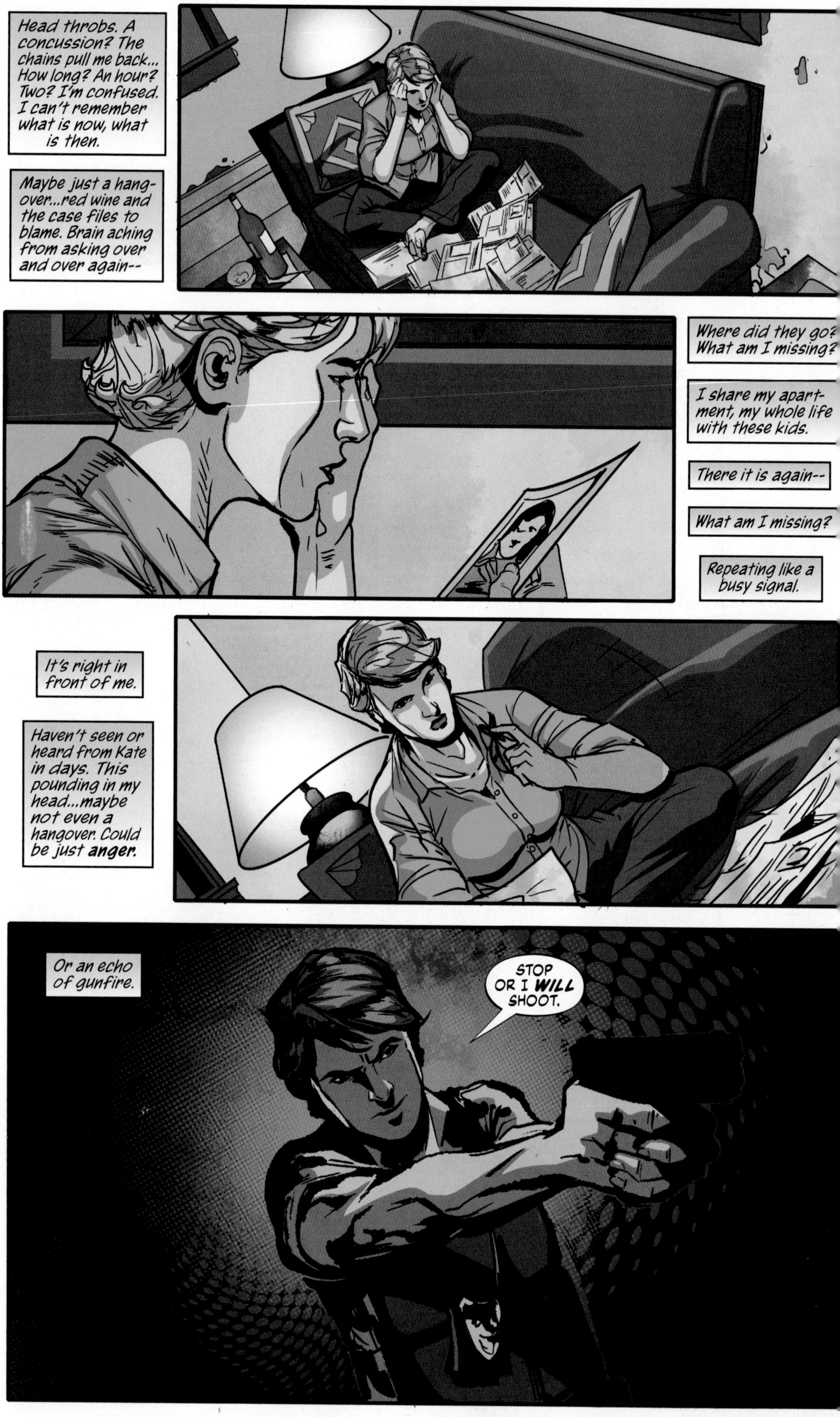
Head throbs. A concussion? The chains pull me back... How long? An hour? Two? I'm confused. I can't remember what is now, what is then.
Maybe just a hang-over...red wine and the case files to blame. Brain aching from asking over and over again--
Where did they go? What am I missing?
I share my apart-ment, my whole life with these kids.
There it is again--
What am I missing?
Repeating like a busy signal.
It's right in front of me.
Haven't seen or heard from Kate in days. This pounding in my head...maybe not even a hangover. Could be just **anger**.
Or an echo of gunfire.
STOP OR I **WILL** SHOOT.

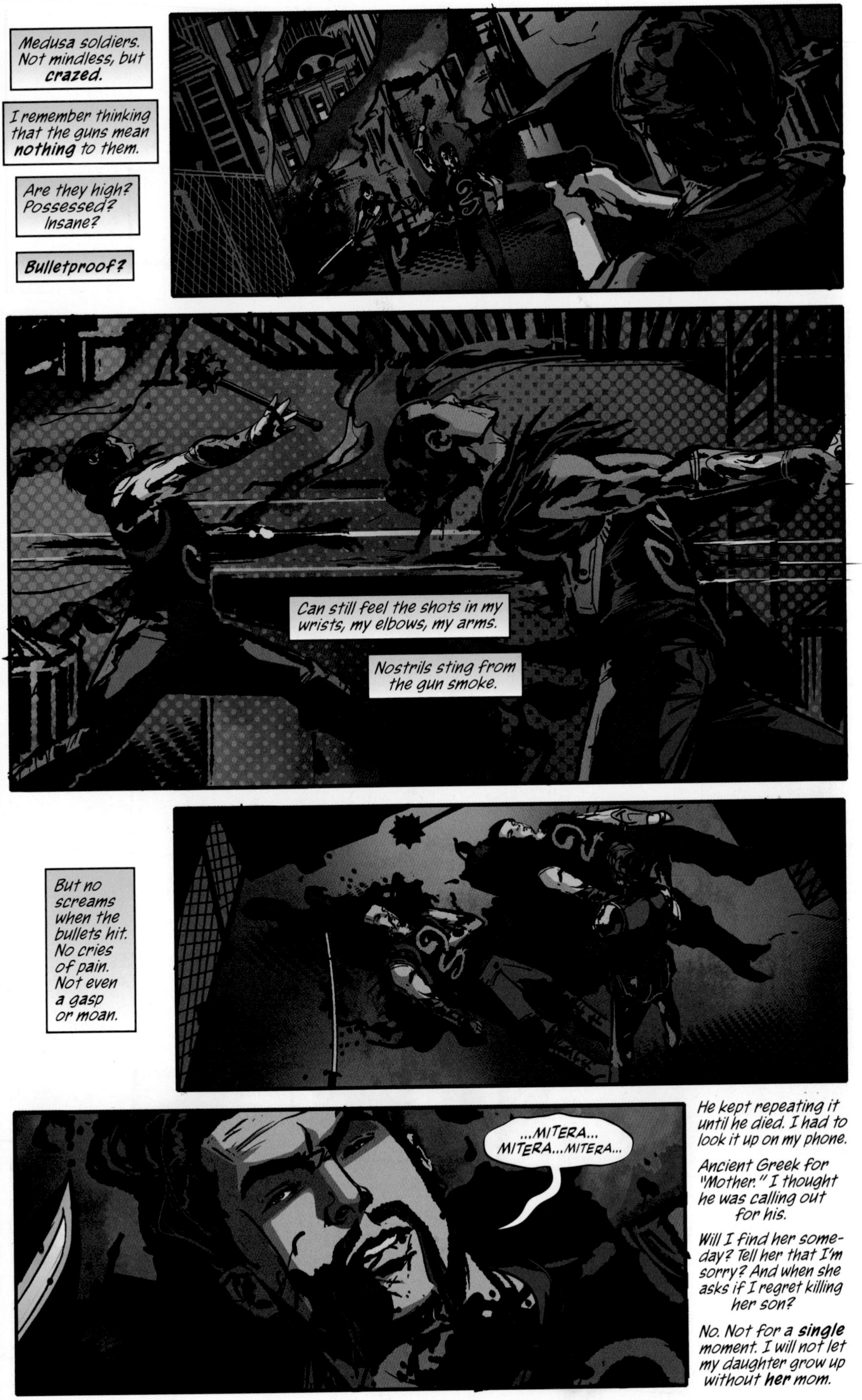
Medusa soldiers. Not mindless, but **crazed.**
I remember thinking that the guns mean **nothing** to them.
Are they high? Possessed? Insane?
Bulletproof?
Can still feel the shots in my wrists, my elbows, my arms.
Nostrils sting from the gun smoke.
But no screams when the bullets hit. No cries of pain. Not even a gasp or moan.
...MITERA... MITERA...MITERA...
He kept repeating it until he died. I had to look it up on my phone.
Ancient Greek for "Mother." I thought he was calling out for his.
Will I find her someday? Tell her that I'm sorry? And when she asks if I regret killing her son?
No. Not for a **single** moment. I will not let my daughter grow up without **her** mom.

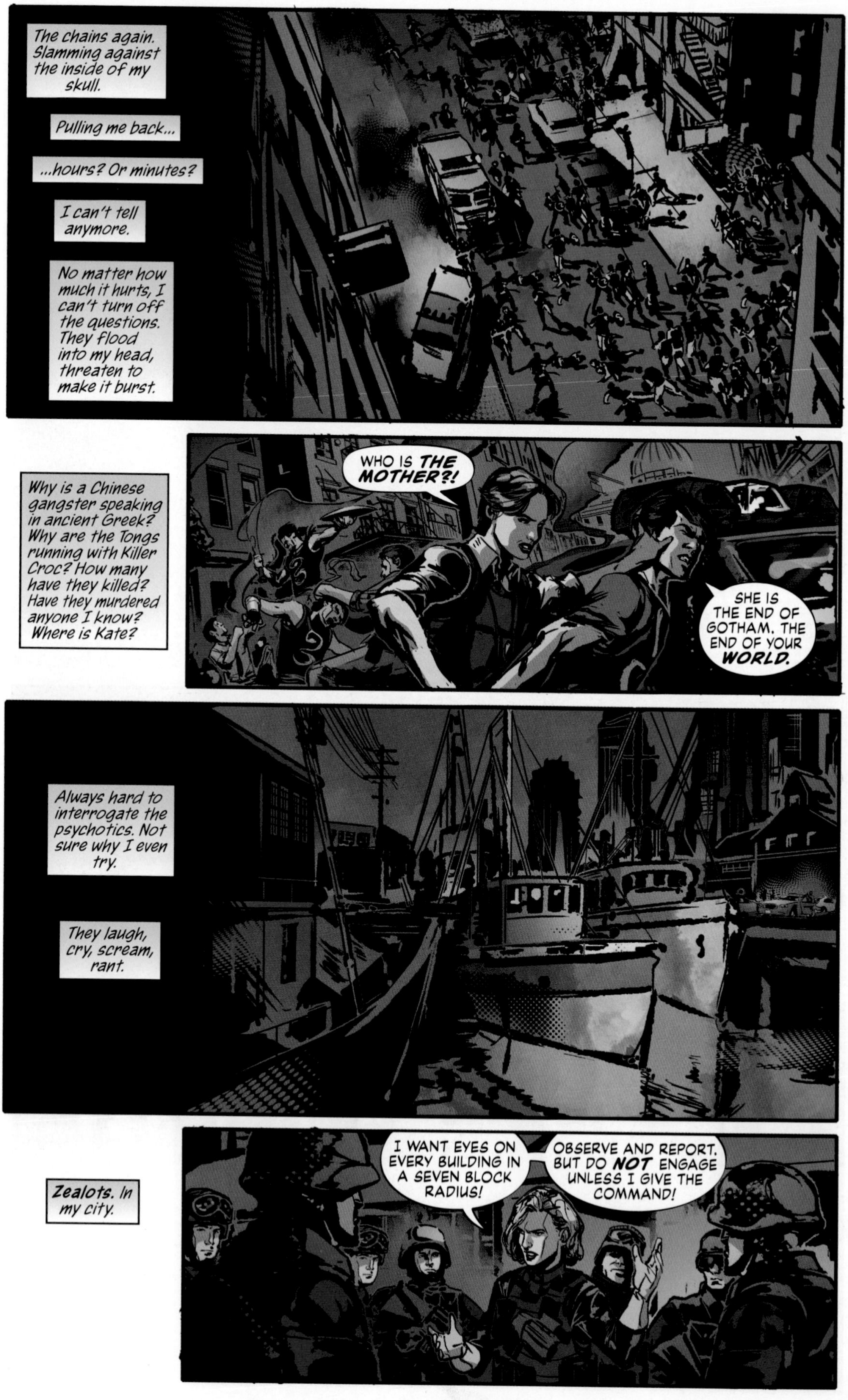
The chains again. Slamming against the inside of my skull.
Pulling me back...
...hours? Or minutes?
I can't tell anymore.
No matter how much it hurts, I can't turn off the questions. They flood into my head, threaten to make it burst.
Why is a Chinese gangster speaking in ancient Greek? Why are the Tongs running with Killer Croc? How many have they killed? Have they murdered anyone I know? Where is Kate?
WHO IS THE MOTHER?!
SHE IS THE END OF GOTHAM. THE END OF YOUR WORLD.
Always hard to interrogate the psychotics. Not sure why I even try.
They laugh, cry, scream, rant.
Zealots. In my city.
I WANT EYES ON EVERY BUILDING IN A SEVEN BLOCK RADIUS!
OBSERVE AND REPORT. BUT DO NOT ENGAGE UNLESS I GIVE THE COMMAND!

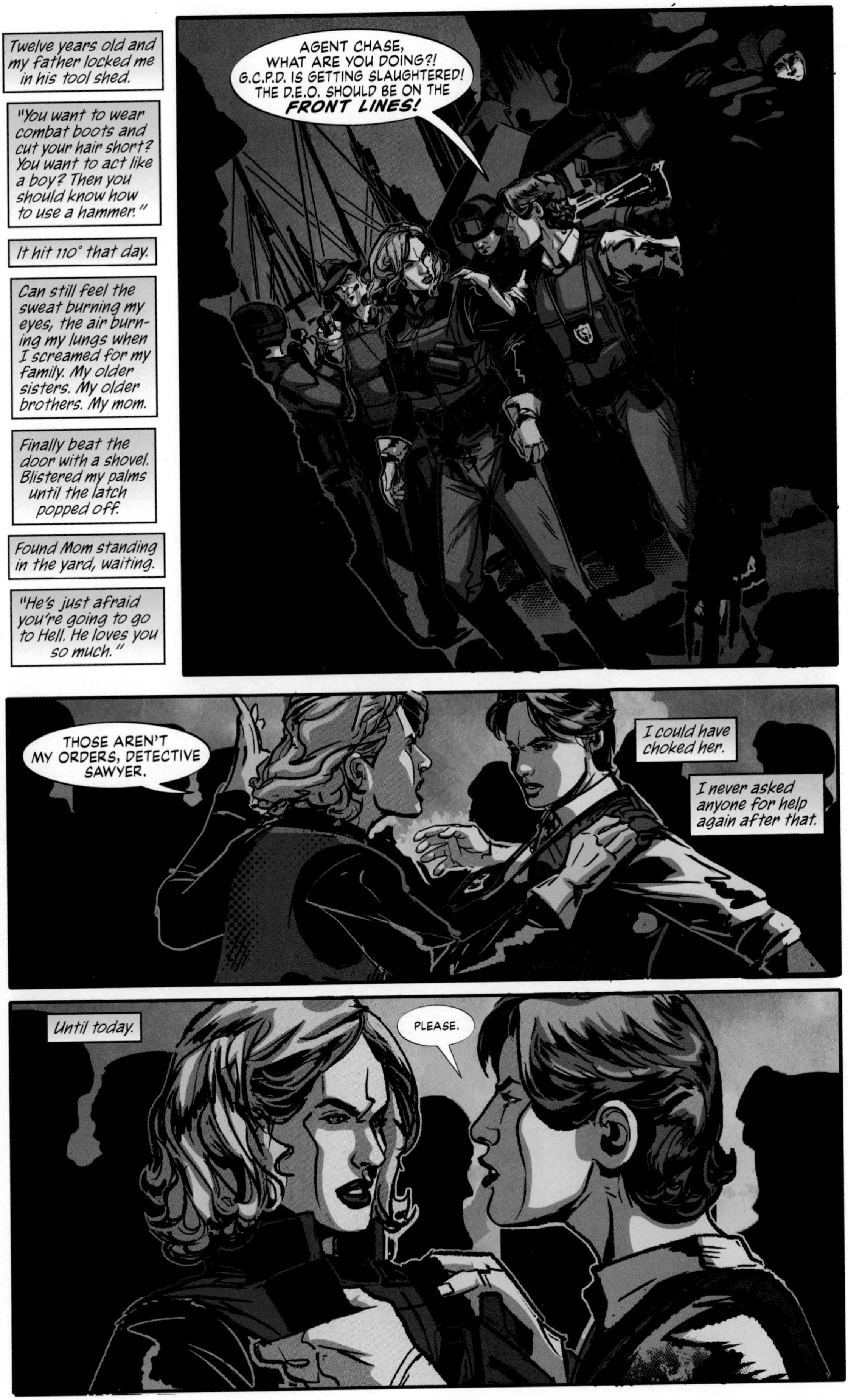
Twelve years old and my father locked me in his tool shed.
"You want to wear combat boots and cut your hair short? You want to act like a boy? Then you should know how to use a hammer."
It hit 110° that day.
Can still feel the sweat burning my eyes, the air burning my lungs when I screamed for my family. My older sisters. My older brothers. My mom.
Finally beat the door with a shovel. Blistered my palms until the latch popped off.
Found Mom standing in the yard, waiting.
"He's just afraid you're going to go to Hell. He loves you so much."
AGENT CHASE, WHAT ARE YOU DOING?! G.C.P.D. IS GETTING SLAUGHTERED! THE D.E.O. SHOULD BE ON THE FRONT LINES!
THOSE AREN'T MY ORDERS, DETECTIVE SAWYER.
I could have choked her.
I never asked anyone for help again after that.
Until today.
PLEASE.

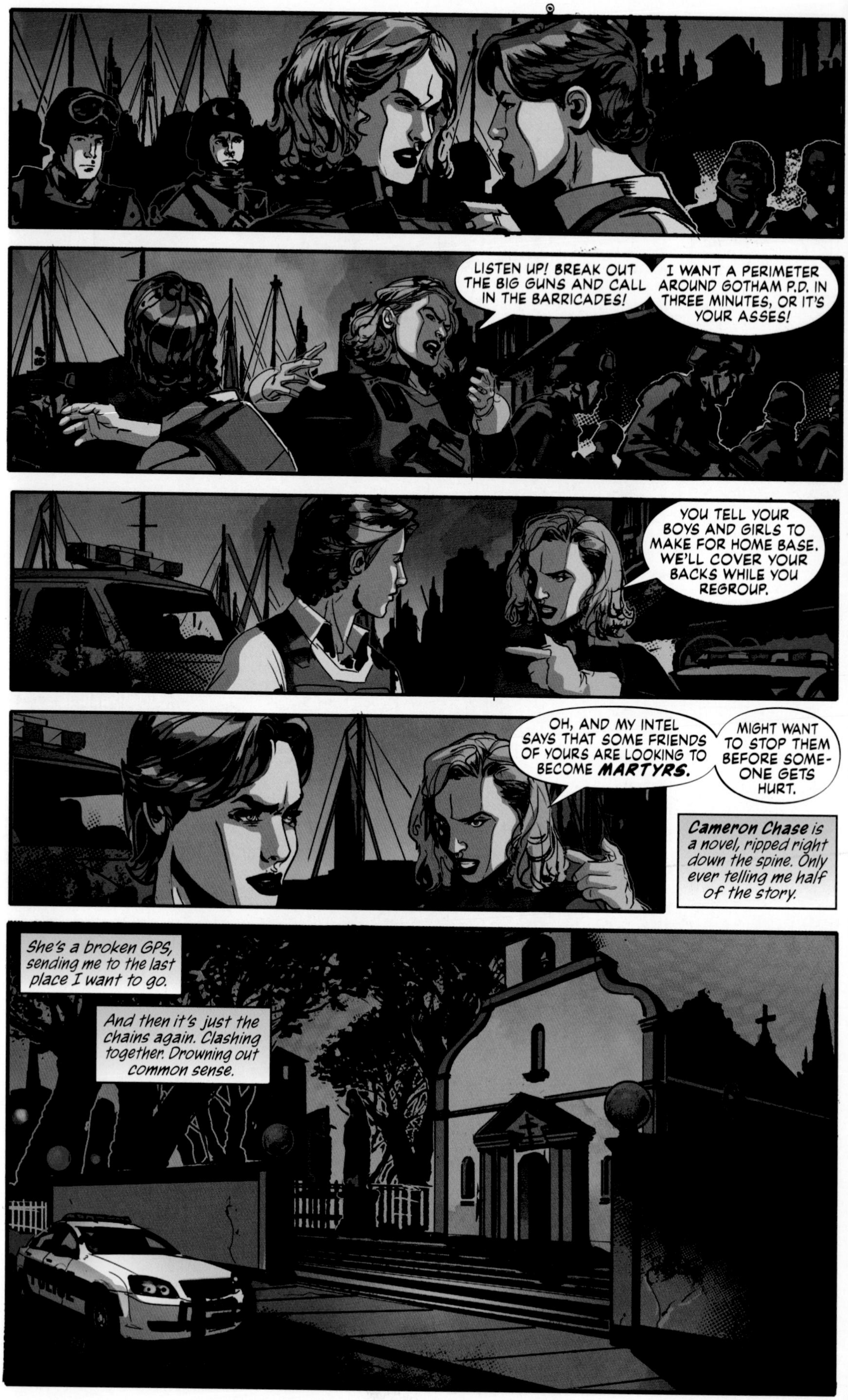
LISTEN UP! BREAK OUT THE BIG GUNS AND CALL IN THE BARRICADES!
I WANT A PERIMETER AROUND GOTHAM P.D. IN THREE MINUTES, OR IT'S YOUR ASSES!
YOU TELL YOUR BOYS AND GIRLS TO MAKE FOR HOME BASE. WE'LL COVER YOUR BACKS WHILE YOU REGROUP.
OH, AND MY INTEL SAYS THAT SOME FRIENDS OF YOURS ARE LOOKING TO BECOME MARTYRS.
MIGHT WANT TO STOP THEM BEFORE SOME-ONE GETS HURT.
Cameron Chase is a novel, ripped right down the spine. Only ever telling me half of the story.
She's a broken GPS, sending me to the last place I want to go.
And then it's just the chains again. Clashing together. Drowning out common sense.

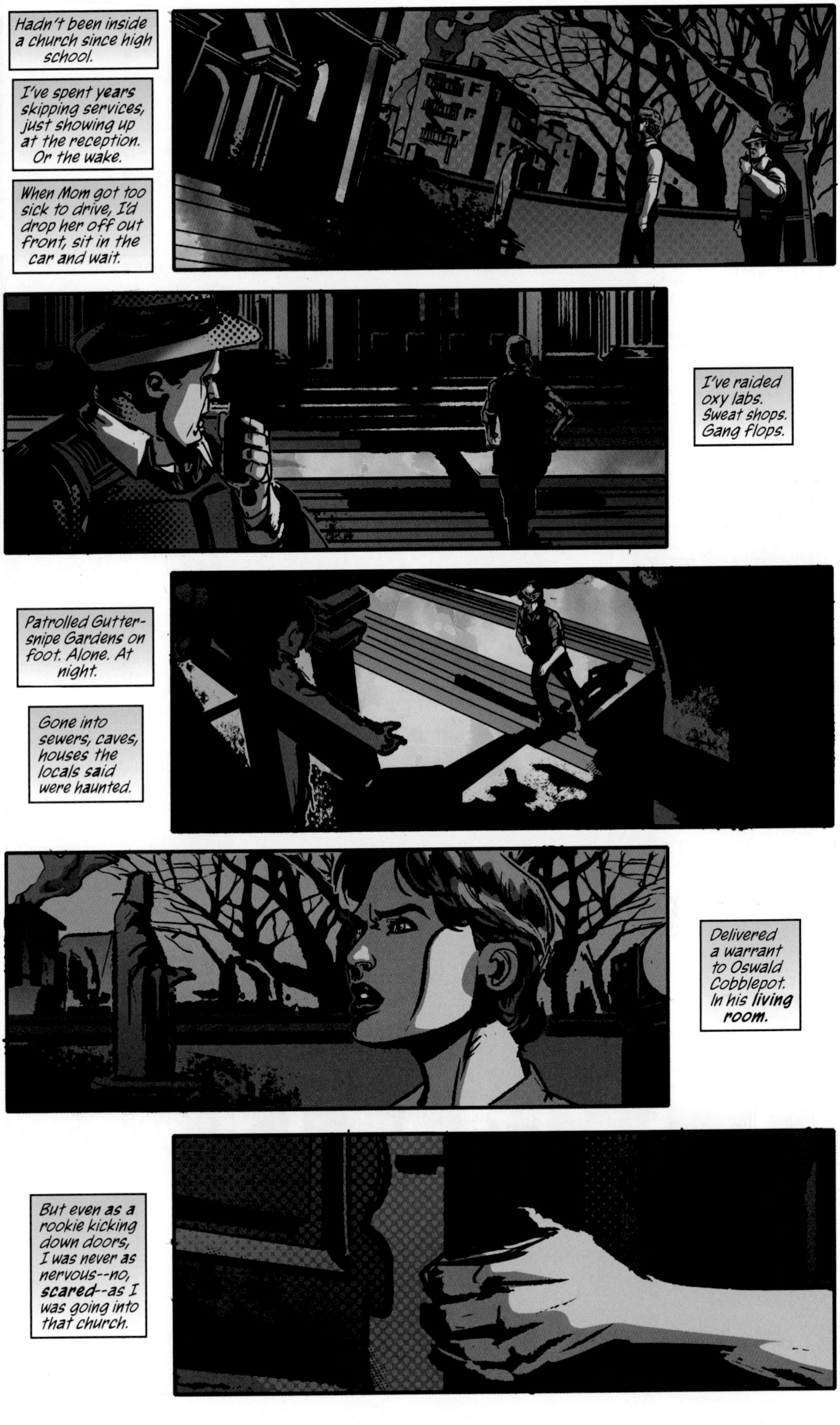
Hadn't been inside a church since high school.
I've spent years skipping services, just showing up at the reception. Or the wake.
When Mom got too sick to drive, I'd drop her off out front, sit in the car and wait.
I've raided oxy labs. Sweat shops. Gang flops.
Patrolled Guttersnipe Gardens on foot. Alone. At night.
Gone into sewers, caves, houses the locals said were haunted.
Delivered a warrant to Oswald Cobblepot. In his **living room.**
But even as a rookie kicking down doors, I was never as nervous--no, **scared**--as I was going into that church.

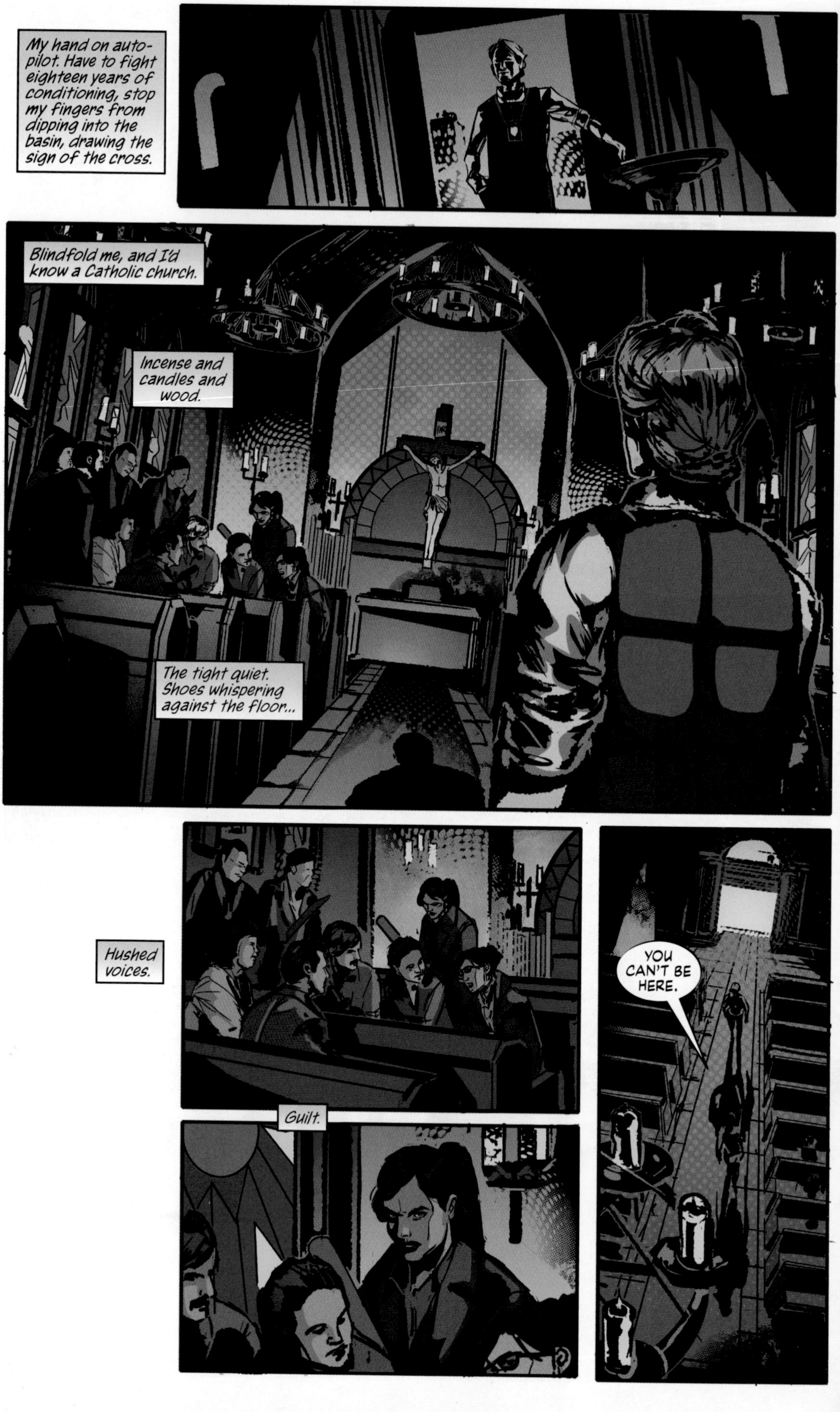
My hand on auto-pilot. Have to fight eighteen years of conditioning, stop my fingers from dipping into the basin, drawing the sign of the cross.
Blindfold me, and I'd know a Catholic church.
Incense and candles and wood.
The tight quiet. Shoes whispering against the floor...
Hushed voices.
Guilt.
YOU CAN'T BE HERE.

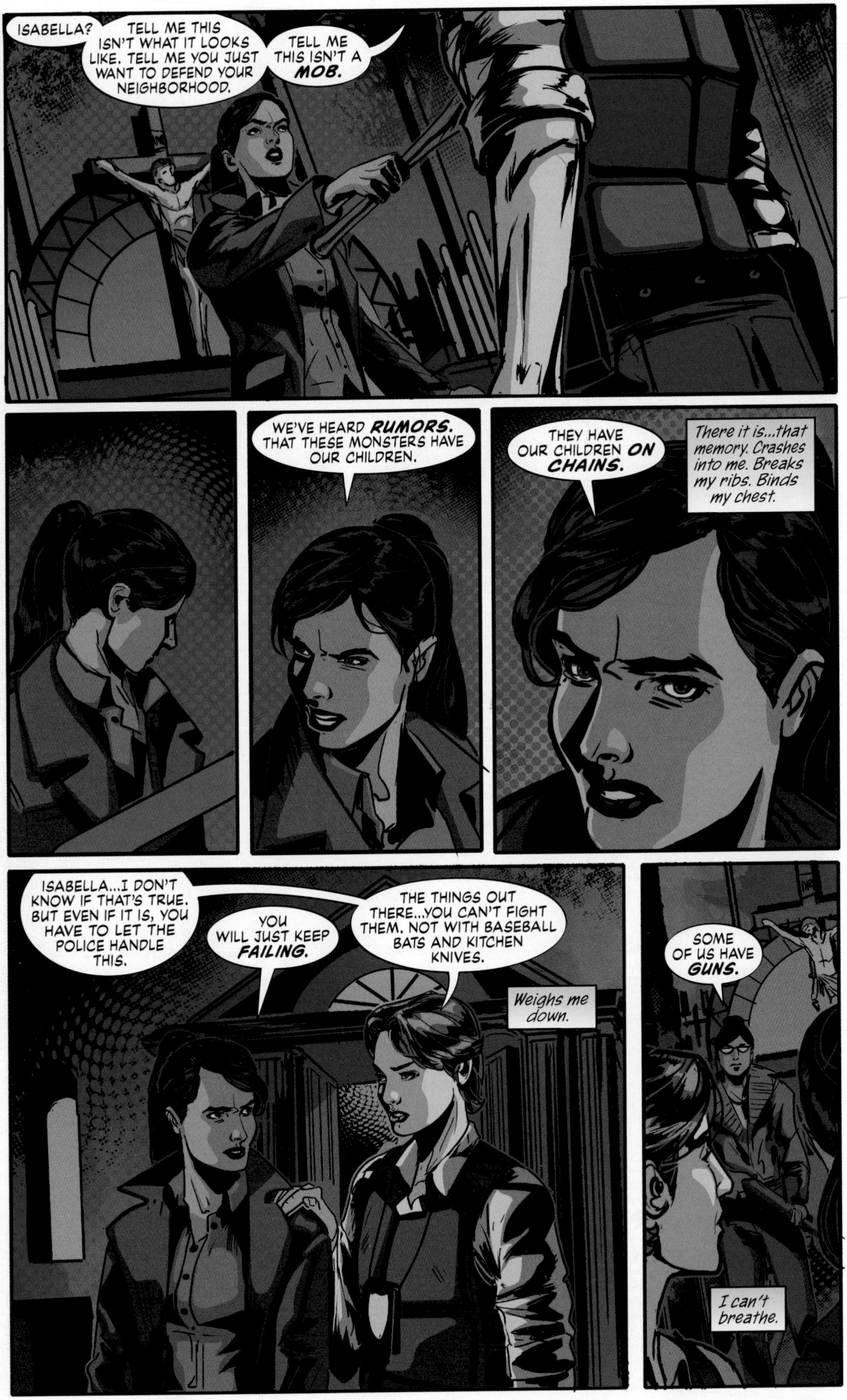
ISABELLA?
TELL ME THIS ISN'T WHAT IT LOOKS LIKE. TELL ME YOU JUST WANT TO DEFEND YOUR NEIGHBORHOOD.
TELL ME THIS ISN'T A MOB.
WE'VE HEARD RUMORS. THAT THESE MONSTERS HAVE OUR CHILDREN.
THEY HAVE OUR CHILDREN ON CHAINS.
There it is...that memory. Crashes into me. Breaks my ribs. Binds my chest.
ISABELLA...I DON'T KNOW IF THAT'S TRUE. BUT EVEN IF IT IS, YOU HAVE TO LET THE POLICE HANDLE THIS.
YOU WILL JUST KEEP FAILING.
THE THINGS OUT THERE...YOU CAN'T FIGHT THEM. NOT WITH BASEBALL BATS AND KITCHEN KNIVES.
Weighs me down.
SOME OF US HAVE GUNS.
I can't breathe.

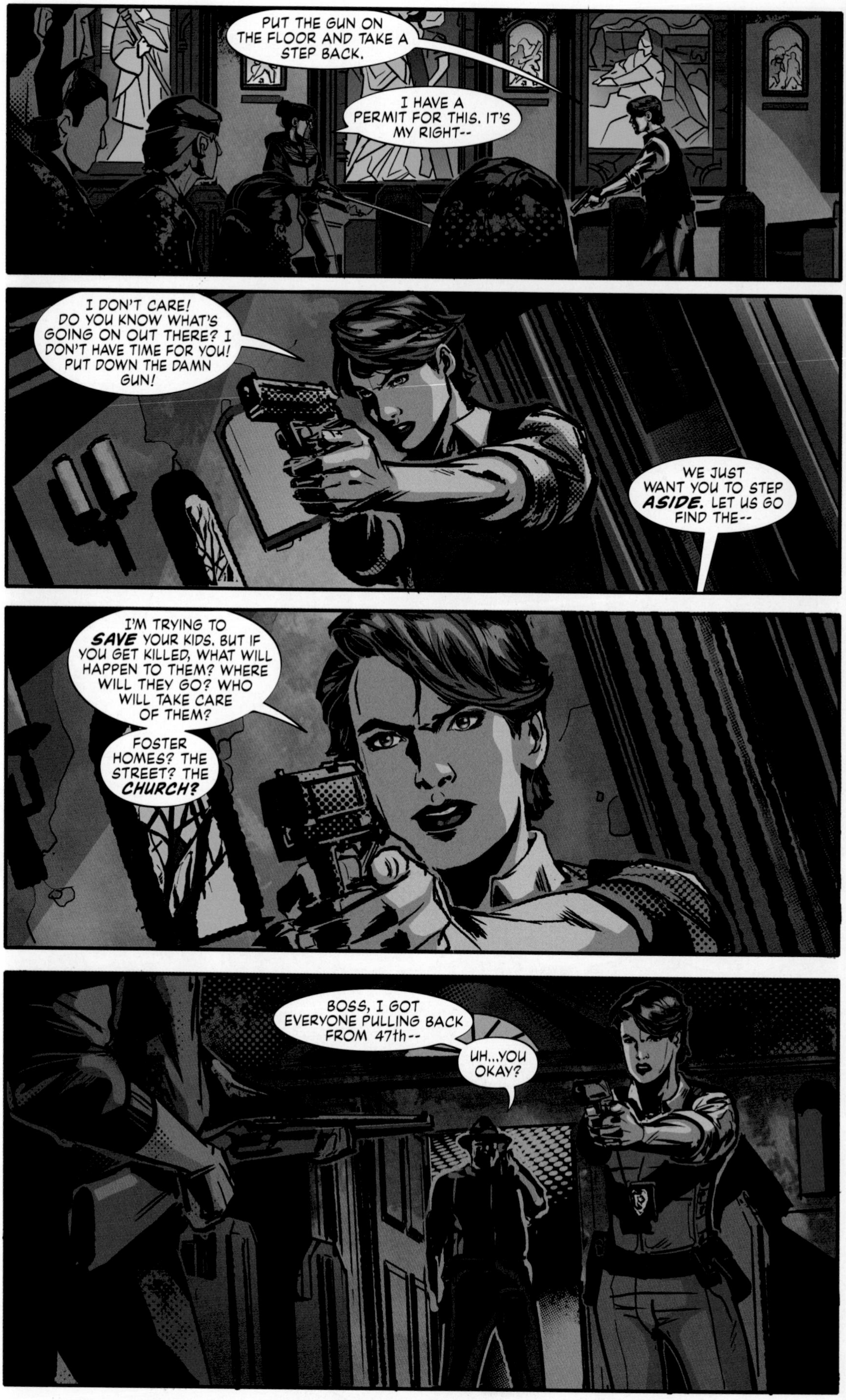
PUT THE GUN ON THE FLOOR AND TAKE A STEP BACK.
I HAVE A PERMIT FOR THIS. IT'S MY RIGHT--
I DON'T CARE! DO YOU KNOW WHAT'S GOING ON OUT THERE? I DON'T HAVE TIME FOR YOU! PUT DOWN THE DAMN GUN!
WE JUST WANT YOU TO STEP ASIDE. LET US GO FIND THE--
I'M TRYING TO SAVE YOUR KIDS. BUT IF YOU GET KILLED, WHAT WILL HAPPEN TO THEM? WHERE WILL THEY GO? WHO WILL TAKE CARE OF THEM?
FOSTER HOMES? THE STREET? THE CHURCH?
BOSS, I GOT EVERYONE PULLING BACK FROM 47th--
UH...YOU OKAY?

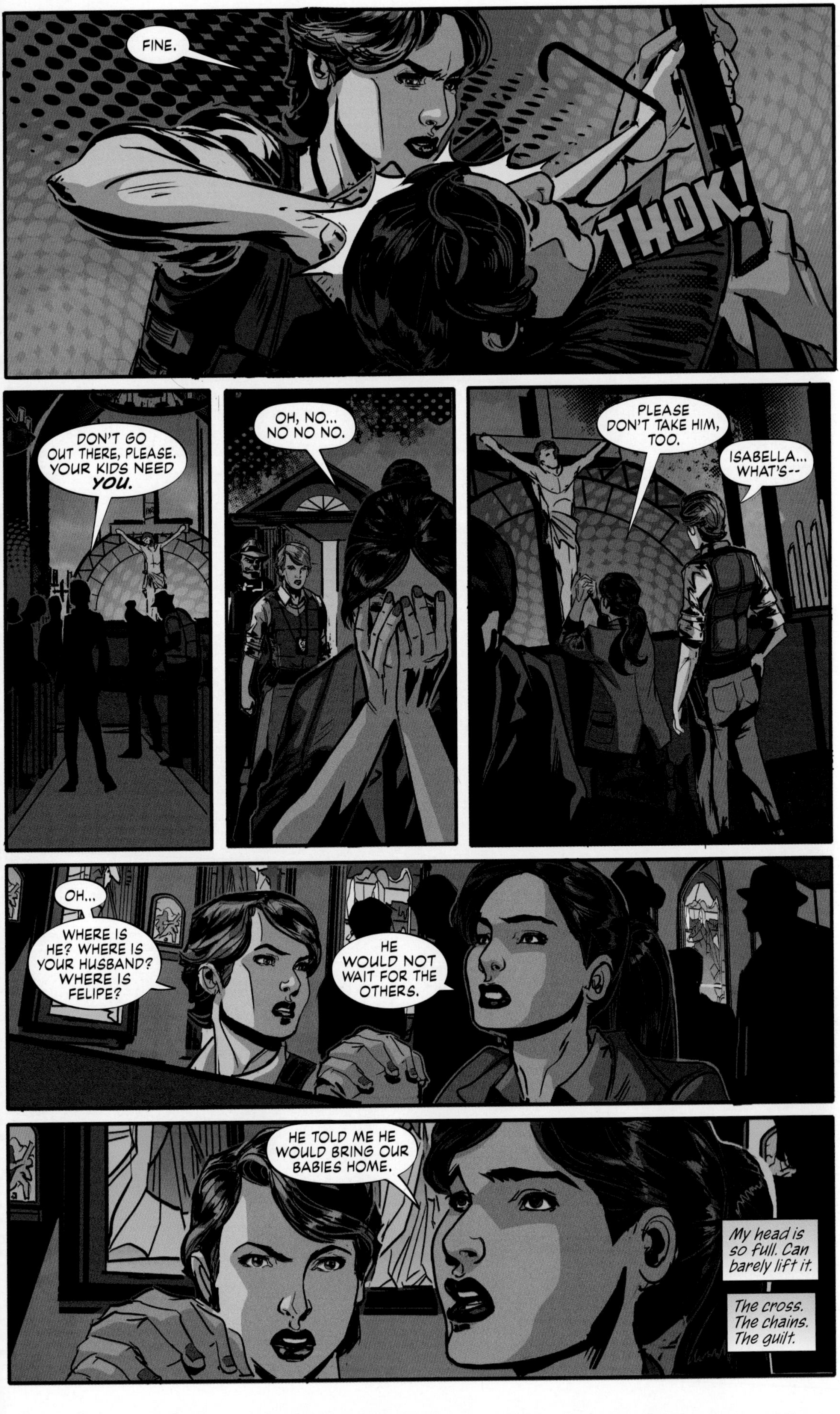
FINE.
THOK!
DON'T GO OUT THERE, PLEASE. YOUR KIDS NEED YOU.
OH, NO... NO NO NO.
PLEASE DON'T TAKE HIM, TOO.
ISABELLA... WHAT'S--
OH...
WHERE IS HE? WHERE IS YOUR HUSBAND? WHERE IS FELIPE?
HE WOULD NOT WAIT FOR THE OTHERS.
HE TOLD ME HE WOULD BRING OUR BABIES HOME.
My head is so full. Can barely lift it.
The cross. The chains. The guilt.

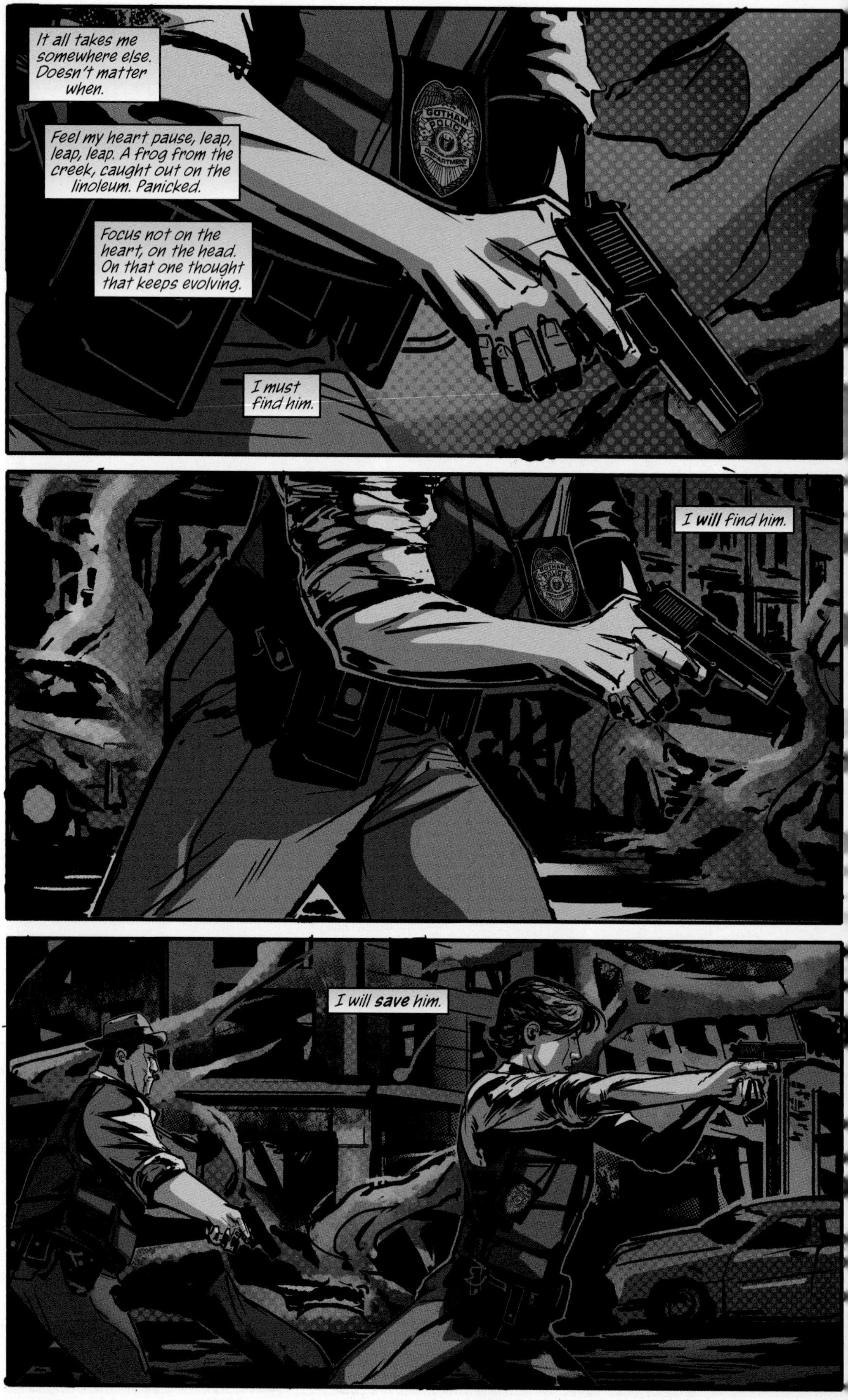
It all takes me somewhere else. Doesn't matter when.
Feel my heart pause, leap, leap, leap. A frog from the creek, caught out on the linoleum. Panicked.
Focus not on the heart, on the head. On that one thought that keeps evolving.
I must find him.
GOTHAM POLICE DEPARTMENT
I will find him.
I will save him.

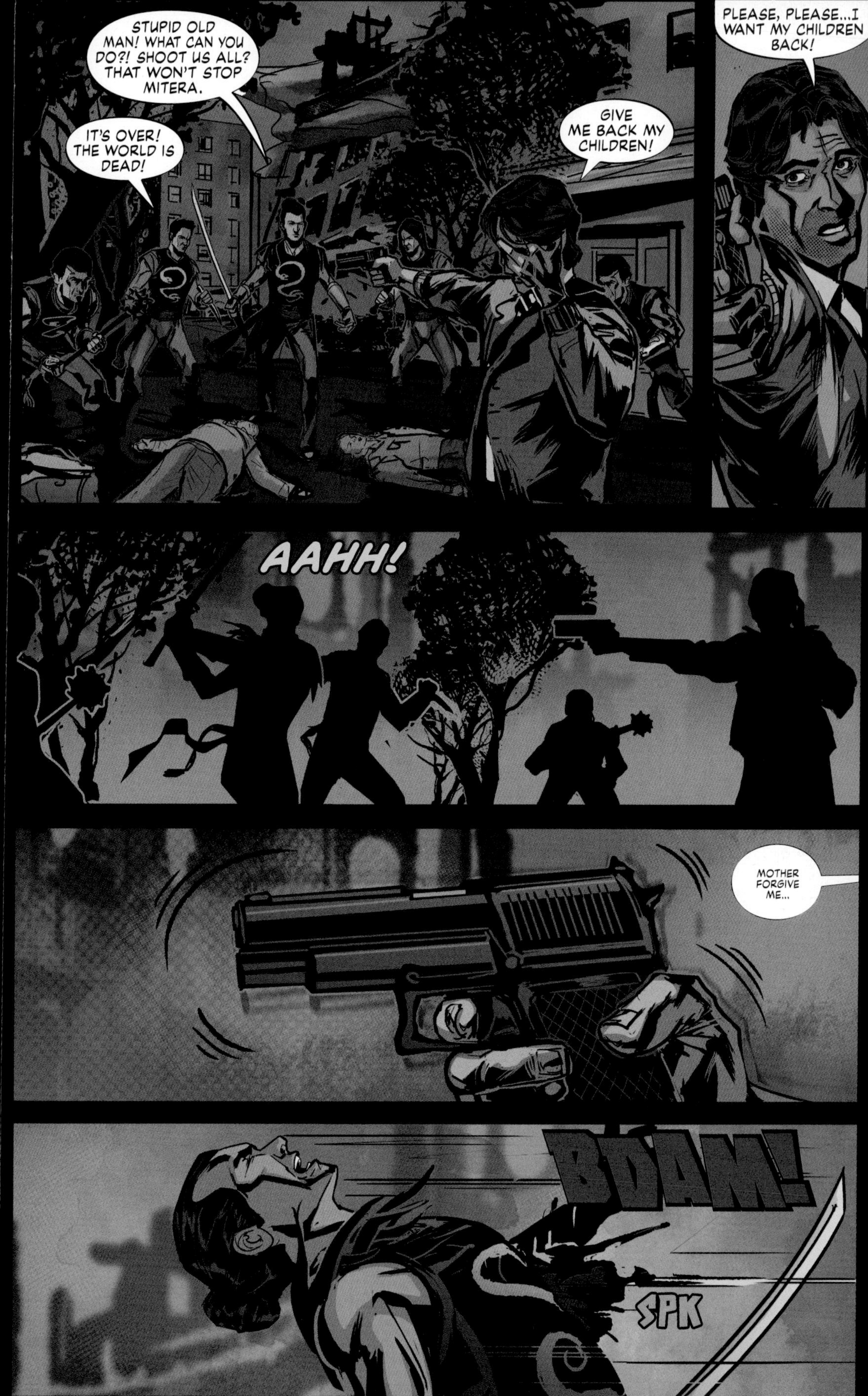
STUPID OLD MAN! WHAT CAN YOU DO?! SHOOT US ALL? THAT WON'T STOP MITERA.
IT'S OVER! THE WORLD IS DEAD!
GIVE ME BACK MY CHILDREN!
PLEASE, PLEASE...I WANT MY CHILDREN BACK!
AAHH!
MOTHER FORGIVE ME...
BDAM!
SPK

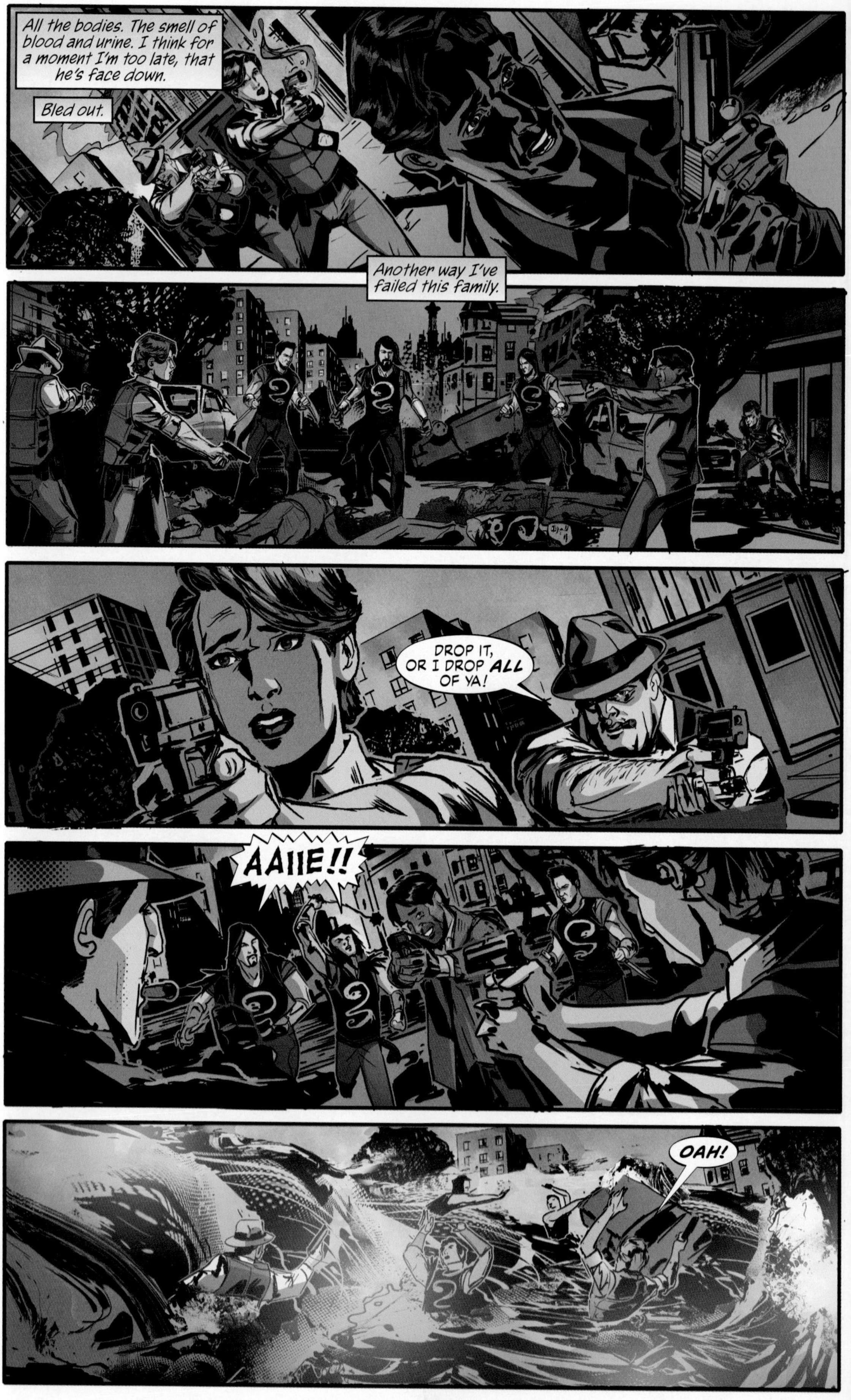
All the bodies. The smell of blood and urine. I think for a moment I'm too late, that he's face down.
Bled out.
Another way I've failed this family.
DROP IT, OR I DROP ALL OF YA!
AAIIE!!
OAH!

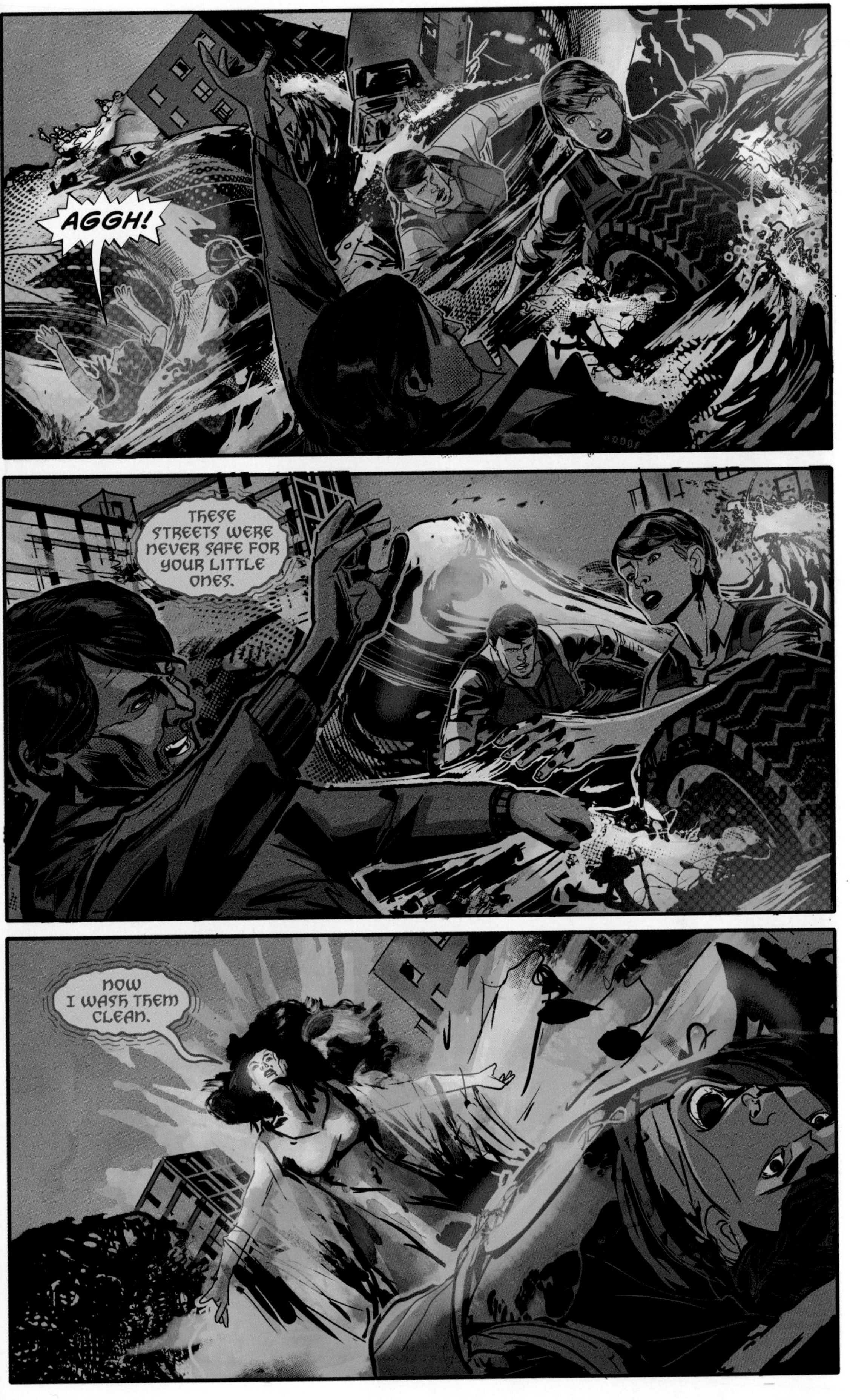
AGGH!
THESE STREETS WERE NEVER SAFE FOR YOUR LITTLE ONES.
NOW I WASH THEM CLEAN.

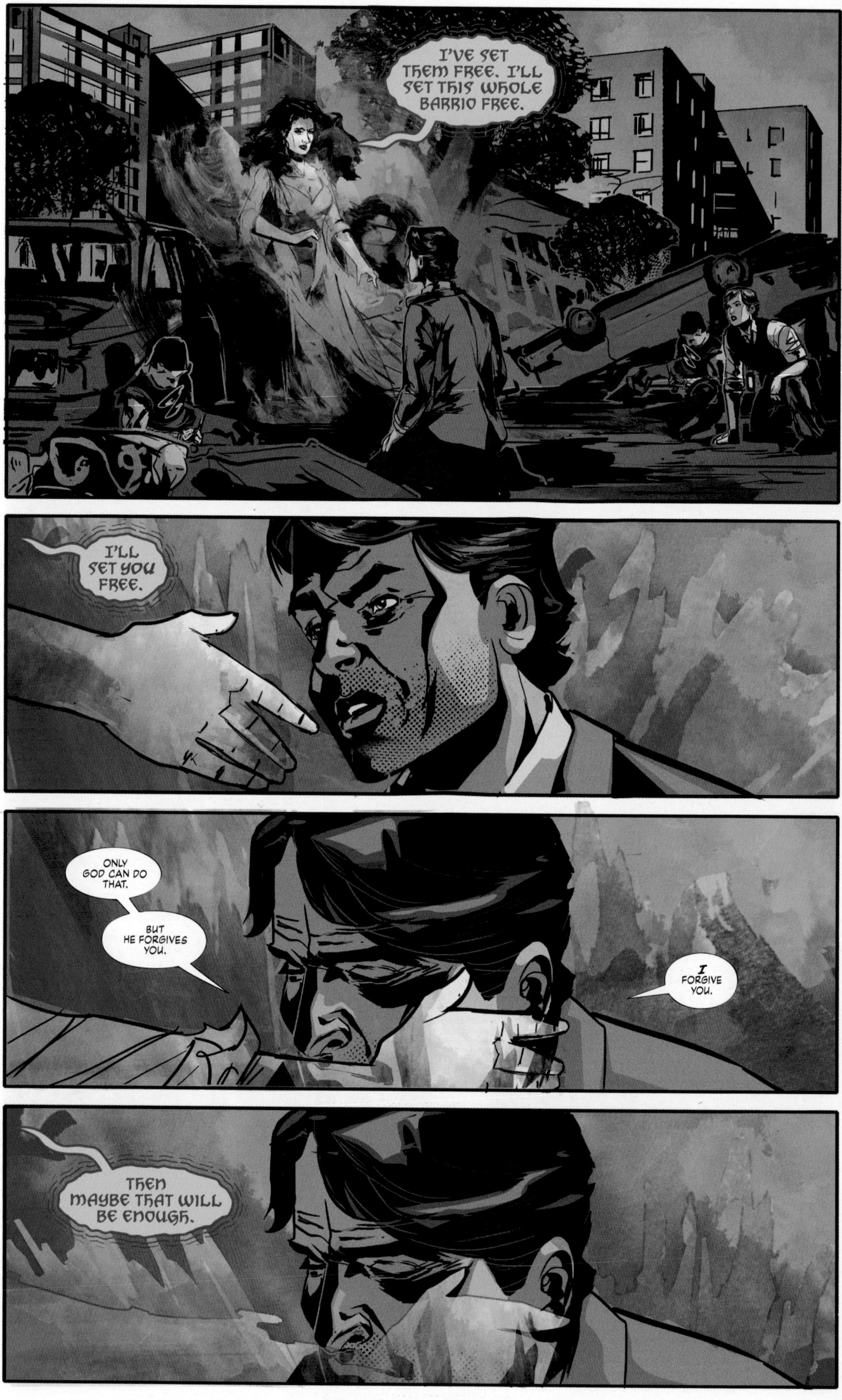
I'VE SET THEM FREE. I'LL SET THIS WHOLE BARRIO FREE.
I'LL SET YOU FREE.
ONLY GOD CAN DO THAT.
BUT HE FORGIVES YOU.
I FORGIVE YOU.
THEN MAYBE THAT WILL BE ENOUGH.

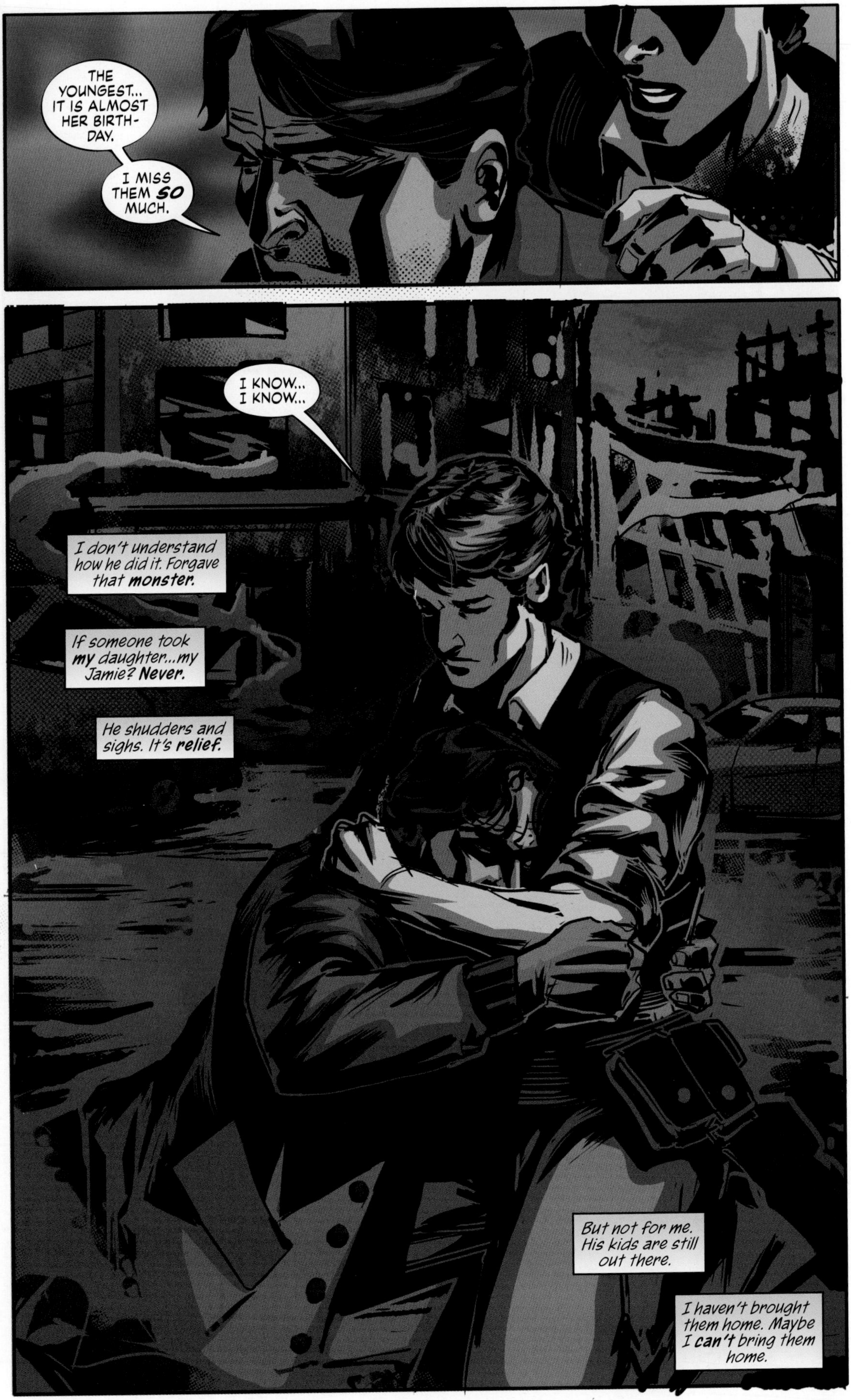
THE YOUNGEST... IT IS ALMOST HER BIRTH-DAY.
I MISS THEM **SO** MUCH.
I KNOW... I KNOW...
I don't understand how he did it. Forgave that ***monster.***
If someone took ***my*** *daughter...my Jamie?* ***Never.***
He shudders and sighs. It's ***relief.***
But not for me. His kids are still out there.
I haven't brought them home. Maybe I ***can't*** *bring them home.*

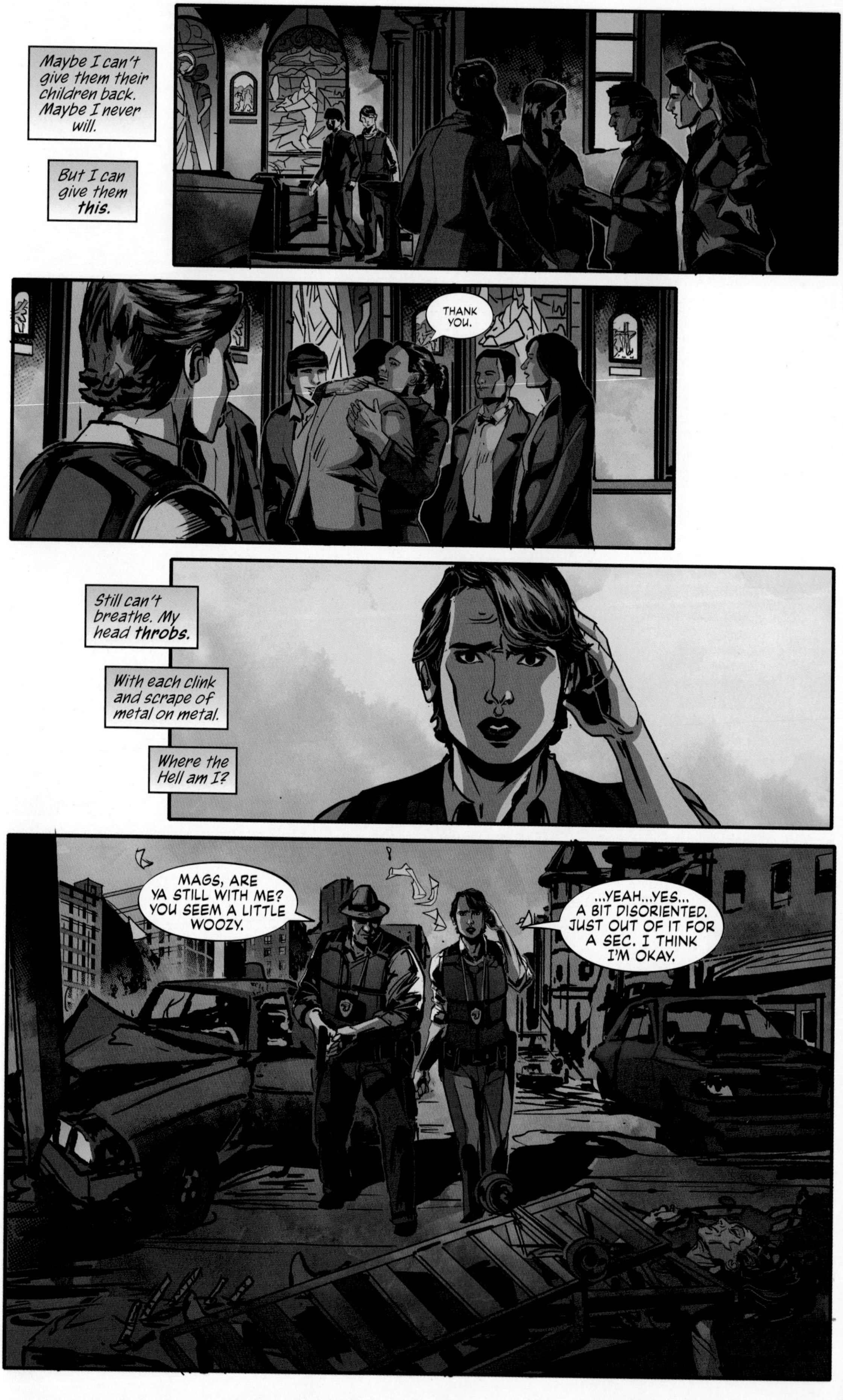
Maybe I can't give them their children back. Maybe I never will.
But I can give them this.
THANK YOU.
Still can't breathe. My head throbs.
With each clink and scrape of metal on metal.
Where the Hell am I?
MAGS, ARE YA STILL WITH ME? YOU SEEM A LITTLE WOOZY.
...YEAH...YES... A BIT DISORIENTED. JUST OUT OF IT FOR A SEC. I THINK I'M OKAY.

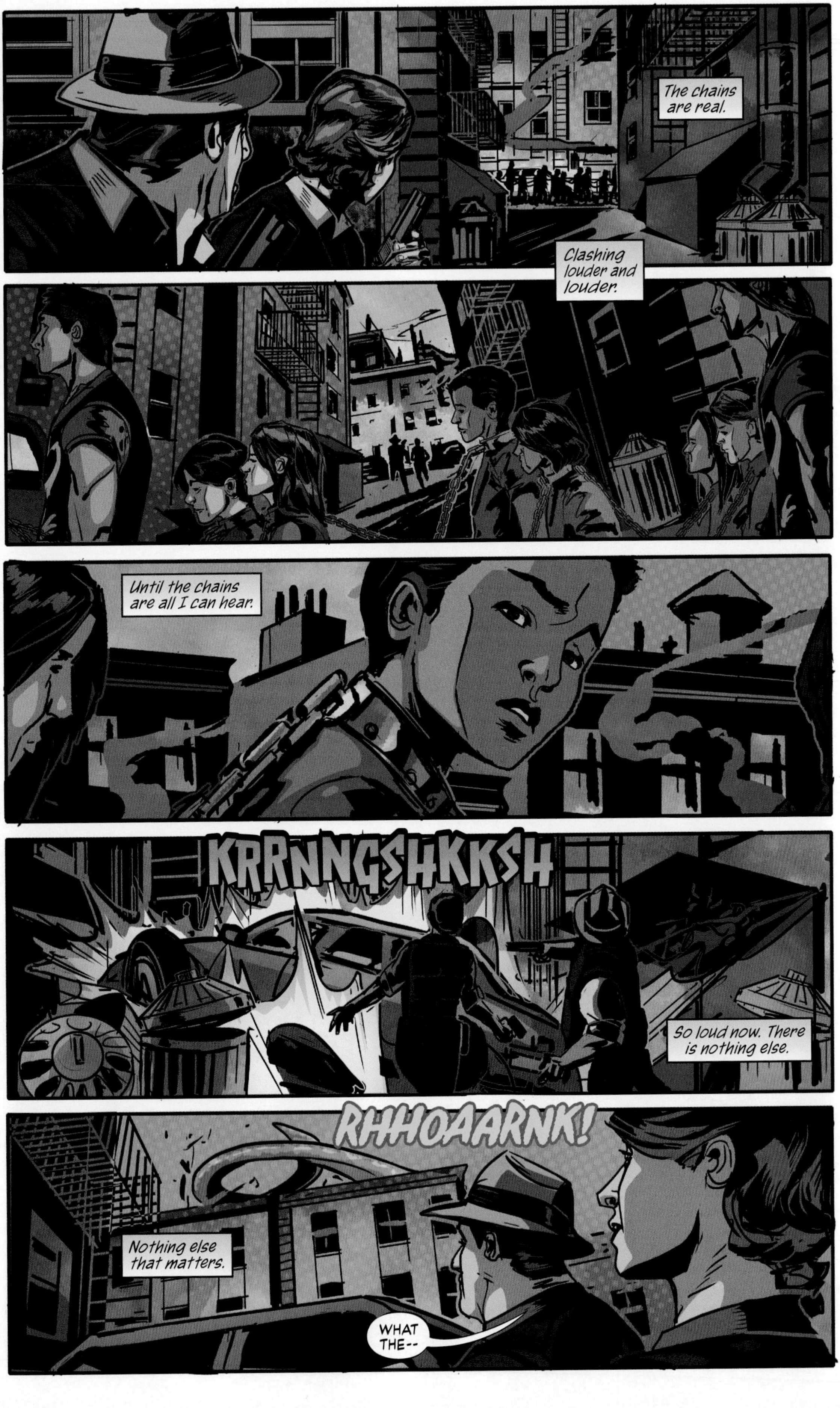

The chains are real.
Clashing louder and louder.
Until the chains are all I can hear.
KRRNNGSHKKSH
So loud now. There is nothing else.
RHHOAARNK!
Nothing else that matters.
WHAT THE--

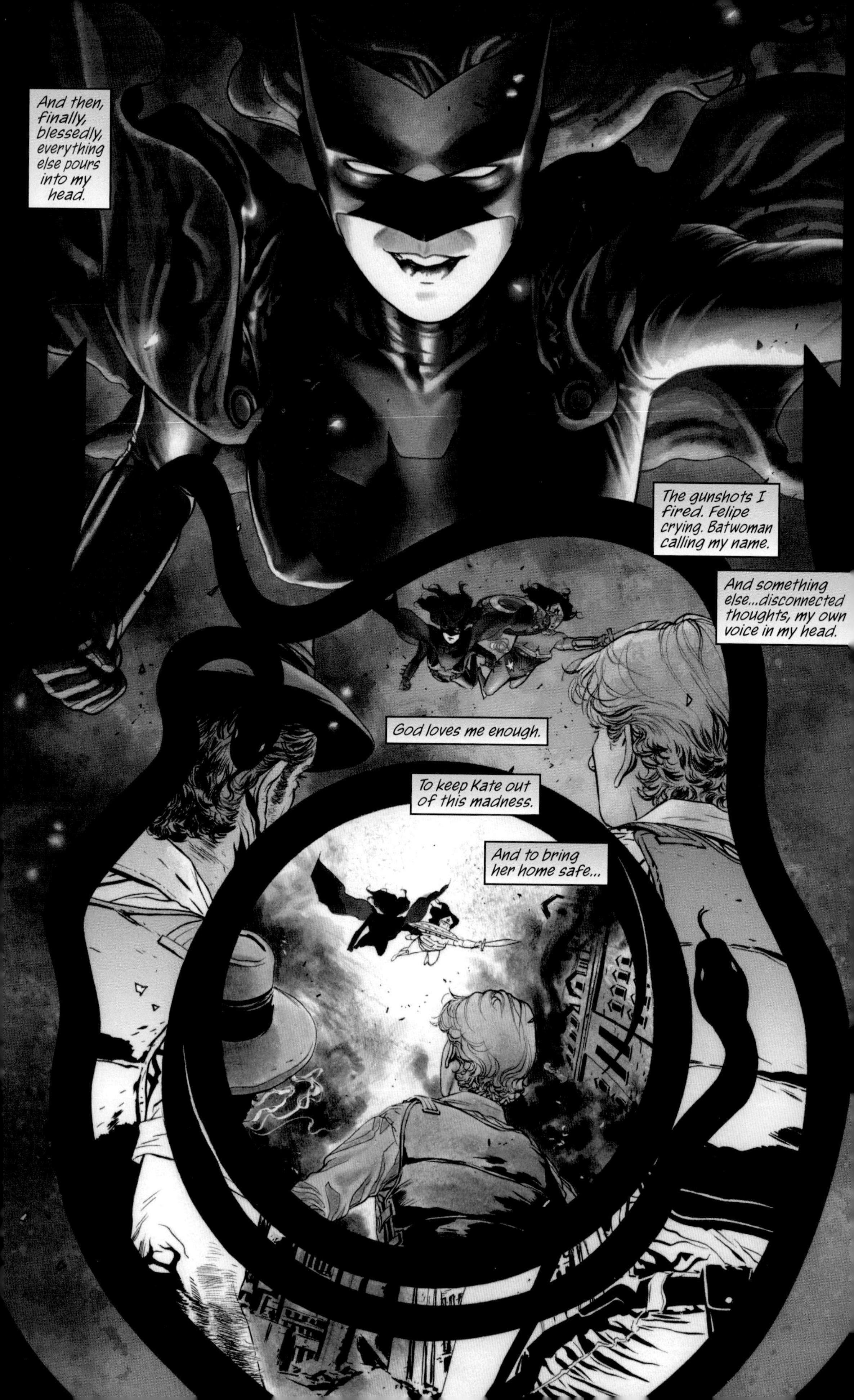
And then, finally, blessedly, everything else pours into my head.
The gunshots I fired. Felipe crying. Batwoman calling my name.
And something else...disconnected thoughts, my own voice in my head.
God loves me enough.
To keep Kate out of this madness.
And to bring her home safe...

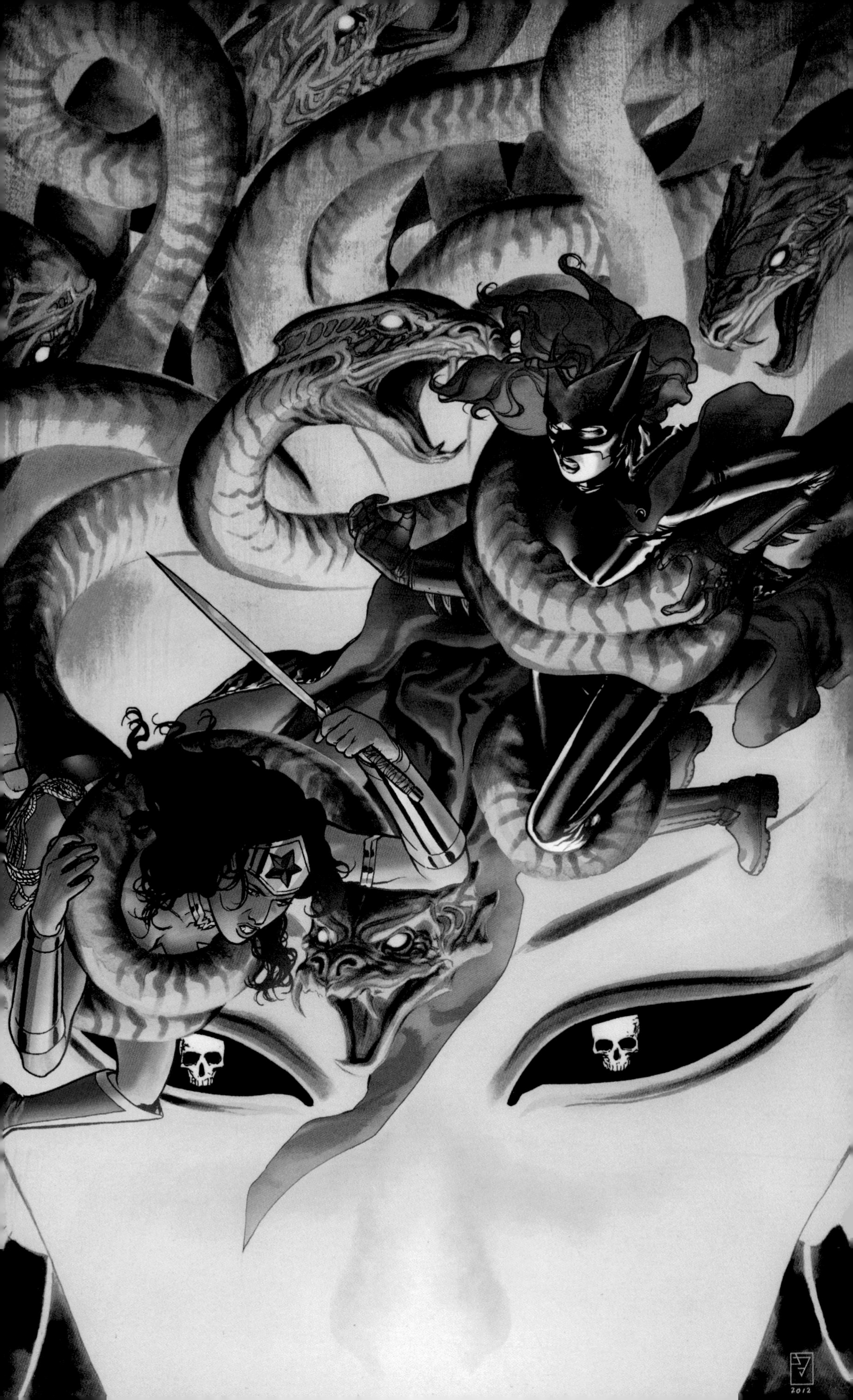
2012

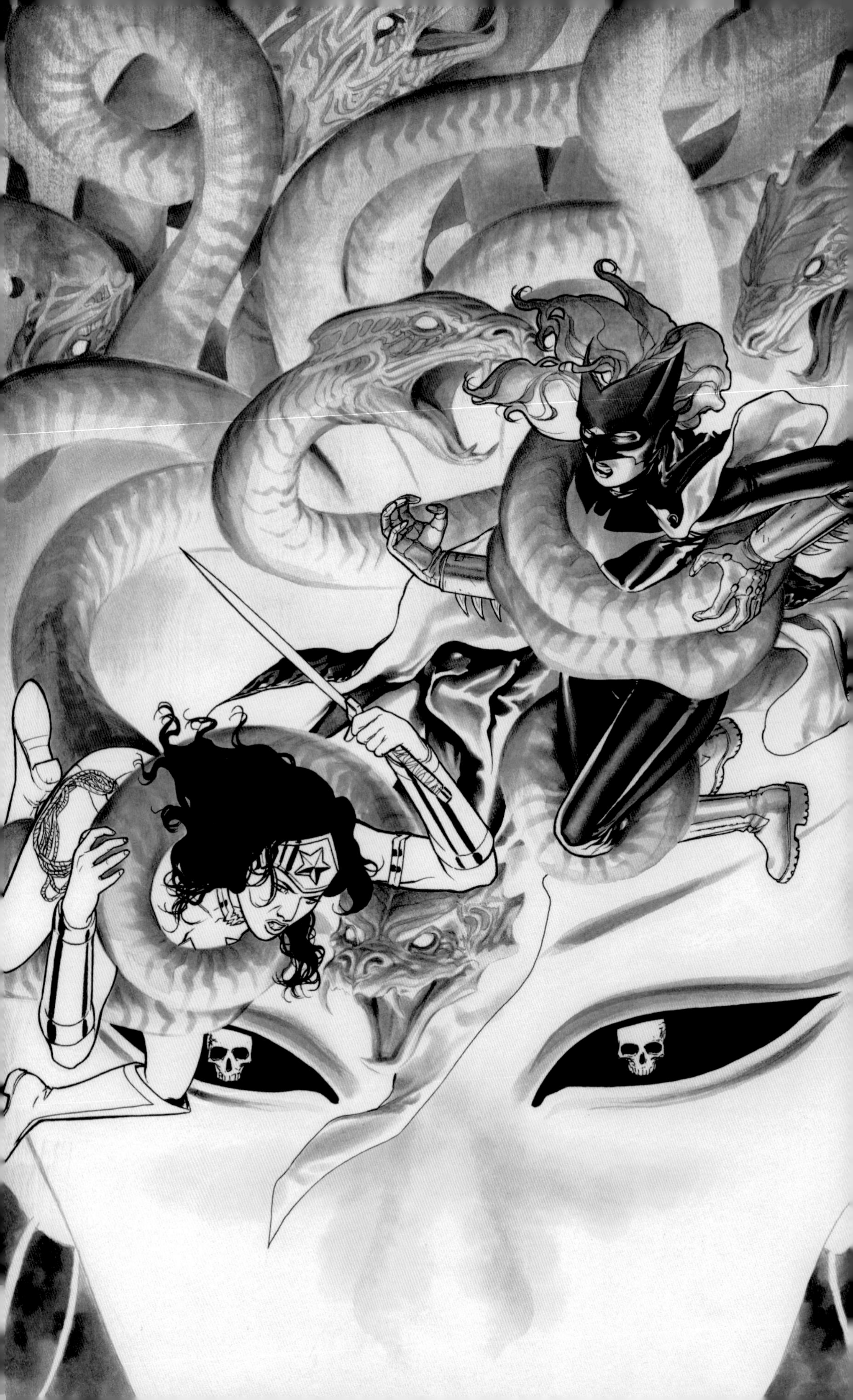

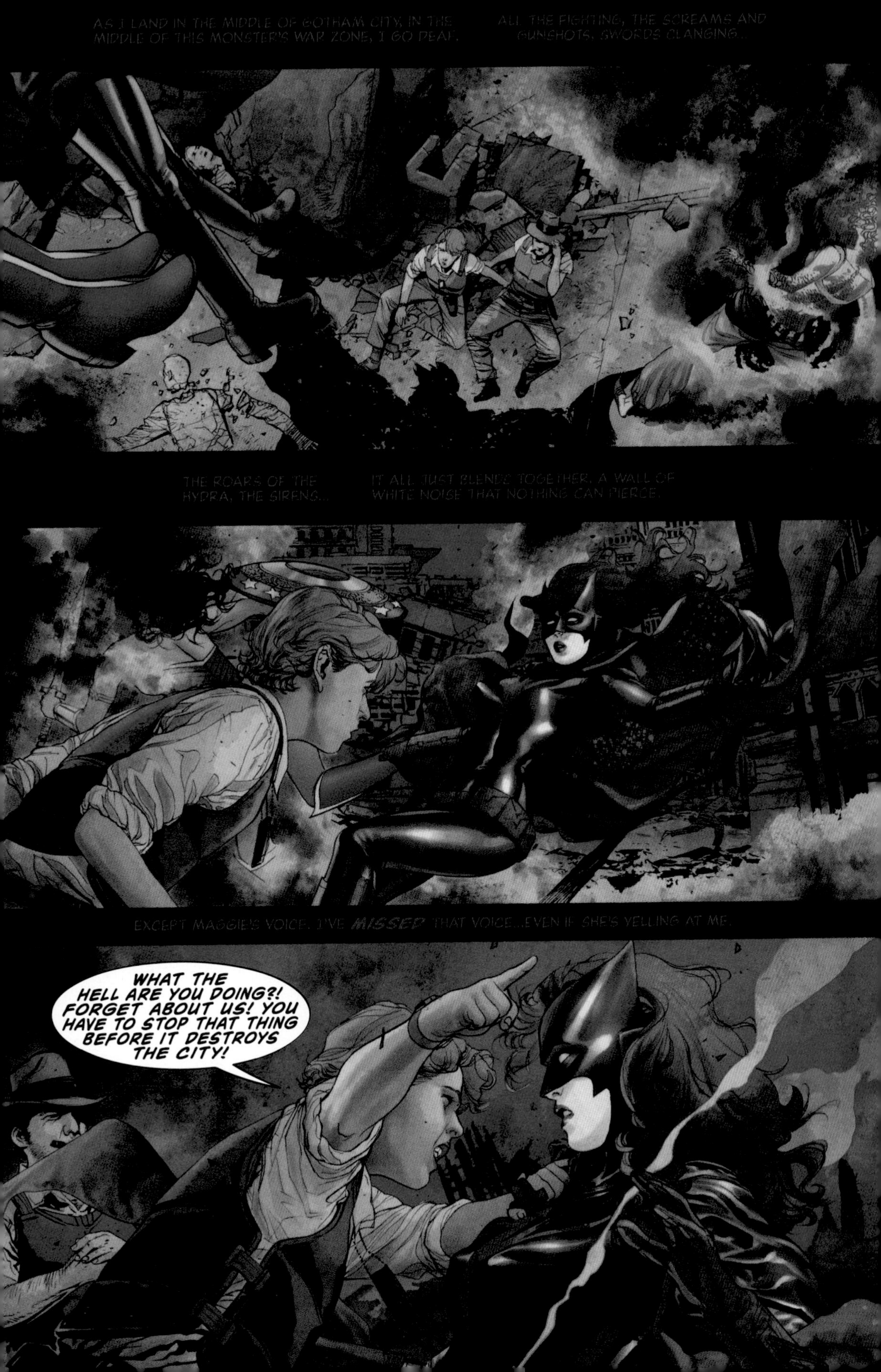
AS I LAND IN THE MIDDLE OF GOTHAM CITY, IN THE MIDDLE OF THIS MONSTER'S WAR ZONE, I GO DEAF.
ALL THE FIGHTING, THE SCREAMS AND GUNSHOTS, SWORDS CLANGING...
THE ROARS OF THE HYDRA, THE SIRENS...
IT ALL JUST BLENDS TOGETHER. A WALL OF WHITE NOISE THAT NOTHING CAN PIERCE.
EXCEPT MAGGIE'S VOICE. I'VE *MISSED* THAT VOICE...EVEN IF SHE'S YELLING AT ME.
WHAT THE HELL ARE YOU DOING?! FORGET ABOUT US! YOU HAVE TO STOP THAT THING BEFORE IT DESTROYS THE CITY!

I WADE IN. THE THUGS SMELL
LIKE A BAR. MALT LIQUOR AND
UNFILTERED CIGARETTES SWEATING
FROM THEIR PORES. BUT THERE IS SOME-
THING ELSE...AT FIRST, IT'S HARD TO PLACE.
WET AND DUSTY, ALL AT ONCE. *HUMID.*

THEN I REMEMBER TAKING DOWN AN OXY LAB OUTSIDE
THE CITY. THE GOON RUNNING IT HAD DOZENS OF SNAKES,
ALL CRAMMED INTO TINY TERRARIUMS. BALL PYTHONS AND
ANACONDAS AND BOA CONSTRICTORS.

THESE THUGS...THEY SMELL LIKE THAT   THEY HAVE MEDUSA'S
OXY LAB, LIKE THE REPTILE HOUSE AT   *STENCH* ALL OVER
THE ZOO, LIKE *SERPENTS.*   THEM.

          BUT SO MUCH MORE   ...OH MY GOD, IT'S
          OVERWHELMING IS THE   DESTROYING MY
          STENCH OF THAT GIANT   BUILDING...MY BASE-
          BEAST...*THE HYDRA*...   MENT...*EVERY-
                                             THING.*

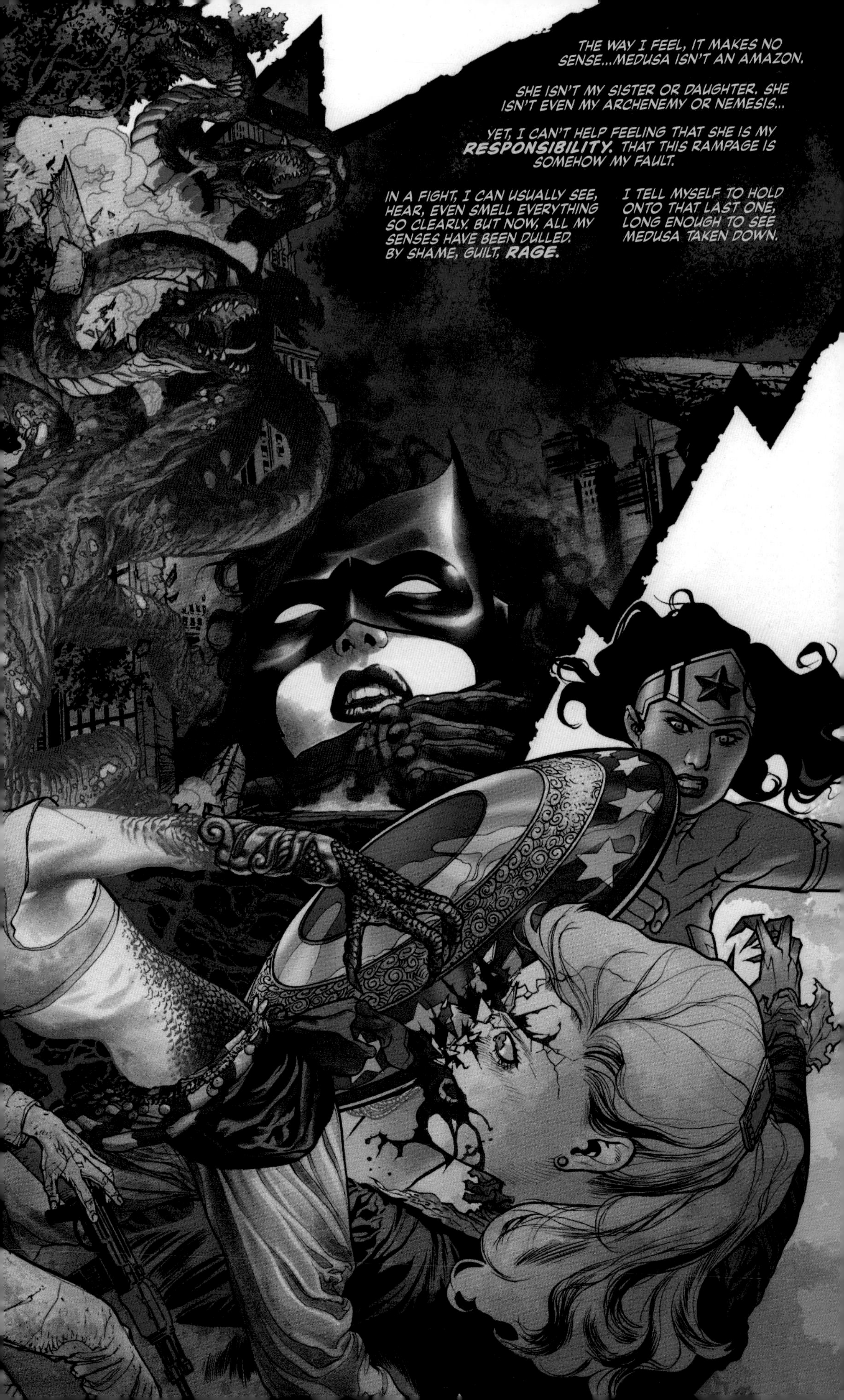
THE WAY I FEEL, IT MAKES NO SENSE...MEDUSA ISN'T AN AMAZON.
SHE ISN'T MY SISTER OR DAUGHTER. SHE ISN'T EVEN MY ARCHENEMY OR NEMESIS...
YET, I CAN'T HELP FEELING THAT SHE IS MY RESPONSIBILITY. THAT THIS RAMPAGE IS SOMEHOW MY FAULT.
IN A FIGHT, I CAN USUALLY SEE, HEAR, EVEN SMELL EVERYTHING SO CLEARLY. BUT NOW, ALL MY SENSES HAVE BEEN DULLED. BY SHAME, GUILT, RAGE.
I TELL MYSELF TO HOLD ONTO THAT LAST ONE, LONG ENOUGH TO SEE MEDUSA TAKEN DOWN.

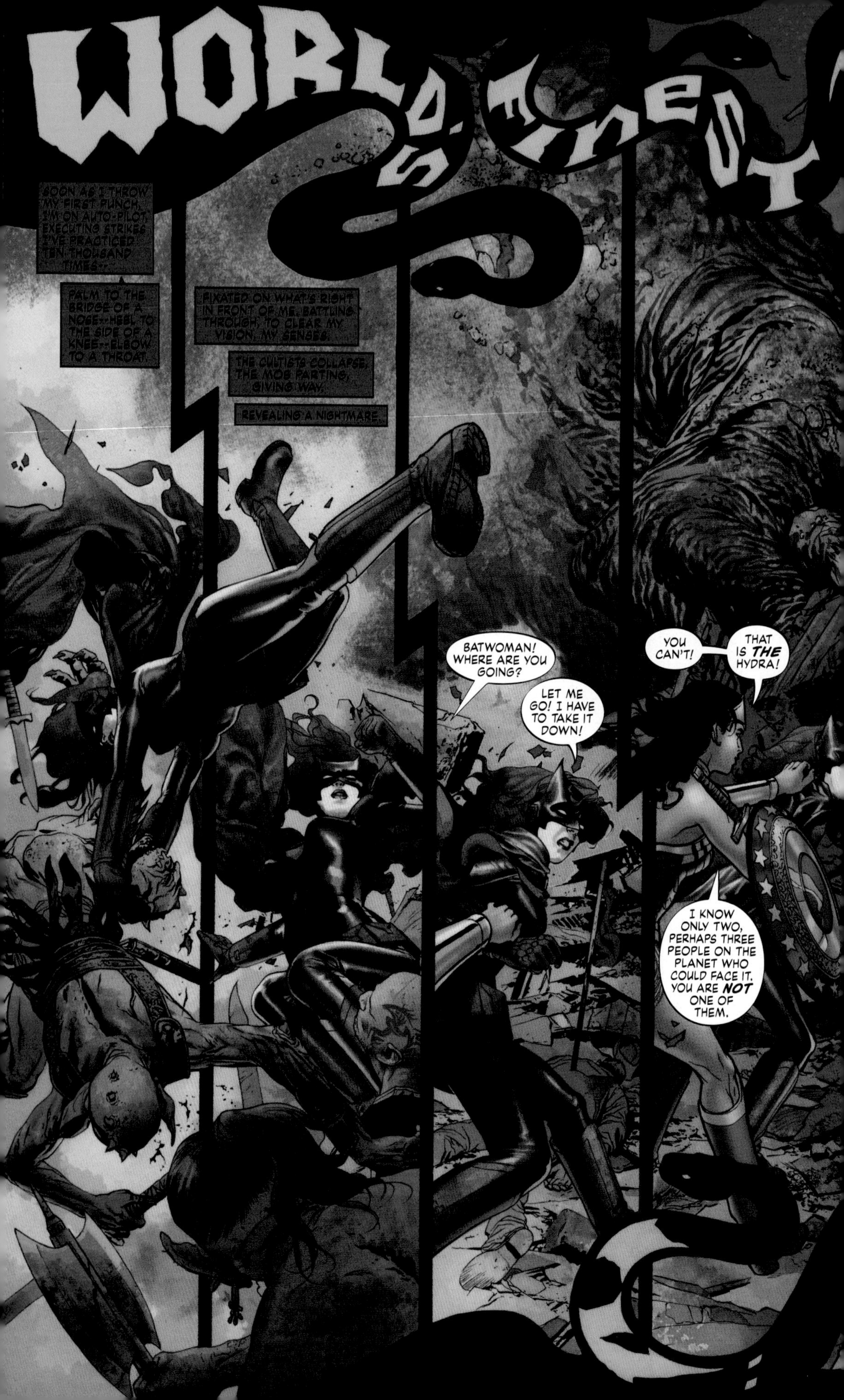
WORLD'S FINEST
SOON AS I THROW MY FIRST PUNCH, I'M ON AUTO-PILOT, EXECUTING STRIKES I'VE PRACTICED TEN THOUSAND TIMES--
PALM TO THE BRIDGE OF A NOSE--HEEL TO THE SIDE OF A KNEE--ELBOW TO A THROAT.
FIXATED ON WHAT'S RIGHT IN FRONT OF ME, BATTLING THROUGH, TO CLEAR MY VISION, MY SENSES.
THE CULTISTS COLLAPSE, THE MOB PARTING, GIVING WAY.
REVEALING A NIGHTMARE.
BATWOMAN! WHERE ARE YOU GOING?
LET ME GO! I HAVE TO TAKE IT DOWN!
YOU CAN'T!
THAT IS *THE* HYDRA!
I KNOW ONLY TWO, PERHAPS THREE PEOPLE ON THE PLANET WHO COULD FACE IT. YOU ARE *NOT* ONE OF THEM.

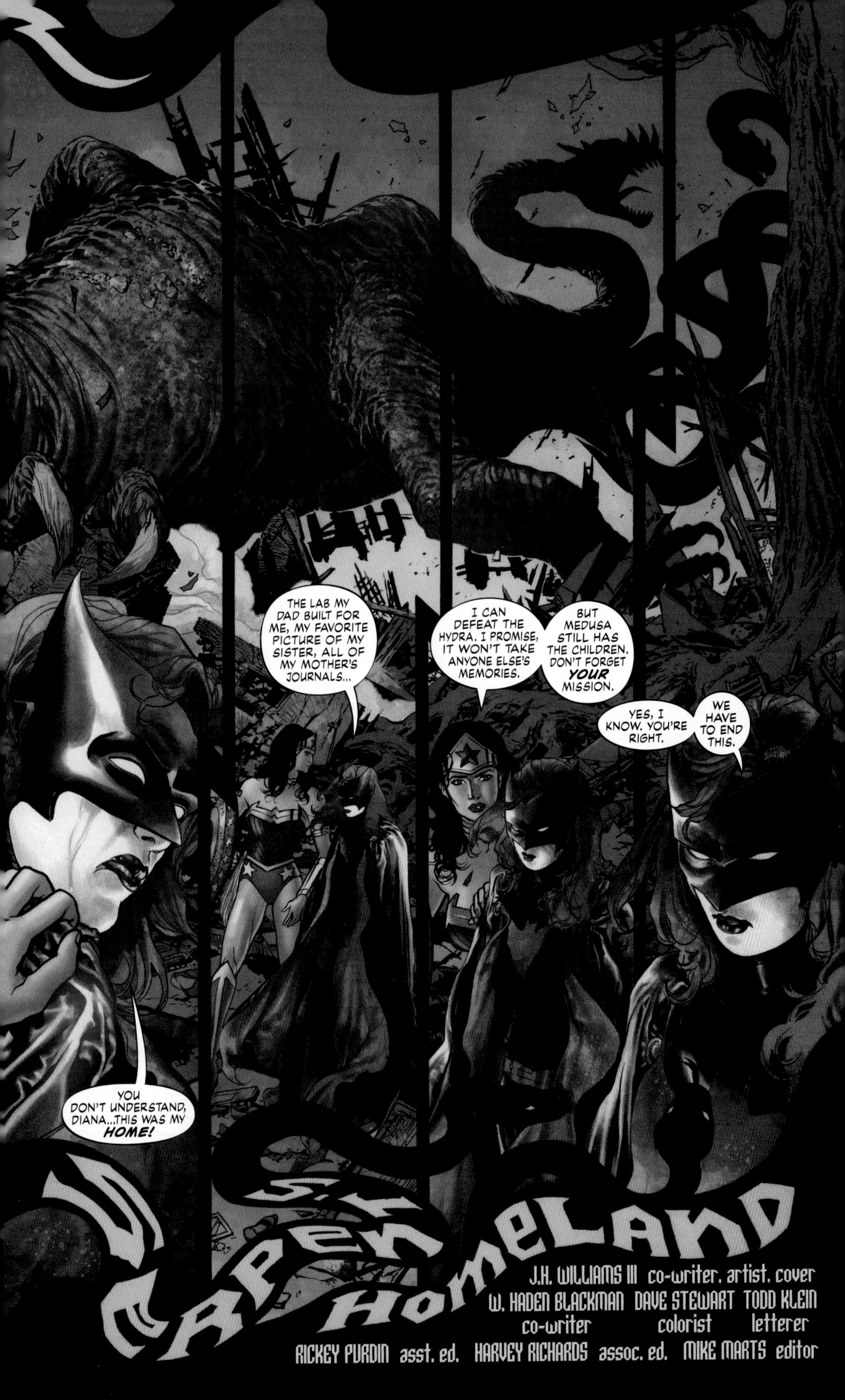
YOU DON'T UNDERSTAND, DIANA...THIS WAS MY *HOME!*
THE LAB MY DAD BUILT FOR ME, MY FAVORITE PICTURE OF MY SISTER, ALL OF MY MOTHER'S JOURNALS...
I CAN DEFEAT THE HYDRA. I PROMISE, IT WON'T TAKE ANYONE ELSE'S MEMORIES.
BUT MEDUSA STILL HAS THE CHILDREN. DON'T FORGET *YOUR* MISSION.
YES, I KNOW. YOU'RE RIGHT.
WE HAVE TO END THIS.
J.H. WILLIAMS III co-writer, artist, cover
W. HADEN BLACKMAN co-writer
DAVE STEWART colorist
TODD KLEIN letterer
RICKEY PURDIN asst. ed. HARVEY RICHARDS assoc. ed. MIKE MARTS editor

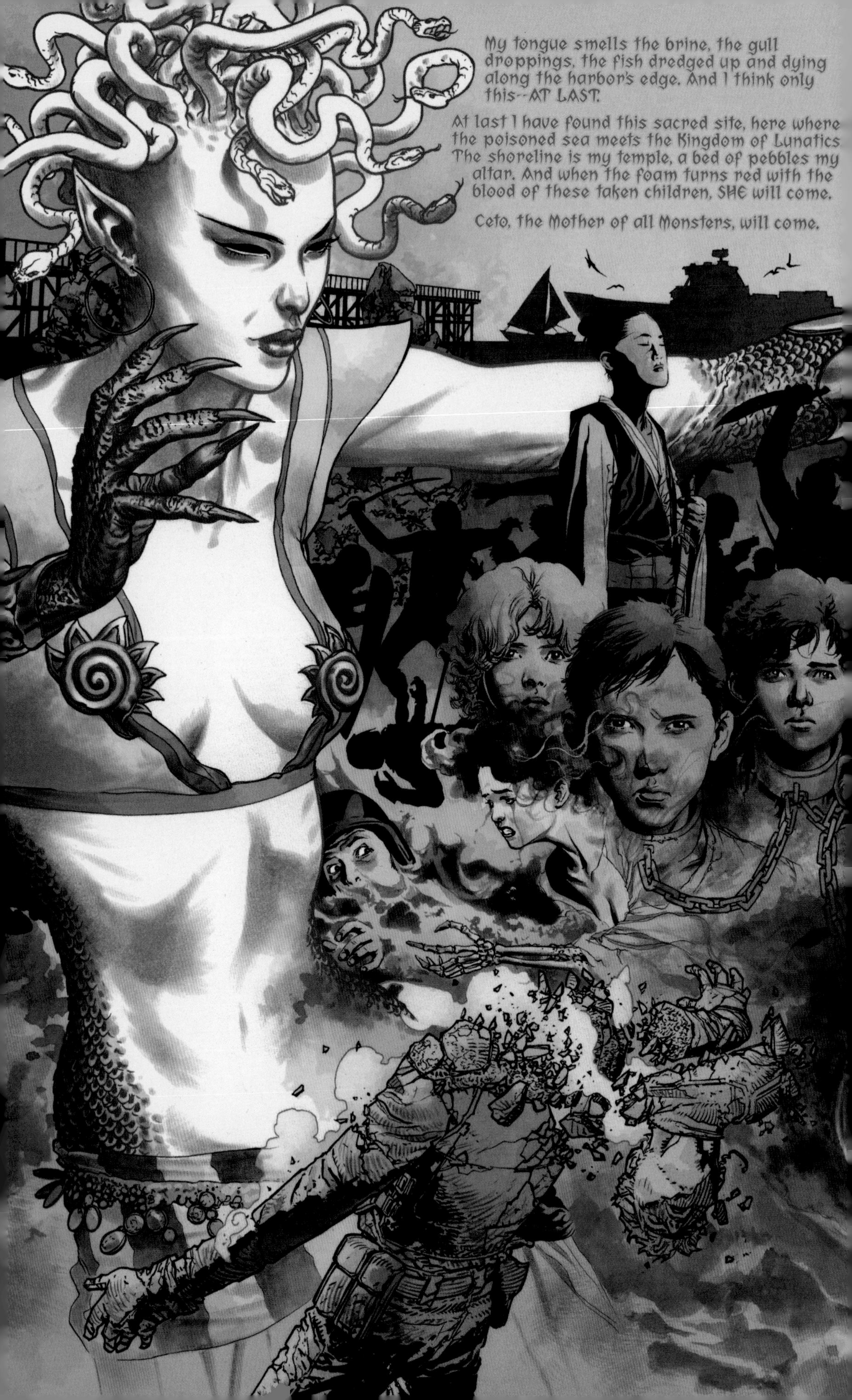
My tongue smells the brine, the gull droppings, the fish dredged up and dying along the harbor's edge. And I think only this--AT LAST.
At last I have found this sacred site, here where the poisoned sea meets the Kingdom of Lunatics The shoreline is my temple, a bed of pebbles my altar. And when the foam turns red with the blood of these taken children, SHE will come.
Ceto, the Mother of all Monsters, will come.

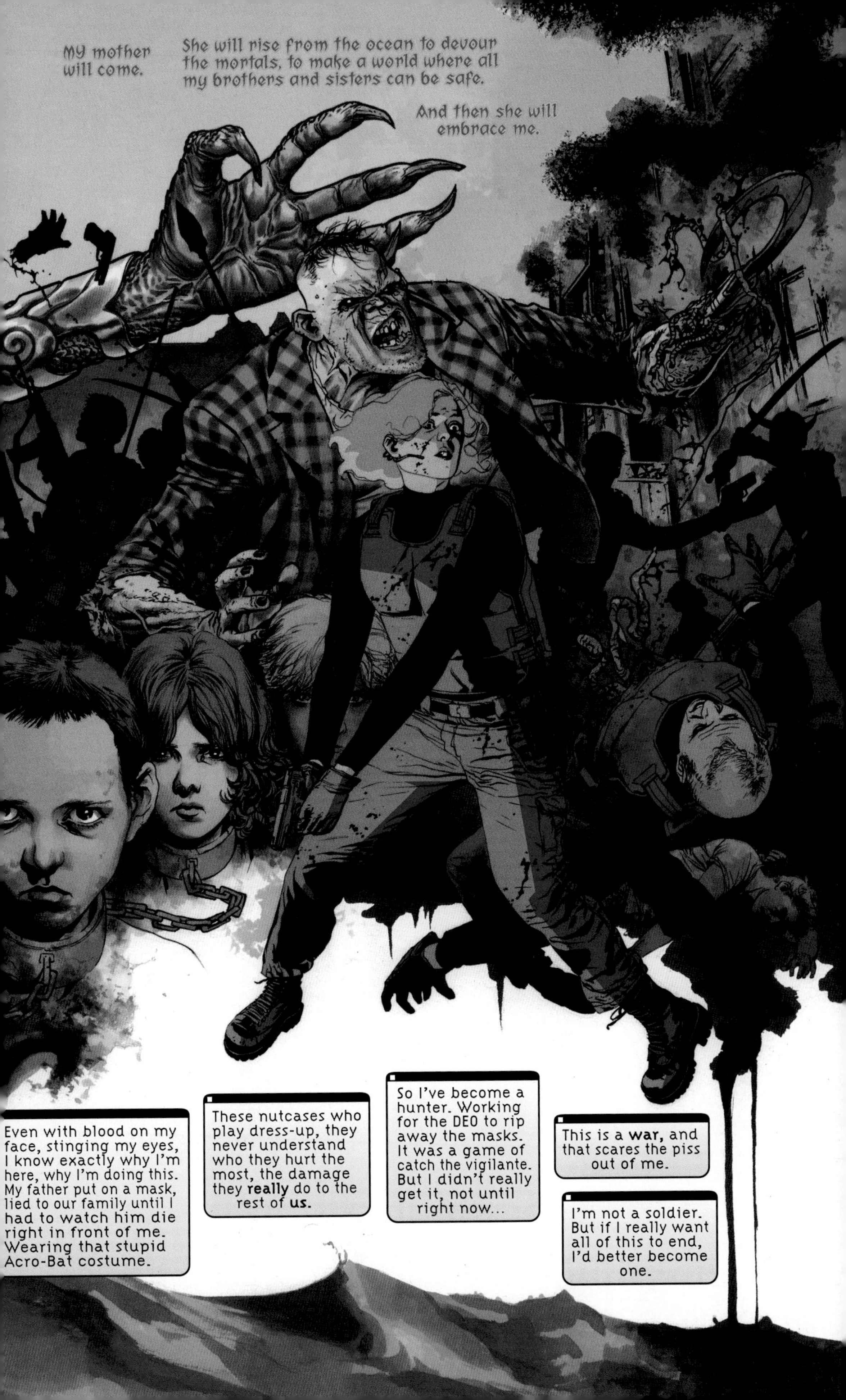
My mother will come.
She will rise from the ocean to devour the mortals, to make a world where all my brothers and sisters can be safe.
And then she will embrace me.
Even with blood on my face, stinging my eyes, I know exactly why I'm here, why I'm doing this. My father put on a mask, lied to our family until I had to watch him die right in front of me. Wearing that stupid Acro-Bat costume.
These nutcases who play dress-up, they never understand who they hurt the most, the damage they **really** do to the rest of **us.**
So I've become a hunter. Working for the DEO to rip away the masks. It was a game of catch the vigilante. But I didn't really get it, not until right now...
This is a **war,** and that scares the piss out of me.
I'm not a soldier. But if I really want all of this to end, I'd better become one.

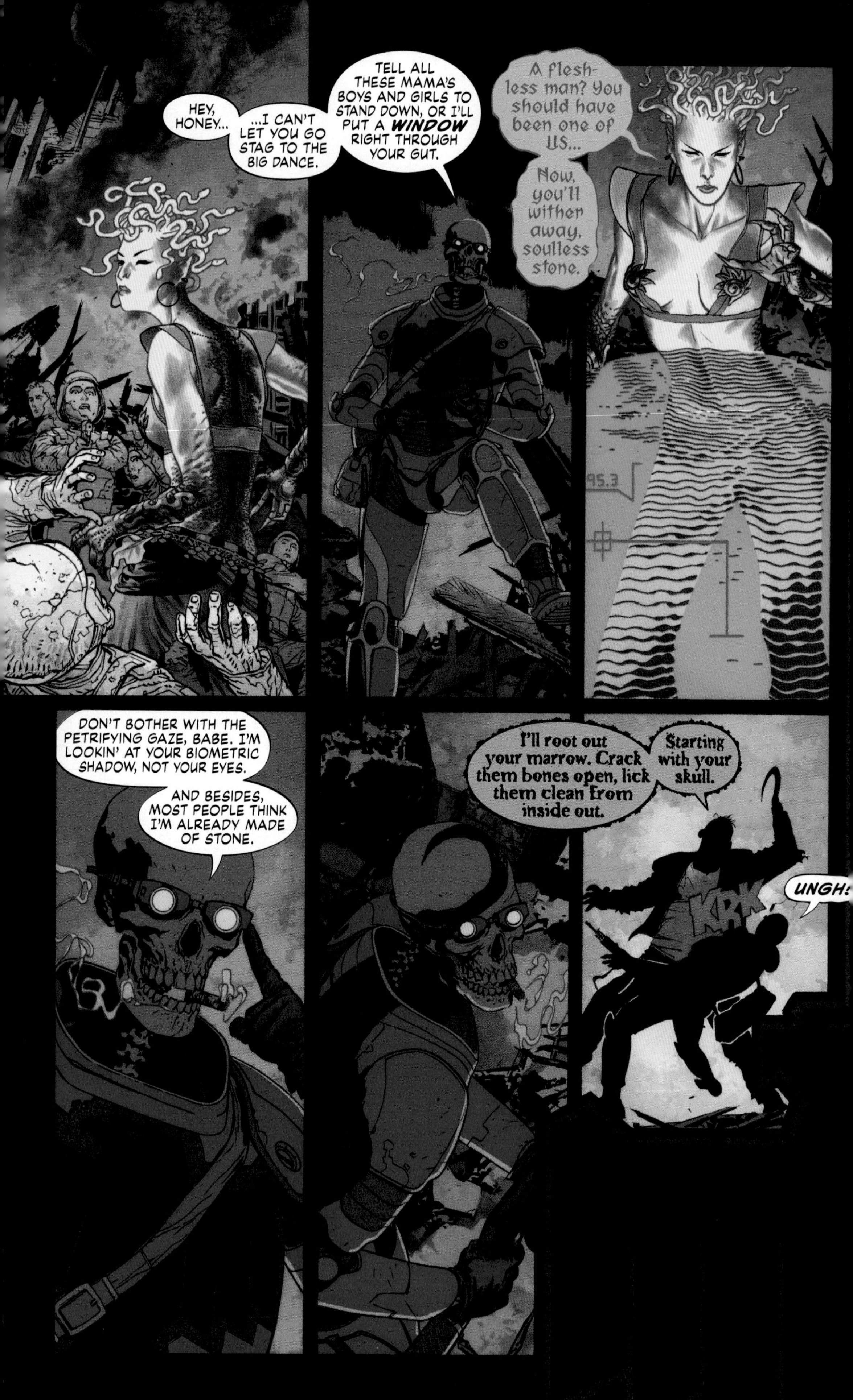
HEY, HONEY...
...I CAN'T LET YOU GO STAG TO THE BIG DANCE.
TELL ALL THESE MAMA'S BOYS AND GIRLS TO STAND DOWN, OR I'LL PUT A WINDOW RIGHT THROUGH YOUR GUT.
A flesh-less man? You should have been one of US...
Now, you'll wither away, soulless stone.
95.3
DON'T BOTHER WITH THE PETRIFYING GAZE, BABE. I'M LOOKIN' AT YOUR BIOMETRIC SHADOW, NOT YOUR EYES.
AND BESIDES, MOST PEOPLE THINK I'M ALREADY MADE OF STONE.
I'll root out your marrow. Crack them bones open, lick them clean from inside out.
Starting with your skull.
KRK
UNGH!

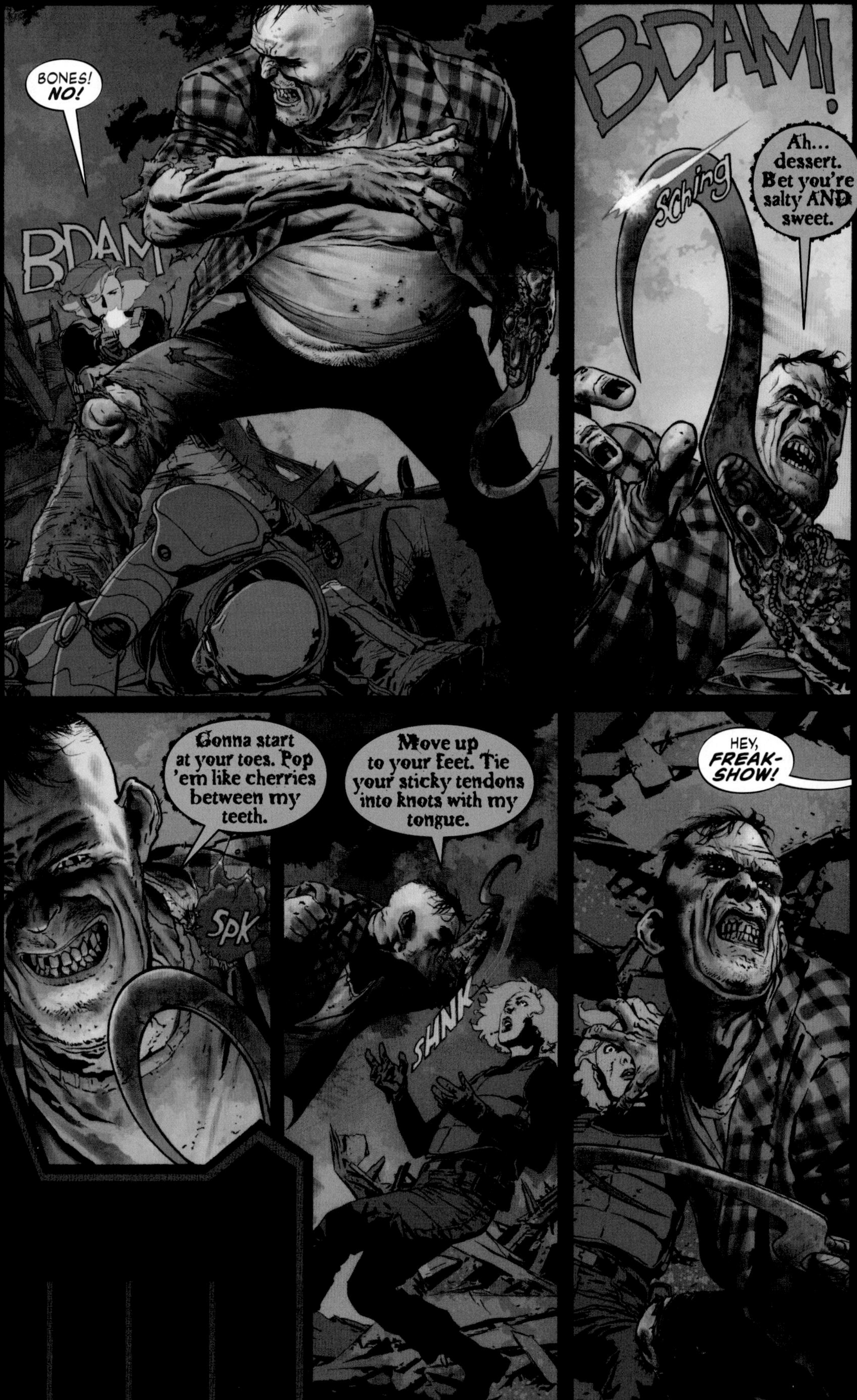
BONES! NO!
BDAM
BDAM!
Sching
Ah... dessert. Bet you're salty AND sweet.
Gonna start at your toes. Pop 'em like cherries between my teeth.
Spk
Move up to your feet. Tie your sticky tendons into knots with my tongue.
SHNK
HEY, FREAK-SHOW!

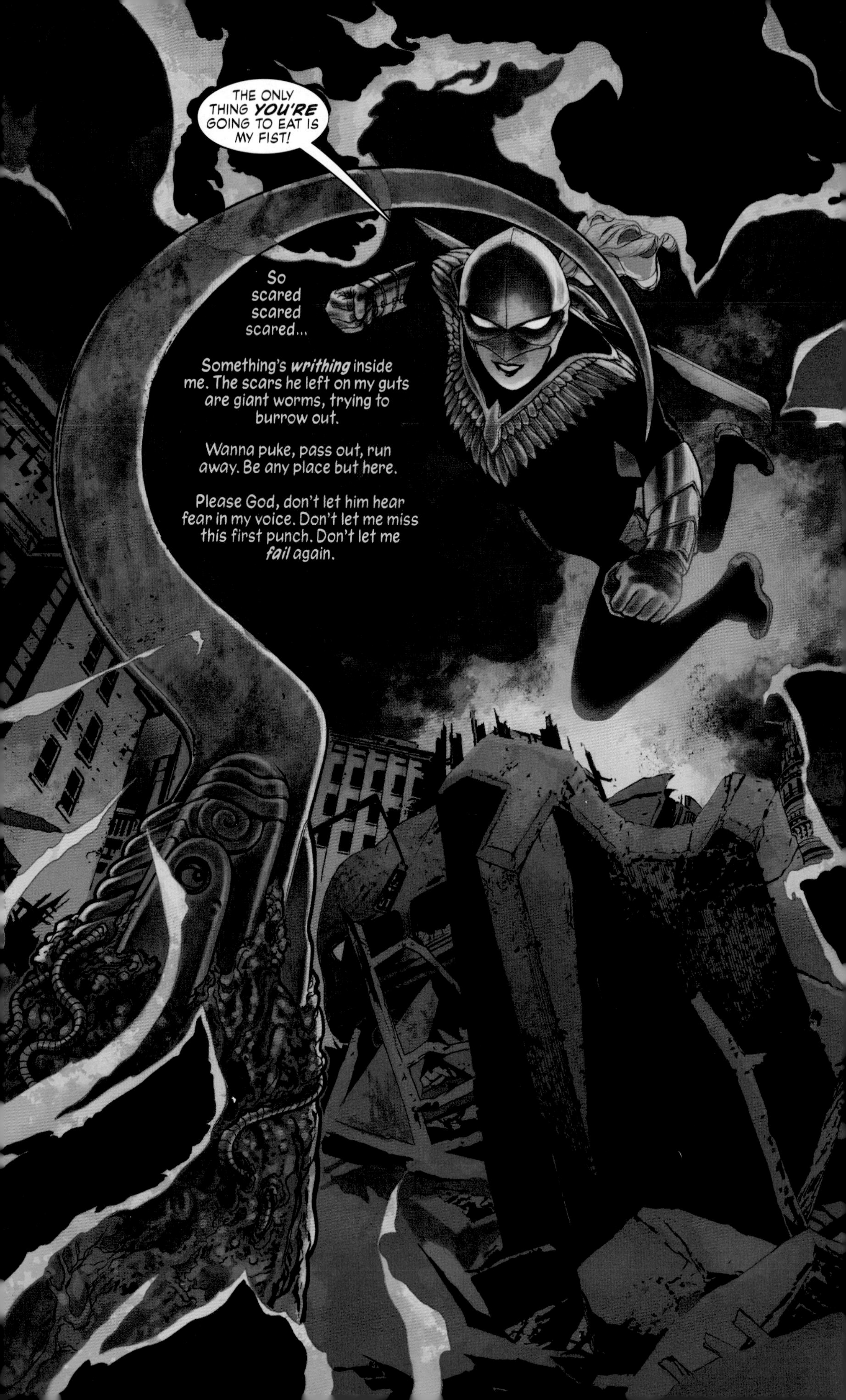

THE ONLY THING ***YOU'RE*** GOING TO EAT IS MY FIST!
So scared scared scared...
Something's ***writing*** inside me. The scars he left on my guts are giant worms, trying to burrow out.
Wanna puke, pass out, run away. Be any place but here.
Please God, don't let him hear fear in my voice. Don't let me miss this first punch. Don't let me *fail* again.

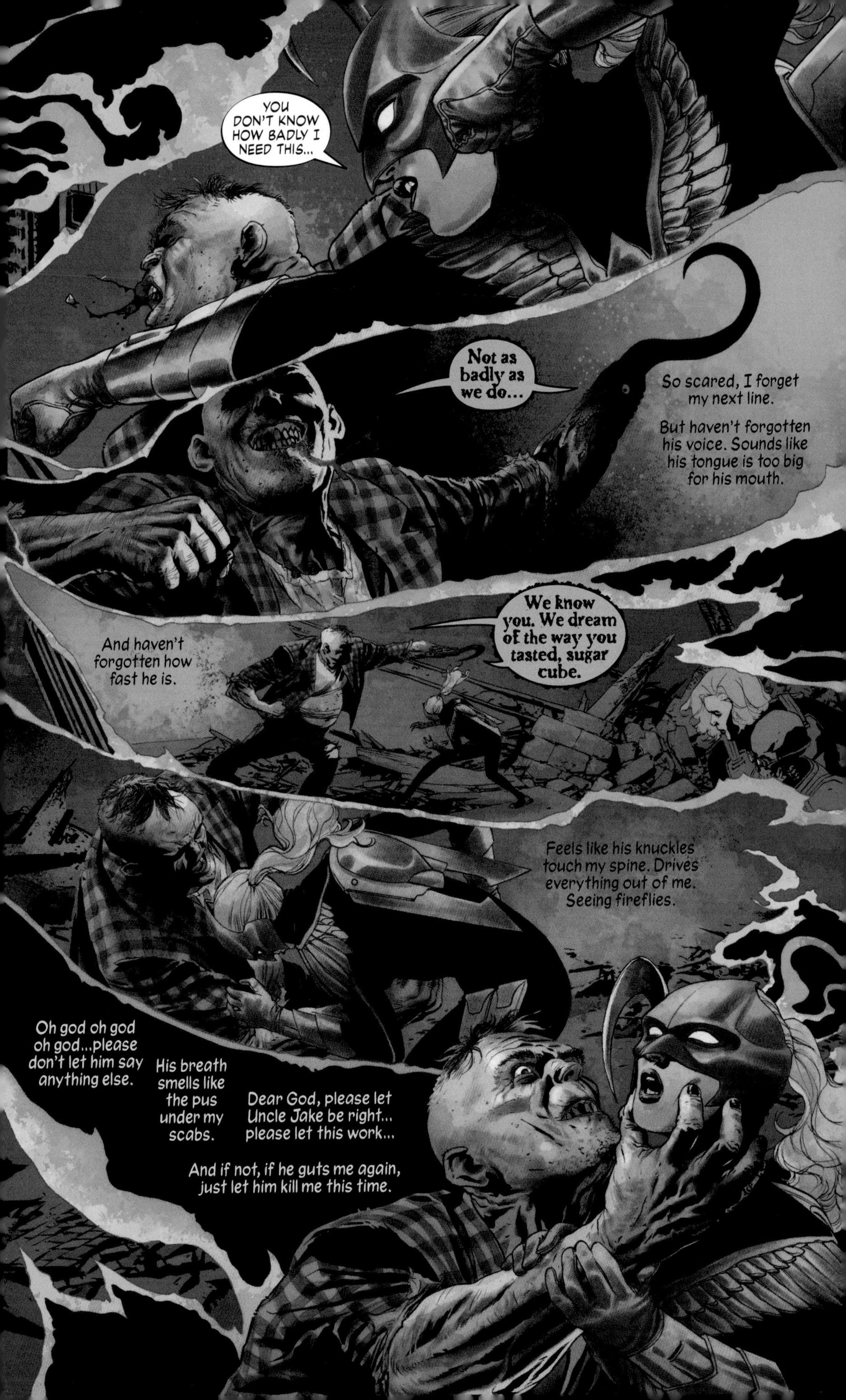
YOU DON'T KNOW HOW BADLY I NEED THIS...
Not as badly as we do...
So scared, I forget my next line.
But haven't forgotten his voice. Sounds like his tongue is too big for his mouth.
And haven't forgotten how fast he is.
We know you. We dream of the way you tasted, sugar cube.
Feels like his knuckles touch my spine. Drives everything out of me. Seeing fireflies.
Oh god oh god oh god...please don't let him say anything else.
His breath smells like the pus under my scabs.
Dear God, please let Uncle Jake be right... please let this work...
And if not, if he guts me again, just let him kill me this time.

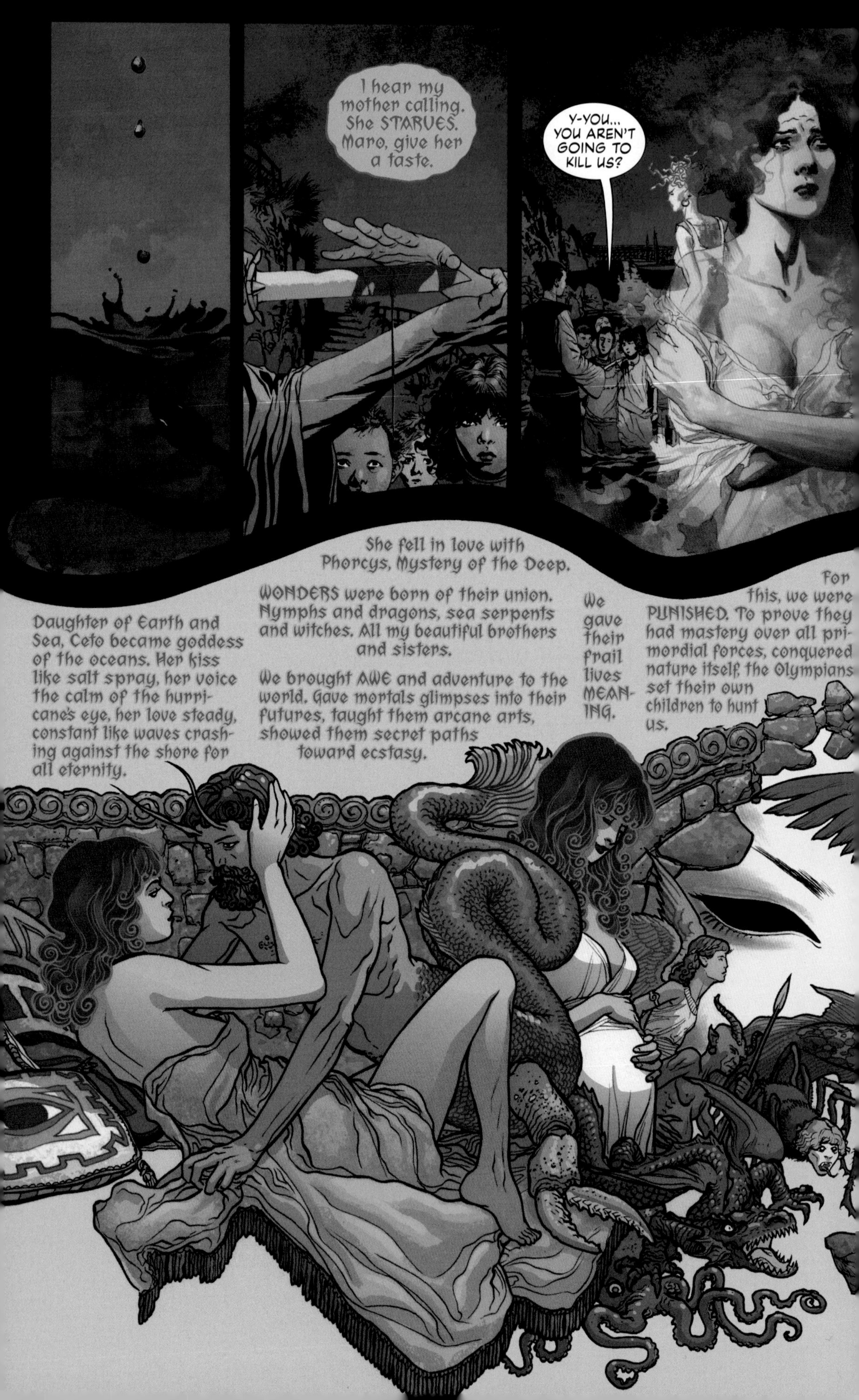
I hear my mother calling. She STARVES. Maro, give her a taste.
Y-YOU... YOU AREN'T GOING TO KILL US?
She fell in love with Phorcys, Mystery of the Deep.
Daughter of Earth and Sea, Ceto became goddess of the oceans. Her kiss like salt spray, her voice the calm of the hurricane's eye, her love steady, constant like waves crashing against the shore for all eternity.
WONDERS were born of their union. Nymphs and dragons, sea serpents and witches. All my beautiful brothers and sisters.
We brought AWE and adventure to the world. Gave mortals glimpses into their futures, taught them arcane arts, showed them secret paths toward ecstasy.
We gave their frail lives MEANING.
For this, we were PUNISHED. To prove they had mastery over all primordial forces, conquered nature itself, the Olympians set their own children to hunt us.

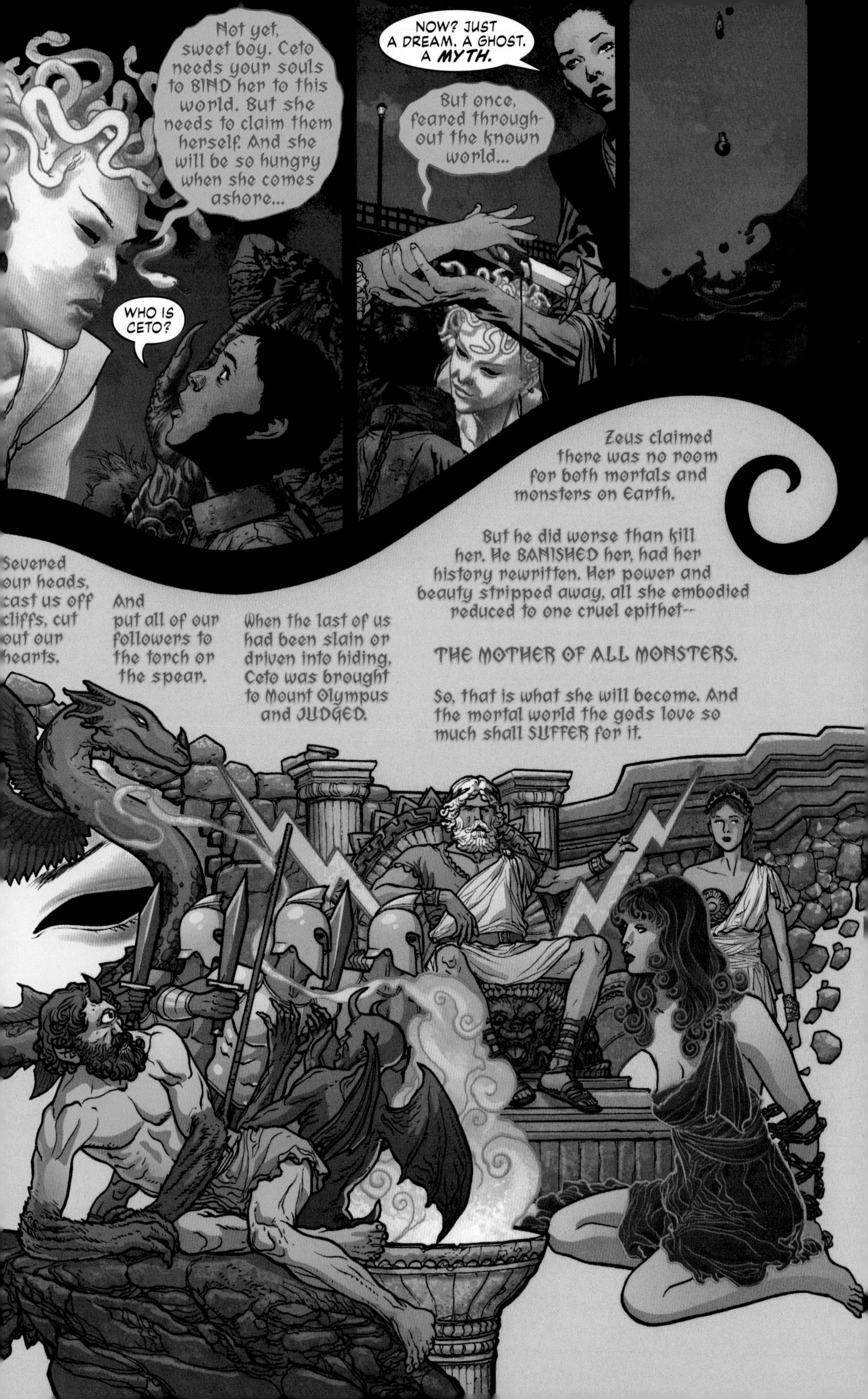
Not yet, sweet boy. Ceto needs your souls to BIND her to this world. But she needs to claim them herself. And she will be so hungry when she comes ashore...
WHO IS CETO?
NOW? JUST A DREAM. A GHOST. A MYTH.
But once, feared throughout the known world...
Zeus claimed there was no room for both mortals and monsters on Earth.
But he did worse than kill her. He BANISHED her, had her history rewritten. Her power and beauty stripped away, all she embodied reduced to one cruel epithet--
THE MOTHER OF ALL MONSTERS.
Severed our heads, cast us off cliffs, cut out our hearts.
And put all of our followers to the torch or the spear.
When the last of us had been slain or driven into hiding, Ceto was brought to Mount Olympus and JUDGED.
So, that is what she will become. And the mortal world the gods love so much shall SUFFER for it.

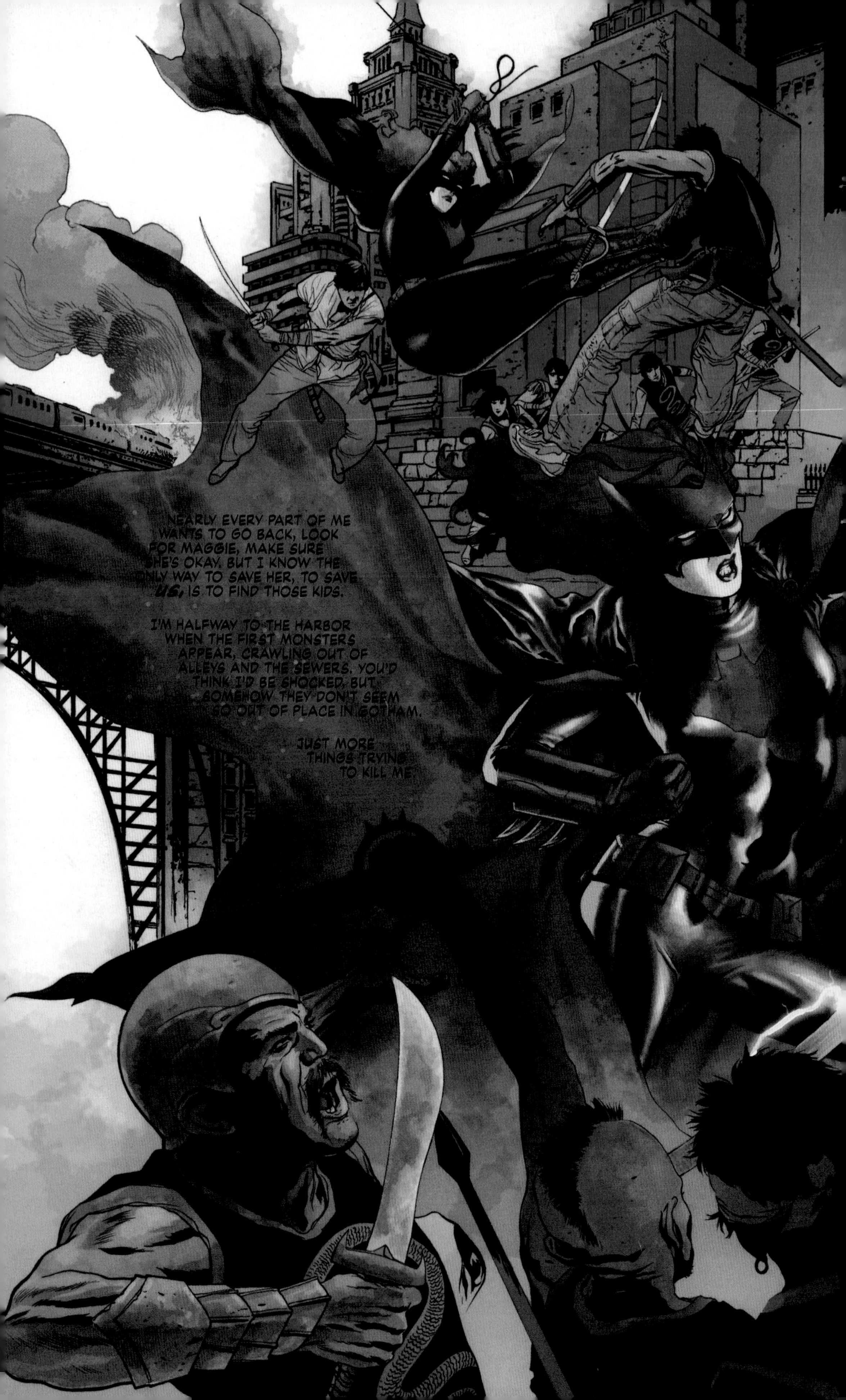
NEARLY EVERY PART OF ME WANTS TO GO BACK, LOOK FOR MAGGIE, MAKE SURE SHE'S OKAY. BUT I KNOW THE ONLY WAY TO SAVE HER, TO SAVE US, IS TO FIND THOSE KIDS.
I'M HALFWAY TO THE HARBOR WHEN THE FIRST MONSTERS APPEAR, CRAWLING OUT OF ALLEYS AND THE SEWERS. YOU'D THINK I'D BE SHOCKED, BUT SOMEHOW THEY DON'T SEEM SO OUT OF PLACE IN GOTHAM.
JUST MORE THINGS TRYING TO KILL ME.

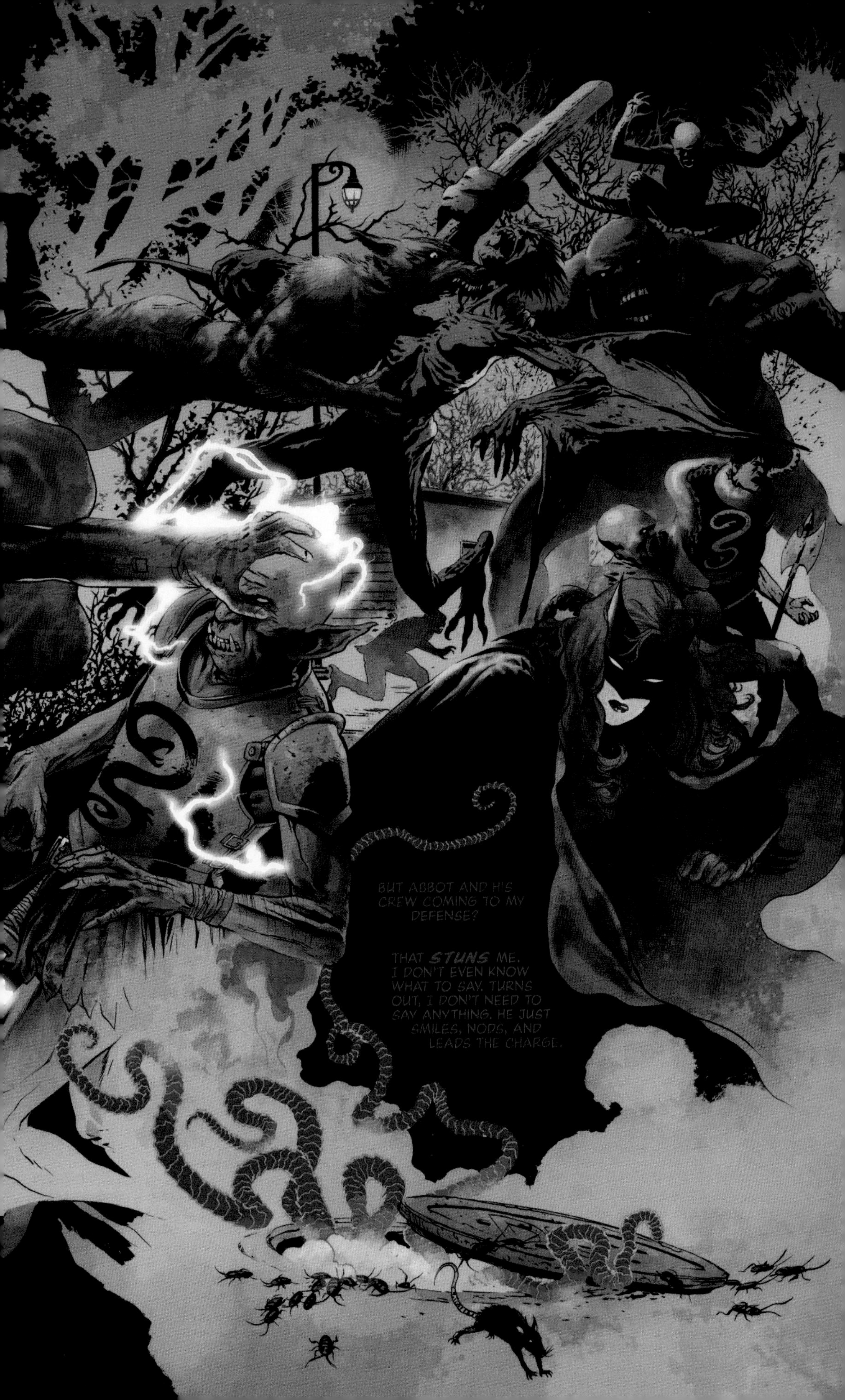
BUT ABBOT AND HIS CREW COMING TO MY DEFENSE?
THAT STUNS ME. I DON'T EVEN KNOW WHAT TO SAY. TURNS OUT, I DON'T NEED TO SAY ANYTHING. HE JUST SMILES, NODS, AND LEADS THE CHARGE.

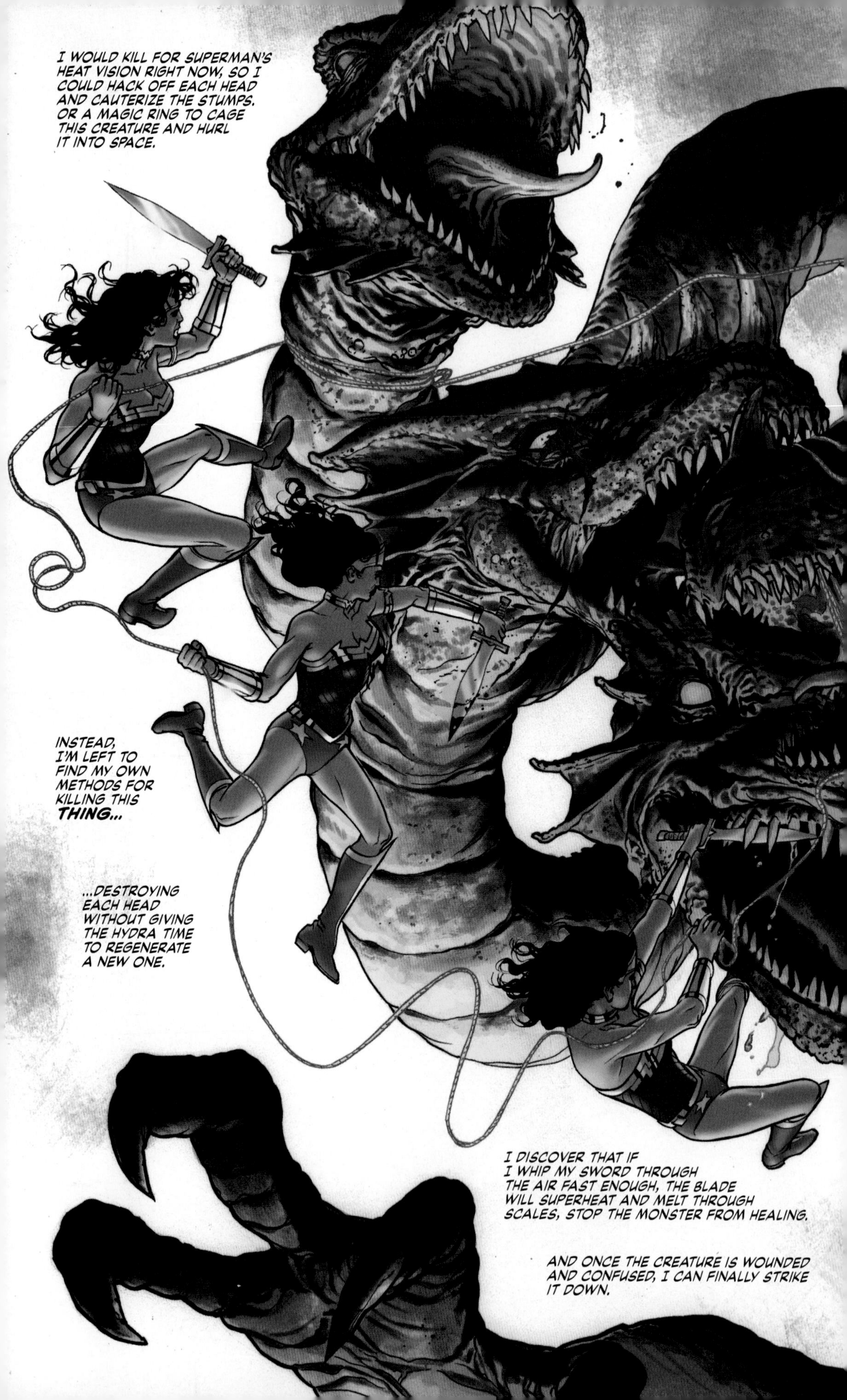
I WOULD KILL FOR SUPERMAN'S HEAT VISION RIGHT NOW, SO I COULD HACK OFF EACH HEAD AND CAUTERIZE THE STUMPS. OR A MAGIC RING TO CAGE THIS CREATURE AND HURL IT INTO SPACE.
INSTEAD, I'M LEFT TO FIND MY OWN METHODS FOR KILLING THIS **THING...**
...DESTROYING EACH HEAD WITHOUT GIVING THE HYDRA TIME TO REGENERATE A NEW ONE.
I DISCOVER THAT IF I WHIP MY SWORD THROUGH THE AIR FAST ENOUGH, THE BLADE WILL SUPERHEAT AND MELT THROUGH SCALES, STOP THE MONSTER FROM HEALING.
AND ONCE THE CREATURE IS WOUNDED AND CONFUSED, I CAN FINALLY STRIKE IT DOWN.

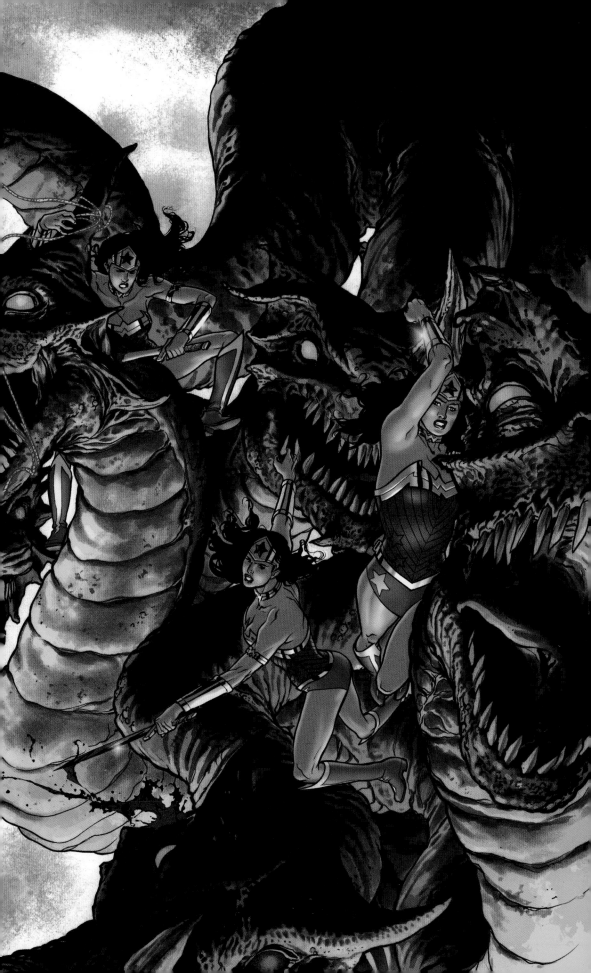

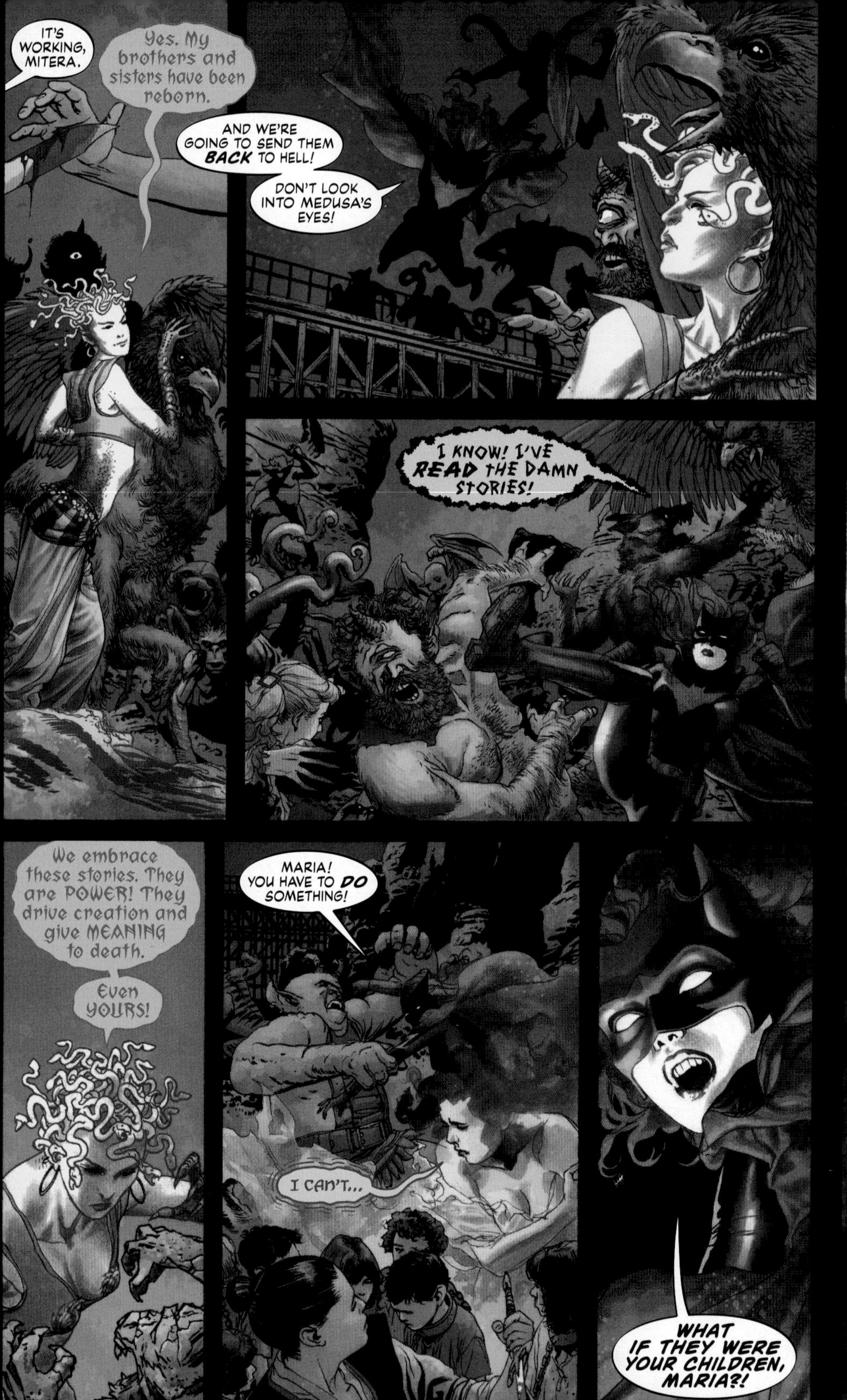
IT'S WORKING, MITERA.
Yes. My brothers and sisters have been reborn.
AND WE'RE GOING TO SEND THEM BACK TO HELL!
DON'T LOOK INTO MEDUSA'S EYES!
I KNOW! I'VE READ THE DAMN STORIES!
We embrace these stories. They are POWER! They drive creation and give MEANING to death.
Even YOURS!
MARIA! YOU HAVE TO DO SOMETHING!
I CAN'T...
WHAT IF THEY WERE YOUR CHILDREN, MARIA?!

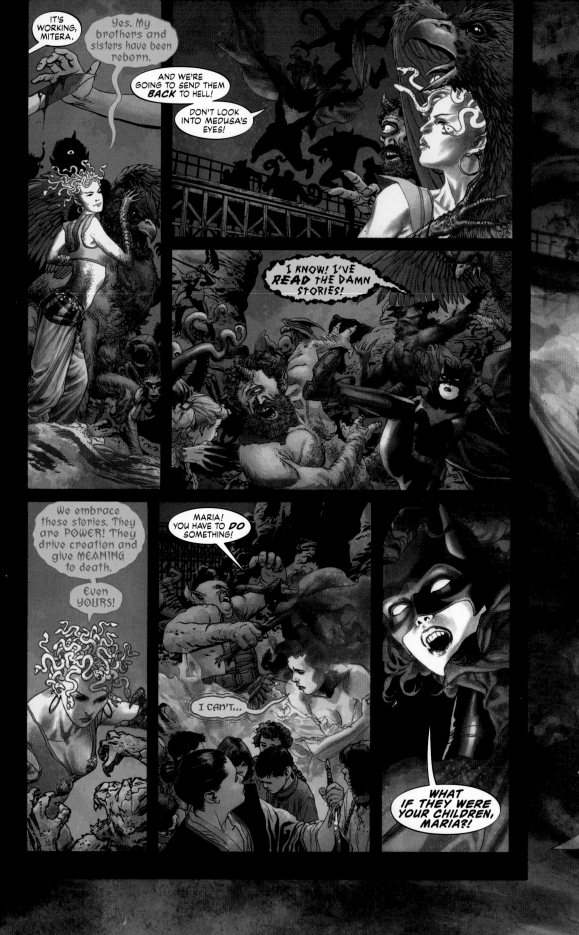

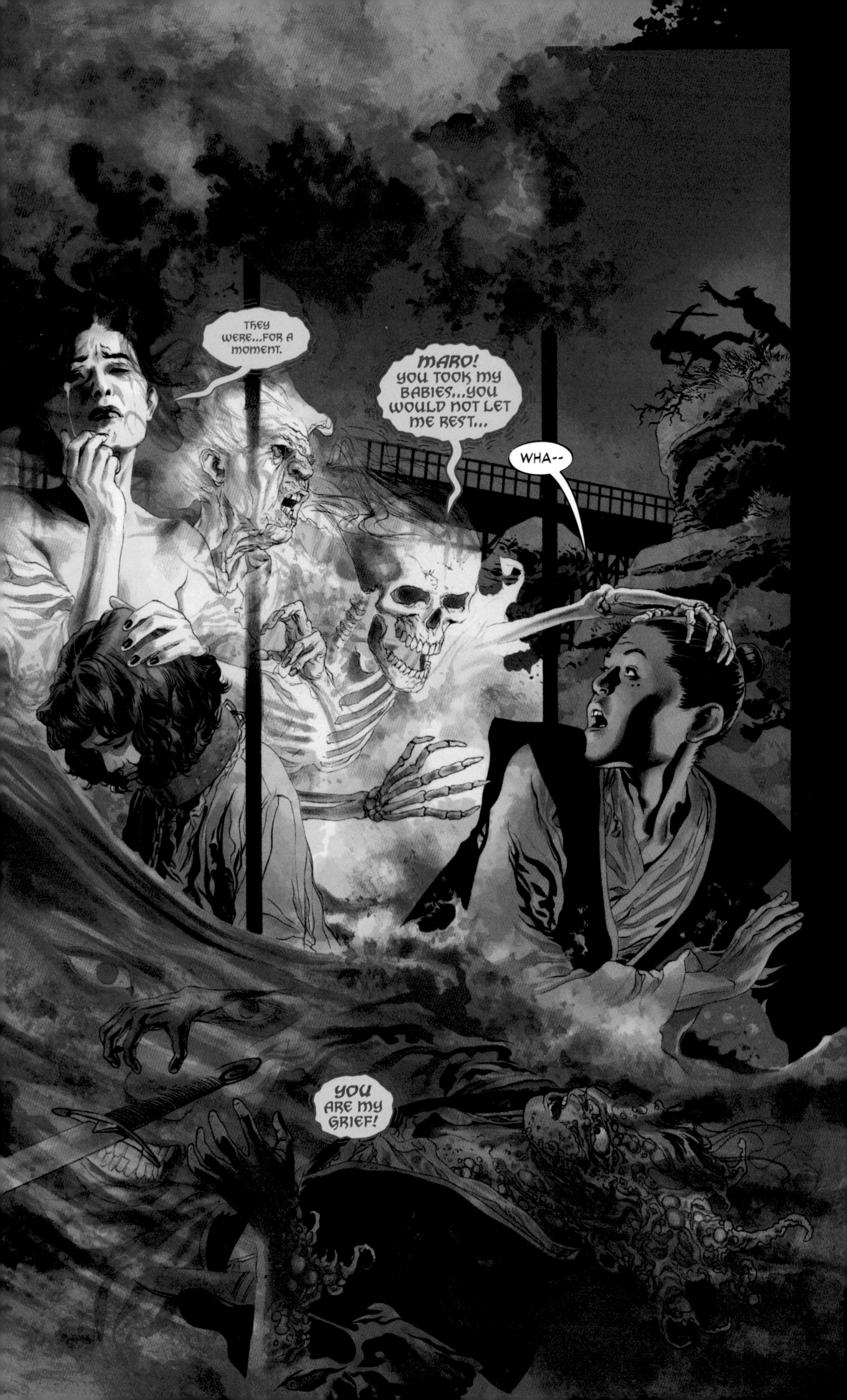
THEY WERE...FOR A MOMENT.
MARO! YOU TOOK MY BABIES...YOU WOULD NOT LET ME REST...
WHA--
YOU ARE MY GRIEF!

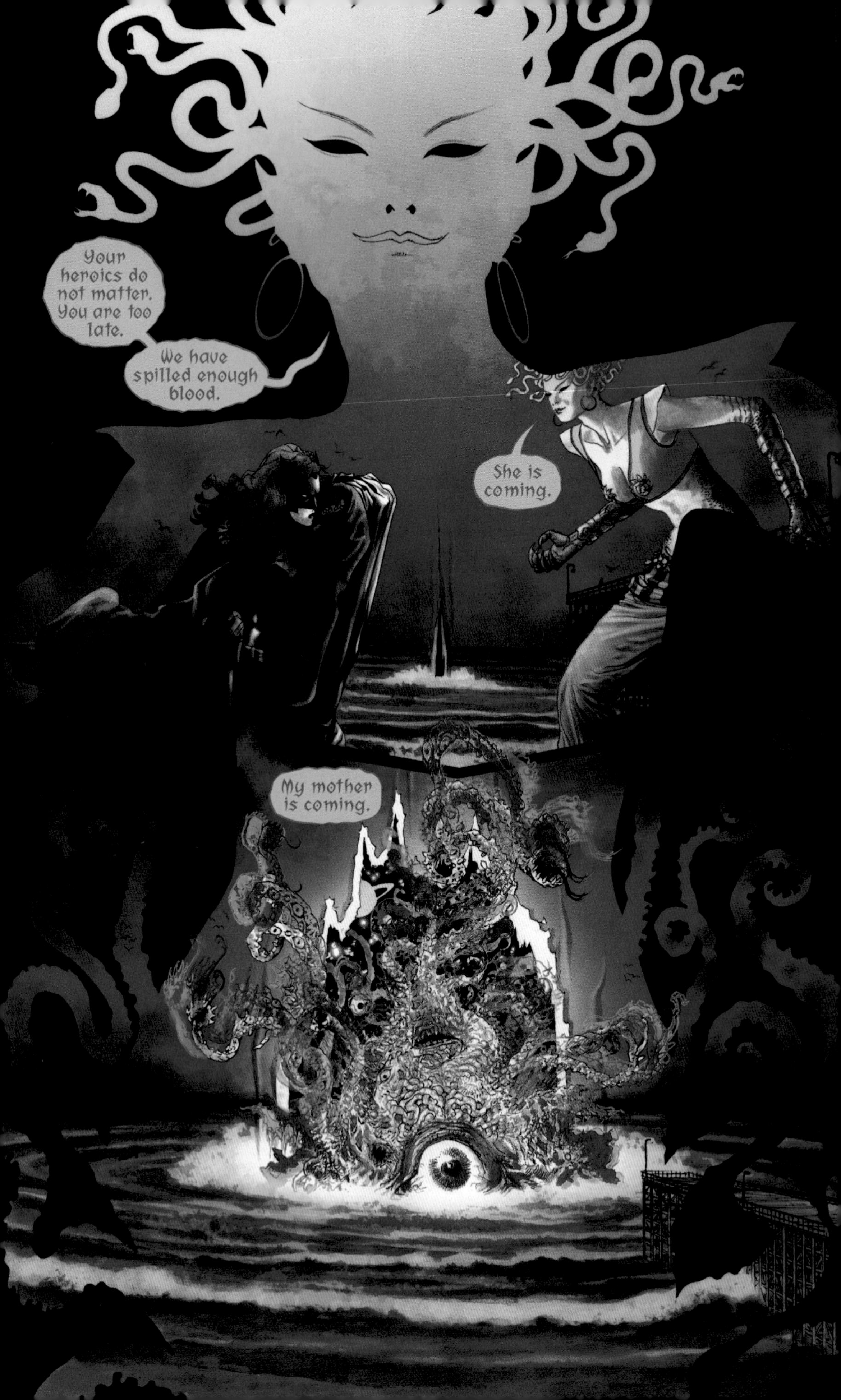
Your heroics do not matter. You are too late.
We have spilled enough blood.
She is coming.
My mother is coming.

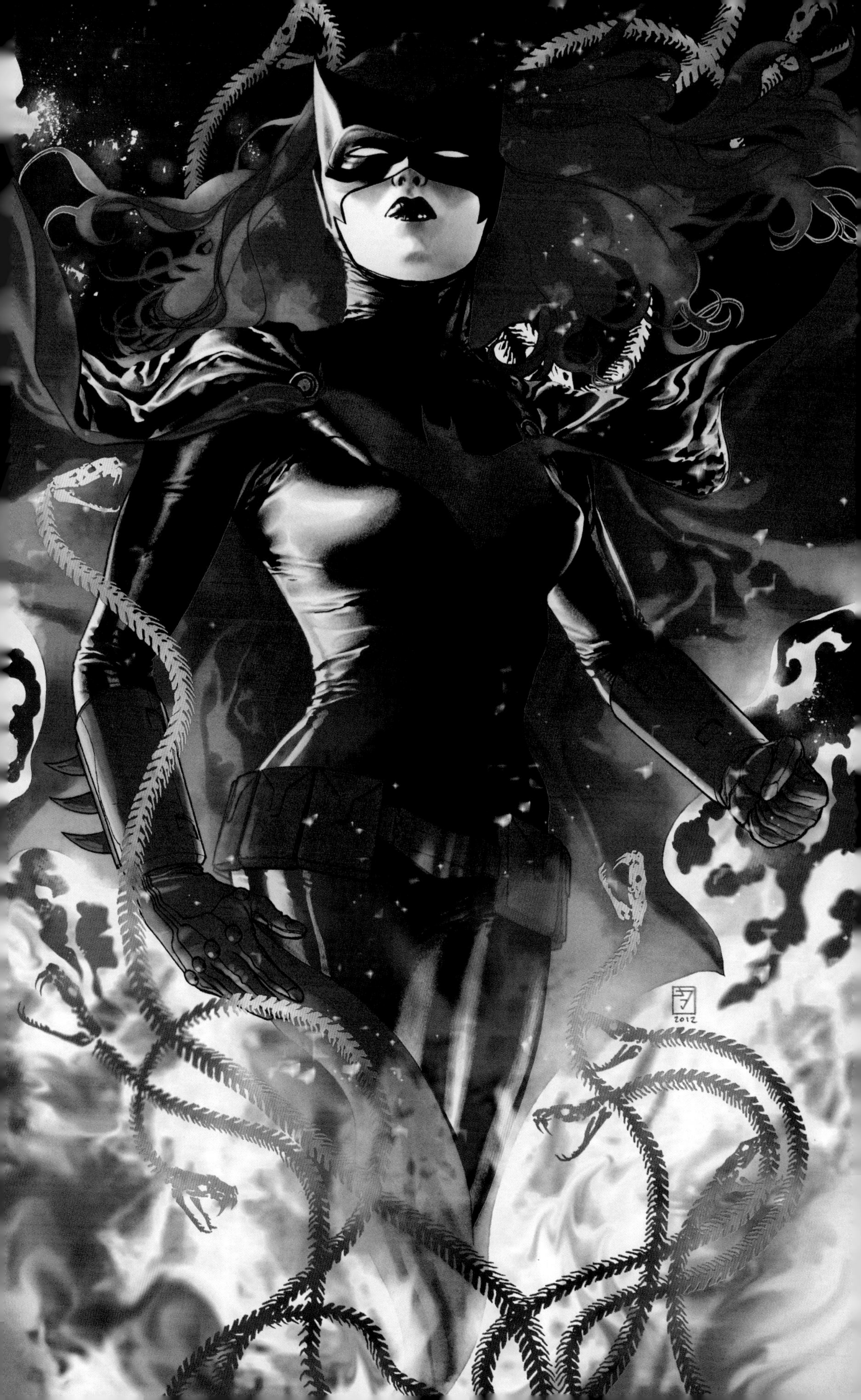
2012

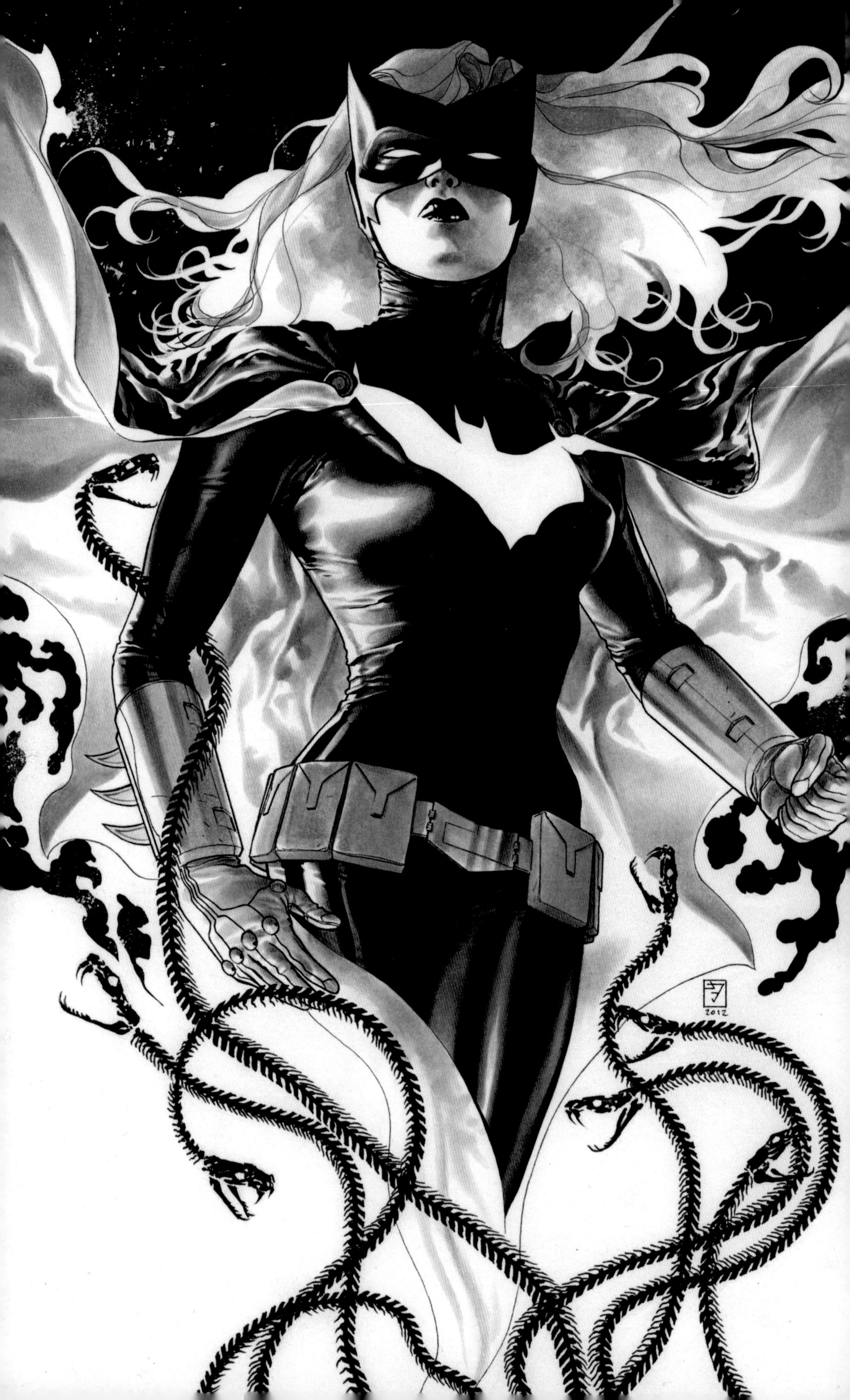
2012

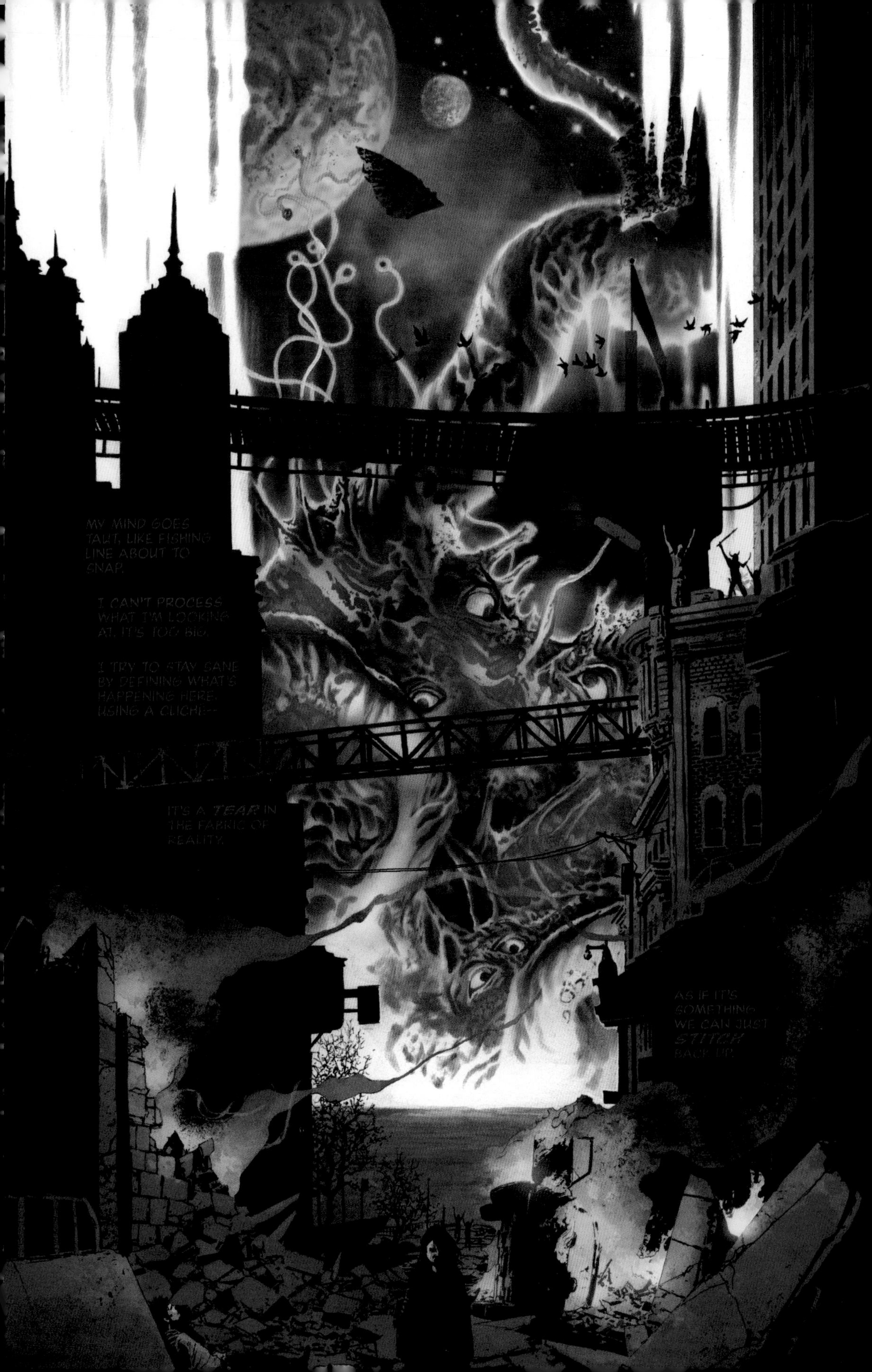
MY MIND GOES TAUT, LIKE FISHING LINE ABOUT TO SNAP.
I CAN'T PROCESS WHAT I'M LOOKING AT. IT'S TOO BIG.
I TRY TO STAY SANE BY DEFINING WHAT'S HAPPENING HERE. USING A CLICHE--
IT'S A *TEAR* IN THE FABRIC OF REALITY.
AS IF IT'S SOMETHING WE CAN JUST *STITCH* BACK UP.

BUT REALITY DOESN'T TEAR AT THE SEAMS LIKE CLOTH. REALITY GETS *DISEMBOWELED* AND HAS ITS INTESTINES PULLED OUT.

THAT'S WHEN I REALIZE THERE ARE SOME THINGS YOU CAN ALWAYS SEE, AND SOME YOU CAN NEVER UN-SEE.

PLEASE TELL ME YOU KNOW WHAT THE HELL THIS *IS*, BATWOMAN.

MEDUSA AND MARO HAVE PERFORMED SOME KIND OF RITUAL...

...SUMMONING SOMETHING CALLED THE MOTHER OF ALL MONSTERS.

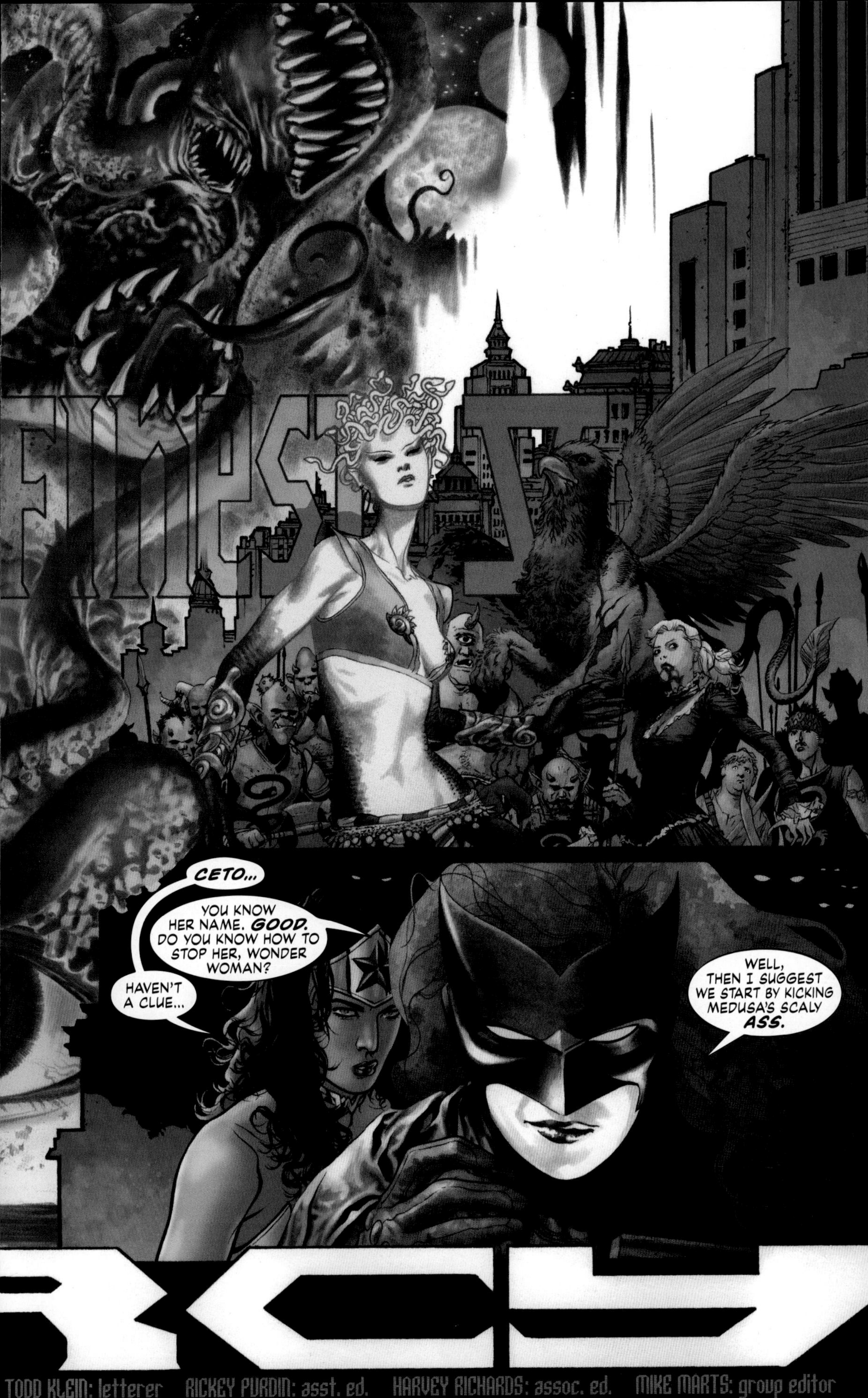
CETO...
YOU KNOW HER NAME. GOOD. DO YOU KNOW HOW TO STOP HER, WONDER WOMAN?
HAVEN'T A CLUE...
WELL, THEN I SUGGEST WE START BY KICKING MEDUSA'S SCALY ASS.
TODD KLEIN: letterer RICKEY PURDIN: asst. ed. HARVEY RICHARDS: assoc. ed. MIKE MARTS: group editor

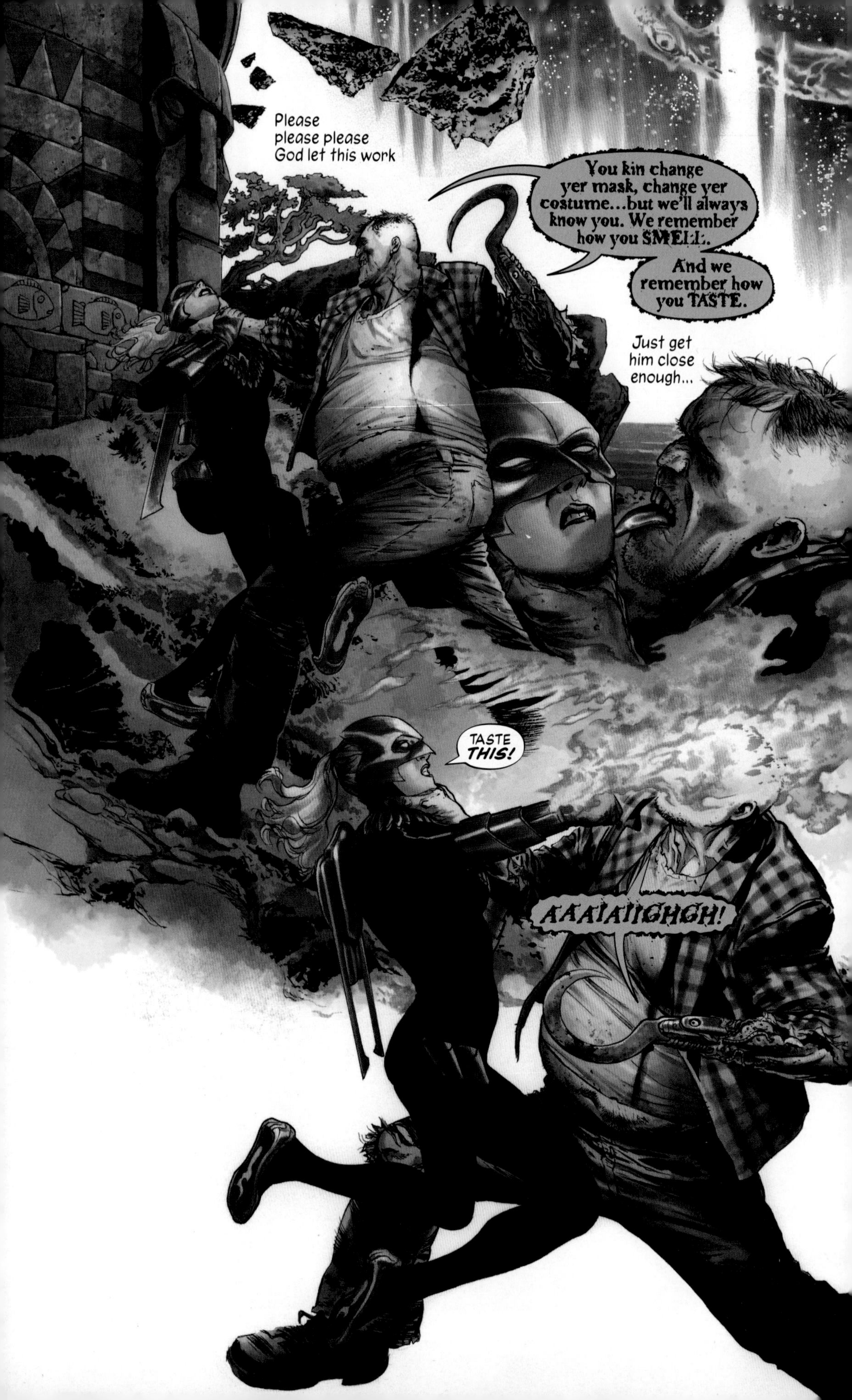
Please
please please
God let this work
You kin change yer mask, change yer costume...but we'll always know you. We remember how you SMELL.
And we remember how you TASTE.
Just get him close enough...
TASTE THIS!
AAAIAIIGHGH!

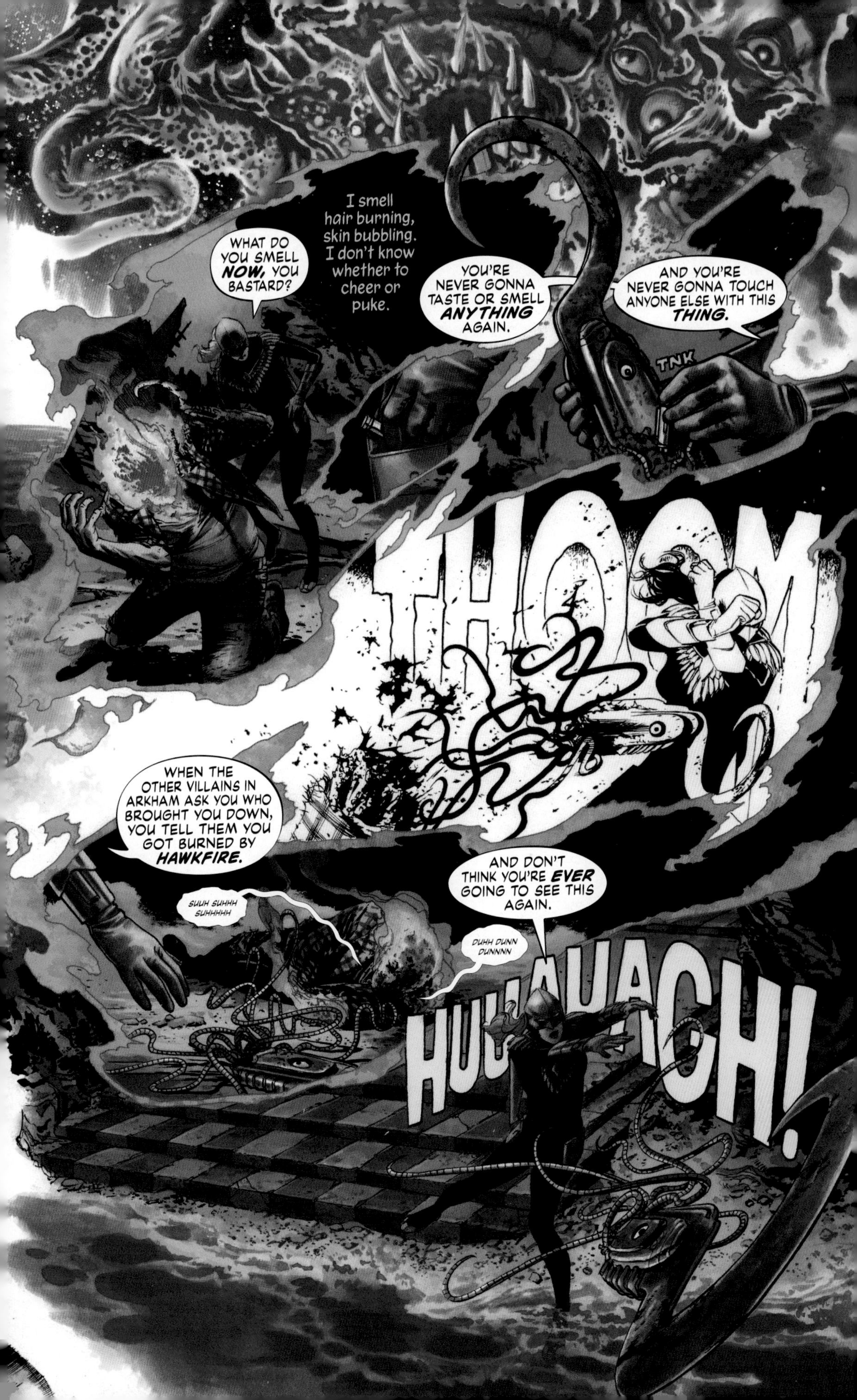
WHAT DO YOU SMELL *NOW,* YOU BASTARD?
I smell hair burning, skin bubbling. I don't know whether to cheer or puke.
YOU'RE NEVER GONNA TASTE OR SMELL *ANYTHING* AGAIN.
AND YOU'RE NEVER GONNA TOUCH ANYONE ELSE WITH THIS *THING.*
TNK
THOOM
WHEN THE OTHER VILLAINS IN ARKHAM ASK YOU WHO BROUGHT YOU DOWN, YOU TELL THEM YOU GOT BURNED BY *HAWKFIRE.*
SUUH SUHHH SUHHHHH
AND DON'T THINK YOU'RE *EVER* GOING TO SEE THIS AGAIN.
DUHH DUNN DUNNNN
HUUAUACH!

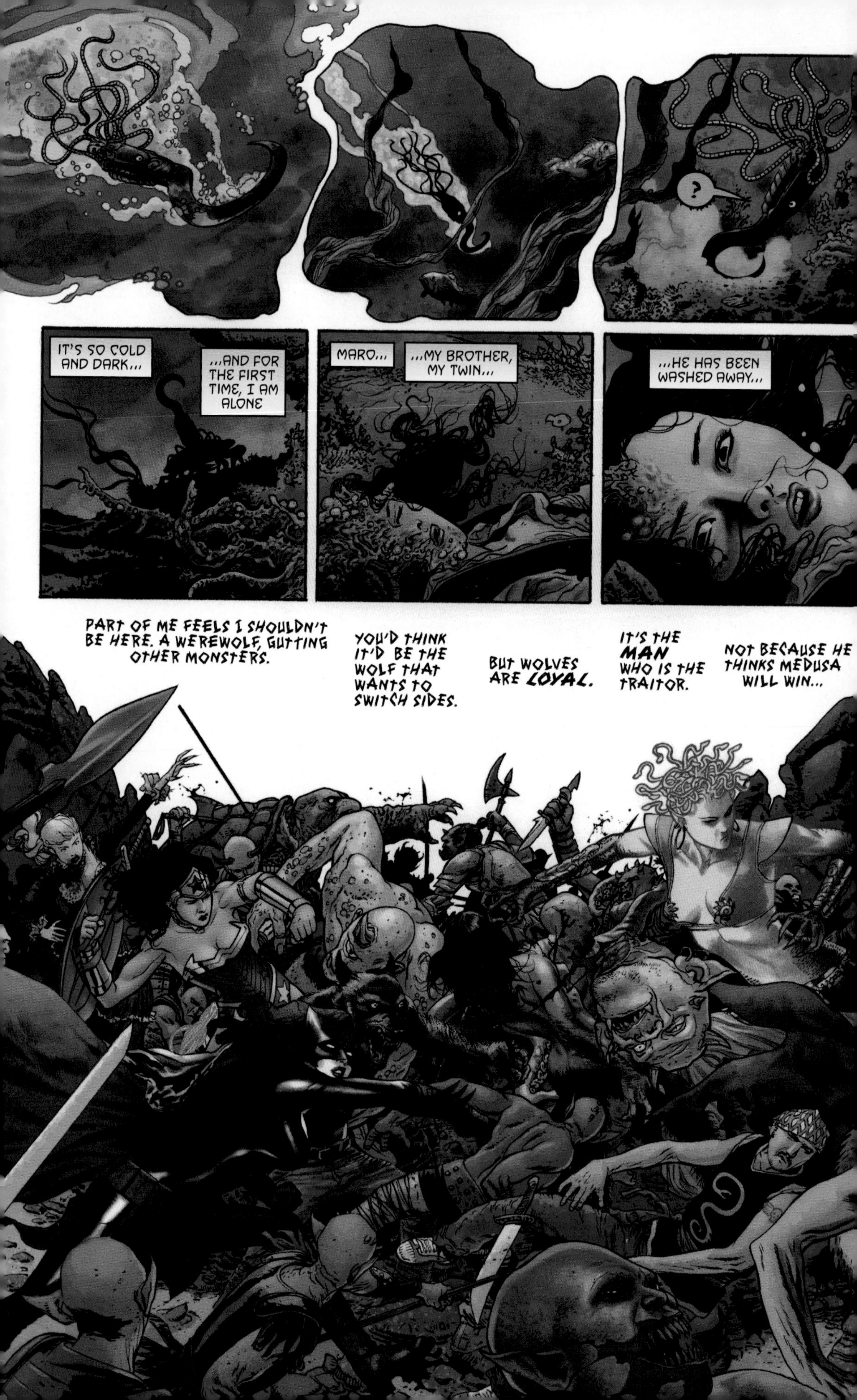
?
IT'S SO COLD AND DARK...
...AND FOR THE FIRST TIME, I AM ALONE
MARO...
...MY BROTHER, MY TWIN...
...HE HAS BEEN WASHED AWAY...
PART OF ME FEELS I SHOULDN'T BE HERE. A WEREWOLF, GUTTING OTHER MONSTERS.
YOU'D THINK IT'D BE THE WOLF THAT WANTS TO SWITCH SIDES.
BUT WOLVES ARE LOYAL.
IT'S THE MAN WHO IS THE TRAITOR.
NOT BECAUSE HE THINKS MEDUSA WILL WIN...

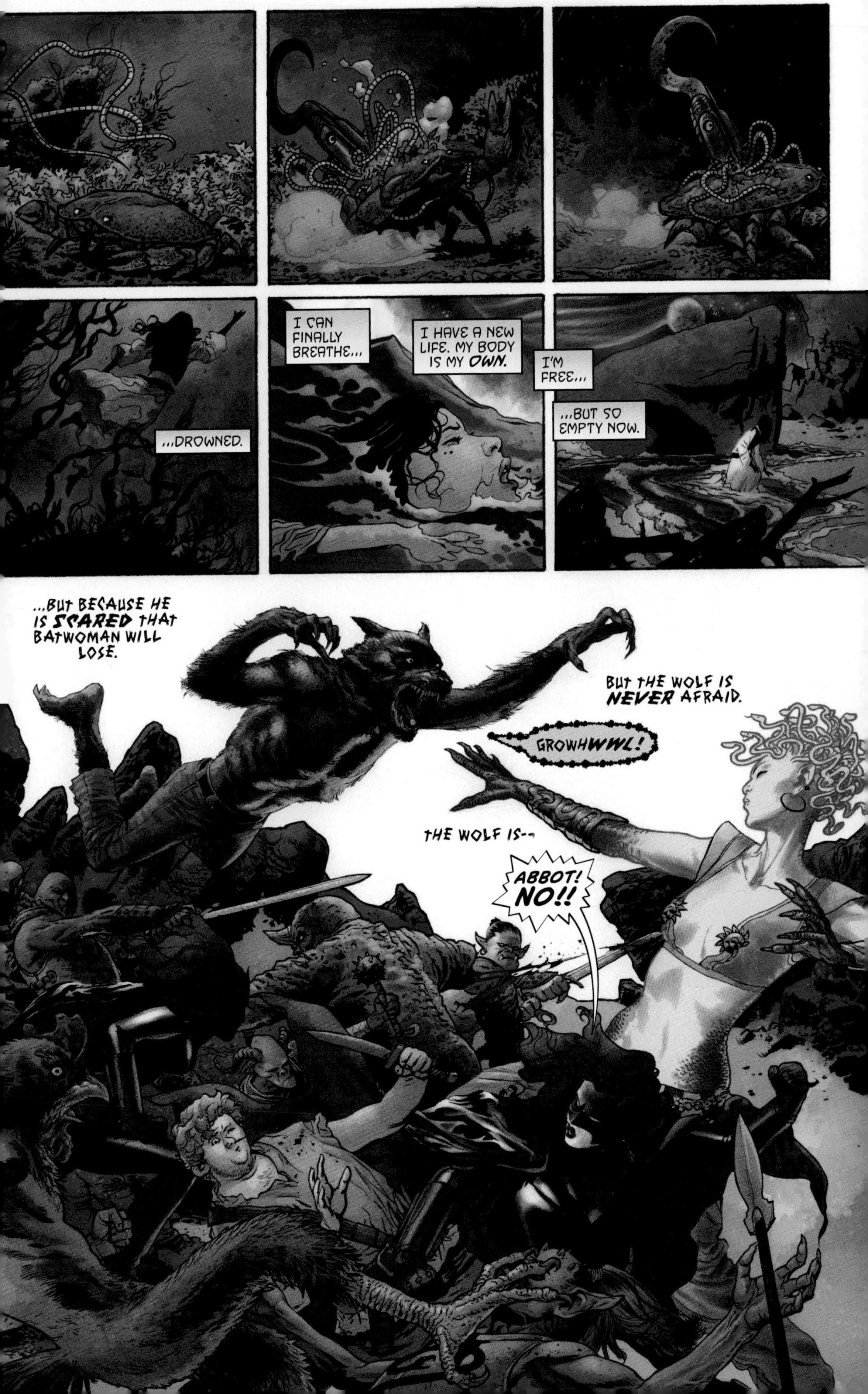

...DROWNED.
I CAN FINALLY BREATHE...
I HAVE A NEW LIFE. MY BODY IS MY OWN.
I'M FREE...
...BUT SO EMPTY NOW.
...BUT BECAUSE HE IS SCARED THAT BATWOMAN WILL LOSE.
BUT THE WOLF IS NEVER AFRAID.
GROWHWWL!
THE WOLF IS--
ABBOT! NO!!

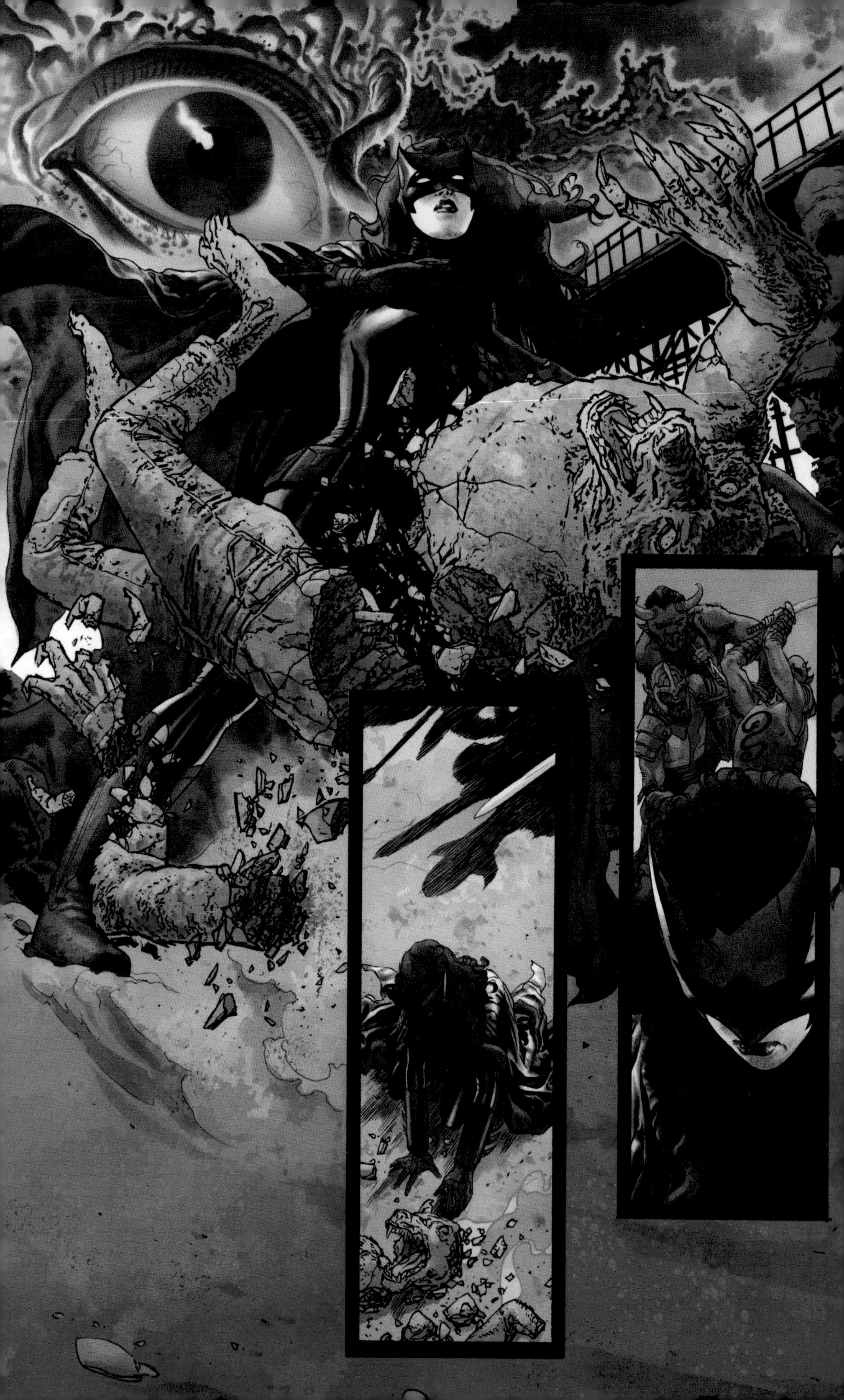

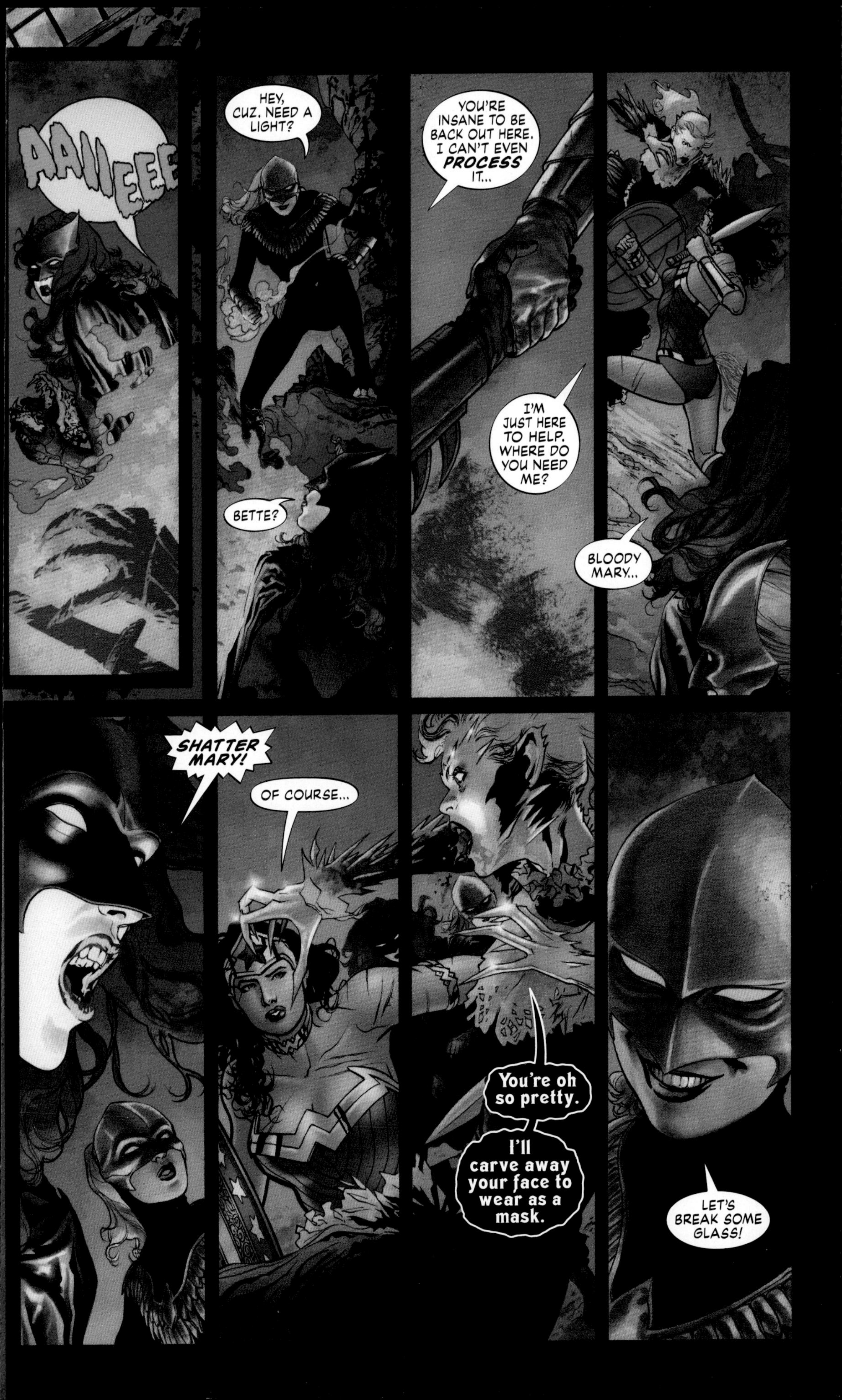
AAIIEEE
HEY, CUZ. NEED A LIGHT?
BETTE?
YOU'RE INSANE TO BE BACK OUT HERE. I CAN'T EVEN PROCESS IT...
I'M JUST HERE TO HELP. WHERE DO YOU NEED ME?
BLOODY MARY...
SHATTER MARY!
OF COURSE...
You're oh so pretty.
I'll carve away your face to wear as a mask.
LET'S BREAK SOME GLASS!

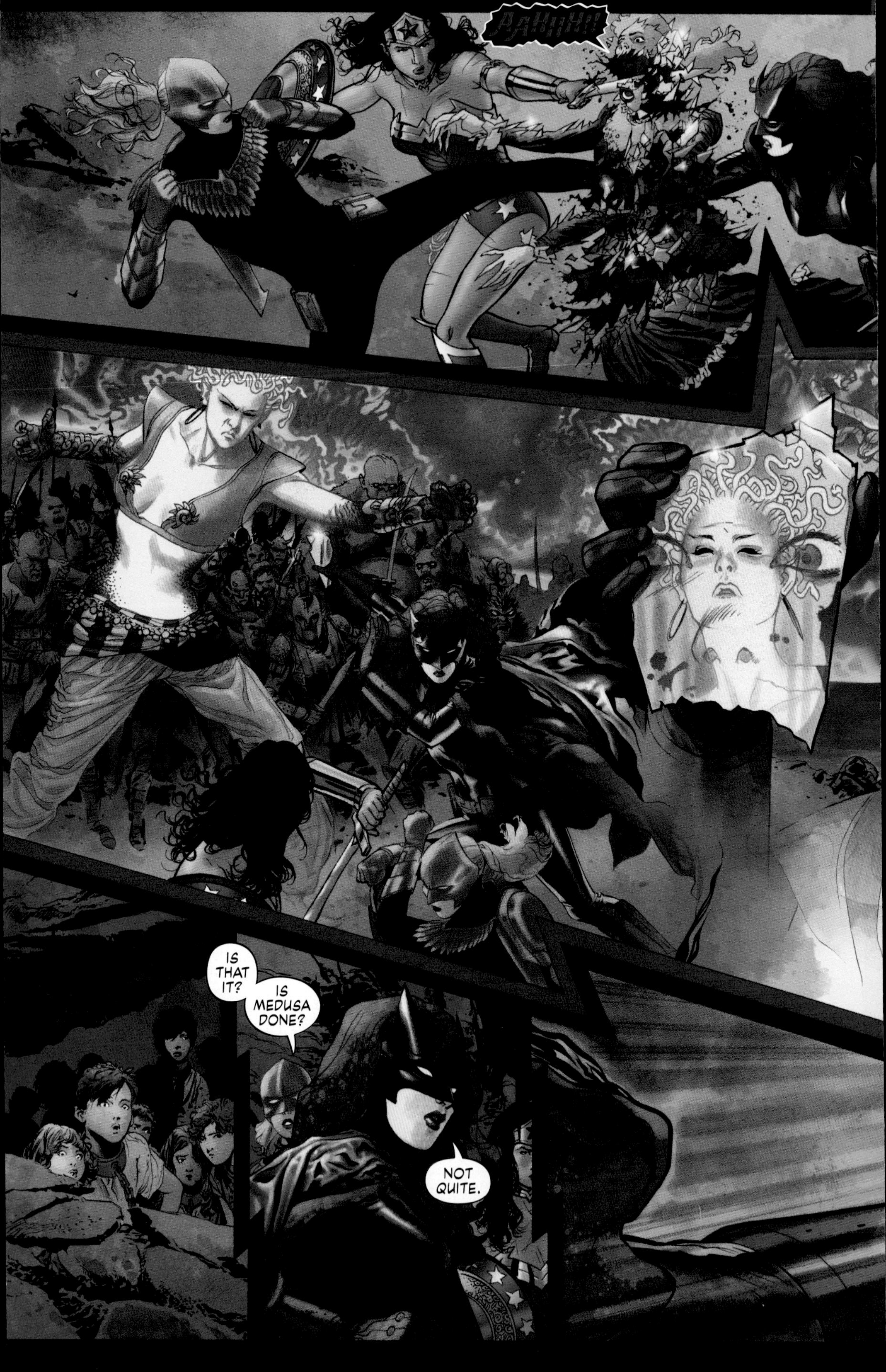
AAHHHH!!
IS THAT IT?
IS MEDUSA DONE?
NOT QUITE.

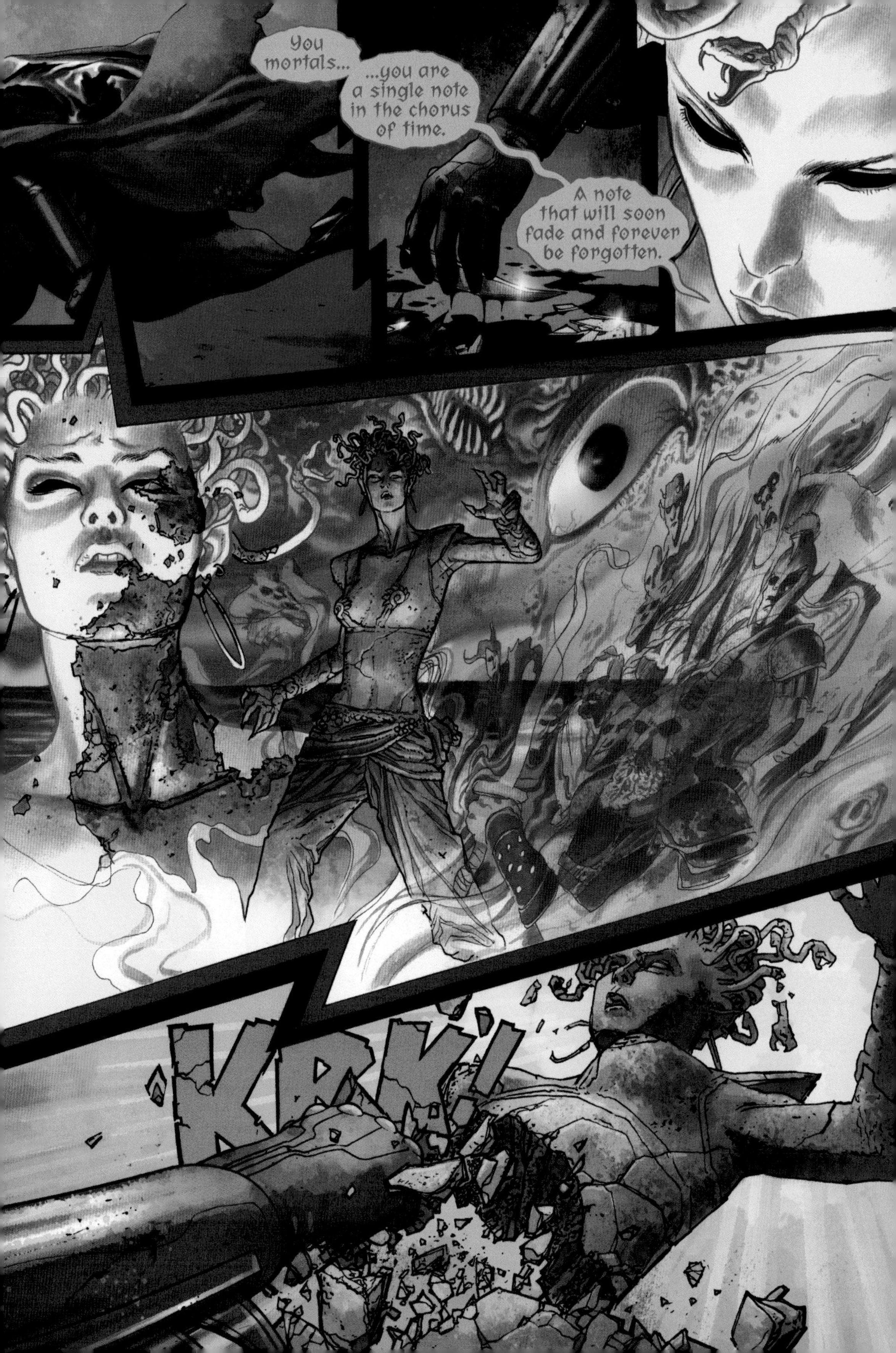
You mortals...
...you are a single note in the chorus of time.
A note that will soon fade and forever be forgotten.
KRAK!

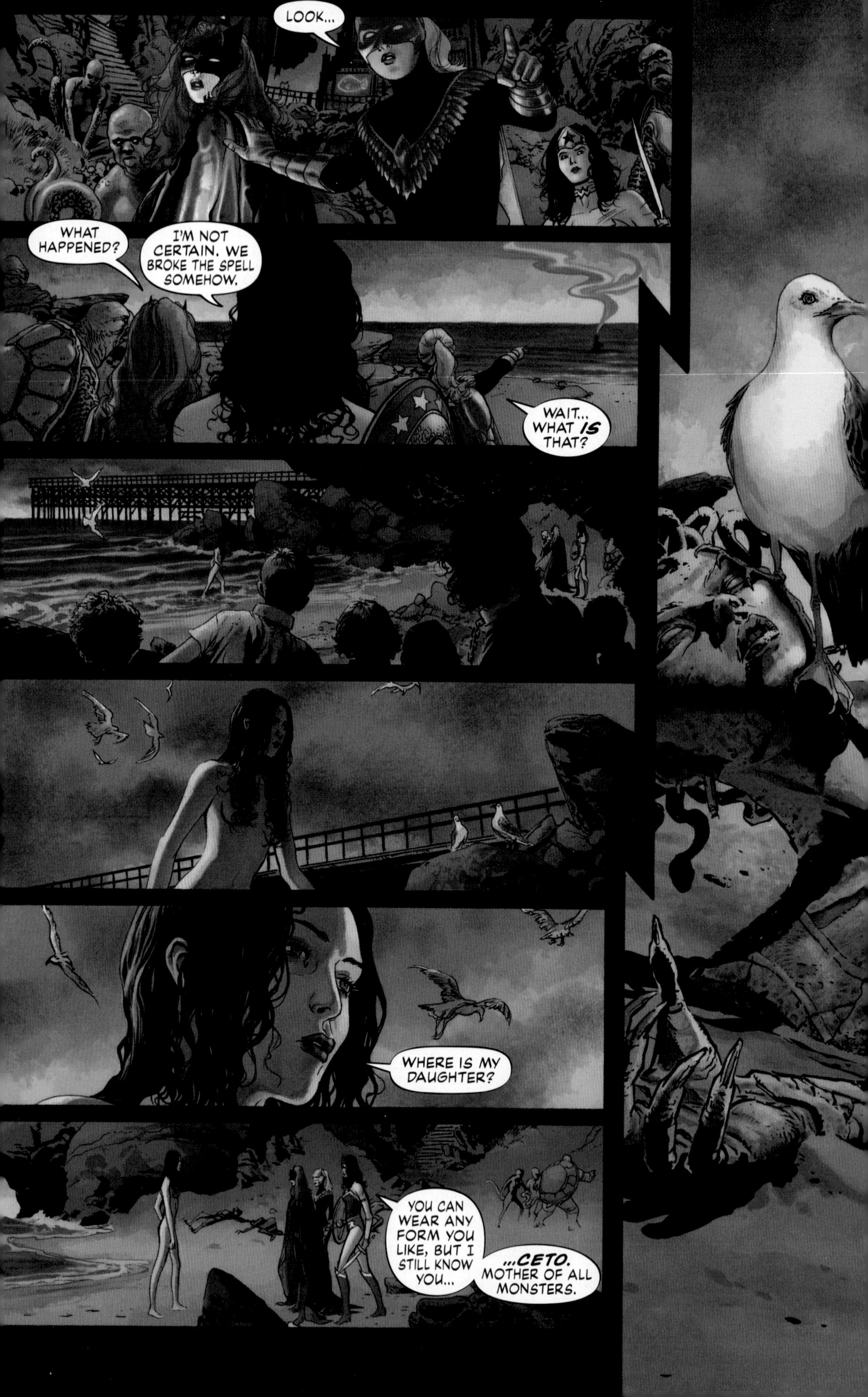
LOOK...
WHAT HAPPENED?
I'M NOT CERTAIN. WE BROKE THE SPELL SOMEHOW.
WAIT... WHAT *IS* THAT?
WHERE IS MY DAUGHTER?
YOU CAN WEAR ANY FORM YOU LIKE, BUT I STILL KNOW YOU...
...**CETO.** MOTHER OF ALL MONSTERS.

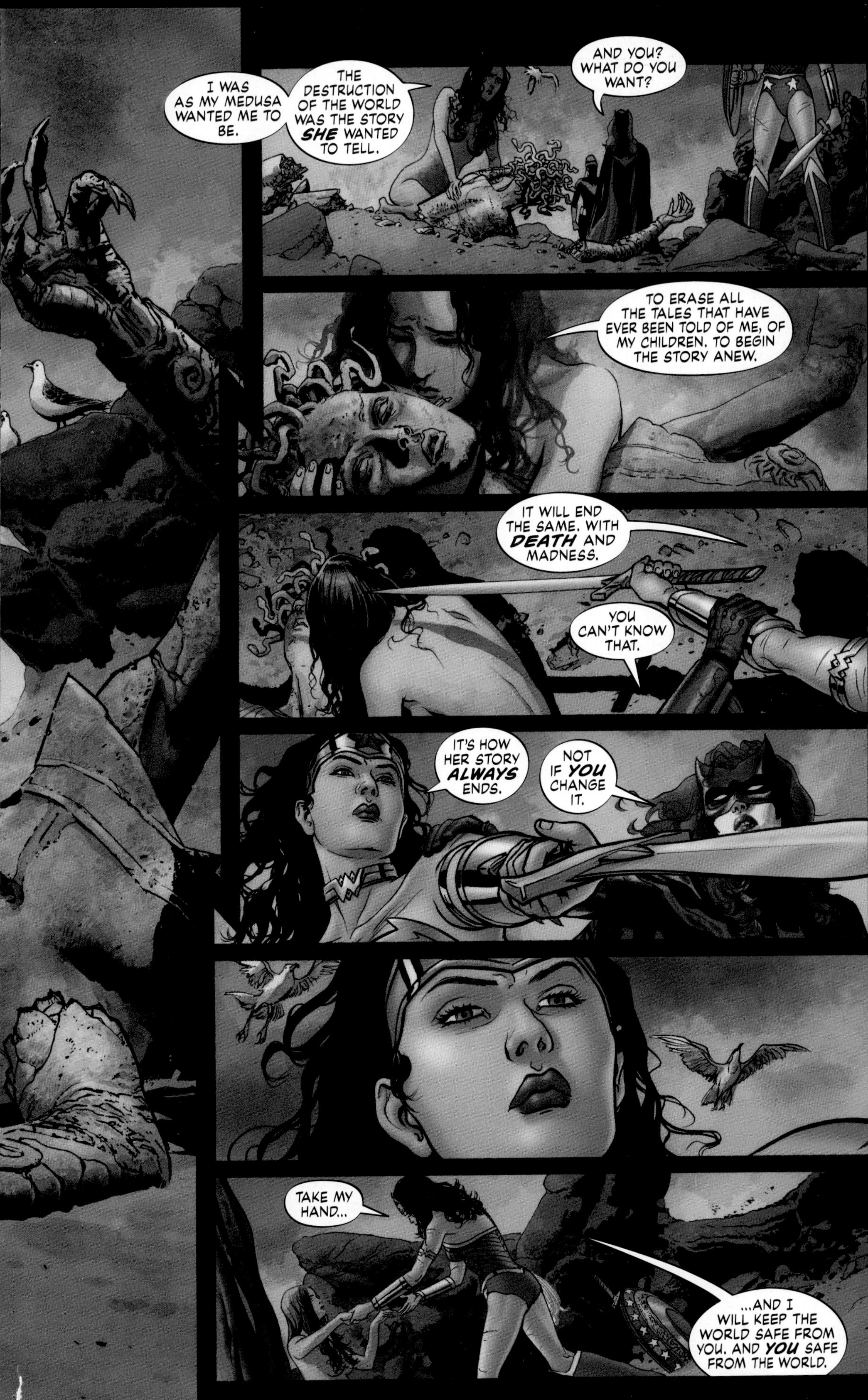
I WAS AS MY MEDUSA WANTED ME TO BE.
THE DESTRUCTION OF THE WORLD WAS THE STORY SHE WANTED TO TELL.
AND YOU? WHAT DO YOU WANT?
TO ERASE ALL THE TALES THAT HAVE EVER BEEN TOLD OF ME, OF MY CHILDREN. TO BEGIN THE STORY ANEW.
IT WILL END THE SAME. WITH DEATH AND MADNESS.
YOU CAN'T KNOW THAT.
IT'S HOW HER STORY ALWAYS ENDS.
NOT IF YOU CHANGE IT.
TAKE MY HAND...
...AND I WILL KEEP THE WORLD SAFE FROM YOU. AND YOU SAFE FROM THE WORLD.

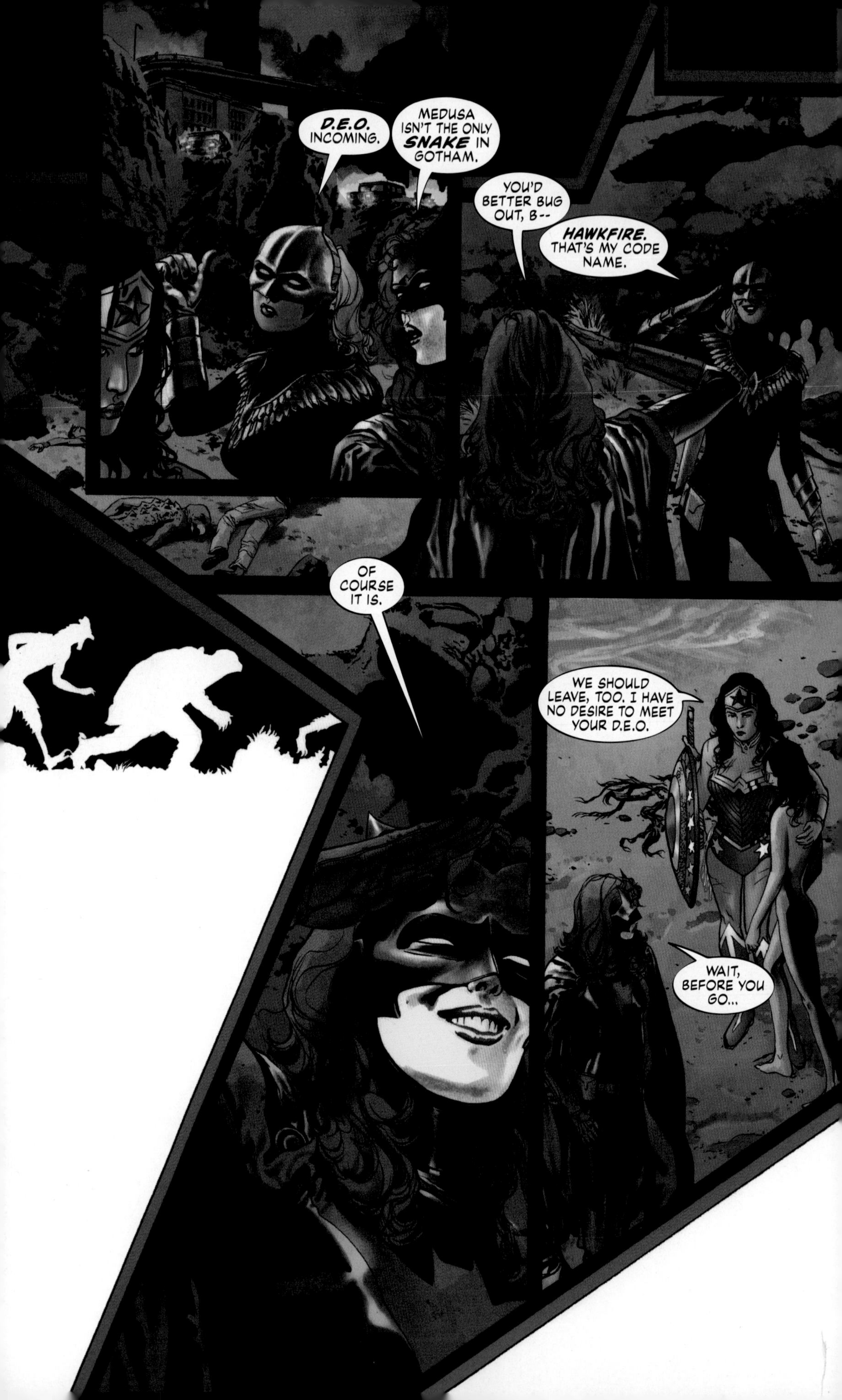
D.E.O. INCOMING.
MEDUSA ISN'T THE ONLY SNAKE IN GOTHAM.
YOU'D BETTER BUG OUT, B--
HAWKFIRE. THAT'S MY CODE NAME.
OF COURSE IT IS.
WE SHOULD LEAVE, TOO. I HAVE NO DESIRE TO MEET YOUR D.E.O.
WAIT, BEFORE YOU GO...

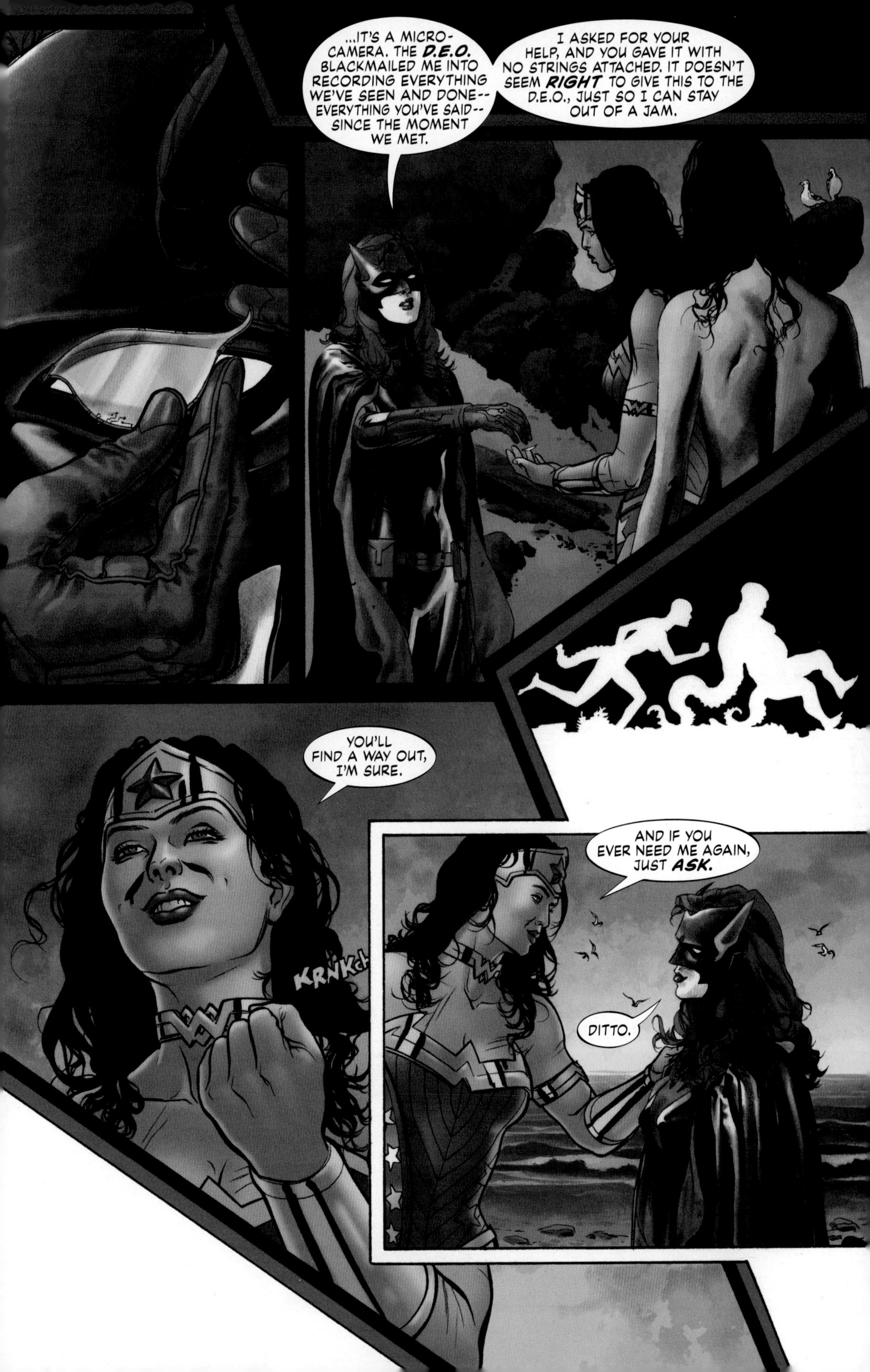
...IT'S A MICRO-CAMERA. THE D.E.O. BLACKMAILED ME INTO RECORDING EVERYTHING WE'VE SEEN AND DONE--EVERYTHING YOU'VE SAID--SINCE THE MOMENT WE MET.
I ASKED FOR YOUR HELP, AND YOU GAVE IT WITH NO STRINGS ATTACHED. IT DOESN'T SEEM RIGHT TO GIVE THIS TO THE D.E.O., JUST SO I CAN STAY OUT OF A JAM.
YOU'LL FIND A WAY OUT, I'M SURE.
KRNKch
AND IF YOU EVER NEED ME AGAIN, JUST ASK.
DITTO.

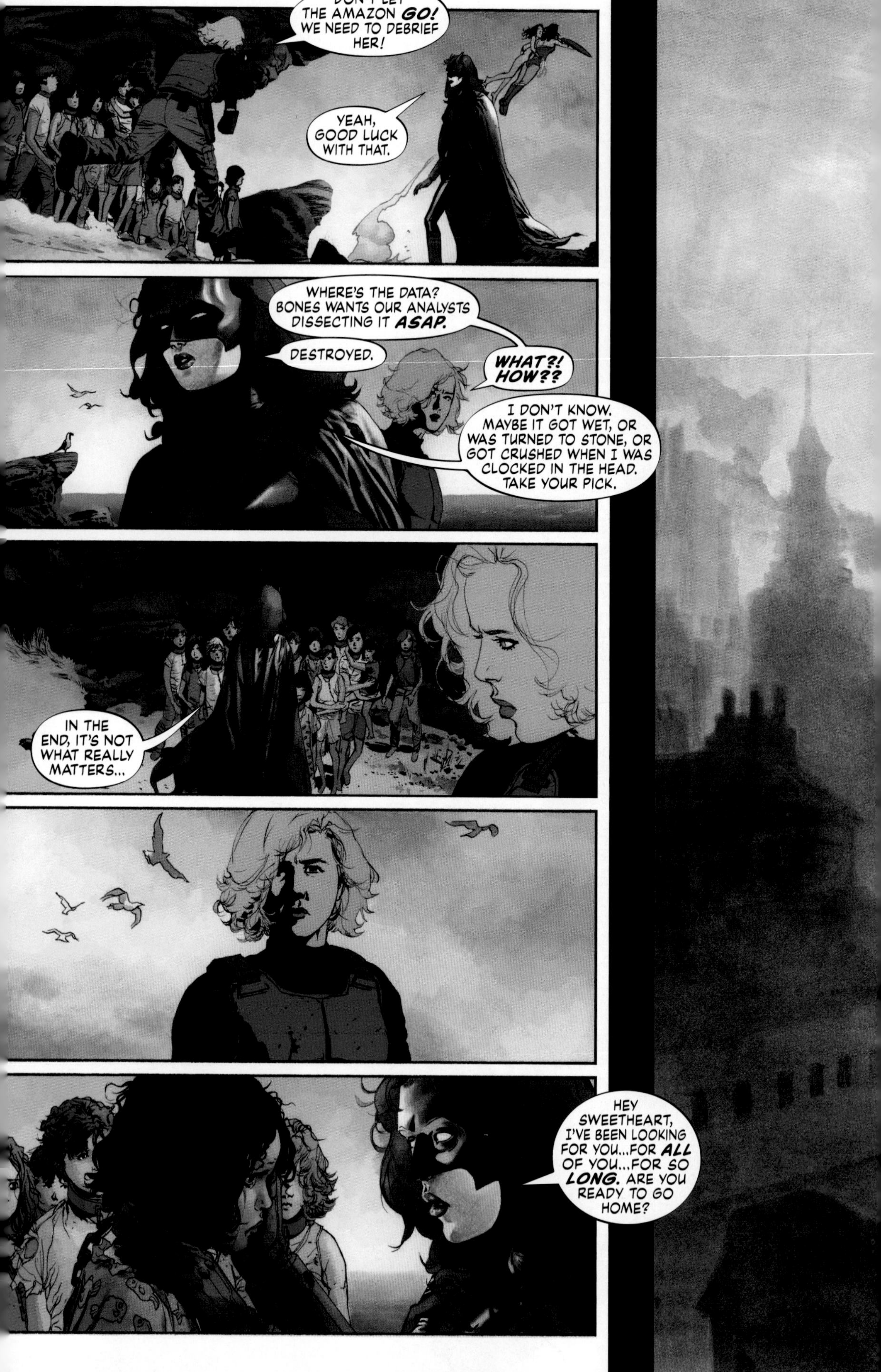
DON'T LET THE AMAZON GO! WE NEED TO DEBRIEF HER!
YEAH, GOOD LUCK WITH THAT.
WHERE'S THE DATA? BONES WANTS OUR ANALYSTS DISSECTING IT ASAP.
DESTROYED.
WHAT?! HOW??
I DON'T KNOW. MAYBE IT GOT WET, OR WAS TURNED TO STONE, OR GOT CRUSHED WHEN I WAS CLOCKED IN THE HEAD. TAKE YOUR PICK.
IN THE END, IT'S NOT WHAT REALLY MATTERS...
HEY SWEETHEART, I'VE BEEN LOOKING FOR YOU...FOR ALL OF YOU...FOR SO LONG. ARE YOU READY TO GO HOME?

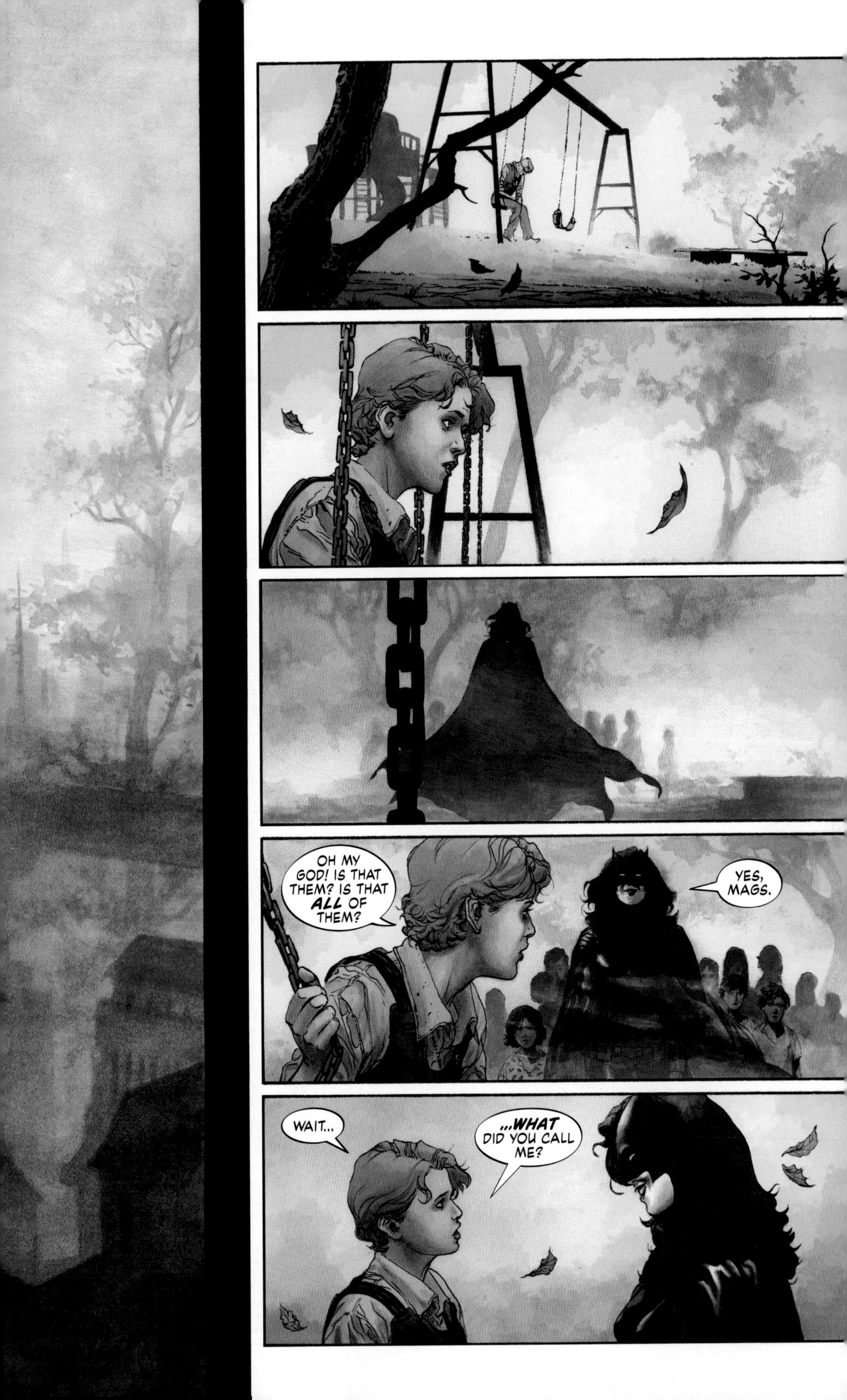
OH MY GOD! IS THAT THEM? IS THAT ALL OF THEM?
YES, MAGS.
WAIT...
...WHAT DID YOU CALL ME?

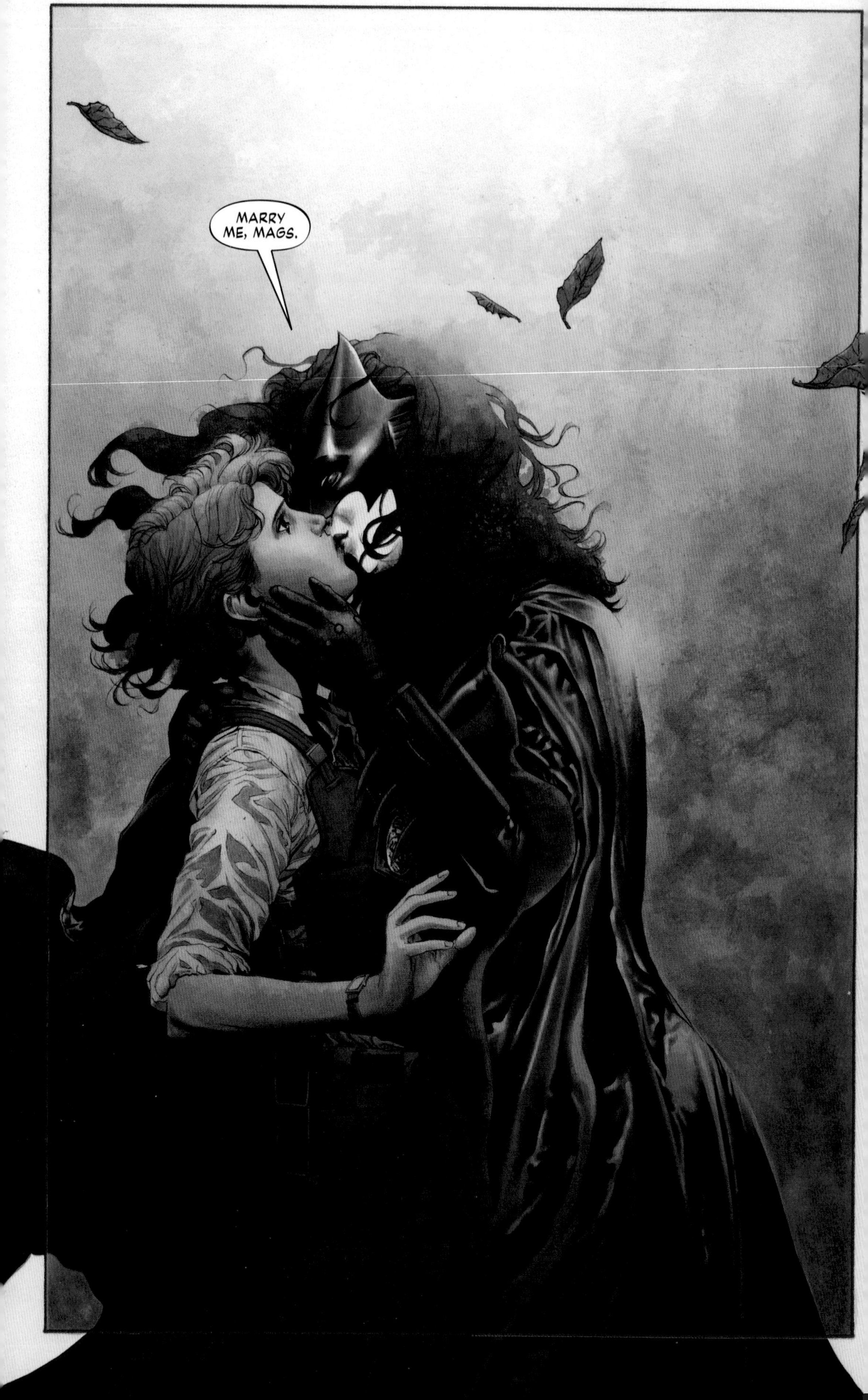
MARRY ME, MAGS.

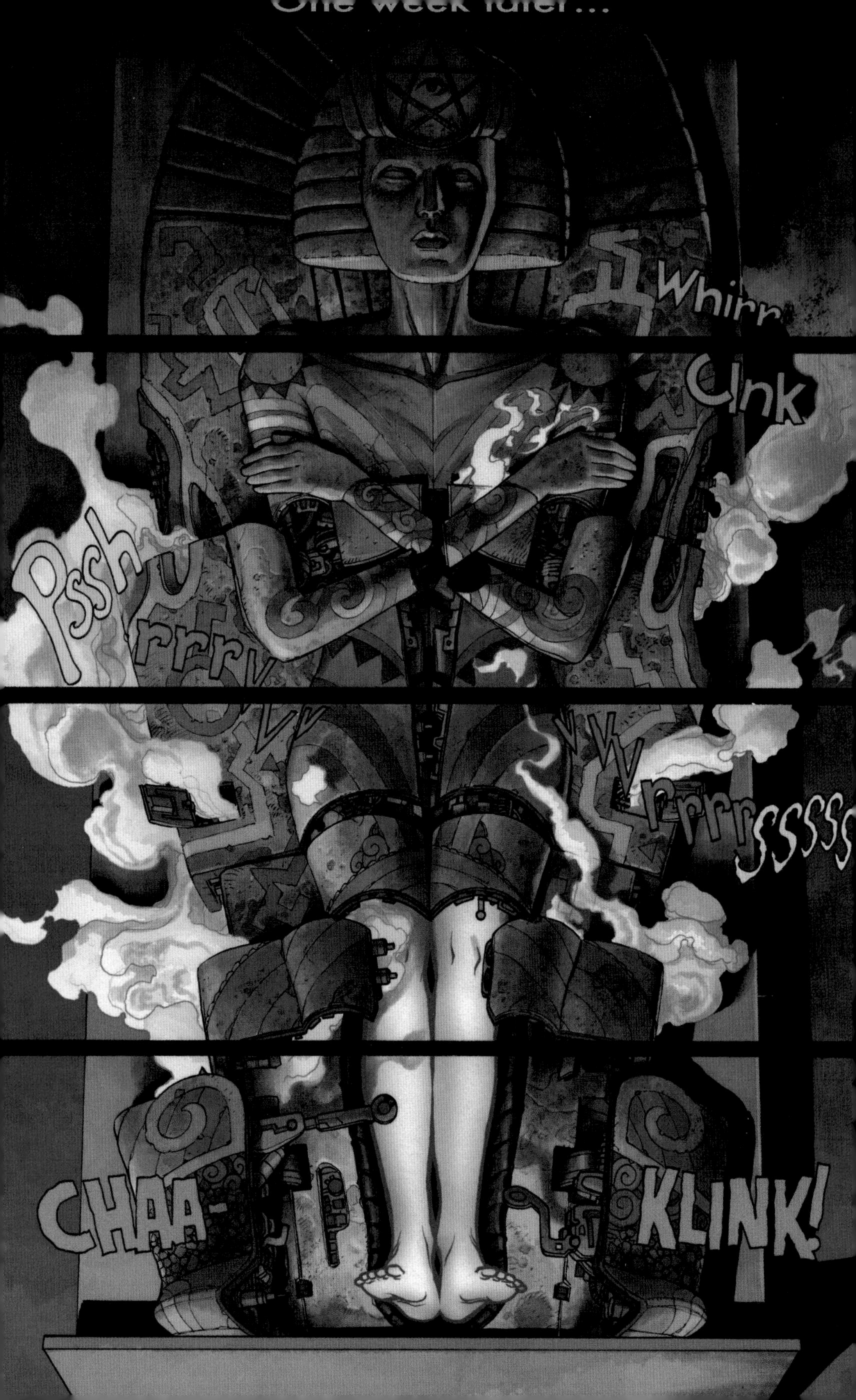
One week later...
Whirr
Clnk
Pssh
CHAA-KLINK!

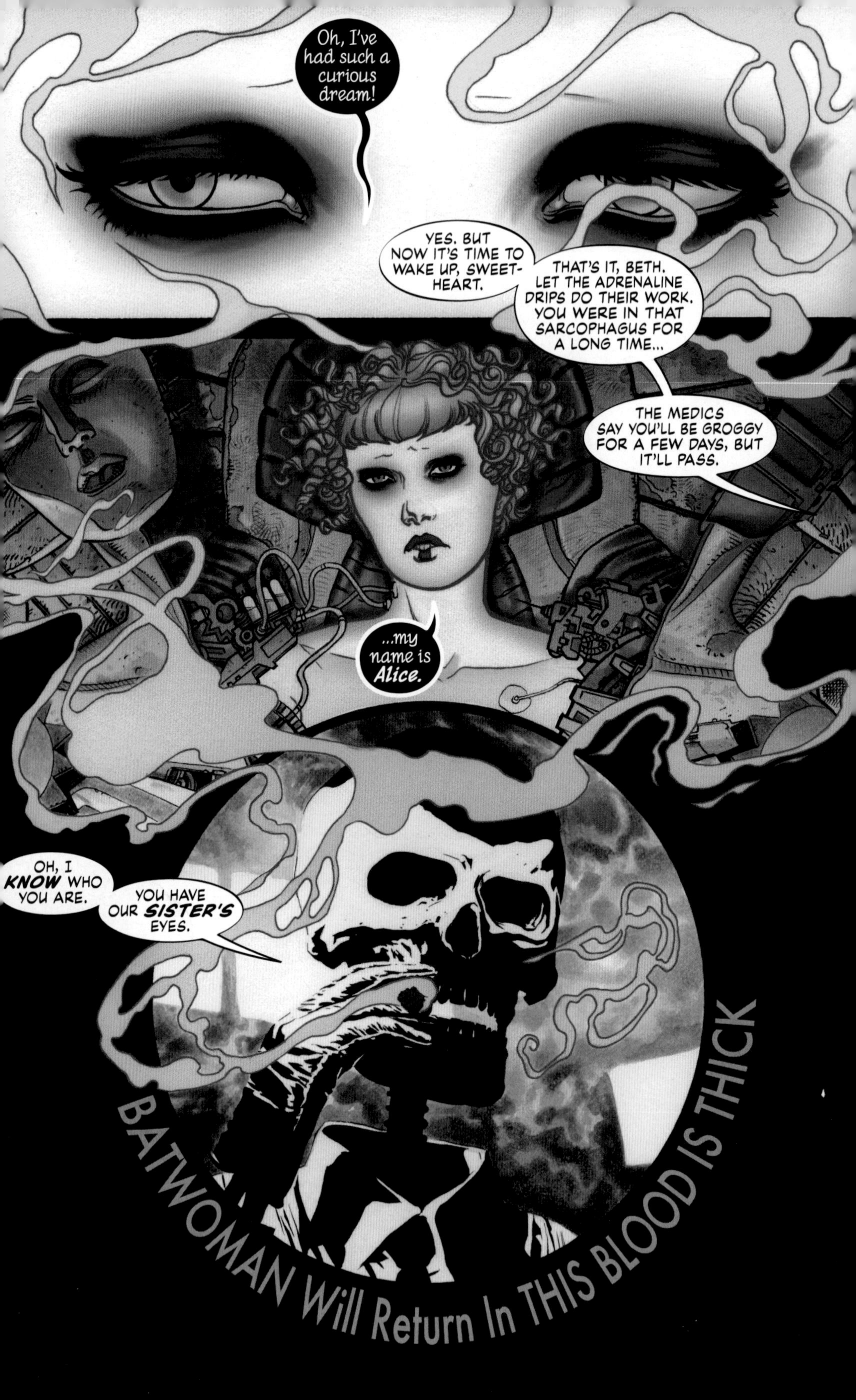
Oh, I've had such a curious dream!
YES. BUT NOW IT'S TIME TO WAKE UP, SWEET-HEART.
THAT'S IT, BETH. LET THE ADRENALINE DRIPS DO THEIR WORK. YOU WERE IN THAT SARCOPHAGUS FOR A LONG TIME...
THE MEDICS SAY YOU'LL BE GROGGY FOR A FEW DAYS, BUT IT'LL PASS.
...my name is Alice.
OH, I KNOW WHO YOU ARE.
YOU HAVE OUR SISTER'S EYES.
BATWOMAN Will Return In THIS BLOOD IS THICK

BATWOMAN

ISSUE #12 INKED PAGES BY J.H. WILLIAMS III

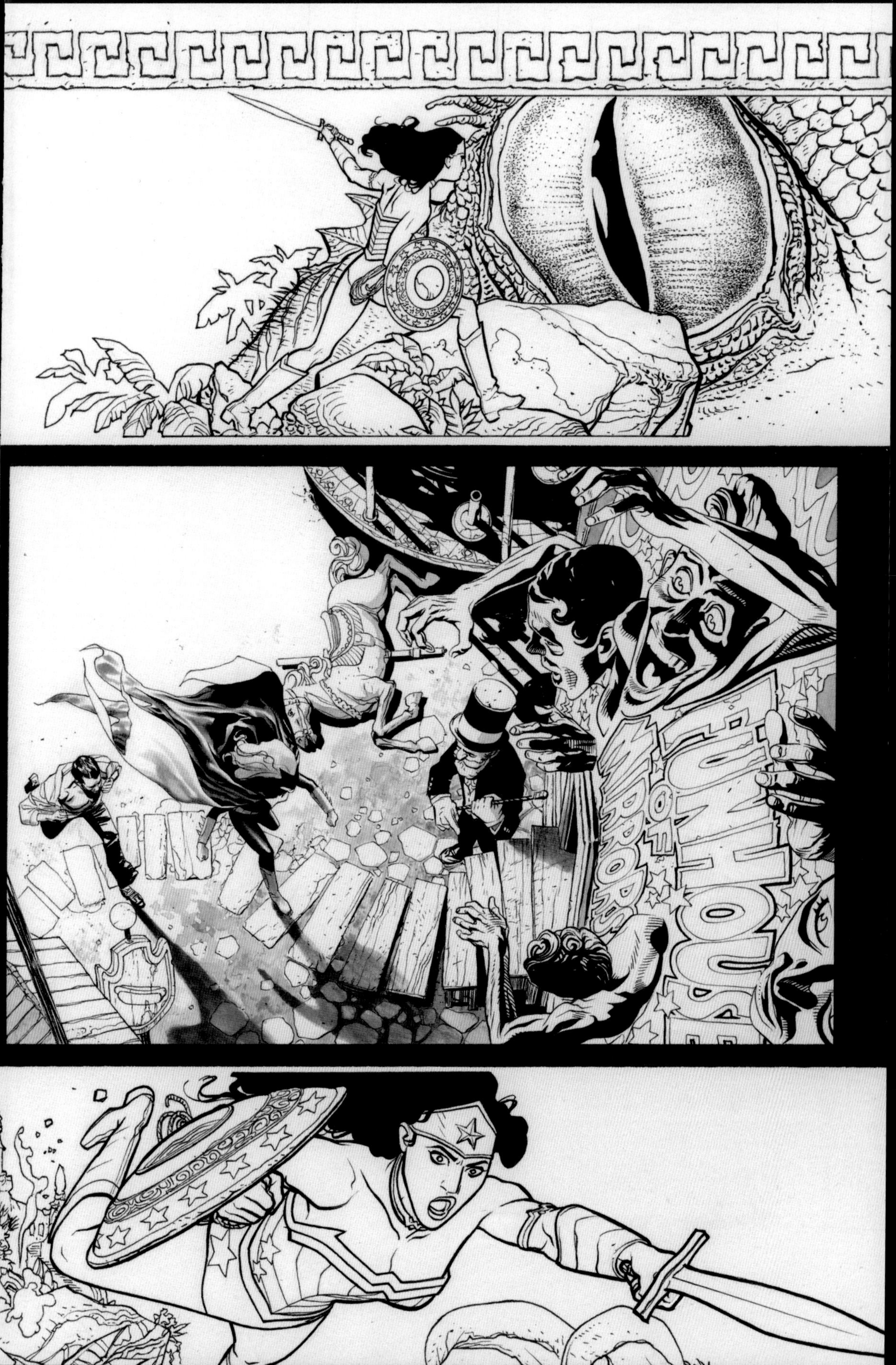

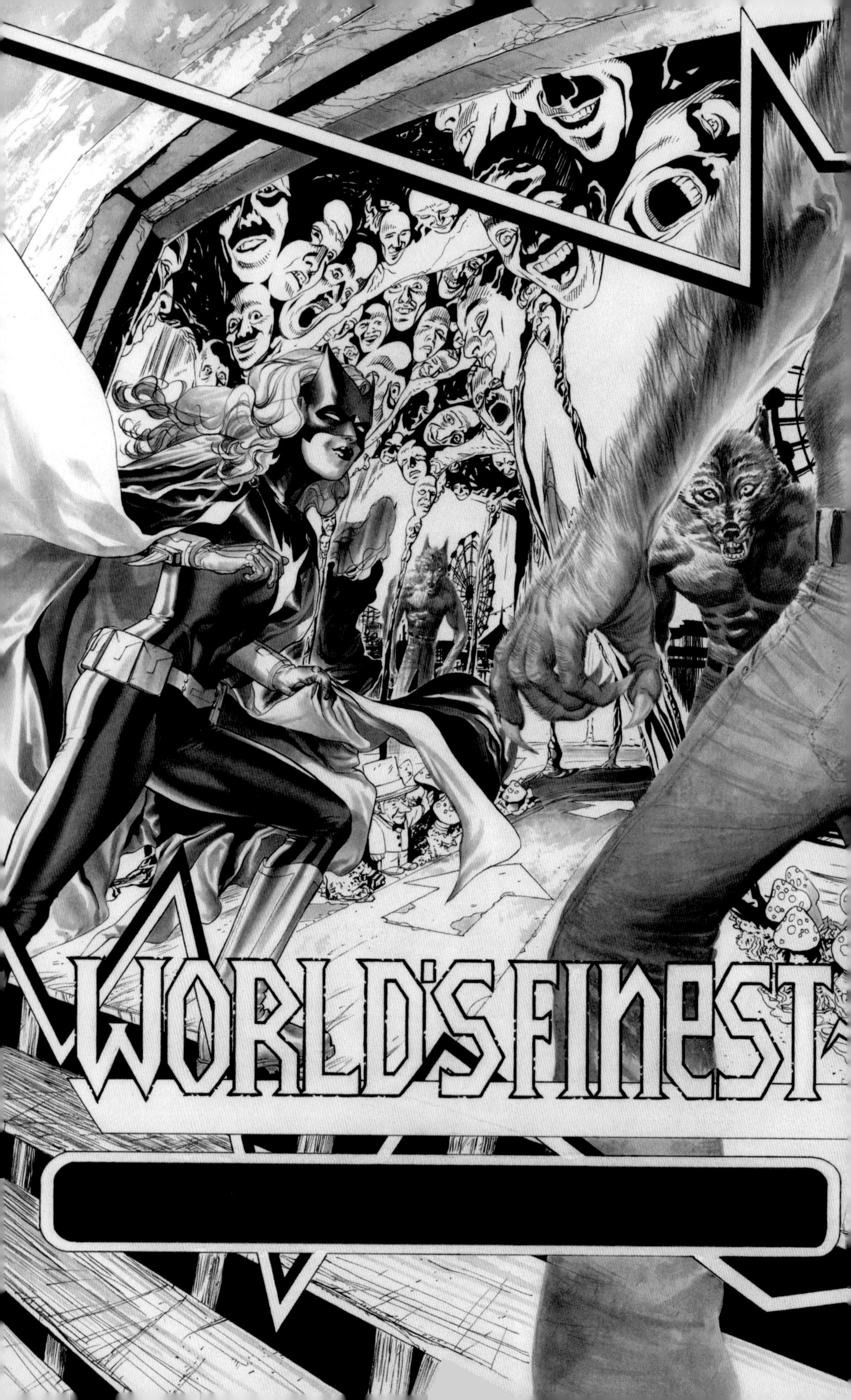
WORLD'S FINEST

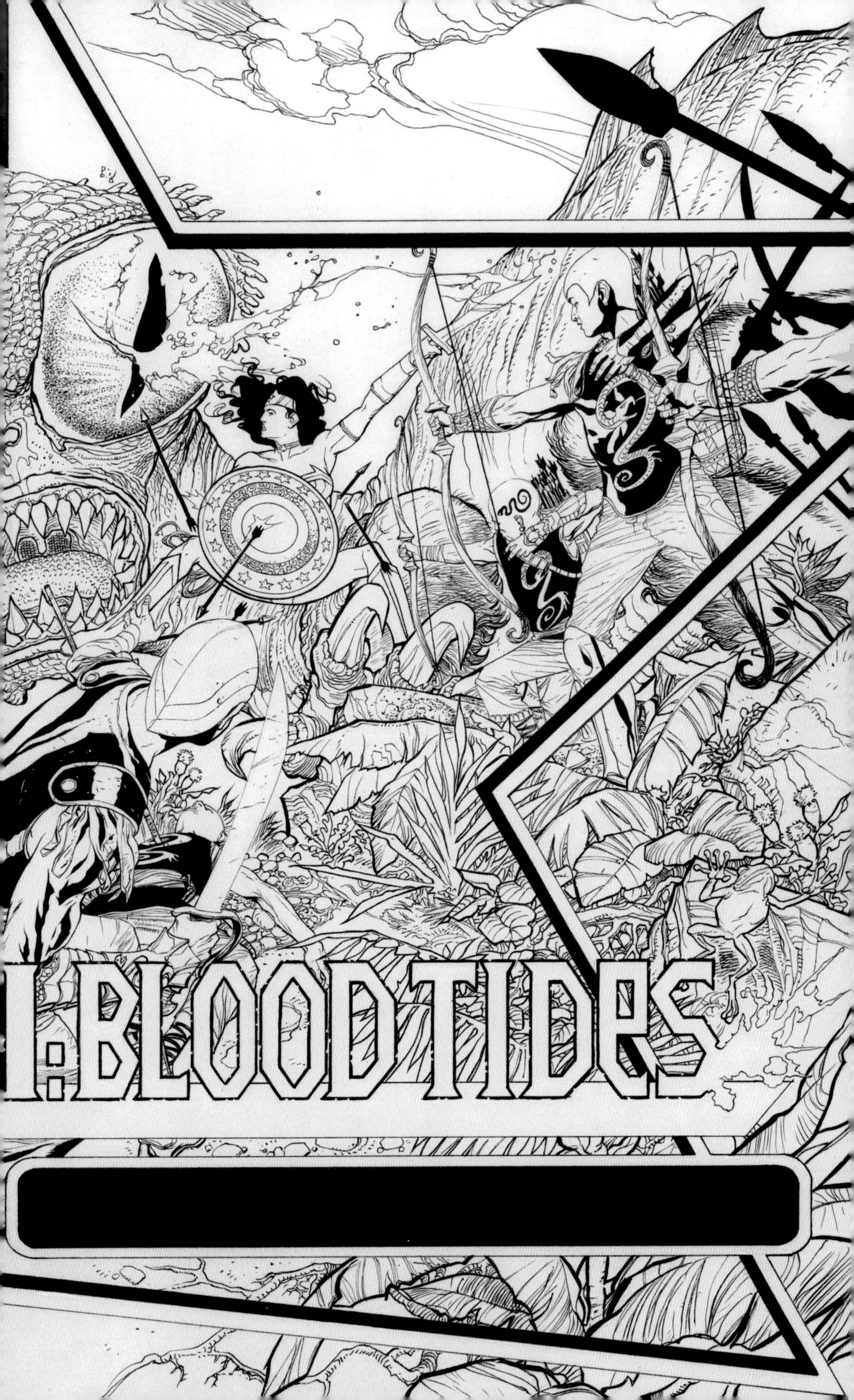
I: BLOODTIDES

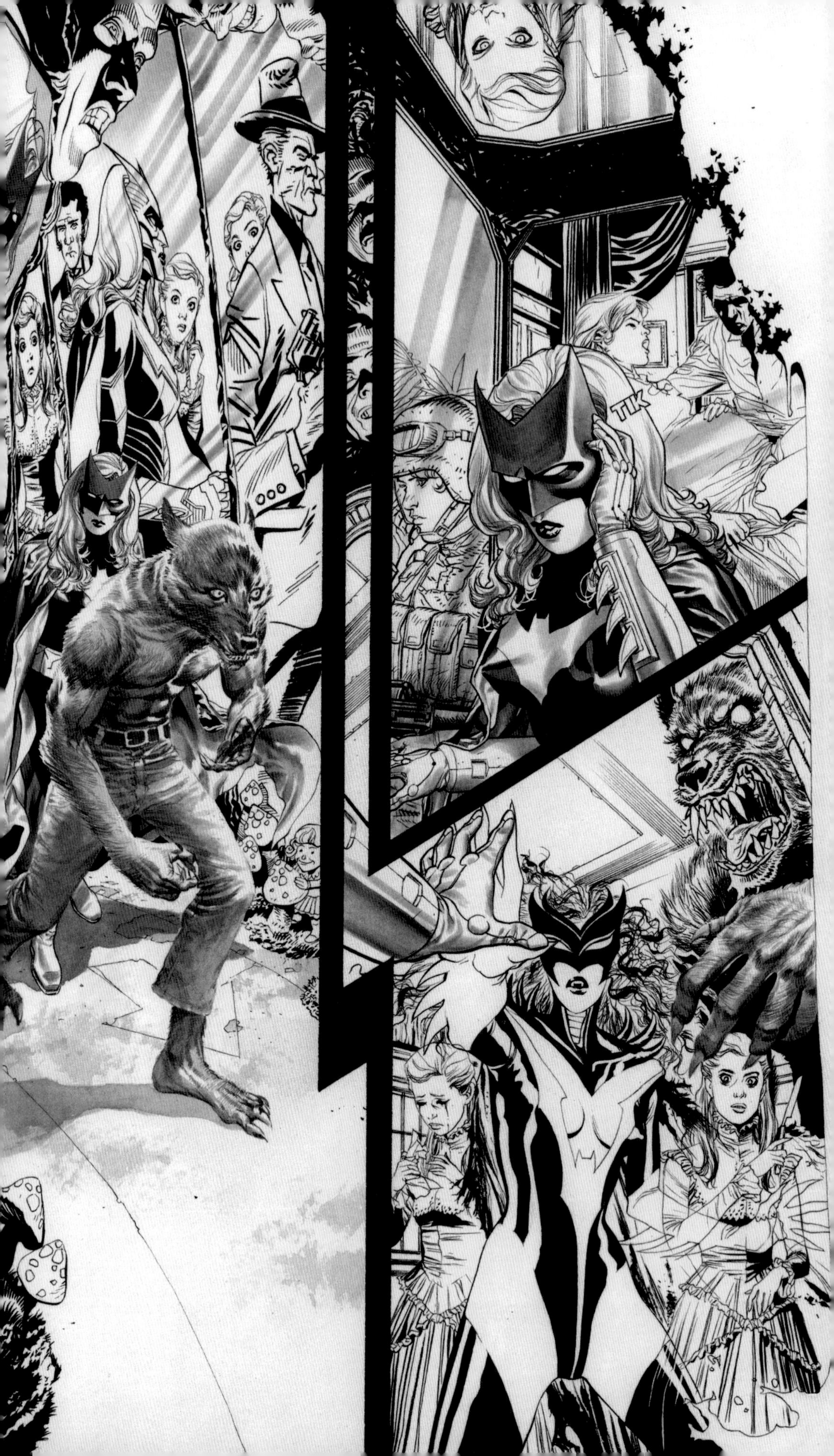
TIK

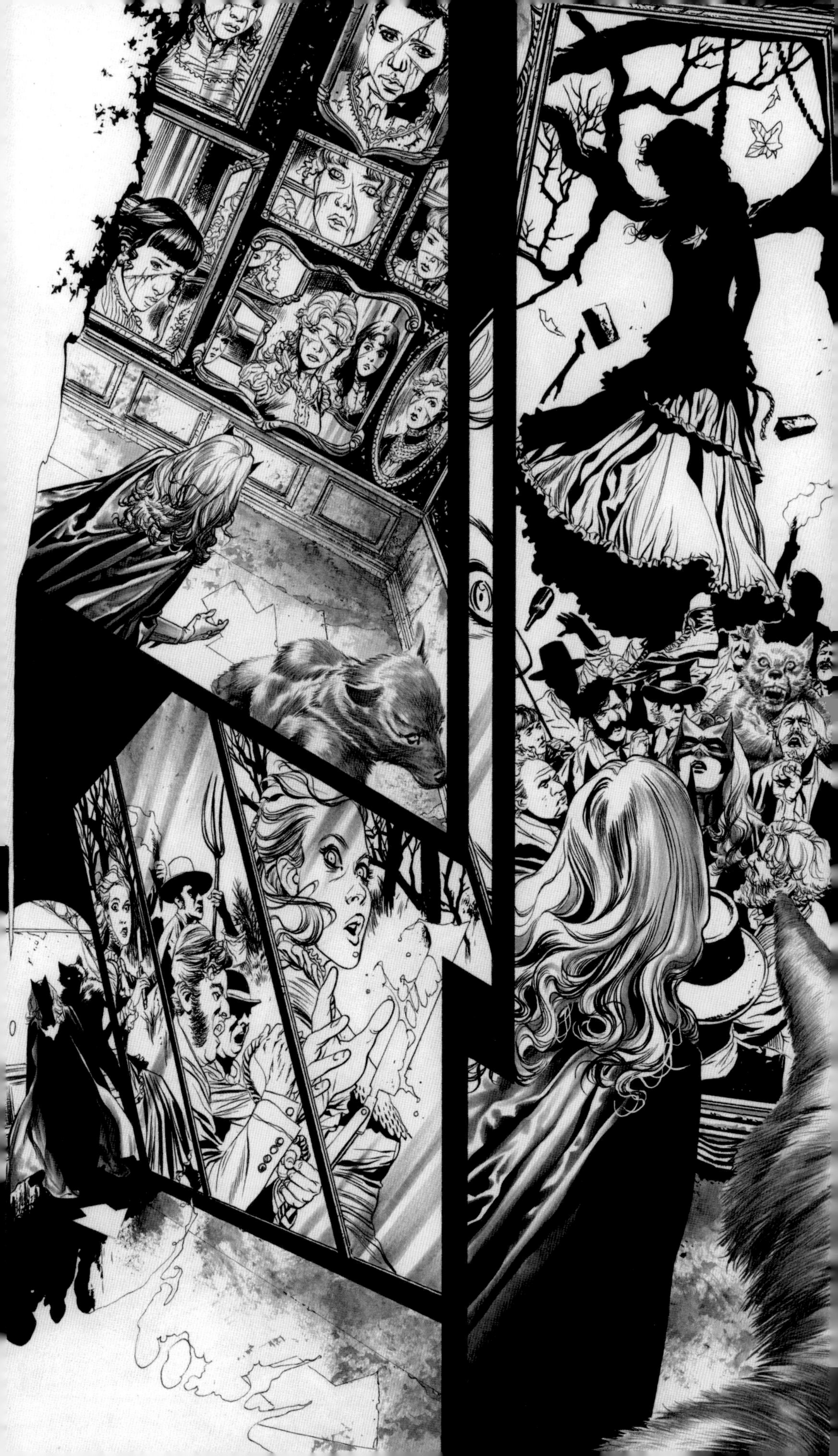

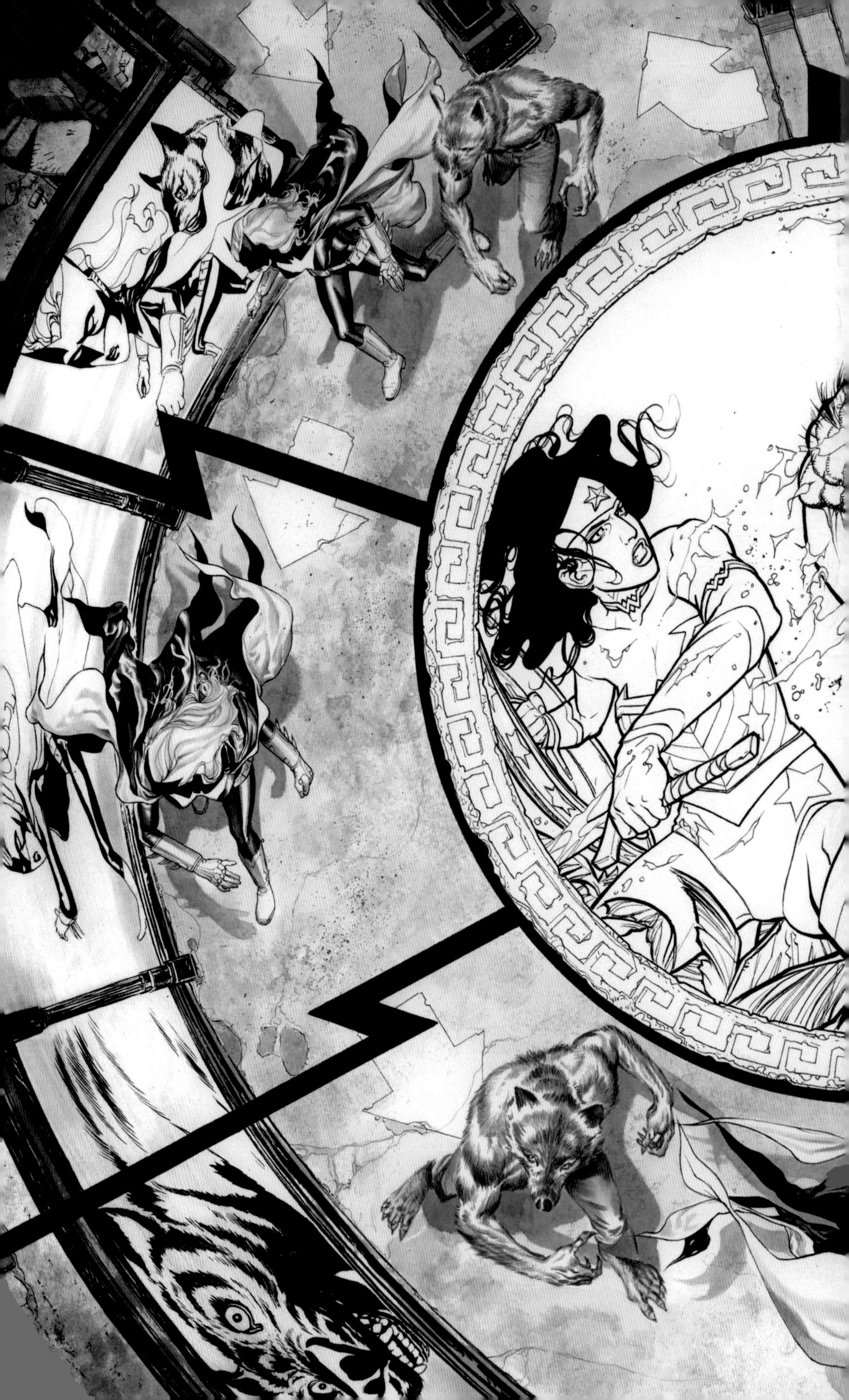

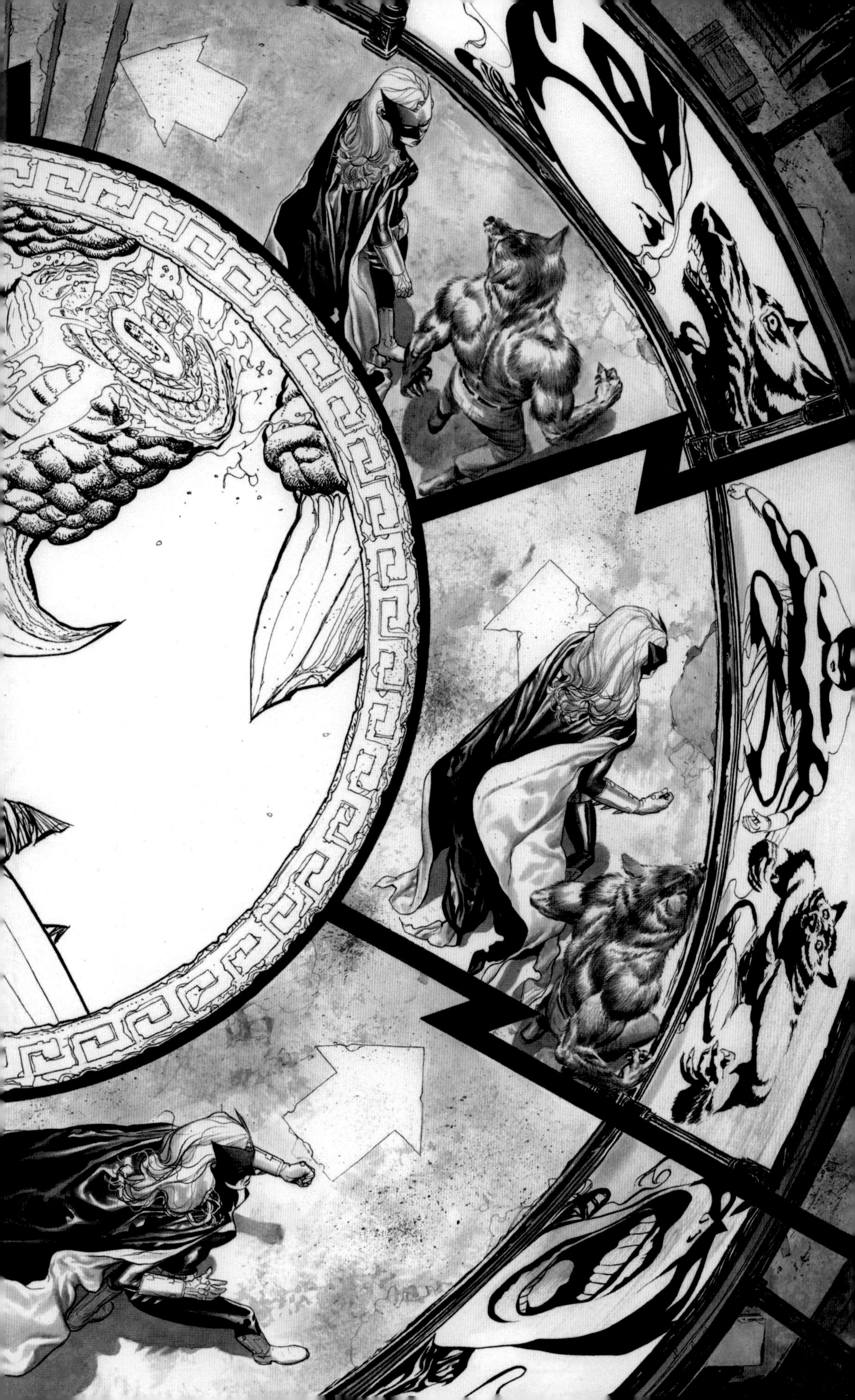